TREASON

ALSO BY ANN COULTER

HIGH CRIMES AND MISDEMEANORS
The Case Against Bill Clinton

SLANDER
Liberal Lies About the American Right

AND LOOK FOR
HOW TO TALK TO A LIBERAL (IF YOU MUST)
The World According to Ann Coulter

TREASON

LIBERAL TREACHERY FROM THE COLD WAR TO THE WAR ON TERRORISM

ANN COULTER

THREE RIVERS PRESS · NEW YORK

Published by Three Rivers Press, New York, New York.
Member of the Crown Publishing Group, a division of Random House, Inc.
www.crownpublishing.com

THREE RIVERS PRESS and the Tugboat design are registered trademarks of
Random House, Inc.

Originally published in hardcover by Crown Forum, a division of Random House,
Inc., in 2003

Printed in the United States of America

Design by Barbara Sturman

Library of Congress Cataloging-in-Publication Data
Coulter, Ann H.
    Treason : liberal treachery from the cold war to the war on terrorism /
Ann Coulter.
Includes bibliographical references and index.
    1. Liberalism—United States—History—20th century.
2. Anti-communist movements—United States—History.   3. United
States—Politics and government—1945–1989.   4. United States—Foreign
relations—1945–1989.   5. United States—Politics and government—
1989– .   6. United States—Foreign relations—1989– .   I. Title.
    E743.C68   2003
    320.51'3'097309045—dc21   2003009311

ISBN 1-4000-5032-4

10   9   8   7   6   5   4   3   2   1

First Paperback Edition

FOR MY FATHER, JOHN V. COULTER

THE NEW BLACKLIST: ACKNOWLEDGMENTS

Deserving of the most hysterical liberal blacklisting for helping me with this book are: M. Stanton Evans, the world's leading authority on Senator Joseph McCarthy, who gave me—gratis—original research for my brief version of a topic he will cover in meticulous detail in his forthcoming book; Allan H. Ryskind, who gave me an enormous amount of historical material for this and the next several books; Tom Winter and *Human Events*, for their decades of relentless truth-telling; and Jim Jerome for many things, including brilliant editorial assistance.

The next tier of blacklistees helped me with this book beyond the call of friendship, giving me invaluable jokes, historical facts, editorial advice, and arguments: Trish Baker, Robert Caplain, Andy Devlin, Jim Downey, Ted Forstmann, Melanie Graham, James Higgins, Merrill Kinstler, Jeremy Rabkin, Ned Rice, Jon Tukel, and Younis Zubchevich.

Also deserving of Senator Schumer's crusading wrath for being thanked in my book are friends who have helped me in various ways, sometimes intentionally, including: Hans Bader, Jon Caldera, George Conway, the Danahers, Miguel Estrada, John Harrison, Mark and Kara Joseph, Mark Kielb, David Limbaugh, Jay Mann, Gene Meyer, Jim Moody, Mac Owens, and Dan Travers.

Finally, the most blameless and important group, worthy of at least a cocktail party snub, are the people who did a lot of work, but are stuck with me: my magnificent agent, Joni Evans; my truly amazing editor, Doug Pepper; my brave publisher, Steve Ross; and the long-suffering production editor, Camille Smith.

Also, long-overdue thanks to my superb editors at Universal Press Syndicate, Greg Melvin and Alan McDermott, who have edited my contemporaneous arguments about the war on terrorism in my columns since 9-11, some of which I have expanded in the terrorism chapters of this book.

And always, with special thanks to my family—my parents, John and Nell; my brothers, John and Jim; my sisters-in-law, Pam and Diane; and my precocious Republican nieces, Kimberly and Christina. Also God, but He's already on the liberals' blacklist.

CONTENTS

TREASON

1

FIFTY YEARS OF TREASON

Liberals have a preternatural gift for striking a position on the side of treason. You could be talking about Scrabble and they would instantly leap to the anti-American position. Everyone says liberals love America, too. No they don't. Whenever the nation is under attack, from within or without, liberals side with the enemy. This is their essence. The left's obsession with the crimes of the West and their Rousseauian respect for Third World savages all flow from this subversive goal. If anyone has the gaucherie to point out the left's nearly unblemished record of rooting against America, liberals turn around and scream "McCarthyism!"

Liberals invented the myth of McCarthyism to delegitimize impertinent questions about their own patriotism. They boast (lyingly) about their superior stance on civil rights. But somehow their loyalty to the

1

United States is off-limits as a subject of political debate. Why is the relative patriotism of the two parties the only issue that is out of bounds for discussion? Why can't we ask: Who is more patriotic— Democrats or Republicans? You could win that case in court.

Fifty years ago, Senator Joe McCarthy said, "The loyal Democrats of this nation no longer have a Party."[1] Since then, the evidence has continued to pour in. Liberals mock Americans who love their country, calling them cowboys, warmongers, religious zealots, and jingoists. By contrast, America's enemies are called "Uncle Joe," "Fidel," "agrarian reformers," and practitioners of a "religion of peace." Indeed, Communists and terrorists alike are said to be advocates of "peace."

Liberals demand that the nation treat enemies like friends and friends like enemies. We must lift sanctions, cancel embargoes, pull out our troops, reason with our adversaries, and absolutely never wage war—unless the French say it's okay. Any evidence that anyone seeks to harm America is stridently rejected as "no evidence." Democratic senators, congressmen, and ex-presidents are always popping up in countries hostile to the United States—Cuba, Nicaragua, North Korea, Iraq—hobnobbing with foreign despots who hate America. One year after Osama bin Laden staged a massive assault on America, a Democratic senator was praising bin Laden for his good work in building "day care centers." At least we can be thankful that in the war on terrorism, we were spared the spectacle of liberals calling Osama bin Laden an "agrarian reformer."

The ACLU responded to the 9-11 terrorist attack by threatening to sue schools that hung GOD BLESS AMERICA signs. Is the ACLU more or less patriotic than the Daughters of the American Revolution? Public schools across the nation prohibited the saying of the Pledge of Allegiance. Is it more patriotic or less patriotic to prevent schoolchildren from saying the Pledge of Allegiance? University professors called patriotic Americans "naive" and described patriotism as a "benign umbrella for angry people."[2] Is it more patriotic to love your country or to ridicule those who do as "naive" and "angry"? These are not questions impenetrable to human logic.

Liberals want to be able to attack America without anyone making an issue of it. Patriotism is vitally important—but somehow impossible to measure. Liberals relentlessly oppose the military, the Pledge of Allegiance, the flag, and national defense. But if anyone calls them on it, they say he's a kook and a nut. Citing the unpatriotic positions of liberals constitutes "McCarthyism."

In the 1988 presidential campaign, Vice President George Bush pointed out that his opponent Michael Dukakis had vetoed a bill requiring students to begin their day with the Pledge of Allegiance. Liberal heads spun with the dark reminders of the McCarthy era. Dukakis instantly compared Bush's dastardly trick of citing his record "to Sen. Joseph McCarthy's Red-baiting during the 1950s."[3] Despite this slur against his patriotism, Dukakis said, "The American people can smell the garbage."[4] At least *sophisticated Americans* could smell the garbage. As one journalist said of Bush's unwarranted reference to Dukakis's record, it was intended to "rile up" ignoramuses in the American populace: the "folks who don't know any better," whose inferior "education or experience has not taught them that the right to speak out is the rudder of this great big boat we call America."[5] The only people whose "right to speak out" is not part of this great big boat we call America are Republicans who dare to mention that a Democrat vetoed the Pledge of Allegiance. Free speech is a one-way ratchet for traitors. While journalists assailed Bush for creating an atmosphere of intolerance for those who "object to patriotic oaths," they didn't mind creating an atmosphere of intolerance toward those who support patriotic oaths.[6]

Later, while campaigning at a naval base, Bush said of Dukakis, "I wouldn't be surprised if he thinks a naval exercise is something you find in the Jane Fonda Workout Book."[7] Again, there were wails of "McCarthyism" all around. Showing the left's renowned ability to get a joke, one reporter earnestly demanded to know: "Did Bush mean to imply that Dukakis is anti-military?"[8] Bush responded to the hysteria over his Jane Fonda joke, saying, "Was that funny? Reasonably funny? A naval exercise—I thought that was pretty funny."[9]

Historians claimed they had not seen "patriotism used with such cynical force" since the fifties. It was "disturbing," historians and political analysts said, for Bush to manipulate symbols to "raise doubts about the Democratic nominee's patriotism."[10] Historian William Leuchtenburger, at the University of North Carolina, said, "I don't recall anything like this before. I don't think there has been an issue like this—an issue so irrelevant to the powers of the presidency."[11] *Washington Post* columnist Mary McGrory complained about the "McCarthyesque form" to Bush's language: "The subliminal message in all the nastiness and bad taste is that Dukakis is somehow un-American: doesn't salute the flag or dig defense."[12] The *New York Times* denounced Bush for "wrapping himself in the flag." Through his "masterly use of the subliminal" Bush had used "political code." The code was "pledge plus flag plus strong defense equals patriotism."[13] (Evidently true patriotism consists of hatred of flag plus hatred of Pledge plus weakness on national defense.) Not going for subtlety, this was under the headline "Playing Rough; Campaign Takes a Turn onto the Low Road."

A frenzy of "McCarthyism" arose again in Bush's next presidential campaign against noted patriot Bill Clinton. While a Rhodes scholar, Clinton joined anti-war protests abroad. One year after the USSR crushed Czechoslovakia, Clinton had taken what the media called a "sightseeing trip to Moscow." For mentioning Clinton's anti-war protests abroad, Bush was called a nut and a McCarthyite. Clinton campaign aide George Stephanopoulos said Bush was "off the wall, lost his compass."[14] Clinton's running mate, Al Gore, accused Bush of "smear tactics, McCarthyite techniques."[15] Meanwhile, CNN's Robert Novak defended McCarthy, saying, "Joe didn't do any innuendo, Joe would have said the guy is a Communist."[16]

"McCarthyism" means pointing out positions taken by liberals that are unpopular with the American people. As former president Bush said, "Liberals do not like me talking about liberals."[17] The reason they sob about the dark night of fascism under McCarthy is to prevent Americans from ever noticing that liberals consistently attack their own country.

Liberals unreservedly call all conservatives fascists, racists, and enemies of civil liberties with no facts whatsoever. Reviewing the movie *8 Mile* in *The New Yorker*, David Denby praised the interracial friendships portrayed in the movie and then said, "Perhaps the specter of such friendships is what right-wingers actually hate most." Conservatives are prohibited from citing actual facts that reflect poorly on a Democrat's patriotism, but liberals regularly fire off shots like that from their little movie reviews.[18]

Liberals malign the flag, ban the Pledge, and hold cocktail parties for America's enemies, but no one is ever allowed to cast the slightest aspersion on their patriotism. The very same article that attacked Bush for questioning Dukakis's patriotism questioned Bush's sensitivity to civil rights—for mentioning Dukakis's veto of the Pledge. The writer scoffed: "George Bush will really be a stand-up guy when it comes to civil liberties. You betcha."[19] We could draw no conclusions from Dukakis's veto of the Pledge. It was a "smear" merely to state the implacable fact that Dukakis had vetoed the Pledge of Allegiance. But apparently it was not a smear to attack Bush's stand on "civil liberties for mentioning Dukakis's veto of the pledge."[20]

Only questions about patriotism are disallowed—unless it is to say that liberals are the "real patriots." Phil Donahue said the "real patriots" were people who aggressively opposed their own country's war plans: "Are the protesters the real patriots?"[21] It is at least counterintuitive to say that it is more patriotic to attack America than to defend it. Even Donahue couldn't continue with such absurd logic, and quickly condemned patriotism as "the last refuge of scoundrels," and warned: "Beware of patriotism."[22]

In addition to opposing any action taken by your own country, "real patriotism" also consists of promoting the liberal agenda. After 9-11, Mario Cuomo said real patriotism consisted of fighting the "war on poverty."[23] Liberal columnist David Broder said "real patriotism" consisted of expanding the Peace Corps and Clinton's worthless Americorp.[24] A writer for the *Kansas City Star*, Bill Tammeus, said real patriots "support education, especially the public schools."[25] The only "unpatriotic" act he identified was trying to "silence dissident voices."[26] A man protesting the Pledge of Allegiance in public schools said, "True Americans separate church and state."[27] A woman opposing the Pledge said, "Real patriotism, and real love for your country, is . . . dissent, or people fighting against the closure of hospitals."[28] Liberals don't mind discussing who is more patriotic if patriotism is defined as redistributing income and vetoing the Pledge of Allegiance. Only if patriotism is defined as supporting America do they get testy and drone on about "McCarthyism."

In June 2002, an American-born Muslim named Abdullah al-Mujahir was arrested on charges of trying to build a dirty bomb. Most Americans were worried about a terrorist taking out Lower Manhattan. But the *New York Times* was worried about an outbreak of "McCarthyism." According to the *Times*, the arrest reminded many people of "McCarthyism and of zealous F.B.I. agents defining the limits of political orthodoxy." Al-Mujahir's arrest had "revived a fear that has permeated popular history: that a homegrown fifth column is betraying fellow Americans on behalf of a foreign foe."[29] Historian Richard Hofstadter diagnosed the country's attempts at self-preservation as a form of "political paranoia."[30] Even Benedict Arnold was thrown in to the *Times*'s enumeration of victims of America's "paranoia," raising the question: Is there no traitor liberals won't defend?

Liberals attack their country and then go into diarrhea panic if anyone criticizes them. Days after 9-11, as the corpses of thousands of our fellow countrymen lay in smoldering heaps in the wreckage of the World Trade Center, Professor Eric Foner of Columbia University said, "I'm not sure which is more frightening: the horror that engulfed New York City or the apocalyptic rhetoric emanating daily from the White House."[31] On the basis of exhaustive research, apparently the events of September 11, including the wanton slaughter of three thousand Americans, were worse than Bush's rhetoric—frightening and disturbing though it may be. Whenever a liberal begins a statement with "I don't know which is more frightening," you know the answer is going to be pretty clear.

Foner claimed to be the victim of McCarthyite tactics for not being lavished with praise for his idiotic remark. A report by the American Council of Trustees and Alumni—founded by Lynne Cheney and Senator Joseph Lieberman—cited Foner's remark as an example of how universities were failing America. This was, Foner said, "analogous to McCarthyism." These "self-appointed guardians" were "engaging in private blacklisting" and "trying to intimidate individuals who hold different points of view." A private group issuing a report criticizing him was "disturbing" and a "cause for considerable alarm."[32] The eminent historian Ronald Radosh is blacklisted from every university in the nation because he wrote the book definitively proving the guilt of executed spies Julius and Ethel Rosenberg. But if someone fails to agree with tenured Columbia professor Foner, he screams he is being intimidated. "There aren't loyalty oaths being demanded of teachers yet," Foner said, "but we seem to be at the beginning of a process that could get a lot worse."

If Eric Foner wants to claim he is patriotic, doesn't he have to do something to show he supports America, someday? Why is it assumed that patriotism is an unmeasurable quality? Is Eric Foner more or less patriotic than Irving Berlin? Berlin wrote the great patriotic song "God Bless America." He donated all profits from the song in perpetuity to the Boy Scouts of America—an organization so patriotic it removed President Clinton as honorary president. Berlin served in World War I and entertained the troops in World War II with a play he wrote for the troops, *This Is the Army*. He greeted prisoners of war returning from Vietnam at the White House, playing "God Bless America."[33] If only Berlin were around today, he could write us a new song for the war on terrorism, something like "Good-bye Walla Walla, I'm Off to Smash Allah."

Meanwhile, Foner compared the malevolent terror of Islamic terrorists to "rhetoric" from President Bush. He defended Soviet atrocities.[34] He is still defending proven Soviet spy Julius Rosenberg. If only Foner could see beyond what is bad for the United States, he might see that fighting terrorism and Communism might be good for people of other nations, too. In a long tradition of patriotism, in 1941, Foner's father was fired from his job as a state college teacher under the New York State law that prohibited state-supported teachers from engaging in seditious or treasonous speech. (Inasmuch as this happened in New York State while Joe McCarthy was still a young circuit court judge in Wisconsin, the *New York Times* referred to Foner's firing as a "pre-McCarthy Red scare.")[35] Isn't someone who opposes his own country less patriotic than someone who loves his country?

While consistently rooting against America, liberals have used a fictional event forged of their own hysteria—"McCarthyism"—to prevent Americans from ever asking the simple question: Do liberals love their country?

IN McCARTHY'S DAY, A BATTLE AGAINST COMMUNISM HUNG IN the balance even more than the battle against terrorism hangs in the balance today. Time and again, in all crucial matters of national self-defense, the Democratic Party has shirked the honor of leading this country in war, be it cold or hot. Such a party must not be allowed in the Oval Office. That was McCarthy's central point a half century ago; and it's even more obvious today. America's enemies change, but the treason remains the same.

A full accounting of the left's perfidy throughout the second half of the twentieth century is incalculable. Will and Ariel Durant could not document it (*Story of Civilization*, eleven volumes). But it is impossible to understand their naysaying in the war on terrorism today, their vicious wrath, and even their maniacal defense of Bill Clinton, without a brief review of their treachery at the onset of the Cold War.

In the early fifties, ex-Communist Whittaker Chambers said, "In this century, within the next decades, [it] will be decided for generations whether all mankind is to become Communist, whether the whole world is to become free, or whether, in the struggle, civilization as we know it is to be completely destroyed." It had been his fate, he said, to have been "in turn a witness to each of the two great faiths of our time"—God and Communism.[36] Communism, he said, is "the vision of man without God." It was man's second oldest faith: "Its promise was whispered in the first days of the Creation under the Tree of the Knowledge of Good and Evil 'Ye shall be as gods.'" These were the "irreconcilable opposites—God or Man, Soul or Mind, Freedom or Communism."[37]

Liberals chose Man. Conservatives chose God. The struggle between the two great faiths was the subtext of every great political conflict in America in the second half of the twentieth century. It was this conflict that fueled the Chambers-Hiss hearings, "McCarthyism," Vietnam, Watergate, and the elites' abiding hatred for Ronald Reagan. At the end of the century, and against the odds, the free world won.

It was a crushing defeat for liberals. Not because liberals were necessarily Communists, though many were, but because they had been morally blind to Communism. Democratic administrations contained archipelagos of Communist spies, but Democrats had never, not once, responded with genuine anger to Soviet espionage. Liberal elites defended traitors. In response to the Soviet threat, the Democrats consistently counseled defeat, supplication, and retreat.

Indeed, they spent most of the Cold War jeering at phrases like "Soviet threat." They said Communist advances were inevitable and Communist dictators were "agrarian reformers." No one "lost" China. Detente—not victory—was the best the free world could hope for. Phrases like "captive nations" and "freedom fighters" were invariably put in derisive quotes. As long as the Soviet Union thrived, the "inevitability" argument fell within the range of patriotic behavior. If Soviet domination really was inevitable, liberals were just being brutally frank messengers. But then Reagan won the Cold War. It turned out Communism's triumph wasn't inevitable after all. The left's teleological argument for Communist domination was a lie. Liberals were either dupes or traitors in the greatest battle of the twentieth century.

In his own way, Nixon was as crucial as Reagan in defeating Soviet Communism. Nixon exposed the Truman and Roosevelt administrations as having appointed known saboteur Alger Hiss to positions of influence within the government. The Hiss case marked the point at which liberals became conscious of themselves as a conspiracy. There was no turning back. Nixon showed the American people that liberals had failed to meet the challenge of Communist espionage in the highest reaches of government. No matter how many Harvard men spoke on Hiss's behalf, liberals could not stave off the moment of truth. Naturally, therefore, they engaged in lying to ward off Nixon's exposure of Hiss, just as they would again a half century later to save Clinton.

The Republican Party would fail to meet other challenges—there was a reason for liberal political hegemony in the decades preceding the Hiss affair. But with the Hiss case, Nixon created a new universe. He had exposed liberals as dupes of totalitarianism. The Democratic Party could never be trusted again in the same way. Democrats and Republicans ceased being viewed as uniformly American. For this, liberals would never forgive Nixon. Watergate would be the left's ultimate revenge against him for telling the truth about Hiss. To rehabilitate Hiss, they would destroy Nixon. As the *New York Times* put it in Hiss's obituary: Hiss's reputation seemed "to wax and wane with each new turn in the fortunes of Mr. Nixon."[38]

While reacting with unblinking ennui to Soviet spies in high government office, Democrats engaged in drama queen theatrics over "McCarthyism." The myth of "McCarthyism" is the greatest Orwellian fraud of our times. The portrayal of Senator Joe McCarthy as a wild-eyed demagogue destroying innocent lives is sheer liberal hobgoblinism. Liberals weren't cowering in fear during the McCarthy era. They were systematically undermining the nation's ability to defend itself while waging a bellicose campaign of lies to blacken McCarthy's name. Everything you think you know about McCarthy is a hegemonic lie. Liberals denounced McCarthy because they were afraid of getting caught, so they fought back like animals to hide their own collaboration with a regime as evil as the Nazis'. They scream about the dark night of fascism under McCarthy to prevent Americans from ever noticing that liberals sabotaged their own country. As Whittaker Chambers said: "Innocence seldom utters outraged shrieks. Guilt does."[39]

At the time, everyone knew liberals were lying. But after a half century of liberal mythmaking, it would be Judgment Day for liberals on July 11, 1995. On that day, the U.S. government released a cache of Soviet cables that had been decoded during the Cold War in a top-secret undertaking known as the Venona Project. The cables proved the overwhelming truth of McCarthy's charges. It was a mind-boggling discovery. Professors would be forced to retract their theses about the extent of Soviet espionage. Alger Hiss, Julius Rosenberg, even American journalist I. F. Stone were exposed as agents of Moscow. And yet, most people reading this book are hearing about the Venona Project for the very first time. The release of decrypted Soviet cables was barely mentioned by the *New York Times*. It might have detracted from stories of proud and unbowed victims of "McCarthyism." They were not so innocent after all, it turns out.

Soviet spies in the government were not a figment of right-wing imaginations. McCarthy was not tilting at windmills. He was tilting at an authentic Communist conspiracy that had been laughed off by the Democratic Party. The Democrats had unpardonably connived with one of the greatest evils of the twentieth century. This could not be nullified. But liberals could at least hope to redeem the Democratic Party by dedicating themselves to rewriting history and blackening reputations. This is what they had done repeatedly throughout the Cold War. At every strategic moment this century, liberals would wage a campaign of horrendous lies and disinformation to dull the discovery that the American people had made. They had gotten good at it.

There were, admittedly, a few rare and striking exceptions to the left's overall obtuseness to Communist totalitarianism. The Democratic Party was certainly more patriotic then than it has become. Throughout the sixties, the Democrats could still produce the occasional Scoop Jackson Democrat. John F. Kennedy's pronouncements on Communism could have been spoken by Joe McCarthy. His brother Robert worked for McCarthy. For all his flaws, President Harry Truman was a completely different breed from today's Democrats: He unquestionably loved his country. Through the years, there were various epiphanic moments creating yet more anti-Communist Democrats. The Hitler-Stalin Pact,

Hiss's prothonotary warbler, Stalin's show trials, and Aleksandr Solzhenitsyn's *The Gulag Archipelago*—all these had their effect.

But after World War II, the Democratic Party suffered from the sort of pusillanimous psychosis that seized all of France after World War I. The entire party began to lose its nerve for sacrifice, heroism, and bravery. Beginning in the fifties, there was a real fight for the soul of the Democratic Party. By the late sixties the contest was over. The anti-Communist Democrats had lost. In 1972, George McGovern, darling of left-wing radicals, was the Democratic presidential candidate. SDS (Students for a Democratic Society) leader and Chicago riot instigator Tom Hayden became a Democratic state senator in California. In 1968, Staughton Lynd said of Tom Hayden: "On Monday, Wednesday, and Friday he was a National Liberation Front guerilla, and on Tuesday, Thursday, and Saturday, he . . . was on the left wing of the Democratic Party."[40] Black Panther Bobby Rush would go on to become a Democratic congressman. Todd Gitlin, a former president of SDS, would soon be a university professor and frequent op-ed columnist for the *New York Times*.[41]

This was the new Democratic Party. By the time of the 1991 Gulf War, only ten Senate Democrats voted with President Bush to use troops against Saddam Hussein. If the old Democratic Party was merely obtuse, the new Democratic Party was a beachhead of domestic anti-Americanism.

Clinton was the left's last best hope for proving they could too handle the presidency. Having tricked the American people into entrusting a Democrat with the White House—on a bare plurality vote—they had to defend him from any lie, any felony, any reprehensible, contemptible conduct he threw their way. When Clinton first showed his fat, oleaginous mug to the nation, the Republicans screamed he was a draft-dodging, pot-smoking flimflam artist. Had the Republicans turned out to be right again, it would have sounded the death knell for the Democratic Party. So the Democrats lied. Through their infernal politics of personal destruction, liberals stayed in the game for a few more years.

Unless we fight for proper treatment of history and counter the nonsense images of McCarthy, no history can be safe from the liberal noise machine. Schoolchildren will be taught that all of America cringed with terror at Ken Starr, whose evil designs on the nation were frustrated only through the sacrifice of brave liberals. People will have vivid images of the pounding boots of Starr's subpoena-servers and the Gestapo-like wails of alarms as Ken Starr arrived to kick in the doors of innocent Americans and storm through their bedrooms. It will be the Reign of Terror under Ken Starr.

Bill Clinton will be revered in history books as the George Washington of his day who, along with patriots Larry Flynt and James Carville, "saved the Constitution." He will be honored with a memorial larger than the Washington Monument (though probably with the same general design). People will believe that. And liberals will continue unabashedly invoking a lie in order to shield their ongoing traitorous behavior.

THE CREDIBILITY OF DEMOCRATS ON NATIONAL DEFENSE IS now at stake as it has not been since McCarthy's day. Democrats are on the precipice of securing their reputation as the Chamberlains of our time. In fact, today's appeasers are worse than Neville Chamberlain: Chamberlain didn't have himself as an example. In the latest round of liberal demoralization techniques, they are once again rooting against America. You would think the most destructive terrorist attack in the history of the world would call for something new, but liberals have simply dusted off the old clichés from the Cold War and trotted them out for the war on terrorism. The only patriotic liberal in the world is Tony Blair, and he's in England.

Every once in a while their tempers get the best of them and, like Dr. Strangelove trying to restrain the Nazi salute, liberals say what they really mean. Their own words damn them as hating America. One week before the first anniversary of 9-11, Reuters ran a photo of Ground Zero with a caption that said, "Human rights around the world have been a casualty of the US 'war on terror' since September 11."

Arguably, thousands of Americans dying hideous deaths is a more comment-worthy "casualty" than any alleged death of "human rights" around the world. Also, was it really necessary to put "war on terror" in quotation marks?

As the country was beginning to contemplate war with Iraq in the summer of 2002, a Hollywood cast of mostly has-beens and never-beens calling their cause "Not in Our Name" issued a statement imploring "all Americans to RESIST the war and repression that has been loosed on the world by the Bush administration." America's war on terrorism, they said, was "unjust, immoral, and illegitimate." The devastation of September 11 was dismissively compared to "similar scenes in Baghdad, Panama City, and, a generation ago, Vietnam." Among the signers were "Hanoi Jane" Fonda, Ed Asner, Susan Sarandon, Casey Kasem, Noam Chomsky, Gore Vidal, Edward Said, Ben & Jerry's Ben Cohen, Kurt Vonnegut, and noted cop-killer Mumia Abu-Jamal. It was a group nearly indistinguishable from those who had enthusiastically backed the Soviet Union during the Cold War.

Liberals spent most of the war on terrorism in a funk because they didn't have enough grist for the anti-war mill. They nearly went stark raving mad at having to mouth patriotic platitudes while burning with a desire to aid the enemy. Having to suppress their glee at possible failure, they posted droll rambling narratives with no apparent point on the nation's op-ed pages. Liberals write essays like little kids making up a melody. They meander along, issuing contradictory snide remarks about Bush, until they run out of energy and finally conclude with some incongruous, throaty peroration. Is fighting terrorism worth "tearing up the Constitution"? And boo hoo hoo—we have to get the French on board. Just as liberals went into a panic when Ronald Reagan referred to Russia as an "evil empire," they were in a state of frenzy over Bush's "axis of evil" speech. If liberals were half as indignant about Osama bin Laden as they were about President Bush, their objections might rate more with real Americans.

When the Democrats' bluff was called in a roll call vote in Congress, many voted for war with Iraq. Inadvertently performing a great service, *New York Times* columnist Maureen Dowd revealed the Democrats' treasonous calculations. She explained that Democrats would be forced to fake enthusiasm for the war on terror or lose the American people forever. Democrats, she said, "fear that if they approach" Iraq the same way they did during the Gulf War in 1991, "they will be portrayed as McGovernite wimps."[42] Consequently, liberals would lie and pretend to support America. With their votes duly recorded, they went right back to attacking the war. But why were they against it? Saddam Hussein was a madman developing weapons of mass destruction stewing in the same swamp as the 9-11 terrorists. We could beat him. Why were the Democrats against doing that? What do liberals want? Freud would have gone crazy with these people. Figuring out what women want is easy compared to liberals.

The only two living former Democratic presidents publicly opposed the Bush administration's plan to invade Iraq. Jimmy Carter couldn't land a helicopter in a desert, but he seemed to imagine the public was hungry for his counsel in the war on terrorism. Carter is so often maligned for his stupidity, it tends to be forgotten that he is also self-righteous, vengeful, sneaky, and backstabbing. In a vituperative piece in the *Washington Post*, Carter peremptorily announced, "There is no current danger to the United States from Baghdad."[43] The real threat to world peace and global human rights, he said, came from President Bush. The Bush administration, with its "belligerent and divisive voices," was becoming "similar to those of abusive regimes that historically have been condemned by American presidents."

This for incarcerating members of al-Qaeda at Guantánamo without regulation tennis courts. The only subject fewer authentic Americans cared about than the treatment of prisoners at Guantánamo was World Cup Soccer. America is in an epic global battle with ruthless savages who seek our destruction, and liberals are feeling sorry for the terrorists. Unlike the "belligerent and divisive voices" here in America, Carter believed that the great statesman Saddam Hussein could be reasoned with, despite the fact that Hussein was a habitual liar and cold-blooded murderer. But surely Saddam would realize, Carter said, that actually using a weapon of mass destruction "would be suicidal." Unless, of course, a Democrat were in the White House, in which case Saddam could rest assured that there would be no "belligerent and divisive voices" to counsel retaliation.

Bill Clinton, who bombed an aspirin factory in the Sudan to distract from the investigation of his criminal offenses at home, also had a lot of advice for President Bush. The impeached former president unleashed the canard about having to get Osama bin Laden "first"— as if there could ever be sufficient predicates for a Democrat to support their own country in war. "Saddam Hussein didn't kill 3,100 people on September 11," Clinton said. "Osama Bin Laden did, and as far as we know he's still alive."[44] This came roughly one month after Clinton suggested that resources being used to pursue Osama bin Laden could be better spent combating AIDS. Clinton had proposed that the country spend another $1.5 billion fighting AIDS—which was, he pointedly noted, "less than two months of the Afghan war" and "less than 2 percent of the requested increases for defense in America."[45] So first we abolish AIDS, then we produce Osama's DNA, and then the time will be ripe to take out a madman frantically developing weapons of mass destruction who longs to annihilate Americans. Liberals' attitude toward a swamp is that we have to go around killing mosquitoes individually only after proving the targeted mosquito is about to bite us. Otherwise, we might make the mosquitoes mad.

Whatever the left's last-minute hawkishness, all their behavior is calculated to demoralize Americans and to suppress anger. Liberals' principal contribution to the war on terrorism has been to bill themselves as a corrective to "jingoism." Their real goal is too appalling to state out loud.

Whether they are defending the Soviet Union or bleating for Saddam Hussein, liberals are always against America. They are either traitors or idiots, and on the matter of America's self-preservation, the difference is irrelevant. Fifty years of treason hasn't slowed them down.

2

ALGER HISS, LIBERAL DARLING

In what would turn out to be one of the most significant events of the twentieth century, in 1938, Whittaker Chambers broke with the Communist Party. The political battle lines were drawn over Chambers and they have never been redrawn. His story would become the story of the nation. Years later, Chambers would write of his fear that the Communist Party would murder him, as it had murdered so many other apostates, saying, "They must sometimes have thought bitterly since about their failure to do so."[1]

Chambers had planned his break for months. In addition to the practical concern of avoiding a "suicide," leaving the Communist Party was more than "leaving one house and occupying another."[2] He was "reversing the faith of an adult lifetime, held implacably to the point of criminality."[3] When he took up the cause of the free world against the

Communists, he said he had moved to a house "manifestly in collapse and the caretakers largely witless."[4] But he had no choice. Agonizingly, he had come to the realization that he had been working on the side of evil—for terror, torture, fascism, and death. A fellow ex-Communist, Walter Krivitsky, would force him to state the painful truth out loud: The Soviet government was a fascist government and it had been from the beginning.

Krivitsky was the first to tell Chambers of Stalin's feverish efforts to align with Hitler in 1939. The proposed alliance, Chambers said, was "thoroughly justified" as Communist strategy, but from "any human point of view, the pact was evil."[5] As Chambers imagined the coming conflict, he rued that conservatives would be "all but helpless." He said the fate of the free world could only be decided in a struggle between the Communists and the ex-Communists, for "no other has been so deeply into the total nature of the evil with which communism threatens mankind."[6] After meeting with Krivitsky, Chambers said, "I knew that, if the opportunity offered, I would inform."[7] Soon thereafter, the Hitler-Stalin Pact was signed. Days later, as Hitler's armies marched into Poland, Chambers was on a plane from New York to Washington, D.C.

A friend of Chambers had arranged a private audience with President Roosevelt's assistant secretary of state, Adolf Berle. After dinner at Berle's home, Chambers spent several hours detailing the Communist espionage network of which he had been a part. He gave Berle the names of at least two dozen Soviet spies working for the Roosevelt administration. Among them was Alger Hiss, a top State Department official, as well as his brother Donald Hiss. Berle urgently reported to President Roosevelt what Chambers had said, including the warning about Alger Hiss. The president laughed and told Berle to go f— himself.[8] No action was ever taken against Hiss. To the contrary, Roosevelt promoted Hiss to the position of trusted aide who would go on to advise him at Yalta. Chambers's shocking and detailed reckoning of Soviet agents in high government positions eventually made its way to William C. Bullitt, former ambassador to Russia and confidant of the president. Alarmed, Bullitt brought the news to Roosevelt's attention. He, too, was laughed off.[9]

Berle also told Dean Acheson, then Roosevelt's undersecretary of the Treasury, what Chambers had said about the Hiss brothers. As Berle described the meeting, Acheson "said he had known the family and these two boys since childhood and could vouch for them absolutely."[10] When Acheson later became assistant secretary of state, he immediately requested Donald Hiss as his assistant. Berle again stepped in to remind Acheson that Chambers had identified Donald Hiss as a Soviet agent. Acheson investigated the matter much as Democrats investigated Paula Jones's claims against Bill Clinton. He asked Hiss if he was a Communist, Hiss denied it, and Acheson summarily announced that "the matter was closed."[11] The Democrats' nonchalance about Soviet agents on their staffs was scandalous. It would be as if President Bush were promoting Islamic terrorists after being informed they were members of al-Qaeda.

Years later, Berle would soft-pedal the Democrats' promotion of two traitors with an inane straw-man argument: "The idea that these two Hiss boys . . . were going to take over the United States government did not strike me as any immediate danger." It was also not an "immediate danger" that al-Qaeda was going to "take over the United States' government." It still might not be wise for the U.S. government to employ them. As even Berle admitted, "We were all trying not to tell anything that ought not be told, and there were pretty consistent leaks whenever anything went through [Alger Hiss's] office."[12]

In 1948, almost a full decade later, when he was working at *Time* magazine, Chambers was called to testify before the House Un-American Activities Committee, more famously known as HUAC. Chambers again named Hiss as a Soviet agent. HUAC showed somewhat more heightened interest in this fact than had the Democratic administration of Franklin Roosevelt. Here at last, Chambers said, was "a force that was fiercely, albeit clumsily, fighting Communism."[13] Rumors had long dogged Hiss, but as Chambers said, "for the first time, a man had stood up and said, 'I was there, I knew them. The rumors are facts.'"[14]

Hiss soon took his turn before the committee and categorically denied Chambers's accusations. With a Clintonian lie, he said he did not even know a man "named Whittaker Chambers." Chambers, it seems, had gone by another name in the Communist underground. Still, Hiss and Chambers had made sworn statements diametrically opposed to each other: Chambers said he knew Hiss and knew him to be a Soviet spy; Hiss said he didn't know Chambers at all. One of them was lying.

At the risk of giving away the ending, it has now been proved beyond cavil that Alger Hiss was a Soviet spy. For all but the willfully stupid, Chambers would soon produce the definitive evidence from a hollowed-out pumpkin: the famous "Pumpkin Papers." Any remaining Hiss defenders would be confronted by the implacable truth in secret Soviet cables released some fifty years later.

The gist of Hiss's rebuttal is captured by this statement he made at one HUAC hearing: "May I interrupt at this point, because I take it this will take more than 10 or 15 minutes. Would it be possible for one of the members of the committee to call the Harvard Club and leave word that I won't be there for a 6 o'clock appointment?" As Chambers described it, Hiss's defense was to draw "the toga of his official career about him." Hiss was a Harvard man and he wouldn't let anyone forget it.

Springing naturally to their traitorous positions, the adversary press vilified HUAC for persecuting the charming State Department official. Hiss's performance was universally acclaimed as a smashing success. Chambers was portrayed as a "vulgar impostor" who had snowed the "gullible" committee. He was a rumpled journalist at *Time* magazine, without social pedigree. Also he had bad teeth—a point that was endlessly cited in press accounts. The press contemptuously referred to members of HUAC as "the least intelligent in Congress," "uncouth, undignified and ungrammatical."[15] There were titters about a "Red Scare" sweeping Congress.

The angry vituperation in the press, Chambers said, had driven the committee "into a state bordering on anxiety neurosis."[16] Hiss's performance would fail for only one reason—the reason "that is never foreseen," as Chambers said. There was one man on the committee with "an inner ear for the ring of truth"—Richard Nixon.[17] Without the admiration, the *New York Times* concurred, writing in Nixon's obituary: "Because of Mr. Hiss's excellent credentials and Government record, the matter might have been dropped had Mr. Nixon not doggedly pursued it as head of a special subcommittee."[18] Nixon, then a young congressman from California, refused to allow the committee to drop the matter. For not being snowed by Hiss's Harvard law degree like the lemming press, Nixon would be forever branded as resentful toward the Ivy League.

Thanks to Nixon's perseverance, HUAC's investigation continued. Follow-up hearings were held in closed session, out of sight of the press. To prove he knew Hiss, Chambers told the committee all he knew about Hiss—his habits, hobbies, and physical ailments. During one such hearing, Chambers remarked that Hiss and his wife were avid bird-watchers and had once expressed excitement at spotting a rare specimen, a prothonotary warbler. When Hiss later appeared before HUAC, an amateur ornithologist on the committee maneuvered Hiss to the topic of his bird watching. Without prompting, Hiss gushed about his exhilaration at having once seen a prothonotary warbler. The committee was convinced: Chambers knew Hiss.

With cinematic timing, between the two hearings at which Hiss would damn himself by mentioning the bird, the president of the United States denounced the investigation into Hiss as a "red herring."[19] President Truman called the Hiss investigation a cheap political ploy by "do-nothing" Republicans to distract from their own sorry legislative record. Campaigning for president that year, President Truman summarized HUAC's investigation as if the entire case came down to the résumés of the two men: "If you work for *Time*, you're a hero. If you work for the State Department, you're a heel."[20] Democratic National Committee Chairman J. Howard McGrath attacked HUAC, saying it had "no future" if it "continue[d] to act as it had in the past."[21] Indeed, the entire Social Register of the liberal establishment backed the patrician, Harvard-educated Soviet spy. Felix Frankfurter and Adlai Stevenson offered to be character witnesses for Hiss. Eleanor Roosevelt said she believed Hiss. Truman's Justice Department asked the FBI to determine whether Chambers had ever been institutionalized for mental illness and began investigating Chambers for perjury.[22] On one hand, a Soviet spy might have been turning over vital government secrets to the nation's mortal enemy. But on the other hand, a Harvard man was having his reputation besmirched.

HUAC's investigation could no longer be held behind closed doors. When Chambers pleaded with Nixon to continue holding hearings away from public view, Nixon warned Chambers: "The Department of Justice is all set to move in on you in order to save Hiss. They are planning to indict you at once. The only way to head them off is to let the public judge for itself which one of you is telling the truth. That is your only chance."[23] As Nixon said, "If the American people understood the real character of Alger Hiss, they would boil him in oil."

Nixon was right. The public saw and believed Chambers. Despite the press's relentless attacks on HUAC, in September 1948—one month after Truman had scoffed at the Hiss probe as a "red herring"—a Gallup poll showed four out of five Americans supported HUAC.[24] Three out of four disagreed with Truman's charge that Republicans were "playing politics" with the hearings. This included 71 percent of Democrats surveyed, but—judging by their coverage—0 percent of reporters.

Hiss had indignantly demanded that Chambers make his charges outside of a congressional hearing room and thus subject himself to a suit for slander. Chambers would soon have the opportunity to do just that. He agreed to be interviewed on the radio program *Meet the Press.* As Chambers described the program, it was "enlivened by an unprecedented personal venom," consisting of "a savage verbal assault and battery on the guest, without pause and with little restraint or decency."[25] One of the hosts—and three of the four were hysterical Hiss partisans—dared Chambers to restate his charges on the radio. Chambers said, "Alger Hiss was a Communist and may be now." He then added, "I do not think Mr. Hiss will sue me for slander or libel."

For an unusually protracted period of time, Chambers was right. To the bewilderment of his supporters, Hiss did not leap at his chance to sue Chambers. This was despite the fact that he had powerful friends eagerly offering pro bono legal assistance, investigative work, and money of mysterious origin.[26] Yet Hiss waited an interminable three months before finally being shamed into suing Chambers for slander. Hiss's legal team leapt to action in classic Democratic fashion. They launched sadistic attacks on Chambers, claiming he was mentally unstable and a homosexual.

One member of Hiss's psychiatric team worked up a unique theory of Chambers's insanity based on a book Chambers had translated, *Class Reunion.* The psychiatrist found amazing similarities between Chambers and a fictional character from the translated work, who neurotically makes false charges against a more talented and brilliant classmate, ruining his life. Chambers's only connection to the book was that he had been paid to translate it. This is what Chambers did for a living—he translated books not chosen by him. As historian Allen Weinstein said, Chambers had also once translated *Bambi;* that did not prove he "was a gun-shy deer."[27] But Hiss's Harvard-educated legal team was captivated by the harebrained theory. Ed McLean, a named partner at Debevoise, Plimpton & McLean and a Harvard man, urged Hiss to alert FBI investigators to the *Class Reunion* theory.[28] Harvard Law School is precisely what it used to be.

In their depositions of Chambers, Hiss's lawyers seemed unduly interested in Chambers's brother, Richard, who had committed suicide years earlier. Hiss attorney William Marbury maliciously referred to Chambers's deceased brother only as "Dickie." Chambers was perplexed by the obsessive focus on his brother. Only much later did Chambers learn why. It was, as Chambers said, "a story so inconceivable that it seemed to me that only a mind deformed by something more than malevolence could have excreted it. What kind of beasts am I dealing with? The fact that men and women could be found to credit and spread a lie so disgusting and so cruel remains the measure of the Hiss defense and the pro-Hiss psychosis."[29] Chambers says no more about the matter. Allen Weinstein reports in his book *Perjury* that the Hiss defense team was ready to launch the theory that Chambers had a homosexual relationship with his own brother and that "the motivation of Chambers in making his accusations against Hiss" was that "Chambers had a subconscious impulse to be reunited with his brother in death."[30]

Though Hiss's investigators logged many hours in their quest to portray Chambers as a nutcase, they came up dry. This was despite sympathetic mental health professionals anxious to take up Hiss's case. Hiss told his brother about one psychiatrist who "feels so strongly about my case that he would not have allowed considerations of professional ethics to play any part in his actions."[31] In the end, neither Hiss's investigators nor the FBI found any evidence that Chambers was ever hospitalized for mental illness.

One of Hiss's little helpers was Truman's secretary of state, Dean Acheson. There is evidence that Acheson was furtively passing government secrets to Hiss's lawyers to help with his case. Allen Weinstein writes in *Perjury,* "Whether or not Acheson, once he rejoined State, provided the Hiss defense with confidential departmental information in the midst of the Justice Department probe has never been determined, *but some officials at State complained to the FBI the following year about such practices by the Secretary.*"[32] (Emphasis added.) To be sure, it was never proved, much like the case against O. J. Simpson was never "proved." But State Department officials not only believed Acheson was passing on secret information to Hiss's lawyers, but were so appalled that they complained to the FBI about it. It is a sobering thought to realize that, as secretary of state, Acheson was very likely giving confidential State Department information to the legal defense team of a Soviet spy.

Until the Democratic defamation team sprang to action, Chambers had tried to limit the damage to Hiss, his former friend. But Hiss had sued. His lawyers attacked Chambers's wife and made her cry. Hiss had smeared Chambers as a psychotic and homosexual. In Hiss's written response to HUAC's report, Hiss called Chambers a "queer" four times.[33] Chambers would no longer conceal the details of Hiss's espionage. Years earlier, Chambers had entrusted his nephew Nathan Levine with an envelope containing confidential government documents Chambers had received from Hiss. Among the documents were copies and summaries of State Department papers written in Hiss's own handwriting. For years, the documents had been secreted away in the dumbwaiter shaft of a relative's house in Brooklyn, New York. Hiss's lawyers were demanding proof. Chambers, now living in Maryland, took a train to New York and retrieved the envelope. When Chambers produced the documents, Hiss's lawyers were flabbergasted. Presented with such damning evidence, even the Harvard-educated lawyers realized the jig was up. They would have to alert the Department of Justice.

What happened next should stir the hearts of all patriotic Americans. The copied State Department documents were delivered to the head of the Criminal Division at Justice, Alexander M. Campbell. Campbell promptly directed that the documents be examined—quote—"so that it can be determined whether Chambers has committed perjury."[34] Chambers! Chambers had produced breathtaking documentary evidence that Hiss had spied on his own country. In response, the Truman administration decided to indict Chambers and throw a party for the traitor.

Apparently the Truman administration's decision to protect Hiss did not come as a surprise to a lugubrious fellow like Whittaker Chambers. In fact, perhaps fearing just this turn of events, Chambers had withheld the most damning material from Hiss's lawyers. He was about to set off a nuclear explosion with the documents he had withheld. As Truman's Department of Justice prepared to indict Chambers— working hand in glove with Hiss's lawyers[35]—puzzling leaks about the investigation began appearing in the press. Members of HUAC were intrigued. They asked Chambers if he had any more information relevant to the committee's investigation of Hiss. He said he did.

On December 2, 1948, Chambers and two HUAC investigators drove to his farm in Maryland. In one of the most dramatic moments in U.S. history, Chambers reached into a hollowed-out pumpkin and produced microfilm of highly confidential documents from the Navy and State Department. At least three documents had come from Alger Hiss's office. The Pumpkin Papers, as *Perjury* author Allen Weinstein said, "provided definite proof of one of the most extensive espionage rings in the history of the United States."[36]

The pontifical, patrician Hiss launched a series of evasions and outright lies in response to the Pumpkin Papers. He claimed the documents did not come from his typewriter, but was unable to produce the typewriter he owned when the documents were transcribed. He said he could not even recall the kind of typewriter it had been.[37] Later it was determined that the Hisses' typewriter was a Woodstock given to Mrs. Hiss by her father. The FBI located documents typed on the Woodstock typewriter by Hiss's father-in-law and matched the typeface to the State Department documents. When it could no longer be denied that the classified government documents had been typed on Hiss's typewriter, Hiss explained to an inquisitive grand jury: "I am amazed, and until the day I die I shall wonder how Whittaker Chambers got into my house to use my typewriter."[38] The grand jurors laughed at him. But the *New York Times* wondered how Chambers had done that, too. *The Nation* magazine is still wondering.

EVIDENCE OF HISS'S GUILT WAS OVERWHELMING. IT INCLUDED Chambers's Pumpkin Papers, the Woodstock typewriter, Chambers's intimate knowledge of the details of Hiss's life (including the prothonotary warbler sighting), multiple independent witness identifications, and documents from Soviet defectors identifying Hiss as a Soviet spy. Chambers agreed to take a lie detector test without hesitation. Hiss refused. (This was before such tests were largely discredited.) Indeed, Hiss even refused a supporter's offer to examine him privately under a truth serum—something he never told his lawyer.[39]

Eventually, after years of hearings and drama and public turmoil over Chambers's accusations, Hiss was convicted of perjury for denying under oath that he had spied on his own country. He escaped a direct espionage charge only because the statute of limitations had

expired. Every few years for the rest of his life, Hiss would claim to
have unearthed some mythical "new evidence" that would finally
prove his innocence. But despite Hiss's numerous ludicrous appeals,
the court repeatedly upheld his conviction.

Almost fifty years later, the release of the decrypted Soviet cables
proved indisputably that Hiss was a Soviet spy, sending a shock wave
through the *New York Times* building.

President Roosevelt had been warned repeatedly over the course
of a decade that Hiss was a Soviet spy, but continued to promote Hiss
to positions of greater influence. Hiss had been at President Roosevelt's side at Yalta, where Roosevelt notoriously handed over Poland to
Stalin. Britain and France had started World War II over Poland, but at
Yalta Roosevelt cavalierly relinquished Poland to another totalitarian
despot. The man advising Roosevelt during this transaction was Alger
Hiss, Soviet agent.

Truman kept Hiss on as director of the Office of Political Affairs at
the State Department. Hiss supervised the Dumbarton Oaks Conference, which helped create the United Nations, and he later served as
secretary general of the San Francisco Conference, which drafted the
United Nations Charter. In a final gift to his country, the Soviet spy
bequeathed us the United Nations. When Chambers publicly accused
Hiss of being a Soviet spy, Truman's Department of Justice tried to
indict not Hiss but Chambers. Had that prosecution gone forward, the
Truman administration would have destroyed the sole witness against
Hiss. Two FDR-appointed Supreme Court justices, Felix Frankfurter
and Stanley Reed, had testified as character witnesses for Hiss at
his criminal trial. A future Democratic presidential candidate, Adlai
Stevenson, would join them in attesting to Hiss's good character.
Democrats were indignant when Joe McCarthy started referring to
Stevenson as "Alger—I mean, Adlai . . . ," but not so indignant that
their party had become a refuge for traitors.

The usual leftist Kool-Aid drinkers spent decades tirelessly working on Hiss's rehabilitation. As the esteemed literary critic Lionel
Trilling wrote, "The educated, progressive middle class, especially in

its upper reaches, rallied to the cause and person of Alger Hiss, confident of his perfect innocence, deeply stirred by the pathos of what they never doubted was the injustice being visited upon him."[40] Hiss "became a steady, if unspectacular, fixture on the university lecture circuit," attracting a new fan base in the 1960s "among college audiences, faculty and students, both in this country and in England."[41] His first speech after leaving prison was at Princeton, where he was given a standing ovation.[42] He lived in Manhattan(!) and was a celebrity guest at parties on the Upper West Side.[43] Bard College has a chair in his name, the "Alger Hiss professor of social studies."[44] William Reuben, the James Carville of the Hiss case, called Hiss "an American saint."[45]

After Nixon was defeated in the 1962 California gubernatorial election, CBS News ran a special, titled "The Political Obituary of Richard Nixon." Among the expert guests was traitor and social critic Alger Hiss.[46] In 1972, Hiss's membership in the bar was reinstated, making him the "first lawyer ever re-admitted to the Massachusetts Bar following a major criminal conviction."[47]

Decades later, the New York Times was still complaining about "the smarmy air surrounding the House inquiry."[48] The air. Hiss was a Soviet spy, and liberals were snippy about the "air" in the room where he was exposed. Indeed, according to the Times, the air actually "cast doubt on Mr. Chambers's credibility." Hiss may have been a traitor to his country, but at least he was not some flag-waving yahoo Republican. Liberals would never give up on a man who spied for Stalin against America. Right up until the Soviet cables were declassified, they were still heatedly proclaiming Alger Hiss innocent.

In 1992, a few years before Soviet cables proved that Hiss was guilty, the Washington Post ran a news item stating three times that there was "no evidence" that Hiss was a Soviet agent.[49] That same year, the New York Times published a letter by John Lowenthal, director of the Cold War Archives Project, The Nation Institute, stating categorically that Alger Hiss "was not a spy." He said, "All disinterested historians must welcome the closing of this distressing episode."[50] The

Hiss case was "over." That same year, a writer mused in the pages of the *Times* that among the "Cold War mysteries" that might be answered by the Soviet archives was the devilish question of Hiss's guilt.[51] In 1994, the *New York Times* reported, "The Hiss case remains as uncertain as before."[52]

In 1995, it was no longer uncertain. That was the year the Venona Project was unveiled, revealing Soviet cables that established that Hiss was a Soviet agent to everyone's satisfaction except direct relatives of Alger Hiss. Nonetheless, the *New York Times* still instinctively trots out the theory that Hiss was innocent. It's some psychological block liberals have. Their minds are fine, but the woman wells up in them. In 1996, the *Times* described Hiss as "one of the great riddles of the Cold War," and blandly noted that some—"many of them on the left"—continued to revere Hiss.[53] One struggles in vain to think of anyone not "on the left" who believed Hiss after Chambers produced the Pumpkin Papers, much less after the Venona Project was declassified.

As recently as September 8, 2002, the *Times* said of Hiss, "He was convicted [of perjury] in 1951. It was later learned that some evidence supporting his claim of innocence was covered up."[54] Hiss was "accused" but it was "later learned" that evidence of his guilt was cooked! In one of the many official "corrections" to the *Times*'s ritualistic proclamation that all Soviet spies were innocent, a later correction admitted that the "later learned" evidence was merely one of many red herrings thrown up by Hiss. It was never accepted by any court. The *Times*'s correction said the original article had "omitted attribution for the suggestion that documents supporting Hiss's innocence were covered up. This was the position of Hiss and his supporters in a petition to set aside his conviction. The petition was denied and later appeals failed."[55]

Lying about Hiss's innocence was only part of the Hiss Rehabilitation Project. There was also the small matter of Chambers to be dealt with. Interestingly, Chambers's reception in polite society was not so welcoming as Alger Hiss's. After Chambers produced documentary proof that he was telling the truth about Hiss, Chambers was nearly unemployable. In 1950, shortly after Hiss's conviction, publisher Henry Luce invited Chambers to return to *Time* magazine as a writer. Before Chambers had even arrived in *Time*'s offices to discuss the offer, Luce rescinded it. He even withdrew an offer to write for *Architectural Forum*, another Luce publication. Other company executives had nixed Chambers's return on the grounds that he was too "controversial."[56]

"Controversial" means "telling the truth about liberals." It is one of the words, along with "shrill" and "divisive," that liberals apply to conservatives before blacklisting them. Would Chambers have been "controversial" if he had exposed Nazi spies working for the president? As is usually the case with "controversial" writers, Chambers was not so "controversial" with the American people. His eight-hundred-page autobiography, *Witness*, released two years later, became an instant— but not a "surprise"—bestseller.[57]

Two Democratic administrations had employed known Soviet spies at the highest level. Because of inept Democrats, Soviet penetration was so deep that Stalin would learn about the atomic bomb before President Truman did.[58] The Democrats had trifled with Communism. Quick action had to be taken immediately after the Hiss case. Otherwise Americans might dwell on the fact that Democrats cannot be trusted with the defense of the nation.

This is why liberals had to invent the myth of "McCarthyism." Joe McCarthy had absolutely no connection to the Hiss hearings. But as Allen Weinstein wrote in *Perjury*, "Hiss seemed an embodiment of what McCarthyism could do."[59] By screaming about "McCarthyism," liberals would force the nation to "move on" from the subject of their own treachery. It has become a cottage industry of the left to aggressively assert and defend the proposition that McCarthy was stone-evil. After Soviet cables proved the Democrats had been sheltering Soviet spies, we had more of a sense of why they were so upset.

It's not as if Democrats ran for office on a policy of letting Communists dominate Eastern Europe and run wild through China. People like Alger Hiss and hundreds of other Soviet agents were lying about their real intentions. The Soviets had an avowed policy of influencing

U.S. government policy, and the Democrats let them. Even liberals wouldn't have dared use the Clinton defense: *Yeah, okay, I'm a Soviet agent and advising the president at Yalta. So what?* Instead, when McCarthy exposed them, they called him a jackbooted oppressor.

McCarthy's opening salvo was his famous Wheeling, West Virginia, speech, in which he said he had in his hand the names of fifty-seven card-carrying Communists in the State Department. The Wheeling speech is often described as if it might as easily have been a speech on housing, but on a whim, McCarthy decided to give a speech on Communists in the State Department and decided anti-Communism was a good gig. As David Halberstam writes, "Suppose he had gone to pension plans instead of Communists. . . . Would history have been different?" Similarly, in *The Manchurian Candidate,* one of scores of Hollywood movies popularizing lies about McCarthy, the McCarthy figure chooses fifty-seven as the number of Communists in the government after seeing it on a bottle of Heinz ketchup.

This is a ludicrous detachment from all antecedent events. It parallels the theory that Ken Starr just woke up one day and decided to start investigating Clinton's sex life. It is true that McCarthy was a politician and, as such, often jawboned a variety of political issues. It was not a crazy fluke that Communism came to be foremost among them.

The entire liberal establishment had ferociously defended Hiss and attacked Chambers. Even after Chambers produced the equivalent of Monica's DNA-stained dress, they still wouldn't give up on their darling Hiss. After dragging the country through their nonsense defenses, Hiss was finally convicted of perjury for denying he was a Soviet spy. On the day of Hiss's conviction, January 25, 1950, Dean Acheson announced at a press conference, "I do not intend to turn my back on Alger Hiss."[60]

The public was aghast at Acheson's statement, enraged at the willful blindness of the Democrats to Communist espionage. Acheson laid it on thick, citing Scripture in defense of a traitor.[61] Only Clinton was more brazen. Nixon called Acheson's statement "disgusting." Chambers said, "You will look in vain in history for anything comparable to

it." Republican Senator William E. Jenner of Indiana denounced
Acheson as a "Communist-appeasing, Communist-protecting betrayer
of America." Would Democrats ever give a damn about Soviet spies
swarming through the government? What was it going to take? The entire country was in a cauldron of rage at these inept, traitor-supporting
Democrats.

On February 9, 1950—almost precisely two weeks after Acheson
praised Hiss—McCarthy gave his Wheeling, West Virginia, speech.
The idea that there was nothing going on and McCarthy burst onto the
scene like the Terminator is preposterous. There was a determinate
setting in which an explosion was inevitable. It was not an accident
that McCarthy launched his anti-Communist crusade just weeks after
the appalling spectacle of the Democratic secretary of state defending
Alger Hiss, a convicted Communist spy.

Journalist David Frum has written that the country did not need
McCarthy "to convince it that the Soviet Union and its domestic sympathizers were a threat that had to be repulsed."[62] At the time, even
people who were not fans of McCarthy did not take such a rosy view. In
1953, at the height of McCarthy's "reign of terror," political philosopher Sidney Hook wrote that the United States was the "chief remaining obstacle to world domination" by the Soviet Union. And yet, he
said, viewing the Kremlin's assault on the United States, "matters are
growing worse."[63]

Whittaker Chambers said that when he left the Communist Party,
he was "leaving the winning side for the losing side."[64] Communist infiltration, he said, had achieved its "ultimate purpose." In a situation "with
few parallels in history," the "agents of an enemy power" were in a position to "influence the nation's foreign policy in the interests of the nation's
chief enemy, and not only on exceptional occasions, like Yalta . . . but
in what must have been the staggering sum of day-to-day decisions."[65]
In America's battle to save itself, Chambers could name only a few
sparse victories. Among them was the indictment of a Soviet spy at the
Commerce Department, William Remington.[66] In McCarthy's enumeration of security risks in the government, Remington was "Case #19."[67]

The liberal establishment reacted to Soviet spies swarming through the government with the gentle, protective attitude of an Oxford don toward Soviet agents like Kim Philby. It was simply a prerogative of the old WASP ruling class to harbor Soviet spies. It was on the spectrum of things young people did. Some of their young men would grow up to be poets and some would grow up to be Bolsheviks. McCarthy exposed the moral corruption of the entire liberal ruling class. Salon liberals foolishly indulged their infatuation with Communism to the peril of the country.

Even the Hiss case had failed to rouse the Democrats. The Brahmins' true indignation was reserved for a lowborn bum like Chambers who dared attack Hiss—with his Supreme Court clerkship, his hauteur, his good breeding, and his Bryn Mawr–educated wife, Priscilla. The Democratic Party defended Alger Hiss and then brushed it off as a mere nothingness.

They would have gotten away with it, too, but for McCarthy. McCarthy came out swinging and created horrendous fear among the Soviet apparatchiks and their champions in the Democratic Party. Dean Acheson, with his fake British accent, his Groton and Yale degrees, was one of McCarthy's favorite targets. He had no use for mincing Ivy League diplomats with Communist partisans on their staff. After Acheson appeared in the Social Pages on a "Best Dressed" list, McCarthy began referring to him as "the Red Dean of Fashion." Privately, he called Acheson "that striped pants a——h——."[68]

A half century later, when the only people who call themselves Communists are harmless cranks, it is difficult to grasp the importance of McCarthy's crusade. But there's a reason "Communist" now sounds about as threatening as "monarchist"—and it's not because of intrepid *New York Times* editorials denouncing McCarthy and praising Harvard-educated Soviet spies. McCarthy made it a disgrace to be a Communist. Domestic Communism could never recover.

It is an interesting fact that this country does not have anything resembling a European-style left wing. In fact, we can barely sustain a functioning Democratic Party. It didn't have to be this way. As FBI

Director J. Edgar Hoover said, in March 1947 there were only about
one million Americans registered to vote with the Communist Party,
but that was more than there were in Russia in 1917.[69] What held the
Communist left to the madrasahs of the Ivy League was Joe McCarthy.
Sneering at McCarthy today because the only people who call themselves Communists are harmless cranks is like sneering at the Sabin
vaccine since, really, almost no one gets polio anymore. The big argument against McCarthy is that the whole notion of Communist subversion was a joke. It was not a joke. It was real. And the Democrats
didn't care.

In the twentieth century, nearly 100 million people were murdered
in the name of Communism.[70] Stalin held his monstrous Soviet show
trials, committed genocide against the kulaks, and created a forced
famine for the Ukrainians when they resisted collectivization. There
was Mao's "Great Leap Forward" murdering tens of millions of people.
There was the Khmer Rouge's massacre of one quarter of the entire
Cambodian population. Communist mass murder not only predated the
Nazi variety but far surpassed it. Wherever there was Communism,
there was repression, torture, and mass murder.

It is a fact that hundreds of agents of this blood-soaked ideology
became top advisors to Democratic presidents, worked on the Manhattan Project, infiltrated every segment of the United States government.
Stalin's agents held top positions in the White House, the State Department, the Treasury Department, the Army, and the OSS. Because of
Democrat incompetence and moral infirmity, all Americans lived
under the threat of nuclear annihilation for half a century. As Soviet
spies passed nuclear technology to Stalin, President Roosevelt gave
strict orders that the OSS engage in no espionage against the country
ruled by his pal, Uncle Joe.[71]

When it could have been stopped, when, days after the Hitler-
Stalin Pact was signed, an ex-Communist came to the United States
government and informed on Hiss, as well as dozens of other Soviet
spies in the government, President Roosevelt had laughed. McCarthy
punched back so hard, liberals are still reeling.

3

NO COMMUNISTS HERE!

A typical account of the McCarthy era is given in the 1978 book *The Great Fear* by David Caute. As the title suggests, the book portrays a period much like Stalin's "Great Terror," only worse. It seems a baseless "sweat drenched fear" of Communists seized America during the fifties. Caute writes, "There is no documentation in the public record of a direct connection between the American Communist Party and espionage during the entire postwar period."[1] In 1994, McCarthy biographer Ellen Schrecker sniffed at J. Edgar Hoover's "longstanding contention that all Communists were potential Soviet agents" and pronounced, "There was no evidence of espionage and no one confessed. When questioned by federal investigators, the alleged spies either took the Fifth Amendment or . . . denied the charges against them."[2]

Liberals' insistence that there was "no evidence" of Soviet spies apparently meant, "We were Soviet spies." Even before Soviet cables proved the existence of a vast Soviet-run espionage network in America, there was lots of evidence. There were, for example, the detailed accounts given in sworn testimony by various ex-Communists like Whittaker Chambers, Elizabeth Bentley, and Louis Budenz. There were Chambers's Pumpkin Papers. There were Soviet defectors who brought reams of KGB documents with them, identifying Soviet agents in America. There were confessions of arrested spies, such as David Greenglass, who informed on his sister Ethel Rosenberg and her husband, Julius. There was the arrest of Judith Coplon, who was actually apprehended in the act of handing a U.S. counterintelligence file to a KGB officer.

"No evidence"!

It turned out that, all along, there was also evidence in the form of decrypted Soviet cables to their agents in America. Though not revealed for half a century, the U.S. government had broken the Soviet cable code beginning in the forties in a top-secret undertaking known as the Venona Project. In the most patriotic act of his career, Senator Daniel Patrick Moynihan would push through the declassification of the Venona Project, which was finally unveiled on July 11, 1995. After the cables were revealed, liberals became a little less argumentative about evidence of Soviet spies. Here was enough "evidence" even for those who demand a shockingly high level of proof before defending America.

The Venona Project was begun in 1943 by Colonel Carter Clarke, chief of the U.S. Army's Special Branch, in response to rumors that Stalin was negotiating a separate peace with Hitler.[3] Only a few years earlier, the world had been staggered by the Hitler-Stalin Pact. Unaccountably, Colonel Clarke did not share President Roosevelt's trust in the man FDR called "Uncle Joe." Cloaked in secrecy, Clarke set up a special Army unit to break the Soviet code. Neither President Roosevelt nor President Truman was told about the Venona Project.[4] This was a matter of vital national security: The Democrats could not be trusted.

The Soviets used a code that was, in theory, unbreakable. But by the war's end, the Americans had cracked it. And when the Venona cryptographers read the Soviet cables they discovered something far more sinister than Stalin's war plans: The Roosevelt administration was teeming with paid agents of Moscow. Stalin's handmaidens held strategic positions at the White House, the State Department, the War Department, the Office of Strategic Services, and the Treasury Department.

Only a small number of the intercepted Soviet cables have been decoded. But even that much proves McCarthy was absolutely right in his paramount charge: The U.S. government had a major Communist infestation problem. It is treated as a mere truism that McCarthy was reckless, made mistakes, and was careless with his facts. It can now be said that McCarthy's gravest error was in underestimating the problem of Communist subversion.

The scale of the conspiracy was unprecedented. Hundreds of Soviet spies honeycombed the U.S. government throughout the forties and fifties. America had been invaded by a civilian army loyal to a hostile power. There was no room for denying it. Soviet operatives were stealing technical information from atomic, military, radar, aerospace, and rocket programs. The cables revealed the code names of the spies, their technical espionage, and the secret transmission of highly sensitive diplomatic and strategic policies.

McCarthy was accused of labeling "anyone with liberal views" a Communist. As we now know, that wouldn't have been a half-bad system. Contrary to Caute's preposterous claim that Communists were innocent idealists, the American Communist Party was linked to Stalin like an al-Qaeda training camp to Osama bin Laden. As John Earl Haynes and Harvey Klehr wrote in their book *Venona*, the American Communist Party was "a fifth column working inside and against the United States in the Cold War."[5] The cables "expose beyond cavil the American Communist party as an auxiliary of the intelligence agencies of the Soviet Union." They said, "While not every American Communist was a spy, hundreds were."[6] It was a striking admission coming from Haynes and Klehr. In their earlier book on American Communism, they had stated matter-of-factly that "few American Communists were spies." The disgorging of decrypted Soviet cables forced the professors to revise that assessment.

The Soviet cables indisputably proved the guilt of all the left's favorite "Red Scare" martyrs—Alger Hiss, Harry Dexter White, and Julius and Ethel Rosenberg. Appropriately, the Soviet's code name for Communist spy Julius Rosenberg was "Liberal." Because of Venona, the FBI and certain top Justice Department officials were absolutely sure "they were prosecuting the right people."[7] But throughout the trial of Julius and Ethel Rosenberg, J. Edgar Hoover risked acquittal rather than reveal that the U.S. had cracked the Soviet code. Without realizing that the U.S. government had confirmed the accounts of such informers as Whittaker Chambers and Elizabeth Bentley with Soviet cables, the left smeared ex-Communist informers as lunatics and perverts. Now the world knew what J. Edgar Hoover knew at the time: The informers were telling the truth.

Bentley, long maligned the way liberals malign all women who cause them trouble, was known as the "Blonde Spy Queen." Her testimony was roundly dismissed as "the imaginings of a neurotic spinster."[8] With flawless timing, just one year before the Venona Project was declassified, *The Nation* magazine sniffed that Bentley was "hardly a reliable informant." (In 1994, the moral flaws of ex-Communist informants from the fifties were still a burning issue at *The Nation*.) The magazine called Bentley "an alcoholic who embraced both fascism and communism before she turned professional and converted to Catholicism." Though Bentley named "nearly 150 people," *The Nation* said, "the bureau never corroborated her story. It was inconsistent from the start and she kept adding names and details over the years."[9] So there you have it. After fifty years on the case, *The Nation* magazine could proclaim Bentley *still* a liar. In the definitive book about the decrypted cables, *Venona*, Haynes and Klehr state simply, "The deciphered Venona cables show that Elizabeth Bentley had told the truth."[10]

Here was the DNA evidence of Communist crimes during the Cold War. But for some reason, liberals did not brandish this evidence as excitedly as they do newly discovered evidence allegedly "exonerating" murderers on death row. A lot of books, documentaries, articles, movies, and graduate student theses had already been deployed in the effort to portray an irrational hysteria that seized the nation about phantom Communists. The unveiling of Venona was as close to Judgment Day for liberals as we'll ever get in this life.

The only indication that liberals have even heard of the Venona Project is that they haven't been as prolix on the subject of innocent victims of anti-Communism lately. In moments of nostalgia, they will sometimes pretend they missed that day's newspaper and impulsively attach the word "suspected" to the names of proved Soviet spies. But except for a few doddering Stalinists on college faculties and at *The Nation* magazine, it was: Game Over. The long, lachrymose tales of woe have disappeared. All liberals can hold on to now is the slogan "McCarthyism." Just don't ask for details.

After all the righteous indignation at the *New York Times* about "McCarthyism," to say nothing of that paper's vehement defense of Hiss, the Rosenbergs, Owen Lattimore—and for the record, Stalin, in the classic reportage of Walter Duranty—the Venona Project might have been at least as important as the July 2001 story on how, if you don't count the military ballots, George Bush might have won Florida by only two hundred votes. But when the Venona Project was declassified, revealing decades of cable traffic between Soviet espionage agents and their American spies, it was barely noticed at the *Times*. Only about a dozen *Times* articles have ever mentioned the Venona Project even in passing. Not one article on Venona ever graced the front page or the op-ed page.[11]

The *Times* showed a rather more heightened interest in the release of internal documents from the House Un-American Activities Committee six years later. In a lengthy op-ed piece—something the *Times* never accorded the release of the Venona Project—Rick Perlstein complained that the unveiling of the HUAC documents "may have lacked the ceremony" of the declassification of Venona but was just as important nonetheless.[12] The "ceremony" surrounding Venona's release had been a demure affair at the *New York Times*. No matter. The HUAC documents, Perlstein said, should "share its import."

Heretofore we had heard only smears against the beloved Soviet Union. Now, at last, we would hear the other side in the battle of relatively equal evil forces: Soviet gulags and fascistic oppression by HUAC. Needless to say, there was nothing new in the HUAC documents and neither Perlstein nor anyone else ever mentioned them again.[13] If Reagan hadn't defeated the Soviet Union, thereby relieving liberals of their duty to defend Communist spies, they would refuse to acknowledge the existence of the Venona Project even now.

TO UNDERSTAND HOW DEEP WERE THE SOVIET TENTACLES IN the Roosevelt and Truman administrations, try to imagine a parallel universe today.

Paul Wolfowitz, Bush's deputy secretary of defense, would be a member of al-Qaeda taking orders from Osama bin Laden.
   Alger Hiss, assistant to the secretary of state under President Franklin D. Roosevelt. Identified as a Soviet spy in Venona.[14]

The assistant to the secretary of the Treasury would be a member of al-Qaeda. He would be furiously employing a dozen other members of al-Qaeda at the Treasury Department. When their loyalty to America was questioned, he would leap in to defend them and save their jobs. With his secret al-Qaeda allies, he would intervene to block a crucial promised loan to Israel while at the same time encouraging the administration to make an absurdly generous loan to Saddam Hussein. When Israel imploded, historians and experts would rush in to say no one "lost" Israel. Bush would then promote the assistant to run the International Monetary Fund.
   Harry Dexter White, assistant secretary of the Treasury under President Franklin D. Roosevelt. Identified as a Soviet spy in Venona. White secured high-level government positions at the Treasury Department for at least eleven other Soviet agents—

all named in Venona.[15] *White conspired with his fellow Soviet spies Frank Coe and Solomon Adler to kill a critical loan to Nationalist China, while at the same time trying to persuade Roosevelt to give the Soviet Union a $10 billion loan on extremely favorable terms (repayable over thirty-five years at a rate of 2 percent).*[16]

   Despite repeated warnings from the head of the FBI that White was a Soviet agent, President Truman retained White at Treasury and then appointed him the top U.S. official at the International Monetary Fund.

Bush aide Andrew Card would be a member of al-Qaeda, sent on important international missions for President Bush.

   Lauchlin Currie, administrative assistant to President Franklin D. Roosevelt and deputy administrator of the Board of Economic Warfare.[17] *Identified as a Soviet spy in Venona.*

The assistant to CIA Director George Tenet would be a member of al-Qaeda. It would raise no eyebrows in the Bush administration that the assistant was identified as a member of al-Qaeda by an FBI informer. Nor that he had honeymooned in Tora Bora.

   Duncan Lee, chief of staff to the head of the Office of Strategic Services—the precursor to the CIA—under President Franklin D. Roosevelt. Honeymooned in Moscow and identified as a Soviet spy in the sworn testimony of ex-spy Elizabeth Bentley. Confirmed as a Soviet spy in Venona.[18]

Bush aide Karl Rove would be referred to by al-Qaeda leaders as their most valuable asset. He would push the Bush administration to sell military and industrial equipment to Osama bin Laden on a special lend-lease deal. Years later, an al-Qaeda operative would claim Rove was working for them.

   Harry Hopkins, special advisor to President Roosevelt and so described by a member of the Soviet underground, Anatoly

Akhmerov.[19] *In* K.G.B.: The Inside Story, *former KGB agent
Oleg Gordievsky identified Hopkins as a Soviet agent "of major
significance."*[20]

Dick Cheney would be starstruck by Saddam Hussein and would counsel restraint in response to Hussein's every hostile act. At the same
time, he would regularly denounce the U.S. and Britain as empire-
building fascists. In other words, he would be Jimmy Carter.

*Roosevelt's vice president Henry Wallace, 1940–1944, who
believed "America's main enemy was Churchill and the British
Empire." He insisted that peace would be assured "if the United
States guaranteed Stalin control of Eastern Europe."*[21] *When
Stalin seized Czechoslovakia, Wallace sided with Stalin. When
Stalin blockaded Berlin, Wallace opposed the U.S. airlift. After
visiting a Soviet slave camp, Wallace enthusiastically described
it as a "combination TVA and Hudson Bay Company."*[22]

Richard Perle, chairman of the Defense Policy Board, an advisory
panel to Defense Secretary Donald H. Rumsfeld, would surround himself with members of al-Qaeda in and out of government. He would
invariably take the position most advantageous to al-Qaeda.

*Owen Lattimore, the foreign policy sage loitering around the
State Department, surrounded himself with Communist spies,
both as editor of* Pacific Affairs, *the journal published by the
Institute of Pacific Relations think tank, and at the State
Department building, where he kept a desk and was deferred
to as the wise man on China (which no one "lost").*

The American ambassador to Iraq would heatedly deny that Saddam
Hussein had gassed his own people. He would defend Saddam Hussein's nuclear weapons program and state that Iraq has "every moral
right to seek atomic-bomb information"—including by espionage.

*Joseph Davies, a Roosevelt-appointed ambassador to the USSR,
insisted Stalin's show trials were honest searches for the truth.*

He told the Associated Press in 1946 that "Russia in self-
defense has every moral right to seek atomic-bomb information
through military espionage if excluded from such information
by her former fighting allies."[23]

Gale Norton, Bush's secretary of the interior, would be a member of
various al-Qaeda front groups, such as the Benevolence International
Foundation,[24] publicly lending her name to their events.

Harold Ickes, Roosevelt's interior secretary (and father of
Clinton deputy chief of staff by the same name), was a member
of the Stalinist front group League for Peace and Democracy.
He wrote a letter welcoming them to Washington for its fifth
national gathering.[25]

In the midst of all this, President Bush would be referring to America's
mortal enemy with warmth and affection, calling him "Uncle Osama."
In his inaugural address, Bush would explain that his posture toward
al-Qaeda was, "In order to make a friend, one must be a friend."

President Roosevelt, who called Stalin "Uncle Joe," said of
the Soviet Union in his fourth inaugural address: "In order to
make a friend, one must be a friend."

Bush's Republican successor as president would be telling a top aide
that "Saddam was a fine man who wanted to do the right thing." He
would write in his diary, "The Iraqis have always been our friends and
I can't see any reason why they shouldn't always be."

President Truman said this about Stalin in October 1945, and
wrote in his diary that the Russians "have always been our friends
and I can't see any reason why they shouldn't always be."[26]

THE PRINCIPAL DIFFERENCE BETWEEN FIFTH COLUMNISTS IN
the Cold War versus the war on terrorism is that you could sit next to
a Communist in a subway without asphyxiating. The second difference is, by the end of World War II, Roosevelt's pal Joseph Stalin had

murdered twenty million people. ("One death is a tragedy but a million is only a statistic.") Even the Religion of Peace has not come close to that record. In far more time, Islamic terrorists of all nationalities, in all their manifestations, have not murdered even 0.1 percent as many people.

Incredibly, if Roosevelt had died one year earlier, Stalin might have immediately gained control of the United States presidency, Treasury Department, and State Department. Soviet dupe Henry Wallace would have become president, and it is very possible that he would have made Soviet spy Harry Dexter White his Treasury secretary and Soviet spy Alger Hiss his secretary of state.

In a formulation that would make Harvard-educated traitors titter, Joe McCarthy called it "a conspiracy on a scale so immense as to dwarf any previous such venture in the history of man. A conspiracy of infamy so black that, when it is finally exposed, its principals shall be forever deserving of the maledictions of all honest men."[27] With a campaign of lies, liberals have turned McCarthy into the object "forever deserving of the maledictions of all honest men." Summarizing the views of all liberals, President Truman said, "I like old Joe. Joe is a decent fellow."[28] Not McCarthy, of course, but Stalin. Truman loathed Joe McCarthy.

Among the most notorious Soviet spies in high-level positions in the Roosevelt and Truman administrations—now proved absolutely, beyond question by the Soviet cables—were Alger Hiss at the State Department; Harry Dexter White, assistant secretary of the Treasury Department, later appointed to the International Monetary Fund by President Truman; Lauchlin Currie, personal assistant to President Roosevelt and White House liaison to the State Department under both Roosevelt and Truman; Laurence Duggan, head of the Latin American Desk at the State Department; Frank Coe, U.S. representative on the International Monetary Fund; Solomon Adler, senior Treasury Department official; Klaus Fuchs, top atomic scientist; and Duncan Lee, senior aide to the head of the OSS.

The late senator Daniel Patrick Moynihan made a valiant effort to defend Roosevelt's and Truman's maddening obtuseness to Soviet agents in their employ, arguing that since they weren't told of the Venona Project, how could they be sure?

From 1945 to 1946, J. Edgar Hoover deluged Truman, the attorney general, and the secretary of state with increasingly urgent memos indicating that Harry Dexter White was a spy.[29] The evidence was neither flimsy nor ambiguous. In 1945, the prime minister of Canada flew to Washington to warn the director of the FBI about a spy who clearly had to be White. A Soviet defector, Igor Gouzenko, had left the Soviet embassy in Canada, bringing hundreds of pages of documents with him. His information led to twenty-two arrests in Canada. Gouzenko's information identified White as a Soviet spy. Ex-spies Whittaker Chambers and Elizabeth Bentley had also "independently and without knowledge of each other's stories" named White as a Soviet spy.[30] In the words of Sam Tanenhaus, biographer of Whittaker Chambers, Hoover provided the Truman administration with "stark confirmation" that Harry Dexter White (as well as Alger Hiss) was a Soviet agent.[31] Truman responded by making White the top U.S. representative at the International Monetary Fund.

Just months into his presidency, Eisenhower would take the astonishing step of directing his attorney general, Herbert Brownell, to go on national TV and announce that President Truman had appointed a Soviet spy to be the top U.S. official at the IMF with full knowledge that White had been reliably identified as a Soviet agent. It was a breathtaking revelation. This would be like President Bush instructing Attorney General John Ashcroft to hold a press conference announcing that President Clinton had appointed Mohammed Atta to be secretary of the Department of Transportation after being told Atta was a Muslim terrorist. Truman responded to Brownell's statement by indignantly denying he had ever seen an FBI report suggesting that White was a spy. The FBI then produced the report. Next, Truman said he had moved White to the IMF only to get him out of the Treasury Department, expecting the FBI to continue its surveillance of White.[32] So putting a Soviet spy in charge of the IMF was really a security measure. At least there was a good explanation.

But Moynihan claimed that if only Roosevelt and Truman had been told about the precise mechanics of the Venona Project, perhaps the Democrats would have finally expressed curiosity about the many Soviet spies in their employ. More likely, the Democrats would have told their Soviet pals that their cables were being read. In fact, that actually happened. The Venona Project had just gotten under way when trusted Roosevelt advisor Lauchlin Currie informed the Soviets that the Americans were about to crack their code. Thanks to the Soviet work ethic, the KGB reacted by making only superficial changes to the code.[33] (Perhaps a profit motive would have inspired the Soviet code-makers to be more thorough.) Incredibly, a year later, someone in Roosevelt's White House, "most likely" Currie again, directed that the entire code-breaking project be stopped. The head of the Venona Project ignored the order.[34] The problem was not that Democrats were not given sufficient proof of Communist spies in their administrations. It was that they didn't give a damn.

Even before the Venona Project was declassified, there were subtle clues that the Roosevelt and Truman administrations were having staffing problems. After showing up to testify before HUAC with Dean Acheson at his side, Harvard-educated Currie fled to Colombia. Coe pleaded the Fifth Amendment when asked if he was a "Soviet agent," and then escaped to Red China, where he became a top advisor to the Communist government until his death. (His efforts on behalf of totalitarianism were better rewarded than those of another Soviet spy, Noel H. Field, who fled to the workers' paradise in Hungary—and was immediately imprisoned.)[35]

With all the innocent victims of the "Red Scare" flinging themselves from windows in the fifties, you would think you couldn't walk down a street in Manhattan without a body falling on you. In fact, Harry Dexter White and Laurence Duggan were the only casualties. After denying he was a Soviet spy in sworn testimony before HUAC,

White had a heart attack and died. After being questioned by the FBI, Duggan fell from the sixteenth floor of a Manhattan building, an apparent suicide. And now we know why. They were Soviet spies, and House investigators were closing in. It wasn't the "Red Scare" that drove them to their deaths. It was their guilt.[36] At least they spared us the habeas petitions.

A few years earlier, when State Department investigators were circling, Duggan told his KGB handler that he would henceforth "only work openly within American leftist circles."[37] Apparently he made a lot of friends. After Duggan's death, the moaning and gnashing of teeth from the liberal aristocracy almost surpassed Hollywood's bleating about lost movie credits. Such liberal luminaries as Eleanor Roosevelt, poet Archibald MacLeish, journalist Drew Pearson, and broadcasting personality Edward R. Murrow denounced the idea that Duggan could possibly have been a spy. Truman's undersecretary of state, Sumner Welles, defended Duggan. Attorney General Tom Clarke pronounced Duggan "a loyal employee of the United States Government."[38]

Though all half-serious people knew the left's various celebrity martyrs were traitors without having to see Soviet cables, liberals would never, ever relent in their lies.

Most astonishing was the left's defense of the Rosenbergs. There had been mass protests all around the world over the Rosenberg case. The Communists assembled large crowds in Paris, Brussels, Rome, and all the usual hot spots. It was a real international cause célèbre. American liberals were exuberant. They had finally won recognition and support from all over the world. It was a good issue for them. The American left kept carrying on about the horrors of McCarthyism, but even their fellow Communists couldn't quite work themselves into a lather over most of the "horror." *You mean he couldn't do screenplays under his own name and had to fire the gardener and clean his pool in Bel Air by himself? No! That is shocking!*

The Rosenberg case was the sort of thing Europeans could relate to—a bookish middle-aged couple sentenced to die in the electric chair and not even allowed to do forced labor but sent right away to some fiendish capitalist high-technology killing implement! It was also important in the background that everyone knew the Rosenbergs were Jewish. The Communist message was: America is becoming a fascist police state! What better proof than the execution of a harmless Jewish couple from the Bronx. The Rosenbergs became the most compelling proof for the line that Eisenhower was turning the United States into a fascist state. It wasn't easy to put grinning Ike and "fascism" in the same sentence—unless it was to say that Ike destroyed fascism with his resolute wartime leadership. So the left held very tightly to the one piece of evidence that seemed to substantiate their crackpot vision of the fifties.

If liberals ever admitted the Rosenbergs were guilty, they would have to admit that all those people protesting on their behalf—and warning of impending fascist tyranny in America—were total Communist stooges or complete idiots. At least they wanted to hold on to the suggestion of symmetry: "Yes, Stalin committed many excesses—but there was also McCarthyism in America!" So no matter how much evidence kept rolling in, liberals clung to the theory that the Rosenbergs were innocent.

Among the evidence tending to prove the Rosenbergs' guilt was the detailed confession of Ethel Rosenberg's brother David Greenglass implicating his sister and brother-in-law. There were the scores of eyewitnesses who painted a clear picture of a Soviet spy ring with Julius Rosenberg at its center. There was the fact that two members of the Rosenbergs' circle fled the country upon the Rosenbergs' arrest. And, of course, there was a unanimous jury verdict—or as patriot Ethel Rosenberg called it, "American fascism." As Rosenberg prosecutor Roy Cohn said, "To ask for any more, is to ask for the impossible."[39]

In 1983, Ronald Radosh and Joyce Milton wrote a book about the case, *The Rosenberg File: A Search for the Truth.* They, too, had been "idealists," and fervent believers in the Rosenbergs' sublime innocence. And then they looked at the evidence and concluded otherwise. Indeed, so overwhelming was their case against the Rosenbergs, even

O.J. defender Alan Dershowitz proclaimed it "definitive." Henceforth, he said, all "reasonable" discussion of the case must begin with the "fact that Julius Rosenberg was guilty of espionage."[40]

Alan Brinkley, also then a Harvard professor, said *The Rosenberg File* presented "a vast accumulation of small but incriminating facts, an accumulation so large (and thus far so uncontradicted) that even the most determined conspiracy theorist will have difficulty believing that it could have been the result of a calculated frame-up."[41] And yet, the title of Brinkley's book review called it "A Story Without Heroes." The accusations against the Rosenbergs "may have been generally correct," Brinkley admitted, but the government's "tactics were consistently questionable and at times shamefully unethical."[42] On one hand, the Rosenbergs had spied on their own country and turned over atomic secrets to a grisly totalitarian regime that would threaten American citizens with nuclear annihilation for the next fifty years. On the other hand, the prosecutors had played rough. So there were mistakes on both sides.

Yet more evidence of the Rosenbergs' guilt appeared with the publication of Nikita Khrushchev's memoirs in 1990. The late Soviet premier gushed with praise for the Rosenbergs, saying they had provided "very significant help in accelerating the production of our atomic bomb." Indeed, Khrushchev was unrestrained in his gratitude: "Let this be a worthy tribute to the memory of those people. Let my words serve as an expression of gratitude to those who sacrificed their lives to a great cause of the Soviet state at a time when the U.S. was using its advantage over our state to blackmail our state and undermine its proletarian cause."[43]

The *New York Times* reacted to Khrushchev's stunning if inadvertent admission of the Rosenbergs' guilt by saying it was "unlikely to settle a matter that has generated passionate books and an endless debate."[44] As long as liberals refuse to concede a point, it remains "unsettled." Indeed, the *Times* reported that reaction was "fervent and inconclusive."[45] Liberals think they can defeat the truth with loudness.

Unhappy with the way the real evidence was going, in 1993, the American Bar Association staged a "mock trial" of the Rosenbergs and proclaimed them innocent.[46]

And then, two years later, the Soviet cables that had indisputably identified Rosenberg as a spy were declassified.

There wasn't much room for any more nails in the coffin of the Rosenbergs' guilt after that. And still the evidence kept pouring in! In 1997, former KGB colonel Alexander Feklisov gave a television interview in which he identified himself as Julius Rosenberg's Soviet controller. He praised their important contributions to the USSR's acquisition of the bomb. Feklisov said, "Julius and Ethel are heroes, real heroes," and "I don't want to take this story to my grave."[47] He later boasted that "the Rosenberg network was one of the best-producing groups of agents in the history of Soviet technological espionage."[48]

To this day, there are liberals who refuse to admit that Julius Rosenberg was a spy. In 2002, the London *Guardian* would concede only this: "Recent evidence, from the so-called Venona tapes of wireless traffic between Soviet intelligence and its agents in America and from newly opened Soviet archives, strongly suggests that Julius Rosenberg may have been a spy."[49] There is no comparable refusal to accept facts among conservatives. Even the right-wing militias of liberals' fevered imaginations are not this insane.

In 1992, ABC's *Nightline* was puzzling over the guilt of two engineers in the Rosenbergs' spy ring who fled to Russia after the Rosenbergs were arrested. Joel Barr disappeared so fast he left all his possessions behind in a Paris apartment. Alfred Sarant left behind a wife and child—but took his neighbor's wife with him. Once safely ensconced in the mother country, the USSR, Barr and Sarant were set up in fabulous apartments in Leningrad and were paid ten times more than the average Russian worker. They were given their own institute to design technology that would be used to shoot down American planes. Their work helped the USSR develop radar-guided anti-aircraft artillery and surface-to-air missiles later used against American planes in Vietnam.[50] The deciphered Soviet cables revealed that Barr and

Sarant were "among the KGB's most valuable technical spies," as Haynes and Klehr put it in *Venona*.[51]

But in 1992, ABC's *Nightline* didn't know what to make of a Communist Party member fleeing to Russia upon the Rosenbergs' arrest. In a program titled "American Patriot/Soviet Spy?" Ted Koppel interviewed Barr—who had recently returned to America to collect his Social Security benefits. Koppel treated Barr's spy status as an open question. As Koppel put it, "You'll have to make up your own mind." Barr had been a member of the Communist Party. He happened to know America's most notorious spy, Julius Rosenberg. And he fled to the USSR the instant Rosenberg was arrested. What evidence was Koppel waiting for? ABC News has accused American corporations of conspiring to maim and addict consumers with substantially less evidence than the evidence tending to show Barr was a Soviet spy.

Amid occasional clips of FBI agents blind with rage, screaming that Barr was a Soviet spy who had done incalculable damage to America, Koppel informed the audience that Barr had "left" the country because he was "pro-Communist." Koppel quickly explained that being "pro-Communist" was "not such a terrible thing during the U.S.–Soviet alliance of World War II." Only later, he said, being "pro-Communist" was "no longer acceptable."

The allies' compact with Stalin was a military alliance, not an endorsement of Stalin's murderous ideology. No one took seriously the idea that because of an expedient alliance, Stalin was a fine fellow. Churchill had wanted to crush Soviet totalitarianism back in the twenties. Republican presidents Warren Harding, Calvin Coolidge, and Herbert Hoover refused to recognize the Soviet regime (though Franklin Roosevelt's very first diplomatic act as president was to grant the USSR diplomatic recognition, coinciding, as it turned out, with Stalin's forced Ukrainian famine). Referring to the alliance with Stalin, Churchill said that to defeat Hitler he would have allied with the devil. When the United States made an alliance with mad mullahs in Afghanistan against the USSR, no sensible American would go sign up with the Taliban. In forty years, *Nightline* will be running a special on American Taliban

John Walker Lindh: "American Patriot/American Traitor?" You'll have to make up your own mind!

Retired FBI agent Robert Royal said of Barr, "He recruited a minimum of 18 of his classmates as Russian spies. There's no way you can describe the hideous nature of this group of people and what they did to this government, what it cost us." He said the FBI had identified Barr as a spy. To this Koppel retorted: "That may have been what the FBI concluded, but Joel Barr adamantly denies it, and the FBI has never proved it." It was a little difficult to prove, on account of Barr's fleeing the country.

Koppel joshed with the American traitor, telling Barr, "You're a piece of work, you really are." Barr was, Koppel said, "charming, engaging, at times bewilderingly disingenuous." Not disingenuous outright, but "bewilderingly disingenuous." Koppel evidently considered it out of character for Bolshevik traitors to be "disingenuous." Barr's children—who, Koppel noted, "share their father's love for music"—told Koppel the reason their father fled to the Soviet Union was that he "decided to live" there. His decision came, as luck would have it, at the precise instant the Rosenberg cell was broken and David Greenglass began to inform on the cell. Koppel was still unable to draw any firm conclusions. As he said, "Joel Barr makes your head throb."

Barr had retained his American citizenship and had even voted in recent presidential elections. Guess which party he belonged to? Guess!

KOPPEL: You voted?

MR. BARR: Of course I voted. Are you kidding? I'm a Democrat.[52]

Of course—"I'm a Democrat." What else would he be? He should have said—"I'm *still* a Democrat."

Koppel concluded with the mind-bogglingly stupid point that Barr didn't look like a spy: "He still doesn't seem to fit into any easy preconception of what a spy should be." What does Koppel think Soviet spies are supposed to look like? Jim Thorpe? Barr was a first-generation Russian Jew, born in Brooklyn, who joined the Young Communist League at the City College of New York. Apart from being a Harvard-educated patrician WASP, there was no more archetypal Soviet spy.

Only after the Venona cables irrefutably identified Joel Barr as a Soviet spy did the damnable question of whether Barr was a Soviet spy finally come into clearer focus for liberals. Clearer, but still murky. When Barr died in 1998, the *New York Times* wrote in his obituary, "Mr. Barr was *suspected* of passing secret information about technology advances to the Soviets" (emphasis mine). Dozens of Soviet cables had identified Barr as a Soviet spy.[53] He fled to the USSR, where he helped develop Soviet military technology. If the *Times* ever produced half that much evidence in support of global warming, conservatives would concede the point. Perhaps the ABA could stage another "mock trial," this time finding Barr innocent of Soviet espionage.

In 1998, several years after Harry Dexter White's extensive espionage activities were revealed in Soviet cables, the *New York Times* published a letter from White's daughter scoffing at the "flimsy" evidence for the claim that her father was a Communist agent.[54] Among the copious Soviet cables identifying White as a spy, one reveals that the Soviet Union offered to pay the education expenses of White's daughter to help keep him in government service where they needed him.[55]

These are the people who are indignant that McCarthy was not always scrupulous about his facts. Conservatives are compelled to engage in ritualistic self-flagellation over the possibility that Senator Joe McCarthy may have said he had in his hand a list of "205" rather than "57" card-carrying Communists. But liberals will never abandon their provably false assertions about Soviet spies. Listening to liberals discuss Soviet spies is like being trapped in some infernal freshman dorm debate about the meaning of words. How do we know the cat is on the mat and the mat is not on the cat? "Seeing before me a cat on a mat directly causes me to truly believe that the cat is on the mat. Such causation, though, falls desperately short of the call for the epistemic evidence that epistemically justifies beliefs."[56]

In 2002, the *Seattle Times* described the government's case against accused spy Judith Coplon as "entirely circumstantial."[57] The circumstance was this: In March 1949, she was arrested while handing secret government documents to a Russian agent. I suppose you could call that a "circumstance." Needless to say, Soviet cables confirmed that Coplon was a Soviet agent. Liberal refusal to accept any evidence that any person ever spied for the Soviet Union would be exasperating if it weren't so comical.

No amount of evidence proving anyone was a Soviet spy could ever be enough. Blindingly obvious Soviet spies were treated as innocent liberals victimized by anti-Communist hysteria drummed up by Joe McCarthy. Fleeing to the Soviet Union is deemed ambiguous evidence. Handing secret documents to a KGB agent is merely "circumstantial." One could have a more fruitful discussion with a paranoid schizophrenic about his tinfoil hat than with liberals about Soviet spies crawling through Democratic administrations at the onset of the Cold War. This is the atmosphere in which McCarthy's charges have been evaluated for the last half century.

4

THE INDISPENSABLE
JOE McCARTHY

The truth about McCarthy will sound insane, because it has been a major goal of the left to make it sound insane. Your tax money is used to support school textbooks and college professors churning out nonsense about McCarthy. It has been pounded into people that the "Red Scare" was a weird psychological obsession and that McCarthy was the evil genius behind it. Even people who know better are constantly being forced to declaim McCarthy a very bad man just so liberals will leave them alone. It is the code word that must be uttered to gain acceptance into the halls of establishmentarian opinion. Crying "McCarthyism" is the coward's version of fatwa. Traduce the McCarthy myth and you can expect a double-blacklisting.

Despite the fevered associations of Joe McCarthy with Hollywood blacklists, ruined lives, destroyed reputations, broken careers, suicides, divorce, and depression, McCarthy's campaign was somewhat more limited in scope. McCarthy's contribution to "McCarthyism" consisted exclusively of his investigation of loyalty risks working for the federal government. He was not even particularly interested in the Communists themselves. His targets were government officials charged with removing loyalty risks from sensitive government jobs. His campaign lasted only a few years, from 1950 to 1953, until liberals immobilized him in 1954 with their Army-McCarthy hearings and censure investigation. He conducted his investigations from the Senate Permanent Subcommittee on Investigations, the express mandate of which was— surprisingly enough—to investigate the federal government. As we now know, McCarthy was not terrorizing people purposelessly. His targets *were* Soviet sympathizers and Soviet spies.

Liberals use animal-like logic to string together irrelevancies from Hollywood blacklisting to the Smith Act all under the rubric "McCarthyism." It has simply become de rigueur to describe all Communists as hapless victims of "McCarthyism," irrespective of whether McCarthy had ever heard of them and certainly irrespective of whether they were Soviet spies. It would be as if conservatives grouped the violence of the Black Panthers, the Weathermen, SDS, and drunk drivers under the name "Kennedyism." Actual knowledge about McCarthy is a constant impediment to the urgent business of denouncing him. It is simply axiomatic that McCarthy was evil incarnate, just as it is axiomatic that all Republican presidents are stupid. In actual usage, "McCarthyism" means "Anyone looking at a liberal with a dyspeptic expression between 1930 and 1955."

Just a few years ago, the *New York Times* gave as a crossword puzzle clue "Sen. McCarthy's grp," for which the correct answer was supposed to be "HUAC," standing for the House Un-American Activities Committee. The vigilant observer will note that the *H* in HUAC stands for *House*. McCarthy was never in the House. As his title indicates, Senator McCarthy was a *senator*. He hadn't the slightest connection with any of HUAC's investigations, which included probes of

American Nazis, the Ku Klux Klan, Alger Hiss, and Hollywood. The *Times* correction a few days later idiotically stated, "Joseph R. McCarthy was *ideologically akin* to members of the House Committee, but as a senator he had no direct connection with it"[1] (emphasis added; "ideologically akin" meaning "We hate them both").

In May 2000, the *New York Times* headlined an obituary: "Oscar Shaftel, Fired After Refusing McCarthy, Dies at 88." The bulk of the obituary was dedicated to a tearful retelling of Shaftel's suffering at the hands of the reckless demagogue McCarthy:

> He and three other teachers from New York City colleges were called before the investigations subcommittee of the Senate Internal Security Committee headed by Senator Joseph R. McCarthy on Feb. 9 and Feb. 10, 1953. Each witness cited the Fifth Amendment protection against self-incrimination in refusing to answer.
>
> "They asked if you were a Communist," Dr. Shaftel said in a 1980 interview. "If you said no, and they had different information, that was perjury. If you said yes, they said, 'Name everyone that you know, all of your friends.' If you forgot any, that was perjury." . . .
>
> After he was fired, Dr. Shaftel and other dismissed academics had to get by in what they spoke of as "the wilderness," taking poor-paying jobs for which they had little experience. In Dr. Shaftel's case, he became what he called a hack writer. He knocked out profiles of small businessmen for a magazine, wrote a book about house construction, and copyedited other books. He often wrote under a pseudonym.
>
> "It was a very bad time, hard on me, hard on my kids," he said in an interview in 1982. "We have survived, but I don't recommend it."[2]

Shaftel had appeared before only one congressional committee: the Senate Internal Security Subcommittee—a subcommittee of which McCarthy was never even a member. The *Times* eventually ran a correction admitting this more than three months later[3] and then only in response to the relentless demands of two media critics who had protested the *Times*'s mendacity.[4]

Inasmuch as the *Times* characterized Shaftel as an innocent victim of anti-Communist hysteria, it might be of passing interest to know: *"Was he a Communist?"* This is the question it is impolite to ask. In fact, Shaftel had been identified under oath as a Communist operative by an economics professor at Queens College.[5] If any other religious cult knew so few basic facts about its own seminal beliefs as the liberal cult does about Joe McCarthy, Janet Reno would gas them.

In an immoderately effusive review of its own bravery, *The New Republic* claimed in a 1984 article, "Far from succumbing to McCarthyism, TNR fought it every step of the way. In February 1949, it challenged the prosecution of Communist Party members under the Smith Act."[6] McCarthy had nothing to do with the Smith Act—which was, however, supported by the Communist Party on the assumption it would be used aggressively against "fascists" and Trotskyites.[7] Indeed, contrary to their own self-advertisements, liberals were wildly enthusiastic about the most egregious civil liberties violations, provided Communists were not disturbed. The national ACLU, for example, approved of rounding up the Japanese in World War II. (The Korematsu case, which challenged the internment, was sponsored by a chapter of the ACLU without approval from the national executive.) The left's lusty enthusiasm for suspending civil liberties during World War II seems inconceivable until you realize liberals were in favor of that war because they saw it as a war to save Stalin.

In any event, the Smith Act was passed in 1940—six years before McCarthy was even elected to the Senate. The act, which criminalized "teaching and advocating the violent overthrow of the government," was written by a Democratic House and a Democratic Senate; signed into law by a Democrat president, FDR; and enforced by another Democrat president, Harry Truman. This is how *The New Republic* came face-to-face with "McCarthyism."

Liberals explain this history by the simple expedient of lying.

In a 1998 article in *The New Republic*, Michael J. Ybarra essentially reverses the positions of the two parties, saying, "Truman and many liberal anti-Communists believed the best answer [to Communist subversives] was to let the FBI monitor the party and prosecute its members if they broke laws against subversion or espionage; conservatives, however, believed that the party needed to be crippled and exposed before Moscow's minions launched a revolution."[8] In 2088, *The New Republic* will explain the parties' different approaches to sexual harassment by saying, *Clinton and many liberal anti–sexual harassment groups believed the best answer was to wait for several women to step forward with credible, corroborated stories of physical touching, groping, or pants-dropping; conservatives, however, believed that potential sexual harassers needed to be stopped on the basis of a single woman's uncorroborated claim of dirty talk about pubic hairs on a Coke can.*

While McCarthy is blamed for things he didn't do by people who know nothing, he is often dismissed by those who do know something as irrelevant to the honorable task of red-hunting. Even the eminent scholar Sam Tanenhaus has said that by 1948, "scarcely any Communists were left in government." Using the words of Senator Ralph Flanders—whose other reasoned judgments of McCarthy included calling him a Hitlerite, a homosexual, and Dennis the Menace— Tanenhaus said, "The best McCarthy could do was dredge up a 'pink' dentist at a military base in New Jersey."[9]

This is preposterous. As Mary McCarthy said of Lillian Hellman, every word about Joe McCarthy is a lie, including "and" and "the."[10] The neurotically repeated claim that McCarthy "did not discover a single communist anywhere"[11]—as one massive biography of McCarthy states—is akin to the claim that Ken Starr never proved a single crime committed by Bill Clinton. Unless a liberal shouts out "I did it!" in a *Perry Mason* climax, liberals say conservatives have proved nothing.

Among the Soviet operatives who had been in government jobs and named by McCarthy were T. A. Bisson, Mary Jane Keeney, Cedric Belfrage, Solomon Adler, Franz Neumann, Leonard Mins, Gustavo

Duran, and William Remington (later killed with a bar of soap in prison by a patriotic inmate). All victims of "McCarthyism." But it's a trap to quibble about the precise number of Soviet spies McCarthy uncovered. That wasn't his point. Only by bowdlerizing McCarthy's message can liberals make it look like he failed. McCarthy wasn't sleuthing for hidden Communists. He wasn't an ex-Communist, like Whittaker Chambers, informing on his former comrades in an underground spy ring. He wasn't J. Edgar Hoover, investigating domestic espionage. His primary purpose wasn't even to expose individual Communists.

He didn't invent cold fusion or storm the cliffs at Pont du Hoc, either. McCarthy was simply demanding explanations from the liberal establishment: Why were they sheltering traitors? It was the exact same point Eisenhower was making when he directed Attorney General Brownell to inform the public that President Truman had wittingly placed a Soviet spy in a key post at the IMF.

For decades, people who should not have been allowed anywhere near a government job were strolling into sensitive positions with the U.S. government. As Soviet agents wormed their way deep into the U.S. government, loyalty boards were sipping sherry and shuffling papers. McCarthy came in with a blowtorch. As even McCarthy's critics concede, "A host of other right-wing Republicans had sought to dramatize the communism issue, but only McCarthy succeeded. And McCarthy succeeded while the others did not in part because of his thoroughgoing contempt for the rules of political controversy."[12] McCarthy forced liberals to make an accounting of themselves in full view of the American people. To defend themselves, liberals made McCarthy the issue. Ever since, he has been judged under a jurisprudence of epithets.

It is often clucked that McCarthy could not distinguish between a Communist Party member and a Soviet spy. This is said by people who can't distinguish between a criminal offense and a fireable offense. The question wasn't simply whether people like William Remington were agents of Stalin. (He was.) The question was whether he should be working for the U.S. government. The "accused" weren't going to be sent to a gulag, only to private practice. It's not that complicated a point. Fifty years of liberal propaganda has accustomed people to thinking of Communist Party members as lovable idealists and the urge to fire them from government jobs as an irrational anachronistic prejudice, much like "Irish need not apply." Allowing card-carrying members of the Communist Party to handle classified material after the Alger Hiss case would be like allowing avowed members of al-Qaeda to carry box cutters on airplanes after 9-11. As J. Edgar Hoover said of McCarthy, "Thank God somebody's doing it."[13]

A case in point was the "pink dentist," Irving Peress. Even after the scandal of the Rosenberg cell emerging from the Army, the Army was still blithely employing ridiculous security risks. Beginning in early 1953, for one solid year, Army intelligence issued urgent warnings about Captain Irving Peress. The reports said that Peress was an active member of the Communist Party, that he was "very disloyal and untrustworthy."[14] He was thought to be organizing a Communist cell on the Army base.[15] One Army report said, "His very presence creates an uncomfortable feeling."[16] His camp commander wanted him dismissed on grounds of national security.[17] Needless to say, the scrawny pinko was also a failure as a soldier.[18]

Despite all this—and well after the Rosenbergs had been caught— the Army did not dismiss Peress, but promoted him to major. When were they going to learn? Thanks to the Army's incompetence in dealing with the Rosenbergs, nearly 300 million Americans would spend the second half of the twentieth century under threat of nuclear annihilation, to say nothing of the 500 million enslaved by the Soviet Empire. McCarthy exposed the Army's egregious stupidity in dealing with Peress. According to internal Army documents, what finally spurred the Army to get rid of Peress—with an honorable discharge—was their fear of McCarthy finding out about him.[19]

Senator Ralph Flanders—a Vermont Republican in the full sense of the term—instantly grasped the importance of the Peress case. He attacked McCarthy for his brutal excesses. Peress, Flanders said, was merely a "pink dentist in New Jersey." What does it mean to call Peress a "pink dentist"? He was also a major in the Army. It is true that in his civilian life, Peress had been a dentist. Did that make him any less impressive than the various members of the Rosenbergs' cell? Using Flanders's nomenclature, Harry Gold was a "pink college dropout in Pennsylvania"—and one of the Soviet Union's most prolific industrial and atomic spies. Among his sources for atomic secrets was a "pink soldier in New Mexico"—Ethel Rosenberg's brother, David Greenglass.[20]

Another example of the fine job the Army was doing routing loyalty risks from sensitive positions was the case of Annie Lee Moss. Amazingly, the Moss case has gone down in history as one of McCarthy's most laughable blunders. According to lovingly nurtured liberal mythology, McCarthy recklessly hauled a semiliterate black washwoman before the committee and accused her of being a Communist.

In fact, what the Moss case demonstrates is the hysterical resistance McCarthy faced from the press and from his Democratic colleagues. Moss had been "absolutely" identified as a Communist Party member by a reliable FBI informant.[21] She was listed in the Communist Party's records. The party's newspaper, the *Daily Worker*, was delivered to her home—and mysteriously seemed to follow her wherever she lived.[22] Annie Lee Moss was also working in the Code Room of the Pentagon.

Moss played the fool when she testified before McCarthy's committee. Democrats, always eager to portray blacks as stupid for their political advantage, enthusiastically egged on Moss's ignorant washwoman performance. Democrat Senator Stuart Symington spoke to Moss as if she were a child, asking her, "Would you ever do anything to hurt your country?" (No, she would not.) Symington said, "Did you ever hear of Karl Marx?" To gales of laughter from sensitive liberals in the press, Moss said, "Who's that?"[23]

Still, the evidence against Moss was not insignificant. To claim Moss was not a security risk, the Democrats would need something more persuasive than their ability to laugh at black people. When

Moss innocently mentioned that there were three other people named Annie Lee Moss in the Washington, D.C., phonebook, everyone in the hearing room breathed a sigh of relief. The press accepted this explanation and happily returned to calling McCarthy a reckless demagogue. In front of the entire hearing room, "Sanctimonious Stu" Symington offered Moss a job if the Pentagon would not take her back. CBS's Edward R. Murrow used the Moss case as critical evidence of McCarthy's reckless cruelty in his "See It Now" broadside against McCarthy.[24]

One thing hard-nosed reporters like Murrow did not do was open a Washington, D.C., phonebook to see if Moss was telling the truth. If they had, they would have seen there were not three people named "Annie Lee Moss." The poor put-upon washwoman was lying. There was an Anna Lee Moss and an Annie Moss. But there was only one Annie Lee Moss—and she lived at 72 R Street S.W., Washington, D.C.[25] That was the precise address where Communist Party records listed their "Annie Lee Moss."[26] Indeed, in her testimony before the committee, Moss had specifically given her address as 72 R Street while explaining another wacky coincidence. It seemed that wherever Moss lived, the *Daily Worker* kept being delivered to her door. First she received it at a rooming house, and then, she explained, we "didn't get this Communist paper anymore until after we had moved southwest, at 72 R St."[27] There is no question: McCarthy had the right Annie Lee Moss.

It was a breathtaking security breach. Even after the Rosenberg case, the Army was employing a Communist Party member in the Code Room of the Pentagon. The Army briefly suspended Moss during McCarthy's investigation and then—thanks to great patriots like Edward R. Murrow—the Army soon rehired her. Only because of the ruckus McCarthy had caused, the Army at least did not put Moss back in the Code Room.

The blabocracy portrays the Moss case a little differently. In one of many glorious accounts of how brave liberals stood up to Joe McCarthy, a Broadway play titled *A Question of Loyalty* showed the McCarthy character browbeating Moss until—in a triumphant moment—Moss produces a telephone book proving there are three other Annie Lee Mosses. A *New York Times* theater review called this the "most satisfying moment" of the play.[28] So apparently liberals were aware of the looking-in-the-phonebook trick. They just didn't bother using it in the actual Annie Lee Moss case.

One of the most Orwellian lies of the McCarthy myth is that he "named names," as the slogan goes, ruining people's lives with reckless accusations. Apart from distracting questions of guilt or innocence, it is a fact that McCarthy doggedly resisted releasing anyone's name to the public. As is usually the case when liberals are the historians, the truth was just the opposite. Blinded by their own loathing, Democrats literally forced McCarthy to name names.

McCarthy had raised the issue of loyalty risks working for the government—not proven cases of espionage. There are many reasons a person should not be handling classified materials, short of proof beyond a reasonable doubt that he was a Soviet spy. McCarthy said he would attach names to the cases only in a closed committee hearing but would not release names to the public because he didn't want to blacken the names of government employees who could be completely innocent. When he presented his case against the State Department on the Senate floor, for example, McCarthy described the loyalty risks anonymously, as case #1, case #2, and so on.

The Democrats subjected him to a barrage of catcalls and interruptions demanding that he name names. Democrat Senate Majority Leader Scott Lucas (D-Ill.) said, "I want to remain here until he names them. That is what I am interested in. . . . Will the Senator tell us the name of the man for the record? We are entitled to know who he is. I say this in all seriousness."[29] That was one of Lucas's sixty-one interruptions that day.[30] Another Democrat, Senator Withers of Kentucky, said, "I should like to ask the Senator what reason he has for not calling names. Does not the Senator think it would be a fine thing to let the public know who the guilty are? Is not the Senator privileged?"[31] That was one of Senator Withers's twenty-three inter-ruptions of McCarthy.[32]

Despite McCarthy's repeated insistence that he would provide names to only the senators in closed session, the Democrats voted to compel him to name security risks openly, in front of the press.

Before McCarthy ever named his first name he said, "The Senator from Illinois demanded, loudly, that I furnish all the names. I told him at that time that so far as I was concerned, I thought that would be improper; that I did not have all the information about these individuals . . . I have enough to convince me that either they are members of the Communist Party or they have given great aid to the Communists: I may be wrong. That is why I said that unless the Senate demanded that I do so, I would not submit this publicly, but I would submit it to any committee—and would let the committee go over these in executive session. It is possible that some of these persons will get a clean bill of health."[33]

The sine qua non of "McCarthyism" came about because of the Democrats' own hatefulness.

Even McCarthy's most celebrated "victim," Owen Lattimore, was not named publicly by McCarthy. It was liberal journalist and anti-McCarthy zealot Drew Pearson who leaked Lattimore's name to the public—the better to revile McCarthy for ruining people's reputations. Lattimore became one of the most well-compensated victims of "McCarthyism." Upon being found a "conscious, articulate instrument of the Soviet conspiracy"[34] by a unanimous Senate Committee, Latti-more was assured a spot lecturing at Harvard.

It is indignantly reported that McCarthy exaggerated. His claim that Owen Lattimore *was* a Soviet agent—as opposed to *behaved like a Soviet agent*—is a hyperbole deserving of a hundred-year condemna-tion. Liberals' threshold for outrage dropped when it came to McCar-thy. In fact, McCarthy's rhetoric was mild by the standards of his time. In President Truman's 1948 campaign, he railed, "If anybody in this country is friendly to the Communists, it is the Republicans." Truman also compared the Republicans to fascists: "In our time we have seen the tragedy of the Italian and German peoples, who lost their freedom to men who made promises of unity and efficiency and sincerity . . . and it could happen here."[35] At least Republicans came up with new arguments in the intervening fifty years. This is still the Democrats' best argument.

Moreover, there is no question but that McCarthy's errors were infinitesimal compared to liberals' tearful testimonials to their own victimization. Roosevelt's secretary of the interior, Harold Ickes, summarized the period by sadly observing that "if a man is addicted to vodka he is, ipso facto, a Russian, therefore a Communist."[36] The editor of the Sunday *New York Times*, Lester Markel, described "a black fear in the country brought about by witch hunters."[37] University of California librarian Lawrence Clark Powell maniacally claimed, "In this time of inquisitional nationalism, I know that I run a risk in confessing that I possess a French doctor's degree and own an English car. And what dire fate do I court when I say that I prefer English books."[38] As is now indisputably proved by Soviet cables, hundreds of Stalin's agents swarmed through government jobs. Gee, it's so outrageous that McCarthy exaggerated.

When questioned by the FBI in 1947, suspected spy Helen Silvermaster lamented that "anyone with liberal views seemed to be called a communist now-a-days."[39] Soviet cables now prove absolutely Silvermaster was a Soviet spy, her husband, Gregory, was a Soviet spy, and her son was a courier for their spy ring.[40] Her husband was literally on the payroll of Moscow and the United States government at the same time. He worked for the Board of Economic Warfare and later, the War Assets Division of the Treasury Department. Among his services for the Soviet Union, Silvermaster smuggled out "huge quantities of war production Board data on weapons aircraft, tank, artillery, and shipping production."[41] While working for the Roosevelt administration, Silvermaster was given a medal for his service to the USSR.[42]

He got his job at the Treasury from another Soviet agent, Harry Dexter White. When Mr. Silvermaster's loyalty was questioned by the

Office of Naval Intelligence and War Department counterintelligence, Harry Dexter White (Soviet spy) and Lauchlin Currie (Soviet spy) enthusiastically vouched for his patriotism. Roosevelt's undersecretary of agriculture, Paul Appleby, wrote a righteous letter saying Silvermaster had been questioned simply because he happened to have been born in Russia.[43]

Denouncing McCarthy is the establishment's loyalty oath. A professor who puts in a kind word for McCarthy would end his career—or spend the rest of it explaining himself. Even Haynes and Klehr, the authors of *Venona,* utter the ritualistic malediction before cheerfully returning to identifying another hundred liberals who were Soviet spies. U.N. weapons inspectors got more honest answers from Iraqis living under Saddam Hussein than one can expect from American professors about McCarthy.

In one of the milder summaries of McCarthy's failings, historian Douglas Brinkley argues that McCarthy had frightened off "responsible" anti-Communists. Brinkley cites "the vast difference between responsible anti-communists of the early years of the Cold War— Walter Reuther, Arthur Schlesinger, Jr., Reinhold Niebuhr and Hubert Humphrey come to mind—and an unprincipled, opportunistic bully like McCarthy."[44]

Had Joe McCarthy offended Arthur Schlesinger's delicate sense of dignity in the government? If so, his standards of dignity must have changed by 1998. Schlesinger attacked the impeachment of President Clinton as a "strictly partisan" operation based on a "revolutionary theory of impeachment" with "ominous implications" for the country.[45] To refresh the memory, Clinton had procured the services of an intern for oral sex in the Oval Office, lied, perjured himself, suborned the perjury of others, and obstructed justice to cover it up. He blamed Rush Limbaugh for the Oklahoma City bombing, described the Republicans' Contract with America as a hit man's assignment, allowed his henchmen to look into the private lives of Paula Jones, Gennifer Flowers, Kathleen Willey, Henry Hyde, Newt Gingrich, Bob Livingston, Ken Starr, and Starr's associates. That didn't bother Schlesinger. But

Joe McCarthy calls a raving fellow senator an "alleged man" and Schlesinger was nearly lost to the cause of anti-Communism forever!

Right up until the Venona decrypts positively proved Laurence Duggan was a spy, Schlesinger bitterly denounced anyone who said Duggan was a spy.[46] If McCarthy had ever made a mistake of that magnitude, the McCarthy mythmakers would finally have had one cold hard fact McCarthy got wrong. It's nice that a few liberals eventually found the strength to formulate carefully worded objections to Communism, but the importance of Jackie Kennedy's poodle to the anti-Communist crusade may be somewhat overrated.

The Thomas Pynchon of his day, Reinhold Niebuhr was the subject of much platitudinous, worshipful characterization, but no one ever read him. Niebuhr spent decades writing about the bright side of Marxism. His eventual "responsible anti-communism" led him to oppose the Vietnam War because—as he pompously and incorrectly said—"we are in fact dealing with the nationalism of a small nation in Asia." America's attempt to save Vietnam from Communist totalitarianism led Niebuhr to proclaim himself "ashamed of our beloved nation."[47] Fortunately, Niebuhr's influence was limited by the fact that he was a big, sonorous bore.

Walter Reuther and Hubert Humphrey are interesting additions to Douglas Brinkley's list of "responsible anti-communists" inasmuch as they were far rougher with Communists than McCarthy ever was. In a wild overreaction common to liberals, in 1954 Senator Humphrey introduced a bill that would have outlawed the Communist Party.[48] Outlawed it. That was the year the Senate voted to censure McCarthy, who had been engaged in the far more reasonable task of exposing inept government bureaucracies that were ignoring serious loyalty risks on the government payroll.

Reuther presided over a brutal factional campaign in the CIO with lots of red-baiting.[49] A few years later, the sanctimonious fraud signed a letter urging that McCarthy be censured. Adopting the hatreds and prejudices of the ruling class evidently buys you exemptions. (Interestingly, the United Mine Workers and the Teamsters—the crotchety old Republican unions—were the only unions to reject loyalty oaths for their members.)

To be sure, there were a few genuine anti-Communists among the ponderers, and they are to be commended. But the country was not in vital need of soporific academics at windbag conferences put on by the Congress for Cultural Freedom. It did not need tepid rebukes of Stalinism in *Encounter* magazine or cherished little homilies warning that "quite noble attempts to defeat evil may, in sufficiently perverse circumstances, be mistaken for evil."[50]

What the country needed was Joe McCarthy. His appeal was directed to a sturdier set—the mass of ordinary Americans. It's interesting that Democrats keep claiming to speak for the working man, but somehow it's always right-wing Republicans who make a direct connection to workers. (What liberals mean by "working families" is "nonfamilies in which no one works.") From McCarthy to Richard Nixon to Ronald Reagan, it is conservatives who appeal to workers. When Republicans ignite the explosive energy of the hardhats, liberals had better run for cover. When that force is squandered, Republicans fall back. Nixon clearly recognized this, saying, "When you have to call on the nation to be strong—on such things as drugs, crime, defense, our basic national position—the educated people and the leader class no longer have any character, and you can't count on them." In times of crisis, he said, business and corporate elites "painted their asses white and ran like antelopes." Not the "two-fisted" workers, as Nixon called them admiringly. "They are men, not softies."[51]

McCarthy was beloved by workers. He had a gift for appealing to the great common sense of the American people. He made broad points that captured headlines and rallied Americans. Normal Americans could not believe their fellow countrymen could be so dastardly as not to love their country. For them, McCarthy was a poet. Liberals may have written the history books, but at the time, the instinctual response of the American people prevailed over the left's theatrics. No matter how much the elites ridiculed McCarthy, lots of Americans seemed to like him.

In the summer of 1951, the Truman administration planned an all-out attack on McCarthy, going directly to his base—the Veterans of Foreign Wars.[52] At the dedication of the new American Legion building, both Truman and his not-coincidentally Catholic labor secretary, Maurice Tobin, gave speeches attacking McCarthy. Truman spoke darkly of "hysteria" and "fear" about Communism. Tobin denounced "slanderers" in Congress undermining the public's trust in government. Though neither had mentioned McCarthy by name, the point was clear.[53]

When Tobin mentioned "slanderers," one of the VFW organizers had had enough. He leapt from his chair, grabbed the mike out of Tobin's hand, and announced to the crowd that maybe the VFW should let McCarthy speak for himself. The audience roared its approval. McCarthy flew in the next day to address an enthusiastic VFW crowd. For more than an hour, he laid into Truman, Acheson, and "the whole motley crew."[54] His reception was noticeably more positive than Truman and Tobin's had been. A cheering audience chanted, "Give 'em hell, Joe!" and "McCarthy for President!"[55]

The year of McCarthy's censure, Senator Saltonstall described campaigning through Massachusetts just before the vote: "One day I'd campaign in Pittsfield and the factory workers would plead with me to support McCarthy. The next day I'd drive down to Smith College and the audience would boo every mention of his name."[56] The Communists may have had patricians like Franklin Roosevelt. They may have had the diplomats, the Supreme Court justices, the scribblers, the ponderers, and the Smith College girls. But McCarthy had the hearts of the American workers.

The rote smirking at McCarthy by conservatives is linked to their own psychological compulsion to snobbery. McCarthy was a popularizer, a brawler. Republican elitists abhor demagogic appeals to working-class Democrats. Fighting like a Democrat is a breach of etiquette worse than using the wrong fork. McCarthy is sniffed at for not playing by Marquis of Queensberry Rules—rules of engagement demanded only of Republicans. Well, without McCarthy, Republicans might be congratulating themselves on their excellent behavior from the gulag right now. He may have been tut-tutted on the golf course, but McCarthy made the American workers' blood boil.

Lost amid all the mandatory condemnations of Joe McCarthy's name—he gave anti-Communism a bad name, did a disservice to the cause, was an unnecessary distraction—the little detail about his being right always seems to get lost. McCarthy's fundamental thesis was absolutely correct: The Democratic Party had fallen to the allures of totalitarianism. It was as if Republicans had been caught in bed with Hitler. Liberals would have you believe that Republicans are infinitely susceptible to fascism's lures, but there is no evidence that any American ever connived with Hitler (though FDR was infatuated with Mussolini and had even sent advisors to Italy to take notes on Mussolini's brand of fascism as a model for the National Recovery Act). Even the great aviator Charles Lindbergh, who had once been a Nazi sympathizer, flew combat missions in the Pacific in World War II at an age well beyond expected service years. Conservatives have Charles Lindbergh. Liberals have themselves.

Despite the left's creation of a myth to defeat legitimate charges of treason, McCarthy had so badly stigmatized Communism, his victory survived him. In his brief fiery ride across the landscape, Joe McCarthy bought America another thirty years. For this, he sacrificed his life, his reputation, his name. The left cut down a brave man, but not before the American people heard the truth.

5

VICTIMS OF McCARTHYISM— THE LIBERALS' *MAYFLOWER*

For liberals, "McCarthyism" was the most significant period in human history, darker than the days of the Plague. To hear them tell it, in the forties and fifties, anyone who read the *Village Voice* was liable to be hauled before a congressional Star Chamber and forced to "name names"—presumably of other *Village Voice* subscribers. There are stark images of McCarthy pounding his gavel and angry thugs on HUAC denouncing Communism and driving innocent people to suicide.

Most people who were alive in the fifties have to watch PBS to know it was a frightening period. Liberals simply assert that a certain mood prevailed, and you have to believe it. Liberals' vehemence in declaiming the evils of "McCarthyism" was only equaled by their vehemence in denying that Alger Hiss (Soviet spy), Julius Rosenberg (Soviet spy),

Laurence Duggan (Soviet spy), and Harry Dexter White (Soviet spy) were Soviet spies. People who angrily claimed that scores of now-proved Soviet spies were innocent have forfeited the right to have their characterizations of McCarthy accepted on faith.

Liberals act as if the search for Soviet spies in high government positions was an enterprise equivalent to looking for patterns in wheat fields. Indeed, it was Communists who were the victims—victims of a brute named Joe McCarthy. As Ellen Schrecker ruefully mused in her book *The Age of McCarthyism*, "The Communists never lacked for enemies."[1] Nor for dupes, one might add. As millions of people were enslaved and slaughtered in the Soviet Union, liberals produced nondisprovable claims of school-yard taunts in the United States as examples of comparable suffering.

In a classic account of the fear and suffering wrought by "McCarthyism," the *San Francisco Chronicle* described the horror that befell the children of Soviet spies, such as Robert Meeropol, son of Ethel and Julius Rosenberg. There were "phone taps, FBI surveillances, subpoenas and ostracism." To be sure, their parents were giving atomic technology to the Soviet Union. But the FBI had no right to watch them! Another child victim reported, "The class started to laugh and scream and hoot at me, yelling 'Commie!'" As the *Chronicle* reports, "One by one, these testimonies chill us to the bone, making it clear what totalitarianism once looked like within our own borders."[2] Here was the stark horror of American "totalitarianism." Traitors to their country working on behalf of Communist despotism were treated as badly as College Republicans are treated at Amherst College today.

Conservatives could never catch up with the outburst of liberal indignation. They didn't care as much as liberals did. No one could. Confronted with hysterical zealots demanding that their view of history be acknowledged, conservatives essentially said, *Fine, if it means that much to you—okay, fine, the human spirit was crushed by Joe McCarthy.*

The moment you concede some small point to liberals, they go to work building an enormous elaborate edifice on top of the first lie. Con-

servatives were always annoyed by the idea of the United Nations—
bequeathed to us by Soviet spy Alger Hiss. But they resigned themselves to the U.N. with the hope that, while useless, it couldn't do much
harm. The next thing you knew, the U.N. was dominated by ludicrous
despots in countries primarily known for cannibalism issuing lunatic
declarations while Democrats and the media acted as if U.N. approval
was a constitutional prerequisite to the United States acting in its self-
defense. In 1965, the Supreme Court invented a "privacy right" guar-
anteeing married couples the right to obtain contraception. It seemed
churlish and hypertechnical to object that there was no such right in the
Constitution. Thirty years later, the right of married couples to use con-
traceptives had transmogrified into a "constitutional" right to abortion-
on-demand.

Similarly, having ceded the lie of "McCarthyism," now no one is
allowed to call liberals unpatriotic. Liberals relentlessly attack their
own country, but we can't call them traitors, which they manifestly are,
because that would be "McCarthyism," which never existed.

By now, the left's mind-boggling self-righteousness about Senator
Joe McCarthy is so overwhelming, so hegemonic, it seems the record
could never be set straight. This is the only suffering liberals can point
to. The soft existence of cozy environmentalists and Hollywood degen-
erates doesn't provide much in the way of hardship to bleat about.
Safely ensconced in the most affluent and free nation in the history of
the world, liberals' biggest pretend-fear these days is that "anti-
choice" legislation will somehow sweep the Upper West Side of Manhattan. They haven't really thought through the mechanics of how that
would happen. "McCarthyism" is one of the markers on the left's Via
Dolorosa. It is their slavery, their gulag, their potato famine. Otherwise,
liberals would just be geeks from Manhattan and Hollywood.

The McCarthy myth is the pristine example of how you have to say
certain things to be accepted into civilized society. Anyone who fails to
issue the ritualistic denunciation of McCarthy must be instantly
adjudged a "kook" or—in the reasoned formulation of McCarthy
obsessive and author Richard Rovere—"zanies and zombies and com-

pulsive haters."[3] It simply must be accepted that Joe McCarthy was a vicious hoodlum with every known human vice. No one knows any facts about McCarthy, but everyone knows that his name is a malediction. Whenever liberals are hysterical about something, but short on details, your antennae should go up.

THE CASUAL ASSOCIATION OF McCARTHY WITH HOLLYWOOD blacklisting demonstrates the left's renowned respect for the truth. McCarthy's nonexistent crusade has become a fact by sheer repetition. With no explanation, a 2002 *New York Times* article on the movie industry listed "McCarthyism" as among the various "plagues and scourges" that had beset the industry.[4]

Honorable though it was, the Hollywood blacklisting had nothing to do with McCarthy. The Hollywood Ten were called before HUAC in 1947. To repeat, McCarthy was never in the House. In 1947, he had just been elected to the Senate and was so little known that the *New York Times* called him a "moderate Republican." Even Hiss had been exposed, indicted, and convicted before McCarthy took up the anti-Communist cause in his 1950 speech in Wheeling, West Virginia. McCarthy never participated in any investigation of Hollywood.

To be sure, the Hollywood blacklisting was truly heart-wrenching. While people were being forced to eat their shoes in the Ukraine, only a heart of stone could fail to be moved by the stories of Hollywood screenwriters who couldn't sell a *Twilight Zone* episode for up to three years. There are dark tales of writers whose names did not run in the credits for *M*A*S*H.*[5] Some of the persecuted were even forced to flee to Paris and spin their semipornographic essays from the Champs-Elysées. Such suffering is endlessly recounted in lachrymose memoirs, movies, documentaries, museum exhibits, and awards ceremonies celebrating the blacklist "survivors." Claiming to have been "blacklisted" is Hollywood's version of coming over on the *Mayflower*.

Sometimes, their bragging gets the better of them and the "survivors" forget to include the part about how hard it was. "Blacklist survivor" Norma Barzman described her life in "exile" in Paris thus: "We had dinner with Picasso every Tuesday night when we were at our country house in Provence. Yves Montand and Simone Signoret, Jacques Prevert were all friends. Plus we got to work with all the amazing European directors including Vittorio De Sica and Constantin Costa-Gavras. It was hard, but it was also the time of my life."[6]

Meanwhile back in the country they preferred, people were being whisked off to Soviet gulags in the dead of night. They were being sentenced to work in forced labor camps. They were sent to Siberia for five years. They were being shot execution-style after being forced to confess to absurd diabolical conspiracies.

Ten Hollywood scribblers who subscribed to an ideology responsible for murder by the million refused to admit their membership in the Communist Party to a House Committee. All they had to do was 'fess up. But they felt they had a right not to tell the truth, so they were briefly jailed for contempt. This created a slight setback in their dinners with Picasso. The horror.

Clearly, it wasn't the indignity of testifying before a House Committee that tried their troubled souls. Once the atrocity of having to tell the truth about being Communists had passed, actors and actresses began leaping at the chance to appear before congressional committees. When the Democrats controlled Congress in the eighties, you couldn't turn on C-SPAN without being subjected to the spectacle of some movie star eagerly testifying about disease, childhood obesity, Alar on apples, circus elephants, or the plight of farmers. Indeed, a Democratic-controlled House Agriculture Committee once held a hearing on farmers in which not a single farmer testified. But millionaire actresses who had played farmers' wives in movies, such as Jane Fonda, Jessica Lange, and Sissy Spacek, had a lot to say on the subject.[7]

Nor evidently does the concept of blacklisting offend liberals' sense of fair play. How are the job opportunities these days for screenwriters who believe homosexuality is wrong? Would an actress who is "anti-choice" have an easy time finding work? In 1998, the American Film Institute and the Los Angeles Film Critics Association refused to grant Elia Kazan a lifetime achievement award because he cooperated with HUAC's investigation of Communists in Hollywood. Kazan discovered James Dean and Marlon Brando. He had won three Oscars and directed such movies as *A Streetcar Named Desire* and *On the Waterfront*. That same year, Cinecon, a national film organization dedicated to old and silent films, gave its annual film achievement award to Leni Riefenstahl, the Nazi filmmaker most famous for her 1934 film celebrating Hitler, *The Triumph of the Will*.[8] Hollywood's commitment to freedom and civil liberties has always been a one-way ratchet protecting only the admirers of Communist totalitarians.

It is no surprise that the fear of "McCarthyism" comes from Hollywood. Only the movie industry could produce that level of womanly hysteria. Hollywood drama queens told deranged lies about their torment—and their guilt—while adults tried to hold hearings into a serious matter. Whittaker Chambers said of HUAC, "I watched the Committee's members behave with conspicuous patience and composure in the face of repeated, insolent provocation that no body of men in civil life would have endured."[9]

Indeed, the frothing ideological rants of the Hollywood Ten drove away such stars as Humphrey Bogart, Lauren Bacall, Danny Kaye, and Gene Kelly, who had flown to Washington to support—as they thought—free speech. Not realizing "free speech" was a fig leaf for Communism, John Garfield genially proposed, "Why doesn't Congress make it illegal to belong to the Communist Party and clear the whole thing up?" After one day of watching John Howard Lawson rant at the committee, screaming that the congressmen were Nazis, predicting concentration camps in America, and generally "sounding like Pravda," before having to be physically dragged away, the Hollywood delegation left, humiliated. Bogart later called the trip to Washington "ill-advised, even foolish."[10] Bacall said, "We were so naive it was ridiculous."[11]

Unlike the legal proceedings of their hero, Joseph Stalin, the drama queens were granted full due process. Apparently on orders from Stalin, as Michael J. Ybarra reports in *The New Republic*, the

Hollywood Ten refused to answer the committee's questions.[12] Preposterously, they claimed a First Amendment right not to answer questions
pursuant to a subpoena. This would be like a robber claiming a First
Amendment right to say "your money or your life." It was so absurd,
the Supreme Court refused to hear the case and the ten went to jail
for contempt. All had the benefit of legal counsel, trial by jury, and
proof beyond a reasonable-doubt standard. Still, the cosseted, overpampered Hollywood elites were shocked to discover that they could
be held responsible for anything they did, and vowed that the rest of
the country would never hear the end of it.

At about the same time—under the legal system Communists
revered—Stalin executed, starved, exiled, or imprisoned more than
ten million people.[13] From 1935 to 1941 alone, Stalin's secret police
sent more than three million Soviet citizens to the gulag. Beginning in
the thirties, Stalin forced top party officials and prominent Soviet journalists and artists to issue public "confessions" to being "enemies of
the people." The accused were told of their indictments the day before
the trial began and were not permitted counsel. The trials were limited
to ten days. Convictions were not subject to appeal. Witnesses were
murdered, put in insane asylums, and poisoned. Contradictions in the
obviously manufactured evidence, which included faked autopsies,
were dismissed as "camouflage." Those convicted were shot immediately. Within just a few weeks time, in December 1934, thirty-nine
"guilty" were shot in Leningrad, twenty-nine shot in Moscow, twenty-
eight shot in Kiev, and nine shot in Minsk.[14]

The most spectacular show trials were reserved for top party officials. Devoted Communists publicly confessed to stunning collaboration with the Nazis in comically absurd conspiracies. They were, as
one historian said, "monstrous theatrical productions that had to be
rehearsed many times before they could be shown to spectators."[15]
Confessions were extracted with brutal and prolonged torture and
threats to family members—who were murdered in the end anyway.
The confessions were so unbelievable that it was once thought NKVD
(People's Commissariat of Internal Affairs) agents resembling the

accused had been used to deliver the astonishing confessions in open court.[16] The evidence consisted of "outright lies, deliberately fabricated in the torture chambers of the NKVD and put into the mouths of the accused by sadistic investigators."[17] Following the procedural formalities of many advanced cultures, Stalin's executioners sentenced Leon Trotsky to death in absentia. The show trials of party leaders were only a warm-up act for the bloodbath that was to follow. In what is always a bittersweet moment in the history of Communist regimes, Stalin would soon direct his savagery toward the intellectuals. One historian described Stalin's campaign against the cultural elites as "unprecedented in world history."[18]

Yet in accounts of the period, Stalin is treated as an irrelevant distraction from the real threat to freedom, which was "McCarthyism." The same ilk who would have sworn on a stack of *Communist Manifesto*s to be "frightened" of Senator McCarthy were impressed with the overall fairness and operation of Stalin's show trials. The *New York Times*'s Walter Duranty wrote in *The New Republic* that he was convinced "the confessions are true."

Franklin Delano Roosevelt's ambassador to the Soviet Union, Joseph Davies, was an eyewitness to the trials. Davies reported to the ever-credulous *New Republic*, "We see no reason to take the trial at other than its face value."[19] Davies proclaimed that the trials had exposed the "virus of a conspiracy to overthrow the [Soviet] government."[20] According to Davies, this was the consensus among Western journalists: The trials, he said, were revealing "the truth at least in part."[21] The book in which he wrote that monstrosity, *Mission to Moscow*, was made into a Hollywood movie about our friends, the Soviets. Indeed, there were many movies about our friends the Soviets and good old Uncle Joe. There were also many movies about the horrors of blacklisting, such as *The Front* (1976) and *Guilty by Suspicion* (1991). Amazingly, Hollywood has yet to produce a major movie about the gulag or Stalin's show trials.

One of Stalin's most starstruck admirers, Lillian Hellman, wrote the book *Scoundrel Time*, describing her heroism in standing up to McCarthyism.[22] Hellman also wrote the script for the pro-Soviet movie

The North Star; she defended Stalin through the Hitler-Stalin Pact, through the purges, through the forced starvation. But McCarthy got her goat. Needless to say, McCarthy had absolutely nothing to do with Hellman. Hellman had been called to testify before HUAC. (Remember what the "H" stands for!) This innocent victim of McCarthyism— whom McCarthy never noticed—bequeathed profits from her book to a fund for the advancement of the doctrines of Karl Marx.[23]

Owen Lattimore, poor beleaguered "victim" of McCarthyism, hailed Stalin's murderous show trials as "the sort of habitual rectification" that would encourage others to tell the truth. As he put it, "That sounds like democracy to me."[24] Russia was awash in the blood of this Felliniesque hoax. But Lattimore gushed with admiration. Lincoln Steffens said famously after a visit to Stalin's Russia, "I have been over into the future—and it works."[25] Theodore Dreiser wrote of the abject poverty in the Soviet Union: "There is poverty. There are beggars in the streets. But, Lord how picturesque! The multi-colored and voluminous rags on them!"[26]

From his hideout in Mexico, Trotsky denounced the show trials as a "frame-up," saying the confessions "contain such inherent improbabilities" as to convince "any unprejudiced person that no effort was made to ascertain the truth."[27] American liberals were evidently not the "unprejudiced" witnesses Trotsky had hoped for. In 1992, the *Times* referred to "recent revelations about Stalin's purges and other Soviet deeds."[28] Who was hiding that from the *Times?*

While tens of millions were being executed, torn from their families, subjected to forced starvations as a matter of government policy, packed on trains, and sent to Siberian gulags in the glorious USSR, about two hundred people in America were blacklisted from a single frivolous industry. They could still go to Paris or sell real estate or do any number of things. They just couldn't work in the movies. That was the only price they paid for shilling for a mass murderer.

THERE IS NO EVIDENCE THAT A SINGLE PERSON COMMITTED suicide because of McCarthy. One suicide preposterously but steadfastly attributed to McCarthy was that of Ray Kaplan. The Kaplan suicide is a good example of how risible liberal propaganda becomes historical fact. The story began with McCarthy's investigation of a bitter dispute within the Voice of America about where to locate a satellite transmitter. It appeared to be more than a technical dispute. If, as some of the VOA engineers claimed, locating the transmitter in Seattle would frustrate the signal, it would defeat the whole purpose of VOA. Taxpayer money would be wasted on a useless installation that would not allow America's "voice" to be heard much beyond the greater Seattle area. The peculiar ken of some government engineers to locate the VOA transmitter where it was useless raised obvious questions.

Ray Kaplan was among those who opposed the Seattle installation. Naturally, therefore, when McCarthy held hearings on the transmitter dispute, Kaplan was happy to testify. But before he got the chance, Kaplan committed suicide by leaping in front of a truck. He left a suicide note, saying, "When the dogs are set upon you, everything you have done from the beginning of your life is suspect." Liberals simply assume the "dogs" referred to McCarthy—despite the fact that Kaplan was caught up in a rancorous battle within VOA. But blaming McCarthy was consistent with the left's heartfelt belief that McCarthy was a brute and Communists were gentle little lambs. Whittaker Chambers might have told them otherwise.[29]

A few days after Kaplan's suicide, a particularly charming VOA employee, William Mandel, interrupted McCarthy's questioning to shout out, "You murdered Ray Kaplan!"[30] And thus, notwithstanding its manifest absurdity, the story was set: McCarthy had somehow driven Kaplan to suicide by championing his cause.[31] It would be as if Linda Tripp had turned up dead during the investigation of Bill Clinton, and liberals decided to blame Ken Starr. McCarthy was bewildered by the accusation, saying Kaplan "had no fear of this committee whatsoever." To the contrary, Kaplan had "expressed the desire to appear and testify."[32]

Like so much nonsense about McCarthy, the story of how he drove a sympathetic witness to suicide is now written into the history books. McCarthy biographer David Oshinsky strongly suggests McCarthy was to blame for Kaplan's suicide, sinisterly noting that McCarthy suspected foul play, but "the coroner disagreed."[33] What does that prove? On the basis of the Communist Party's aggressive use of defenestration and other staged "suicides," McCarthy was not making rash assumptions. But whether or not there was foul play, it is an undisputed fact that McCarthy was Kaplan's champion, not his inquisitor.

McCARTHY'S REAL "VICTIMS" WERE NOT SYMPATHETIC WITnesses, frivolous Hollywood screenwriters, or irrelevant blowhard college professors. They were elite WASP establishment policy-makers. Sedition always held a strange attraction for Ivy League types with three names, like John Stewart Service, Harry Dexter White, George Catlett Marshall, and William Sloan Coffin. It was a quirky thing about WASPs. They took perverse pride in harboring the periodic traitor. Their reaction to Alger Hiss was the concentrated expression of that sentiment. Even John Foster Dulles and Dwight Eisenhower had defended Hiss. Eisenhower was better than any Democrat, but he was part of the elite establishment. President Truman had tried to persuade Eisenhower to run as a Democrat, and Barry Goldwater ridiculed Eisenhower's policies as the "dime store New Deal."[34] Damning Eisenhower with robust praise when he won the Republican nomination, the *New York Times* called it "a people's victory."[35]

They all liked one another, these Anglophile blue bloods. They went to Yale, played cricket, became Rhodes scholars, wrestled in the mud together at the Skull and Bones society, and went to parties where Dean Acheson was invariably a guest. They were well-born and looked good in dinner jackets. Protecting traitors was part of the bonhomie of the ruling class. It was as if the WASPs had developed some XXY chromosome that led to overt treason. They had ruled magnificently for many years, but their blood had gotten thin. Angry ethnics like Joe McCarthy made much better Americans.

George Catlett Marshall was the prime example of the ruling elite's exasperating self-satisfaction. Marshall had been a superb military leader in World War II—principally by choosing General Dwight

Eisenhower to lead the Allied forces. But Marshall went on to serve President Truman in various capacities, including as ambassador to China, secretary of state, and secretary of defense, and as a policy-maker. Marshall was the Zelig of disaster. He supported enormous concessions to Stalin at Yalta, including turning over Poland to the USSR. He helped consign a billion people to a totalitarian dungeon in China. He played a central role in Truman's firing General Douglas MacArthur. One has to observe only the veneration of Marshall on the PBS webpage to realize that his civilian career was not all sunshine and song.

There was rarely as incompetent a figure as Marshall, but the blue bloods brooked no criticism of their boy. When McCarthy attacked Marshall, the establishment reacted with sputtering rage. Contrary to popular mythology, McCarthy never called Marshall a "traitor," a "Communist," or a "coward."[36] He simply detailed Marshall's record.

Marshall had been implacably blind to the intentions of Mao's Communists. He doggedly refused to believe Mao was anything other than a simple agrarian reformer. An OSS officer desperately tried to warn Marshall that Mao was a Marxist, but Marshall was too busy putting the final touches on his bow tie for a fancy dinner party to listen. When Mao's second in command, Zhou En-lai, left a notebook on Marshall's private plane containing the names of Maoist spies who had infiltrated the Nationalist Chinese government, Marshall ordered his underling to return the notebook without even taking a little peek.[37]

Marshall's work in losing China to Communism was so impressive, he even won the Nobel Peace Prize for it. This represented a break with long-standing tradition to award the prize only to civilian peaceniks, such as Jimmy Carter, Rigoberta Menchu, Kofi Annan, Woodrow Wilson (for founding the League of Nations in 1919 and putting an end to war just in the nick of time), Amnesty International, International Physicians for the Prevention of Nuclear War, and Linus Pauling.

Though his name adorns the Marshall Plan, it is a fact that George Marshall opposed the whole point of the plan. The Marshall Plan is rightly hailed as a crucial element in preventing a Soviet takeover of all of Europe. The United States poured billions of dollars into Western Europe to jump-start their war-torn economies. By allowing non-Communist European nations to flourish, the Marshall Plan strengthened Western Europe, and immunized it from the allures of Soviet Communism. This precise virtue of the Marshall Plan was opposed by one George Marshall. Marshall never envisioned the plan as a weapon in the Cold War at all, but rather a pointless do-gooder welfare scheme for the world at large. In a proposal of stunning stupidity, Marshall wanted to include the Soviet Union and its satellite states in the Marshall Plan. As he put it in the speech credited with unveiling the plan, "Our policy is directed not against any party of doctrine but against hunger, poverty, desperation and chaos . . . Any government that is willing to assist in the task of recovery will find full cooperation, I am sure, on the part of the United States government."[38]

President Truman continued the charade, allowing Stalin to put in a bid, though the Republicans in Congress would never have approved a massive foreign aid program for the Soviet Union. In the event, Stalin haughtily turned down the Democrats' proposed largesse, not being overly concerned with the material well-being of his subjects. The Marshall Plan is now cited by liberals as a brilliant Democrat stratagem against the Soviet Union. It was—but only despite Truman and Marshall. Fortunately, the actual Marshall Plan bore very little relation to what Marshall had proposed. The Republicans modified the "Marshall Plan" submitted by Truman in another way. Congress included half a billion dollars in aid to Nationalist China and additional military aid to Greece and Turkey. Truman had requested no aid for Nationalist China whatsoever. Prescient little fellow that he was, Truman could already foresee that China would be lost and no one could be accused of "losing" it.

McCarthy was not the only Republican to attack Marshall, but he was the most penetrating.[39] In an erudite sixty-thousand-word speech that was later turned into a book titled *America's Retreat from Victory*, McCarthy recited chapter and verse of Marshall's disastrous policy decisions. He began by saying, "I realize full well how unpopular it is to lay hands on the laurels of a man who has been built into a great hero. I very much dislike it, but I feel that it must be done if we are to intelligently make the proper decisions in the issues of life and death before us."[40] He laid out his case for several hours one day on the Senate floor—with facts and dates and names. Even McCarthy-haters admitted that his case against Marshall was based on a laboriously assembled record.[41]

After detailing Marshall's stunning naiveté toward Stalin and Mao, McCarthy made a remark that stung the entire liberal establishment: "If Marshall was merely stupid, the laws of probability would dictate that part of his decisions would serve America's interests."[42]

Liberals were aghast. Just because millions of people kept being enslaved as a direct result of their policies, it was no reason to get snippy. The *New York Herald-Tribune* proclaimed McCarthy's speech "an offense against good taste." *Colliers* said of McCarthy, "Why not spank him?"[43] In their usual cogent style, liberals simultaneously called the speech a "stink bomb" and attacked McCarthy for the erudition of his speech, claiming it was so well written that he must have had a speechwriter. McCarthy's principal speechwriter on the Marshall speech was widely assumed to be the acclaimed journalist Forrest Davis.[44] When President Kennedy had speechwriters, it was evidence of his elegance and grace. But when McCarthy had a speechwriter, it somehow showed the dark underbelly of the conservative movement. As was usually the case with anyone McCarthy attacked, Marshall was subjected to undeserved praise and liberal emoluments for the rest of his life. Richard Rovere hailed Marshall as "the very image of the strong, noble, gentle Southern man of arms" in the tradition of Robert E. Lee.[45]

No discussion of the victims of "McCarthyism" is complete without mentioning McCarthy's biggest star—Owen Lattimore. Joining a long list, Lattimore boasted that it was he who coined the word "McCarthyism." Lattimore came to McCarthy's attention after he was named as a

Soviet agent by a former Communist. For many years, Louis Budenz had been a leader in the CPUSA (Communist Party USA) and editor of the *Daily Worker*. Other Soviet agents named by Budenz were confirmed by the Venona Project.[46] Among those he identified as a Soviet spy was Owen Lattimore.

Somewhat surprisingly, Lattimore's name has not yet turned up in the Venona cables as a Soviet agent. This glaring oversight can only be attributed to the limited number of cables that have been decoded. As the saying goes, if Lattimore wasn't being paid by Moscow, he was being gypped. Lattimore's friends were Soviet spies. His employees were Soviet spies. His associates were Soviet spies. He was handpicked by a Soviet spy on Roosevelt's staff to "advise" Chiang Kai-shek. Thanks to Lattimore's learned counsel, U.S. policy-makers abandoned Chiang Kai-shek and supported Mao Zedong, the greatest mass murderer in history. If Lattimore was not the Soviet's "top espionage agent," as McCarthy claimed, McCarthy was still more accurate about Lattimore than Al Gore was in anything he ever said about the Internet.

When he was called before two Senate committees in the early fifties, Lattimore's first line of defense to McCarthy's charges was to indignantly deny ever having worked for the government. Evidence tending to contradict Lattimore's denial that he was "mixed up with the State Department" included the facts that he used an office at the State Department, he took phone calls at the State Department, and he answered mail addressed to Lauchlin Currie at the State Department.[47] Currie was a top White House official and also a Soviet agent, proved by Venona.[48] As White House liaison to the State Department, his office was in the State Department Building. In a letter dated June 12, 1942, Lattimore informed an acquaintance, "I am in Washington about 4 days a week, and when there can always be reached at Lauchlin Currie's office, room 228, State Department Building; telephone National 1414, extension 90."[49]

Lattimore also denied under oath that he had reviewed Currie's mail at the State Department:

ROBERT MORRIS, COMMITTEE COUNSEL: "[I]sn't it a fact
    that when Currie went away for a period of time he would
    ask you to take care of his mail at the White House?"
LATTIMORE: "No."
MORRIS: "Is it your testimony that you did not at the request
    of Lauchlin Currie take care of his mail at the White
    House when he was away?"
LATTIMORE: "That certainly is my statement."[50]

Then the committee produced a letter dated June 15, 1942, saying, "Currie asked me to take care of his correspondence while he is
away and in view of your telegram of today, I think I had better tell you
that he has gone to China on a special trip. This news is absolutely
confidential until released in the press."[51] For these and other lies
before a Senate Committee, Lattimore was eventually indicted on
seven counts of perjury. Despite the *New York Times*'s ardent desire,
occasionally printed as fact, Lattimore was never "acquitted" of the
perjury charges. The charges against him were dismissed on technical
grounds. But in the alternative universe created by the *New York Times*
it is factually reported that "Mr. Lattimore was later acquitted of a perjury charge."[52]

    Liberals treated Lattimore like some sort of abstract intellectual,
practically a poet, with no interest in politics whatsoever. To this day,
liberals deny that Lattimore had any connection to the State Department, as if by refusing to admit something they can prevent it from
being true. A 1995 column in the *Washington Post* stated, "Lattimore,
of course, had never been in the State Department nor had he even
served as a consultant to it."[53] To say Lattimore had no effect on America's China policy because he was not a permanent employee of the
State Department would be like saying Dick Morris had no effect on
Clinton's campaign strategy because he was not on the White House
payroll. To be sure, Morris never drew green U.S. Treasury checks, but
he was a close advisor to those who did. Lattimore actually was on the
U.S. payroll, drawing paychecks from both the Office of War Informa-

tion and the State Department as a member of the State Department's Pauley Mission to Japan.

In any event, Lattimore's influence was far greater than his official sinecures suggest. Lattimore's recommendations had a bad habit of becoming official government policy. The left's Poet Laureate Lattimore was hauled out of irrelevance by President Roosevelt—on the recommendation of Soviet agent Currie—and sent to advise Chiang Kai-shek from 1941 to 1942.[54] He also accompanied Vice President Henry Wallace on his trip to Siberia and China in 1944.[55] After Lattimore toured Stalin's slave-labor camps with Wallace, he gushed about the wonderful things Stalin was doing for Russia. Using the standard liberal talking point about Soviet slave-labor camps, Lattimore described the gulags as "a combination Hudson's Bay Company and TVA [Tennessee Valley Authority]." Stalin's other Manchurian candidate, Henry Wallace, used the exact same phrase.[56]

For many years, Lattimore edited *Pacific Affairs*, the journal of the Institute of Pacific Relations (IPR). As editor, he published articles defending Stalin's purges. He loftily dismissed criticisms of the demonic show trials, saying, "A great many abuses have been discovered and rectified." By the time McCarthy called Lattimore a Soviet spy, forty-six people associated with Lattimore's IPR had been named under oath as members of the Communist Party, and eight others as espionage agents for the Soviet Union.[57] Lattimore's entire institute was chock-full of Soviet spies. A meeting of two or more Republicans is treated with greater alarm.[58] Owen Lattimore surely had closer ties to agents of Joseph Stalin than right-wingers do to Richard Mellon Scaife.

Lattimore thought Stalin was a peach, but he equivocated about our Nationalist Chinese ally Chiang Kai-shek. Lattimore had once oozed with praise for Chiang—as long as he served Moscow's interests. When Chiang was fighting the Japanese and thus preventing them from threatening Russia, Lattimore adored Chiang. But as soon as the Soviets didn't need Chiang and Mao's Communists besieged the Chinese Nationalist government, suddenly Lattimore complained that Chiang Kai-shek was nothing to write home about. So Chiang wasn't perfect. It's all relative now, isn't it? In order to be preferable to a satanic dictator in a barbarous land, apparently the alternative has to be Teddy Roosevelt. Is that a fair contest? It was not an opportune moment for the U.S. to be demanding reform from Chiang, inasmuch as he was in the middle of a civil war with Mao's Communists. But Lattimore recommended that the United States begin placing demands on Chiang while simultaneously opening a dialogue with the Communist insurgents. In a stunning development, despite Lattimore's honorable patriotic intentions, China fell to Communism, and more than a billion people were enslaved by a bloodthirsty dictator.

In a fawning profile of Lattimore in the *Washington Post* in 1995, Orville Schell wrote that Lattimore's IPR was attacked for "reasons that are still mysterious." Bear with me here—this is just a guess—but maybe it was the eight Soviet spies working there. That's even more than the *New York Times* had. Schell described critics of IPR as "pesky yet irrelevant cranks with a single-minded agenda."[59] Their pesky single-minded agenda was keeping a quarter of humanity free. This "countercurrent" in intellectual opinion, according to Schell, viewed the "old China hands"—Lattimore and his ilk—as being "soft on communism." By opposing Chiang and supporting Mao, was Lattimore being "tough on communism"?

Owen Lattimore was the original Clinton. He stonewalled the truth, and liberals would never apologize. Conservatives go through agonies of conscience for thirty years after quickly admitting to some minor misstatement. Democrats tolerated the patent risk of allowing Soviet-partisans to loiter around their administrations and to this day, they will not admit the truth.

In the terror that gripped the nation during McCarthy's rule, all respectable opinion supported Lattimore and opposed McCarthy. The left's idea of persecution is an absence of total unanimity in support of Harvard-educated traitors. Lattimore was so cowed by the black night of fascism that when McCarthy first attacked him, he instantly flew to Washington to denounce McCarthy as "base and despicable." He later

boasted of that "short and pithy" response, though by degree, Lattimore proceeded to become considerably less "pithy." He said McCarthy was "a fool or a knave" if he imagined Lattimore had promoted
Communist interests on the flimsy evidence of his having promoted
Communist interests. Furthermore, McCarthy had created "a reign of
terror." Most devastatingly, Lattimore said McCarthy had made
America "the laughing stock of the Communist governments"—a terrifying prospect to liberals everywhere. In April 1995, Lattimore's
harangue was described in the *Washington Post* magazine as "eloquent" and "convincing."[60]

In Lattimore's first round of hearings, he faced the Tydings Committee, a Senate Committee composed of Maxine Waters–style Democrats. The committee refused Senator McCarthy the right to question
witnesses. It pursued no leads and produced no evidence. It glibly dismissed as "hearsay" the testimony of ex-Communist Budenz identifying Lattimore as a Soviet agent. It accepted Lattimore's angry denials
at face value. Lattimore's brave appearance before this committee consisted of his haranguing the committee as un-American. For this, he
was literally applauded. On the basis of no investigation whatsoever,
the Tydings Committee hastily concluded that the charges against Lattimore were "a fraud and a hoax perpetrated on the Senate of the
United States and the American people . . . the most nefarious campaign of half-truths and untruth in the history of the Republic" blah,
blah, blah.

The Tydings Committee was such a joke that a second committee—the McCarran Committee, also dominated by Democrats but of a
very different complexion—was later required to perform an actual
investigation of Lattimore. In round two, the terrified and quaking Lattimore called his accusers "a motley crew of crackpots, professional
informers, hysterics and ex-Communists," "embittered, ruthless and
unprincipled . . . masters of the dark techniques of villainy," and
"artists of conspiracy." Particularly terrifying, evidently, was McCarthy
himself, whom Lattimore shrunk from in fear by calling him a string of

names such as the "Wisconsin Whimperer" and "a graduate witch
burner." One wonders what turns of phrase he would have used if
McCarthy had been a little less intimidating.

Yes, McCarthy held a terrified nation hostage.

Lattimore was defended pro bono by future Supreme Court justice
Abe Fortas and Yale Law School Professor John P. Frank. President
Truman, fresh from denouncing the Hiss hearings as a "red herring,"
said Lattimore was being "shamefully persecuted" by the Senate. All
in all, Lattimore's persecution would not be matched until President
Clinton's ordeal in the black night of fascism was ignited by a man
called . . . *Ken Starr.*

Though Lattimore prattled on about "my seriously damaged reputation," his stock only soared in the nation's editorial pages and universities. He took a paid leave from Johns Hopkins presumably to work
on more derisive adjectives for the committee members. He continued
to lecture, including a once-a-year stint at Harvard. Typical of the contemporaneous fawning over the man who helped condemn a billion
people to a Communist slave state, the *New York Post* editorialized:
"All those who believe in freedom in this country are in the debt of
Owen Lattimore." The millions of Chinese exterminated by Chairman
Mao are also in Lattimore's debt.

The idea of a bowed and terrified liberal minority during McCarthy's "reign of terror" is poppycock. Then as now, all elite opinion was
against McCarthy. The principal result of being called a Communist by
McCarthy was you got to teach at Harvard. In a two-part, four-billion-
column-inch *Washington Post* story detailing the horrors suffered by
Lattimore, the sole suggestion of any professional harm is a bald allegation that Lattimore's annual lecture at Harvard met with "resistance." It was never actually rescinded, mind you. But there were
rumors of "resistance."[61] Harvard resisting a Communist was about as
likely as the American Conservative Union resisting Ronald Reagan.
Contributing to the authenticity of the story, the alleged "dean" who
put up the impotent resistance remained anonymous. Lattimore taught
in Europe for a while, where, the *Post* said, "the academic community

as a whole had been far more supportive of [Lattimore's] scholarly work and admiring of his courage."[62] Unless they were performing the sex acts Monica executed on Clinton, it's difficult to imagine how European academics could have been any more supportive of Lattimore than American academics were.

By 1972, Lattimore himself boasted that his reputation needed no further defense. "President Nixon's record of the same period," he sniffed, "could do with, and is getting, a lavish application of cosmetic art."[63] Lattimore's descent into the hell of "McCarthyism" involved fawning media coverage, legal representation by a future Supreme Court Justice, a paid leave from Hopkins, annual lectures at Harvard, and the adulation of academics everywhere. Having survived his "ordeal," Lattimore took a position at the University of Leeds in Britain. Only by incremental slander did the loudmouthed "victims of McCarthyism" finally convince people that McCarthy held a terrified nation captive. In 1954, critic Leslie Fiedler captured the essence of "McCarthyism": "From one end of the country to another rings the cry, 'I am cowed! I am afraid to speak out!', and the even louder response, 'Look, he is cowed! He is afraid to speak out.' "[64] The *New York Times*, unintentionally hilarious "Herblock" cartoons, and the usual Treason Lobby hysterically attacked McCarthy. Seeking the rewards of apostasy, "moderate Republicans" nodded in agreement. Never has a more powerful oligarchy screamed so long and so loudly about its own victimization.

6

BUT WERE THERE COMMUNISTS IN THE STATE DEPARTMENT?

History is an endless process of liberal brainwashing. The battle for truth is purely propagandistic. Liberals can't persuade, they can only harrumph. But they write the history books. Like all historical myths, arrogant and powerful institutions of liberalism distorted the truth about McCarthy through sheer malice. He was subjected to a relentless stream of abuse the likes of which would not be seen again until Ken Starr had the goods on Clinton. Liberal hysteria has become historical fact. As the critic John Jay Chapman said a century ago, "Give a professor a false thesis in early life, and he will teach it till he dies. He has no way of correcting it."[1]

History textbooks ritualistically include the demonstrably false assertion that McCarthy "did not discover a single Communist anywhere."[2] Schoolchildren are taught in a major American textbook,

A History of US, that McCarthy "was a liar. Not your ordinary small-time fibber. No, Senator Joseph McCarthy was an enormous, outrageous, beyond-belief liar."[3] Upcoming editions will include the dark tale of how Swedes flew planes into the World Trade Center on 9-11 and glorious renditions of how Bill Clinton—shoulder-to-shoulder with Larry Flynt—saved the Constitution.

Flip through any book about McCarthy and notice the footnotes. It is an arresting fact that the supporting documentation rarely consists of primary source material. Academics cite other academics, who cite other academics, with nearly all statements about McCarthy eventually tracing their way back to contemporaneous news accounts from a rabidly anti-McCarthy press. Doing original research on McCarthy is apparently not tenure-track material at American universities. As the saying goes, the first draft of history is written by journalists. And we know who they are. They told us Clinton was only counseling Monica. But trust them on McCarthy. The news industry is the last place you'd go for the truth about McCarthy. It would be as if all historical accounts of the Bush presidency were based exclusively on Maureen Dowd columns.

The press loathed McCarthy. Their idea of investigative reporting was to recycle passages from the Tydings Committee report—a well-known smear job hatched by the segregationist Democratic senator Millard Tydings. Tydings's father-in-law was the infamous Joseph E. Davies, Roosevelt's ambassador to the USSR, who gushed with admiration for Stalin's show trials—later made into a major motion picture, *Mission to Moscow*. When Western journalists wrote a letter pleading with Stalin to spare the life of a prominent Russian journalist, Vladamir Romm, Ambassador Davies refused even to deliver their letter. "Poor devil," Davies glibly wrote of Romm.[4] Davies's son-in-law's concern with Soviet spies was about as honorable.

Historical facts about McCarthy are sourced to the news stories of prominent journalists like I. F. Stone. Needless to say, Stone attacked McCarthy early and often. Stone was an "idealist." He supported

Joseph Stalin in the 1930s, the Soviet-backed "Progressive Party" presidential candidate Henry Wallace in the forties, and Ho Chi Minh in the 1960s.[5] He spoke at the first Vietnam teach-in at Berkeley. Two years later he marched on the Pentagon.[6] After warming to the idea of suppressing "fascist" speech, Stone would later revise that position when it came to Communists. The *Washington Post* said he changed his mind "in light of McCarthyism."[7] Stone famously disdained the wisdom of "the common man"[8]—who adored McCarthy—preferring the wisdom of out-of-touch elites.

Despite the serious risk of being called brave, Stone stood with the' *New York Times*, the *Washington Post*, CBS, NBC, ABC, Hollywood, and every college and university in the nation against the brute McCarthy. The *Los Angeles Times* hailed Stone's raw courage, saying, "Long before it was safe to do so, he attacked McCarthyite loyalty purges."[9] One can only imagine the horror that would befall a journalist who criticized McCarthy. In fact, literally one can only imagine it.

The late Fred Friendly, doyen of American journalism, called Stone "the conscience of investigative journalism." Friendly was a professor at Columbia School of Journalism, where he initiated the tradition of forcing students to gasp in awe at his genius and courage for attacking McCarthy at CBS, where he produced the famous Edward R. Murrow smear job on McCarthy.[10] So honest was I. F. Stone that an Oliphant cartoon showed him refusing to enter heaven because—as Saint Peter is telling God—"he'd rather hang around out here, and keep things honest."[11] Stone's life was the subject of a fawning 1975 documentary, narrated by *New York Times* columnist Tom Wicker.[12]

It has now been overwhelmingly documented that I. F. Stone was a paid Soviet agent.[13] While intrepidly attacking McCarthy, this "conscience of investigative journalism" was on the payroll of a totalitarian regime. Stone was identified as an agent by a former KGB agent in 1992.[14] A few years after that, declassified Soviet cables confirmed that he was an agent. In one cable, Stone's NKVD contact reported Stone was willing to accept money for his services, but "did not want to attract the attention of the FBI."[15] According to professional Soviet apologist Victor Navasky, if you accept the Venona documents, "you have to accept that I. F. Stone . . . was a Communist agent."[16]

Consider that an American journalist on Joseph Stalin's payroll was indistinguishable from other members of his profession. Stone was constantly cited as an exemplar of honest and independent journalism. Michael Beschloss said Stone was a journalist others "came to emulate."[17] The *Washington Post* called Stone a "tough-minded individualist in a time of conformity."[18] The *Los Angeles Times*'s Washington bureau chief Jack Nelson said Stone "was one of the great investigative reporters of the 20th Century."[19] Former Washington bureau chief of the *New York Times* James Reston called Stone "the scholar of our profession."[20]

The "tough-minded individualist"—and Soviet spy—published hysterical diatribes against McCarthy. Without a fig leaf of evidence, Stone called McCarthy an anti-Semite and, for good measure, a fascist.[21] It was standard Communist Party strategy to throw out baseless accusations of anti-Semitism and fascism. In his book *Radical Son,* David Horowitz explains that the [Communist] Party "played up the 'Jewish issue' whenever it could"[22] in order to make comparisons with Nazi Germany seem plausible. Historian Ronald Radosh says, "The tarring of opponents with the 'fascist' brush was the favored course of attack used by American Communists and their supporters."[23] As red-diaper babies, Horowitz and Radosh sat at Communists' dinner tables and heard them speak freely, never suspecting they would be ratted out.

In a shocking development, paid Soviet agent Stone did not like Whittaker Chambers's book *Witness.* Stone was outraged to discover that Chambers had been paid for the book. The fiend. Not only that, but Chambers had betrayed his friends—who happened to be spies against America.[24] Chambers's heartless betrayal of his "friends" became the standard talking point of the "educated, progressive" people, as Lionel Trilling called them. They regarded Chambers "with loathing—the word is not too strong—as one who had resolved, for some perverse reason to destroy a former friend."[25] It's all eerily familiar. What did ever happen to that book by the money-grubbing betrayer Linda Tripp?

Stone also brilliantly foreshadowed the Clinton flacks' "it's just about sex" riposte with his defense of Soviet spy Judith Coplon. When Coplon was caught in the act of handing top-secret government files to a KGB operative, she defended herself by saying it was just about sex. She purported to be having an affair with the KGB agent, and happened to be carrying a sheaf of highly classified government surveillance documents when meeting him for a sexual tryst. By using her sex life as a defense, Coplon put the government to the charming task of proving she was not having an affair with the KGB agent. In making their case, the prosecution produced evidence that, just a week before, she had spent the weekend in a hotel room with another man.

Stone—a journalist so committed to honesty, he would turn down heaven to "keep things honest"—wrote of the government's case: "This is a dirty business. . . . If FBI men can gather sex stories and salt them away in those files of theirs, 'fornication' can be said to obtain conviction in many kinds of cases." Less than one year before Venona was released, proving absolutely that both Stone and Coplon were Soviet spies, an article in the *Washington Post* praised Stone for making this excellent point.[26]

Right up until the Venona Project was declassified, proving the existence of a vast network of Soviet spies in America throughout the forties and fifties, the "Red Scare" industry was still going strong. Literally months before Venona was declassified, Griffin Fariello released an inadvertently hilarious book titled *Red Scare: Memories of the American Inquisition.*[27] The book consisted of scores of "oral histories" describing "how it felt to live amid an ideology now labeled McCarthyism."[28]

Writer and former radical David Horowitz has as much claim to having witnessed the "Red Scare" as anyone. His parents were members of the Communist Party and consequently were fired from their jobs as New York City schoolteachers under the Feinberg Law, which prohibited teachers in New York State from advocating the overthrow of government by force, violence, or any unlawful means. For all the bellyaching, Horowitz says, fired Communists fared pretty well. He says: "What actually happened to my father and American Communists in general bears little resemblance to these lurid images."[29] In his parents' case, they went on to other, better jobs and had their pensions restored in full. The Communist Party's "morality play," Horowitz says, "has become a national myth."[30]

In order to appreciate how the myth of "McCarthyism" was concocted, consider how liberals portray events happening right before our eyes. Only those fresh in the struggle can see how the left's obfuscatory techniques operate. According to the guardians of the McCarthy myth, the most recent efflorescence of "McCarthyism" was the grim zealot Starr persecuting Bill Clinton for no reason whatsoever. A *New York Magazine* review of the anti-McCarthy documentary *Point of Order* expressly recommended the movie for "anyone of any age trying to understand the more obsessional and bizarre elements of Kenneth Starr's investigation of the president." According to the reviewer, David Denby, in ten years Starr's investigation of Clinton will appear as "peculiar" as McCarthy's investigations—"the paranoia, the irrationality, the bullying and toadying and righteousness."[31] If people like Denby write the history, it will.

A *Los Angeles Times* reporter wrote an entire article about the amazing similarities between Starr and McCarthy, saying the "links between the anxiety of [the McCarthy] era and independent counsel Kenneth W. Starr's inquiry in our time are not so far-fetched."[32] Ellen Schrecker, a leading McCarthy-phobe, said the Starr investigation was reminiscent of the McCarthy era because both were "a criminalization of activities, politics or sex, that are not illegal, and this is done through a governmental investigative process."[33] Feminist Betty Friedan said that "sex is going to take the place of the Cold War."[34] This is what liberals mean by "McCarthyism." People who assure us McCarthy presided over a reign of terror also describe Ken Starr's plodding, meticulous investigation as a reign of terror. And they say that when we're watching. Imagine what they'll say when the generation that knows the truth is gone.

The image of McCarthy riding roughshod over civil liberties and terrifying small children is difficult to square with the fact that the public loved him. Even without the truth-monitor of the Internet and Fox News Channel, at the time, people could see McCarthy for themselves. In the words of historian David Oshinsky, McCarthy's campaign was "alarmingly popular."[35] The more he railed against Communists working for the government, the higher his approval ratings soared.

At the height of the left's counterattack against McCarthy, just months away from a Senate censure, Americans told pollsters they approved of the job he was doing by 50 to 29 percent.[36] Excluding those who had no opinion, his approval rating was 63 percent. Gallup polls from 1950 to 1954—the entire run of McCarthy's anti-Communist crusade—showed that Catholics supported McCarthy by 56 to 29 percent; Protestants supported him by 45 to 36 percent. To the eternal annoyance and bewilderment of McCarthy assistant Roy Cohn, Jews opposed McCarthy by 82 to 3 percent.[37] As Michael Paul Rogin writes in *The Intellectuals and McCarthy,* "This man, terribly dangerous in the eyes of sophisticated observers of American politics, had obtained the backing of millions of American people."[38]

Bobby Kennedy worked for McCarthy and held him in such high esteem that he asked McCarthy to be the godfather to his first child, Kathleen Kennedy Townsend, born on the Fourth of July, 1951.[39] This was seventeen months after McCarthy's famous Wheeling, West Virginia, speech, well into McCarthy's "reign of terror." The very year of McCarthy's censure, John F. Kennedy fiercely defended McCarthy on Soviet territory: Cambridge, Massachusetts. In response to a speaker's lighthearted remark that, unlike the law school, Harvard College could be proud of never having produced either an Alger Hiss or a Joe McCarthy, Kennedy erupted: "How dare you couple the name of a great American patriot with that of a traitor?"[40] Kennedy would schedule long-needed surgery in order to avoid having to vote on McCarthy's censure, a vote that was taken largely on partisan lines. Mortified by the Kennedy family's manifest admiration for McCarthy, liberals are always recalling some late-night conversation no one else heard, in which the Kennedys expressed their secret qualms about McCarthy. The facts speak for themselves.

That McCarthy was onto something is evident in the fact that almost everyone knows he was a wretched man, this country's rough equivalent of Stalin, arguably even as bad as Ken Starr. But almost no one knows if he was right. This is the follow-up question that's never asked. That's not the point.

Rather, liberals explained McCarthy was a drunk and a demagogue who played poker for money (shocking the consciences of sissyboys in academia). *But were Communist spies working for the U.S. government?* Moreover, McCarthy's office may have pulled strings to get former staffer David Schine special privileges from the Army. *But were Communist spies working for the U.S. government?* McCarthy's staff attorney Roy Cohn was gay. *But were Communist spies working for the U.S. government?* McCarthy slightly embellished upon his World War II exploits (but not as much as liberals exaggerated his exaggerations). *But were Communist spies working for the U.S. government?* In addition, McCarthy may have said he had a list of 205 Communists in the State Department rather than 57, as he later claimed. *But were Communist spies working for the U.S. government?*

McCarthy was actually accused of "perjury" for denying he said he had the names of 205 Communists in the State Department in his Wheeling, West Virginia, speech. McCarthy plausibly insisted he had claimed to have the names of only 57 Communists. The 205 figure was an important number—but it referred to something else. Just a few years earlier, the Democratic Secretary of State James Byrnes had admitted that 205 identified security risks at the State Department were still on the job.[41] No one seemed to know what had happened to those identified security risks, which was precisely McCarthy's point. He certainly didn't claim to have a list of their names. To the contrary, he was enraged that no one else did, either. The possibility that hundreds of security risks were still employed by the State Department did not interest the Democrats. They just wanted to know whether McCarthy had claimed to have the names of 205 or 57 Communists at the State Department.

To put this controversy in perspective, less than one year before McCarthy's speech, Judith Coplon was arrested in the act of passing government intelligence files to a KGB agent. Only weeks before McCarthy's speech, Alger Hiss had been convicted of perjury for lying about being a Soviet spy. Stalinist spies were passing secret government files to Soviet agents, and the Treason Party sprang to action by vigorously investigating the precise words McCarthy had used in a speech to a women's Republican club in West Virginia. This from the "legally accurate" crowd. Bill Clinton denied under oath that he had engaged in sexual relations with Monica Lewinsky, that Monica Lewinsky had engaged in sexual relations with him, or even that he was ever alone with Monica Lewinsky. This is hailed as Clinton's courageous effort to "save the Constitution." But long, gaseous books have insistently asserted that McCarthy said he had the names of 205 Communists rather than 57 Communists. By now, even normal people have conceded the point. *Fine, if it means that much to you—okay, fine.*

A congressional committee set to work investigating the pressing issue of whether McCarthy had said he had the names of 205 or 57 Communists. Of course, liberals could never manage to produce a tape of his alleged offense. But the committee did produce affidavits from two radio station administrators who a little too eagerly signed affidavits contradicting McCarthy. Even the investigating committee found the affidavits unbelievable and in its report dismissed them as unreliable. The investigators grudgingly concluded that McCarthy had probably claimed to have the names of 57 Communists—just as he had always said. The final report of the committee then dropped the matter and devoted itself to printing several hundred pages of McCarthy's financial records. One will search history books in vain for any mention of the committee's conclusion as to McCarthy's capital offense of misspeaking. This part of the report mysteriously disappeared immediately after it was released and was instantly forgotten. All credible evidence on the subject supports McCarthy.[42] But today, history books universally assert that McCarthy said 205, rather than 57—and then indignantly accuse McCarthy of being sloppy with his facts.

In his initial charges McCarthy named only about a hundred loyalty risks in government jobs—not necessarily spies or even members of the Communist Party, just people who shouldn't be working for the U.S. government. As we now know, he was erring on the low side. So far—and the review is not complete—decrypted Soviet cables have revealed well over three hundred Soviet spies working for the government in the forties and fifties. Hundreds of agents of an enemy foreign power were working for the U.S. government. But McCarthy was a brute for pointing it out.

The primary victim of outrageous persecution during the McCarthy era was McCarthy. Liberals hid their traitorous conduct by making McCarthy the issue. They did to McCarthy everything they falsely accuse him of doing to them. The press didn't mind trafficking in innuendo and smears when McCarthy was the target. Only when Communist spies and sympathizers were exposed did it qualify as a "witch hunt." There was much liberal hilarity over the fact that McCarthy and two of his assistants, Roy Cohn and David Schine, were at one time all unmarried men. The liberal playwright Lillian Hellman giddily gay-baited them as "Bonnie, Bonnie, and Clyde." Hank Greenspun, publisher of the *Las Vegas Sun*, called McCarthy a "disreputable pervert."[43] McCarthy, who would soon be married, laughed off the taunts. In a final payback, the *New York Times* took the occasion of Roy Cohn's death to out him as a homosexual. The obituary referred to "widespread rumors" that Cohn was gay, and noted that one of the secondary causes of his death was "underlying HTLV-3 infections." Many scientists, the *Times* reported, "believe the HTLV-3 virus is the cause of AIDS," which is "statistically most common among homosexual men."[44] Cohn was unavailable for comment.

Senator William Benton issued a blast against McCarthy that was so scurrilous that Benton's own lawyer called it the most libelous document he had ever seen. Page after page of Benton's diatribe repeated unsubstantiated gossip and outright lies. Benton falsely accused McCarthy of bribe-taking. It called him "amoral" and said he was of "unsound mind." It denounced McCarthy for having an "admitted homosexual ex-Communist" on his payroll. It cited as hard fact the lies of a delusional nut who claimed to be an international spy working for McCarthy.[45] In an egregious violation of McCarthy's privacy, Benton's committee ordered the Washington postmaster to keep a record of every piece of mail sent to McCarthy's home and the homes of his top assistants.[46]

To get other senators' signatures on his report, Benton preyed on the alcoholism of two members of the subcommittee.[47] Muckraking journalist Drew Pearson, the Larry Flynt of his day, threatened to expose one as an alcoholic unless he signed Benton's report.[48] The other senator had to be plied with alcohol before putting his name on the report—a report he later dismissed as without legal authority.[49]

The press was whipped into a frenzy of hysteria over Benton's baseless charges. Media across the nation recklessly repeated large sections of the report. The *New York Post* ran a sensationalized seventeen-part series on the charges.[50] Journalists began interviewing McCarthy's former neighbors, reporting such allegations as that he was a "bully" as a child. McCarthy sued one of the newspapers that printed the absurd charge that he had funded spies abroad. He won a public apology and $12,000 in damages.[51]

In liberals' most lurid fantasies, McCarthy never authored such a libelous document. He never arranged for the postmaster to spy on the private mail of a fellow senator. He never threatened to expose a man's alcoholism. He was never compelled to pay damages for defaming someone. And yet historians blithely dismiss the unparalleled assaults on McCarthy with such delusional remarks as "Joe was not the only one who could play rough."[52] The "only one"? He may have been the only one who didn't. McCarthy came up with a few witty nicknames for his colleagues and they acted as if he had burned their houses to the ground. He didn't libel them, spy on them, or gay-bait them. All that was done to him.

The *Madison Capital Times,* an anti-McCarthy newspaper, claimed McCarthy had monkeyed around with campaign funds and demanded a government investigation. After a five-year probe by the IRS, McCarthy received a rebate.[53] While overseeing coverage of McCarthy, the Washington bureau chief of the *New York Times* James (Scotty) Reston called McCarthy a "two-bit demagogue." The reporter Reston assigned to cover McCarthy was a former member of the Communist Party, or, for short, "a *New York Times* reporter." This would be like having a former member of Hamas cover Israel for the *New York Times.* When McCarthy mentioned the reporter's Communist ties, Reston is quoted as having said, "There was no evidence of bias in the reporter's work."[54] There probably wasn't—compared to journalists like I. F. Stone.

Even McCarthy's exemplary war record was subject to much gleeful jeering. Exempt from the draft as a sitting judge, McCarthy volunteered for the Marines in 1942. He was too old to fly, and consequently was an intelligence officer. His principal function was to debrief fighter pilots after bombing runs—famously asking them, "What kind of hell did you give the Japs today?" He volunteered to fly about a dozen combat missions, in which he came under enemy fire and fired back. On rickety airplanes from the forties, thousands of miles from home, he took enemy fire from savage Oriental beasts and fired back as a tail gunner.[55] He asked for and received a Distinguished Flying Cross.

McCarthy was literally and inarguably a tail gunner, but the media sarcastically called him "Tailgunner Joe," indignant that not all of his runs came under enemy fire. This, from reporters who need smelling salts for a paper cut. Not only that, but McCarthy did not regularly provide precise and detailed accounts of how he injured his leg during the war. McCarthy broke his leg in one of those atavistic hazing rituals popular with the military, but which the scribbling profession considers highly immature. McCarthy's minor embellishments of an estimable war record were infinitesimal compared to that of most politicians. And yet, to this day, reporters viciously attack McCarthy's war record as a total fraud. Ed Timms, of the *Dallas Morning News,* described exaggerated boasts by politicians about their military service, saying, "There's even a name for it: 'Tailgunner Joe Syndrome.'" Timms said McCarthy's "lies" consisted of his claiming "combat experience as a tail-gunner aboard bombers during World War II, but he actually never saw action."[56] Twelve combat missions. There's even a name for reporters who lie about McCarthy: "Ed Timms Syndrome."

True heroism—as Timms reminded readers—consists of not noticing an approaching Japanese destroyer soon enough to avoid having it sink your PT boat. Or, as Timms more vaguely summarized raw heroism, "John F. Kennedy's PT boat experience."[57] Even Kennedy understood the irony of the Kennedy publicity machine's turning a not particularly heroic moment into the equivalent of sinking three enemy ships. Asked how he became a war hero, Kennedy would reply, "They sank my boat."

McCarthy's embellishments were nothing compared to the delusional exaggerations of Democrats about their war records. Another act of mind-boggling courage was Lyndon Johnson's single flight throughout World War II—as an observer—for which he was awarded the Silver Star, the third highest combat award. For the rest of his life, Johnson wore what historian David Halberstam called "the least deserved and most proudly displayed Silver Star in military history."[58] As CNN has recently reported, the sole surviving member of the crew has always insisted that the plane never came under fire.[59] Mysteriously, Johnson—the observer—was the only member of the crew to receive any sort of decoration for the thirteen-minute flight. And yet for the rest of his life Johnson wore his Silver Star, brandishing it for effect, and boasting that he flew on many missions. He even claimed the other members of the Air Force group were so admiring of him that they called him "Raider Johnson." In a 1962 recorded telephone conversation with then–Speaker of the House John McCormack, Johnson says, "I know foreign aid is unpopular, but I didn't want to go to the Pacific in 'forty-one after Pearl Harbor, but I did. I didn't want to let those Japs shoot at me . . . but I did."[60] It was all part of Johnson's roguish charm.

The mainstream media was also not much interested in Al Gore's lusty exaggerations of his war record. Throughout the years, Gore had repeatedly provided the media with vivid reminiscences of his combat experiences in Vietnam.[61] The basic picture was that upon landing in Vietnam, young Al Gore ripped open his blouse and shouted, "Let the bullets hit me first!" In fact, Gore not only never saw combat in Vietnam, but was assigned a bodyguard so that this senator's son would not come in harm's way.[62] He was never shot at, and he never fired a shot in anger. Little Lord Fauntleroy's tour of duty in Vietnam consisted of a five-month vacation in the Orient with his own Man Friday bringing him mint juleps as he typed illiterate dispatches for the *Stars and Stripes.* Or, as Gore told *Vanity Fair,* "I took my turn regularly on the perimeter in these little firebases out in the boonies. Something would move, we'd fire first and ask questions later."

Unlike Johnson and Gore, McCarthy actually flew a dozen combat missions, taking enemy fire and firing back. But liberal elites were shocked to the core to discover that McCarthy might have added the slightest bit of color to his military exploits. Oshinsky said McCarthy's boasts were important because they showed a pattern of deception. Excellent point, patterns are important. The pattern is this: McCarthy engaged in the slightest embellishments of his military record and then journalists ferociously attacked him with outrageous lies about his admirable military service.[63]

The most vivid image people have of McCarthy is of the bow-tied attorney Joseph Welch rebuking him during the Army-McCarthy hearings: "Have you no sense of decency, sir, at long last? Have you left no sense of decency?" This is treated as comparable to Henry V's speech at Agincourt, only more inspiring. Leaving no doubt as to Welch's heroic status, reporters in the hearing room erupted in thunderous applause at the conclusion of Welch's emotional response to McCarthy.

The viewer can only imagine what horrible cruelty McCarthy had just inflicted on some hapless witness, prompting Welch's cri de couer. The *Washington Post* recently claimed that Welch was responding to the "vicious tactics" of "the Hill's most notorious scandalmonger, distorting the truth and wrecking reputations without remorse."[64] Suspiciously, the details of the exchange are always a bit murky. It simply must be taken on faith that McCarthy, ruthless destroyer of reputations, had just engaged in some outrageous fiendishness. It must be accepted unquestioningly that Welch was David to McCarthy's Goliath. Whenever liberals become hysterical but refuse to give you any particulars, they are up to no good.

Delivering the standard liberal fairy tale of "How Joseph Welch Saved the World by Standing Up to McCarthy," a *Chicago Sun-Times* columnist explained that Welch delivered the "have you no decency" soliloquy during "televised hearings of [McCarthy's] investigation into phantom communists in the military."[65] Before we continue: Communists working for the Army were assuredly not "phantoms." If liberals thought they were, they could have spared us their whining about executed Soviet spies Julius and Ethel Rosenberg—two such phantoms. Rosenberg was an engineer with the Army Signal Corps. Incredibly, even after the Army discovered he was a Communist and dismissed him in 1944, Rosenberg continued to work on classified military projects. He supervised a cell of other Soviet spies still working for the Army.[66] The Army's incompetence at discovering the Rosenberg cell allowed the Soviet Union to build nuclear warheads pointed at United States soil for the next half a century. This is what liberals mean by "phantom communists in the military."

But more important, the Senate hearing was not, as the *Sun-Times* claimed, "McCarthy's investigation" into anything. It was an investigation of Senator McCarthy. Indeed, this was the Senate's fourth investigation of McCarthy—to the delight of a virulently anti-McCarthy press.[67] McCarthy was not the inquisitor; it was he who was on trial. Welch's speech at Agincourt (only better!) did not come in response to McCarthy's browbeating of a witness. It was just the opposite—Welch was in the process of browbeating one of McCarthy's assistants, Roy Cohn.

In this particular run at McCarthy, the Senate was probing whether McCarthy's committee had pressured the Army to grant special privileges to David Schine, a former staff member on the committee. Roy Cohn, a brilliant but deeply flawed individual, applied unseemly pressure on the Army to allow Schine to finish his work with the committee, or at least to be given generous weekend passes to do so. A closeted homosexual, Cohn apparently had a mad crush on Schine. McCarthy's troubles with the Army were entirely of Cohn's making. Still and all, it was surely one of the lamest acts of influence peddling in all of American history.

Among the facts generally omitted from the traditional telling of the Army-McCarthy hearings is that Schine was suddenly drafted in the midst of McCarthy's investigation of the Army's Communist infestation problems. Cohn thought Schine's draft was political payback. McCarthy disagreed, annoyed at the suggestion that anything could have deterred him from pursuing his investigation. He simply viewed the entire controversy as asinine. The watchdog press was not much interested in exploring the question of why the Army had drafted Schine, just as the press showed little interest in why Clinton's IRS audited Paula Jones.

In fact, the Army's motives may have been pure, but Schine's draft was absolutely political. It came about only as a result of the vigorous lobbying efforts of a ferociously anti-McCarthy journalist, Drew Pearson.[68] When Schine was first drafted, he received a deferment because of a slipped disc. His back had since healed, something the draft board would likely have overlooked, but for Pearson's frenetic letter-writing campaign to the Army demanding a review of Schine's deferment.

By all accounts, Schine was perfectly happy to be drafted and McCarthy showed no interest in relieving him of his duty. McCarthy humored Cohn, while quietly confiding in the secretary of the Army, Robert T. Stevens: "You can send [Schine] to Korea for all I care." He said, "Schine's a good boy, but there is nothing indispensable about him." McCarthy even laughed with Stevens about Cohn's machinations, saying Cohn "thinks David should be a general and work from the penthouse of the Waldorf."[69] Despite enormous pressure to fire Cohn when details of his lobbying the Army came out, McCarthy refused. He was fiercely, perhaps suicidally, loyal to Cohn—whom McCarthy did see as indispensable.

In any event, as Soviet spies wormed their way into the government, the U.S. Senate decided to investigate the pressing matter of whether McCarthy's committee had pressured the Army to give Private David Schine a "fur-lined hood" or allow him to "often" ride in the cab of Army trucks. At one point, McCarthy said in exasperation, "Don't you think this is a little ridiculous? Is my committee being charged with pressuring the Army to give David Schine a fur-lined cap?"

Admittedly, McCarthy was not at his best during the Army-McCarthy hearings. He had been under relentless attacks from the press for four solid years. He began drinking more than usual during the hearings, often working in his office all night sipping straight vodka.[70] Still, he was better than his adversaries. Confident that the media would portray them as eloquent and reasonable no matter what they did, the Democrats behaved like animals—sneering, interrupting, and catcalling McCarthy throughout the hearings. McCarthy could not finish a sentence without being interrupted by obstructionist Democrats. The incessant attacks would have tried Mother Teresa's patience. But McCarthy had grown accustomed to liberal scolds and responded with his usual humor.

Welch's "have you no decency" oration came at the conclusion of his two-hour harangue of Roy Cohn. The *Washington Post* has claimed Welch spoke with "eloquence and tenacity"[71] in the sense of "sneering and whining." As attorney for the Army, Welch's technical, legal objective was to demonstrate that McCarthy's committee was putting undue pressure on the Army. The method Welch chose to prove his case was to portray the members of McCarthy's committee as homosexuals and lunatics. This great hero to liberals viciously gay-baited McCarthy's staff, among whom Cohn was the only homosexual. It was all part of the famed Welch "eloquence."[72]

With staggering condescension, Welch sarcastically asked Cohn to give him the names of all Communists "loose today." He taunted Cohn relentlessly, with exaggerated horror: "Whenever you learn of one from now on, Mr. Cohn, I beg of you, will you tell somebody about them quick?" He squealed with mock alarm: "I don't want the sun to go down while they are still in there, if we can get them out." To gales of laughter from the press, Welch told Cohn, "You not only frighten me, you make me ashamed when there are so many in Massachusetts!" Again and again, in his patronizing singsong, Welch asked Cohn to "tell them tonight" about any Communists, so that FBI surveillance can begin "by sundown tomorrow night."

In the face of Welch's sarcasm, Cohn replied to every sneer with immense politeness, nearly sir-ing him to death—"Yes, sir," "I will try, sir."

Absurdly, Welch asked Cohn, "Cannot the FBI put these hundred and thirty men under surveillance before sundown tomorrow?" This was a stupid question and Welch surely knew it. Soviet spies were under surveillance; they needed to be fired from their government jobs. The FBI once had Alger Hiss under surveillance, too, but that didn't stop President Roosevelt from receiving Hiss's counsel at Yalta. The FBI had had Harry Dexter White under surveillance, but that didn't stop President Truman from putting him in a top job at the IMF. Even after the Rosenberg case, the Army was still promoting witting agents of a totalitarian regime. The point was to remove security risks from their government jobs, not to keep them under lifelong FBI surveillance.

Cohn graciously explained this manifestly obvious point to Welch, saying, "Sir, if there is need for surveillance in the case of espionage or anything like that, I can well assure you that Mr. John Edgar Hoover and his men know a lot better than I . . . just who should be put under surveillance." McCarthy was more blunt with Welch. He interrupted Welch's jabberwocky to say, "Mr. Chairman, let's not be ridiculous. Mr. Welch knows, as I have told him a dozen times, that the FBI has all of this information. . . . The only thing we can do is to try and publicly expose these individuals and hope that they will be gotten rid of. And you know that, Mr. Welch."

But Welch was not particularly interested in the truth. He was playing to the peanut gallery. The reporters, the Democrats, and Welch himself were all having a rip-roaring good laugh at the notion of Communists in government. Stalin's show trials must have had them in stitches. Welch concluded his badgering of Cohn with one final jeer: "May I add my small voice, sir, and say whenever you know about a subversive or a Communist spy, please hurry. Will you remember those words?"

It was after all this—Welch's gay-baiting, mocking attack on McCarthy's assistant—that McCarthy stepped in with a knockout punch. He said that in light of the fact that Mr. Welch "has such terror and such a great desire to know where anyone is located who may be serving the Communist cause, . . . we should just call to your attention the fact that your Mr. Fisher, who is still in your law firm today, whom you asked to have down here looking over the secret and classified material, is a member of an organization, not named by me but . . . named by the Attorney General, . . . I quote this verbatim, as 'the legal bulwark of the Communist Party.' He belonged to that for a sizable number of years, according to his own admission, and he belonged to it long after it had been exposed as the legal arm of the Communist Party." Welch had walked right into it. *You want to know where the Communists are? In your law firm, Mr. Welch.* McCarthy continued: "I have hesitated bringing that up, but I have been rather bored with your phony requests to Mr. Cohn here that he personally get every Communist out of government before sundown. Therefore, we will give you information about the young man in your own organization."

It was a devastating rejoinder to Welch's theatrics. Consequently, Welch responded the way liberals always do when they have been outfoxed. He cried. Slowly, deliberately, and with glistening eyes, Welch said, "Until this moment, Senator, I think I never really gauged your cruelty or your recklessness." Boo hoo hoo. He also made the singularly unhelpful point that Fred Fisher had attended Harvard Law School, not exactly an unheard-of training ground for Communists. Welch admitted that yes, he had invited Fisher to work for the committee, but when he found out about the Lawyers Guild, he sent him back to Boston. Welch said he told Fisher that if his work for the Lawyers Guild was ever revealed, it would "just hurt like the dickens."

Oddly, for a man who hoped to spare Fisher that pain, Welch had already told the whole story to the *New York Times.* Telling the *New York Times* of Fisher's Communist past proved an ineffective method of keeping it quiet. Two months earlier, the Newspaper of Record had run a photo of Fisher along with the story: "Mr. Welch today confirmed news reports that he had relieved from duty his original second assistant, Frederick G. Fisher, Jr. of his own Boston law office, because of admitted previous membership in the National Lawyers Guild, referred to by Herbert Brownell, Jr. the Attorney General, as 'the legal mouthpiece of the Communist Party.' "[73] (Years later, in its passion for accuracy, the *New York Times* would falsely state that it was McCarthy who had branded the Lawyers Guild "the legal bulwark of the Communist Party.")[74]

When McCarthy had the temerity to mention this deeply personal and private fact—recently published in the *New York Times*—Welch was shocked to the core. He scolded McCarthy: "Little did I dream you could be so reckless and cruel as to do an injury to that lad" (who had been a member of the legal arm of the Communist Party). The revelation of Fisher's association with the National Lawyers Guild would be a scar "he shall always bear." If so, it was also a scar that Welch had already inflicted. A towering monument of wounded indignation, Welch said he could not forgive McCarthy. "If it were in my power to forgive you for your reckless cruelty, I will do so. I like to think I am a gentleman, but your forgiveness will have to come from someone other than me."

An astonished McCarthy responded to Welch's "cruel and reckless" speech by noting that it was Welch who had just "been baiting Mr. Cohn here for hours, requesting that Mr. Cohn, before sundown, get out of any department of Government anyone who is serving the Communist cause." Welch quickly brushed aside his venomous attacks on Cohn, saying to him, "I meant to do you no injury, sir." Let's move on. Then he returned with gusto to sobbing about Fisher, launching the line about which songs will be sung for generations to come: "Let us not assassinate this lad further, Senator. You have done enough. Have you no sense of decency, sir, at long last? Have you left no sense of decency?"

This is usually when the trumpets blare and the curtain closes. In fact, the hearing continued. By now, McCarthy was completely perplexed. Raising a topic of precisely zero interest to liberals, he said, if "I say anything which is not the truth, then I would like to know about it." The truth was immaterial. Welch was going for an Academy Award. All aquiver with emotion, Welch babbled about "a God in heaven" (at least he did not use the Clintonian "my God") and made the exceptionally stupid point that all this time McCarthy had "sat within six feet of me," and could have asked about Fred Fisher directly. Apparently, that same six feet was an impossible distance for Welch to traverse in order to ask Cohn about Communists "running loose" in the government.

Reporters, who had shown their dispassion throughout the hearing by cackling and hooting at McCarthy, burst into applause. From start to finish, the press gallery performed the same function as the bovine, in-studio audiences for political talk shows. They cheered at every insult thrown at McCarthy, no matter how stupid or humorless. McCarthy's unfailingly witty ripostes were met with stone silence or womanly gasps of horror from the peanut gallery.

Welch's performance was still not complete. In the hallway outside the hearing room, he walked a gauntlet of cameras, managing to evoke a few fresh tears for each one. Woe was the tormented Fred Fisher—

who was about to be made partner at Welch's law firm. Finally, when Welch had rounded a corner and was out of sight of the press, he perked up and chipperly asked an assistant, "Well, how did it go?"[75]

Precisely ten seconds after Welch stopped crying about the permanent scar left by Fisher's association with the Lawyers Guild, liberals reverted to calling the Lawyers Guild a group of idealists who believed in civil rights.[76] Years later the *Legal Times* would refer to the Guild of the fifties as "the *allegedly* subversive student group."[77] The *New York Times* has variously referred to the Guild as "a nationwide organization noted for its concern with liberal causes and civil rights" and "a national lawyers organization that has long been associated with the labor movement and liberal causes."[78] One is left to wonder why Welch thought membership in such a fine organization as the Lawyers Guild could wreck a man's career. Weren't they just a group of idealists?

In a shocking development, despite Welch's predictions of utter ruin, Fisher somehow survived the permanent scar of his association with the National Lawyers Guild. On the occasion of Fisher's death, the *New York Times* described the horror and suffering that befell Fisher: "Despite Mr. Welch's dire predictions, [Fisher] went on to become a partner at Boston's prestigious Hale & Dorr and president of the Massachusetts Bar Association."[79] And he got a nice obituary in the *New York Times*.

Welch's performance at the Army-McCarthy hearings is the essence of liberal argumentation. Welch would say something vicious, McCarthy would reply, and Welch would start crying. This is why no woman worth her salt ever loses an argument. She starts crying, making it unmanly to pursue your victory. With the exception of Senator Stuart Symington, whom McCarthy repeatedly referred to as an "alleged man," McCarthy made the mistake of assuming he was dealing with men, not little girls. As he left the hearing room, McCarthy kept asking everyone around him, "What did I do?"[80]

The press was exultant, thrilled that Welch had gotten the better of McCarthy—or at least he would in their stories about the hearing the next day. No rational person could view that hearing and react with horror at Joe McCarthy. Democrats do the most outrageous things imaginable—collaborate with totalitarian regimes, commit felonies in the Oval Office, gay-bait Senate staffers—and if anyone complains, they scream about fascist oppression. Through the left's infernal slander techniques, the myth of McCarthyism took flower.

In liberal folklore, Welch's tearful response to McCarthy would not be matched until Bill Clinton angrily insisted he would selflessly fight impeachment to vindicate "the plain meaning of the Constitution." Imagine how Ken Starr would have looked to a country with no organized opposition to liberals. No Internet, no Fox News Channel, no Rush Limbaugh. Nothing but Nina Burleigh gushing to the *Washington Post: I'd be happy to give Joe Welch oral sex just to thank him for attacking McCarthy.* (Actual July 1998 quote about Bill Clinton from former *Time* magazine reporter Nina Burleigh: "I'd be happy to give him [oral sex] just to thank him for keeping abortion legal.")

It simply must be accepted that McCarthy is bad because of liberals' capacity to call him names. One article says the Army-McCarthy hearings show McCarthy "in all of his demagogic glory."[81] Another portrays McCarthy as the opposite of a bully, saying Welch's "verbal dexterity render[ed] McCarthy a mountain of quaking, mute terror."[82] So was he a demagogue or a mass of quaking, mute terror? And wasn't inspiring terror a bad thing when McCarthy did it? Liberals can't get their stories straight, which would matter if they were engaged in honest reporting rather than spinning fairy tales.

Another account of the hearings reported objectively, "This is a story of good triumphing over evil, of two men going into battle. McCarthy is the dark knight, his opponent the simple and good Joseph Welch, the Army's counsel."[83] Any normal human who watched the hearings without being told that Joseph Welch was "simple and good" might well mistake him for Uriah Heep. The sniveling and sarcastic Welch made Clinton lawyer David Kendall look manly.

New York Times columnist Paul Krugman has described Welch's speech at Agincourt this way: "When Senator Joseph McCarthy tried to smear one more innocent victim, Welch burst out with a heartfelt soliloquy that earned him a place in the pantheon of liberty."[84] The *Washington Post*'s similarly fatuous account claims that before delivering his speech at Agincourt, "Welch stood up, [and] faced" McCarthy— demonstrating that the *Post* reporter had not even bothered to watch a tape of the hearing before proceeding to describe McCarthy as an utter beast.[85]

Even the documentary of the hearings, *Point of Order*, cannot obscure the truth. The documentary shows 97 minutes of the hearing, cut and edited down from 188 hours of tape to make McCarthy look like a monkey. People know they are supposed to hate McCarthy, so they do, even when the facts in front of them show nothing hateful. After a solid night of drinking, McCarthy still was never at a loss for a clever comeback. When he got the better of Welch, Welch pouted and cried.

Two other incidents from the Army-McCarthy hearings help illustrate what liberals mean when they say McCarthy trampled human decency and crushed the human spirit. First, McCarthy refused to reveal his sources. He had produced an outline of a letter from J. Edgar Hoover to the Army alerting them to the Communist infiltration at Fort Monmouth. The Democrats couldn't have cared less about Communists in the Army. As with Linda Tripp, they simply wanted to prove that the manner by which a Republican had exposed liberals broke some law. Phony folksy country lawyer Joe Welch demanded that McCarthy reveal his source's name. Far from unreasonable, McCarthy described his source generally as someone with Army intelligence, but refused to give up the name. As McCarthy correctly said, no government whistleblower would ever step forward if his confidence could not be kept. Liberals were indignant that McCarthy insisted on protecting his sources.

McCarthy was also the only senator to recognize the significance of a new privilege claimed by President Eisenhower at the hearings. It was during the Army-McCarthy hearings that a U.S. president would invoke executive privilege for the first time. Eisenhower refused to allow anyone from the Army to testify about what steps the Army had taken to screen out possible Soviet spies, claiming "executive privilege." Liberals were awed by the genius and majesty of Eisenhower's position that the president did not have to respond to congressional subpoenas.

They were not so impressed with the concept when Nixon tried it twenty years later. Nixon's mere invocation of executive privilege was one of the grounds Democrats cited for his impeachment. But in the Army-McCarthy hearings, McCarthy was the only person to recognize what a breathtaking privilege Eisenhower had claimed. Saying he had no dispute with Eisenhower, McCarthy warned that there would be other presidents and if Congress accepted the claim of "executive privilege," it would set a dangerous precedent. At this point the viewer is supposed to laugh at McCarthy and forget about Watergate and Nixon. McCarthy was a wicked, wicked man. That's all you need to know.

Liberals could not believe McCarthy would stubbornly refuse to back down in the face of their hysterics. Conservatives are required to lose an argument on purpose whenever some liberal starts sniffling. It's their obligation to let liberals have the last word. Otherwise, the conservative is being arch and cruel. These courageous liberals with their voices of principle were appalled that McCarthy raised objections to a president's blanket claim of "executive privilege." They claimed to be outraged that McCarthy refused to divulge a whistleblower's name. While feverishly assembling a blue-ribbon Senate Committee to investigate whether David Schine wore a "fur-lined" cap, Democrats were indignant that McCarthy insisted on investigating Soviet espionage in the highest reaches of government.

Their passion of hate for McCarthy had only one cause, candidly explained by Hubert Humphrey: "McCarthy's real threat to American democracy [was] the fact that he has immobilized the liberal movement."[86] So they created a hobgoblin for the masses to fear. The *New York Times* campaigned viciously against McCarthy, the Senate was constantly investigating him, the elites turned every Communist named by McCarthy into a national hero. They finally killed him with a thousand cuts.

In 1954, when liberal loathing of McCarthy had reached a fever pitch, CBS ran a vicious, deceptive hatchet piece on him viewed by millions of Americans. It was produced by Edward R. Murrow, friend of Soviet spy Laurence Duggan.[87] Other organs of establishmentarian treason followed suit. The Senate voted to hold hearings on a censure resolution against McCarthy.

Among the grounds being considered for censure were McCarthy's remarks about Senator Ralph Flanders (R-Vt.). In a fire-breathing diatribe on the Senate floor, Flanders had called McCarthy a homosexual and compared him to Hitler. In response, McCarthy said, "I think they should get a man with a net and take him to a good quiet place."[88] For this the Democrats thought McCarthy should be censured. It is intemperate for Republicans to respond to vicious abuse by the Democrats. In the end, that particular censure count was rejected, but McCarthy was censured on two similarly absurd counts: statements he made in defiance of senators investigating him. Senators were free to defame and abuse McCarthy, but it was considered a grave violation of the dignity of the Senate if he criticized them back. McCarthy said Senator Flanders had to be "taken out of mothballs" to pursue the censure resolution.[89] He called one of his inquisitors, Senator Robert Hendrickson (D-Md.), "a living miracle . . . the only man in the world who had lived so long with neither brains nor guts."[90] For these statements, McCarthy was censured by a body that, fifty years later, would do nothing about a president who committed felonies to obstruct a sexual harassment lawsuit.

Here's the story of Joe McCarthy you won't read in history books. This version will be unfamiliar to most Americans inasmuch as it includes facts. Joe McCarthy was an extraordinarily bright Irish farm boy, who rose from humble origins in Wisconsin to become one of the most admired politicians of his day. He skipped high school to start his own egg business, which thrived for several years until he caught the flu one winter and the chickens died. He went back to high school at age twenty, saying he planned to graduate in two years. The principal laughed at him and told him it couldn't be done. And then McCarthy made headlines when he graduated nine months later. He made the honor roll all four quarters that he was in high school. Despite his humiliation at being so much older than his classmates, McCarthy was immensely popular with the other students. His ninth-grade class even elected him president, though he would be in ninth grade for only a few months. After becoming the first member of his family to graduate from high school, he went on to college and law school.[91]

Just four years out of law school, McCarthy again made headlines by becoming the youngest ever Wisconsin circuit court judge. When war came, he volunteered for the Marines, leaving his judgeship behind. After returning from the war, he ran for the United States Senate. He won, becoming the youngest man to serve in the U.S. Senate and also the Senate's first World War II veteran.

Inauspiciously, when he first came to Washington, the *New York Times* called McCarthy a "moderate Republican." Only later, when it became clear that McCarthy strongly opposed a regime that sought the total destruction of the United States, was he reclassified as a "conservative." McCarthy had begun his political career as a Democrat, but quickly realized the Democratic Party was a rotten organization so, while still in his twenties, he left the party of corrupt big-city machines and segregation. After a few years in Washington, McCarthy married Jean Kerr, a ravishing beauty far above him in social class. Kerr had been voted the most beautiful woman at George Washington University and was a bridesmaid at Margaret Truman's wedding. More unyielding an anti-Communist than even McCarthy, Kerr became his chief of staff.

McCarthy supported civil rights for blacks and campaigned as fervently in black neighborhoods as he did in white neighborhoods. Long before it was fashionable, he employed a strikingly diverse staff— women, gays, and Jews. Unlike the segregationist Democrats who opposed him, McCarthy was famously color-blind, religion-blind, gender-blind, sexual orientation–blind. He just thought Communists shouldn't be working in the Code Room of the Pentagon. Progressive liberals took sadistic pleasure in gay-baiting him for having homosexuals on his staff. Segregationist Democrats attacked McCarthy with blind ferocity. Among the segregationists against McCarthy was Bill Clinton's mentor, Senator Fulbright—whom McCarthy called "Senator Halfbright" so often that, as Fulbright complained, people were starting to believe it. McCarthy was such a congenial fellow that, despite these taunts, Fulbright once remarked that he couldn't help but like "the SOB."

Many others before McCarthy had tried to make an issue of the Democrats' outrageous blindness to Soviet subversion. Only McCarthy succeeded. When he spoke at the 1952 Republican National Convention, the crowd went wild. Wisconsin delegates snaked through the convention floor with bouncing signs that read: HISS, LATTIMORE, and ACHESON. That year, Republicans would take back the White House for the first time in twenty years. Though McCarthy is sniffed at even by conservatives for his flamboyant rhetoric, in *Witness,* Chambers explains the importance of a fellow such as McCarthy. Referring to the Hiss hearings, Chambers writes that theatrics were "almost the only weapon the Committee possessed." Without a "flair for showmanship," the committee's extremely important work "exposing the Communist conspiracy would have been smothered in silence and reduced to nullity."[92]

All organs of establishmentarian opinion tenaciously opposed McCarthy. And yet somehow, no matter how bellicose their slanders, McCarthy's popularity continued to skyrocket. By January 1953, liberal columnist Jack Anderson admitted sadly, "We had used up almost our entire bag of tricks against McCarthy, without marked effect."[93] But the wolf pack had caught the scent. The media would not relent. The unending attacks finally wore down McCarthy. Most painfully for him, the attacks wore down his supporters. The cheering crowds and widespread support he had enjoyed through so many battles began to evaporate. As Roy Cohn said, "He had taken more punishment than a normal man could be expected to absorb. . . . Never have so much vituperation and defamation been directed toward a person in public life."[94]

At the age of forty-eight McCarthy died broken and defamed. The *New York Times* did not mention McCarthy's death in an editorial out of pure hatred. *Times* editor Charles Merz said, "Why dignify the bastard; let him pass from the scene without more attention."[95] Weeks before he died, McCarthy exclaimed at Easter dinner, "They're murdering me, they're killing me!" That's what they do. The left's enthusiasm for destroying individual lives still sputters to life occasionally, driving their monumental crusades against Newt Gingrich, Ken Starr, and Linda Tripp, for example. Frustrated in their attempt to enslave the world, liberals' only fun anymore is destroying individuals.

Contrary to today's image of McCarthy as a despised Torquemada, McCarthy was given a rare state funeral with a private memorial service in the Senate chamber, his seat covered with flowers.[96] St. Matthew's Cathedral bestowed him with the highest honor the Catholic Church can confer, performing a Solemn Pontifical Requiem Mass before one hundred priests and two thousand well-wishers. Seventy senators attended his funeral, as did J. Edgar Hoover. Thirty thousand Americans lined up outside the Washington funeral home where McCarthy lay to pay their final respects from early in the morning until late at night.[97] Condolences poured in to McCarthy's wife over the next few days, amounting to more than seventy bags of mail.

Maybe it would have been better if McCarthy had been more measured in his rhetoric. And maybe it would have been better if Ken Starr had the savoir faire of Cary Grant and if Linda Tripp looked like Gwyneth Paltrow, and Monica—no, Monica was perfect. But were there Soviet spies in the State Department?

7

VIETNAM: OH, HOW THEY MISS SAIGON

In the wake of the 9-11 terrorist attack, the nation's editorial pages virtually transformed themselves into Vietnam War updates. Vietnam is the left's favorite war because America lost. Liberals never tire of citing it. Enragingly, liberals talk about Vietnam as if it proves something about the use of force generally rather than the Democrats' own bungling incompetence in military affairs. Historical accounts of the Vietnam War are incomprehensible because liberals refuse to admit the failure of their own national security strategy. The only important lesson from the Vietnam War is this: Democrats lose wars.

Republicans proceed from the assumption of America's virtue. Democrats do not. Consequently, they are squeamish about any projection of U.S. power in the national interest. The Democrat doctrine on use of military force is the precise opposite of the Powell doctrine:

They are gung-ho about deploying the military for no particular purpose, but then insist that insufficient force be used. Otherwise America would look like a bully and France would get mad at us. The
completely predictable result is lost lives, lost credibility, and lost
continents.

Vietnam is merely part of a great heritage of Democratic foreign
policy disasters. President Kennedy allowed brave Cubans to invade
Cuba at the Bay of Pigs and then double-crossed them at the last
minute by refusing to provide air cover. Because of President
Kennedy's failure of nerve, thousands of Cuban liberators were slaughtered or imprisoned by Castro. But at least America didn't look like a
cowboy! Kennedy's failure of will at the Bay of Pigs made a greater
confrontation with the Soviet Union inevitable. In short order,
Khrushchev built the Berlin Wall and sent nukes to Cuba, nearly leading to World War III. The Russians would never have dared to take
advantage of Nixon by delivering nuclear missiles to Cuba, but even
stupid people are cunning enough to smell cowardice, and Kennedy
had just backed down from a confrontation with a tin-pot dictator. Liberals hail Kennedy as a hero for being able to navigate his way out of
the Cuban Missile Crisis, neglecting to mention that it was a crisis of
his own making.

When Colin Powell went before the U.N. Security Council in early
2003 to make the case for war with Iraq, liberals cited Adlai Stevenson's masterful presentation to the U.N. as the sort of overwhelming
proof they were looking for. Concededly, Stevenson had watertight
proof that the Soviets had moved nuclear missiles to Cuba, miles off
the coast of Florida. A Republican president would never be able to
adduce that level of proof—because a Republican president would
never have allowed the Soviets to get so far. Democrats bring the
nation to the brink of all-out nuclear war and then brag about what a
strong case they are able to present to the U.N. In fact, the Cuban Missile Crisis was a humiliating defeat for the United States: In return for
withdrawing Russia's missiles, Khrushchev extracted a promise from
Kennedy that the United States would not invade Cuba and, most
important, that he would remove our missiles from Turkey.

Time and again, Democrats' gutless pusillanimity has emboldened America's enemies and terrified its allies. President Carter allowed Americans to be held by Iranian savages for 444 days. He ordered a poorly conceived rescue attempt that crashed a helicopter in the desert and killed six brave members of the Delta Force. In the war on terrorism, Democrats purported to oppose military action against Iraq if anyone in the military might get hurt. But they don't mind inept commanders in chief who dishonor the military by ordering suicide missions. Carter's pacifist secretary of state, Cyrus Vance, was indignant about the very idea of attempting a rescue and resigned after the failed rescue attempt. He preferred sticking with the Democrat strategy of doing nothing in response to brutal foreigners taking Americans hostage. In another show of America's force to the world, when the Soviets invaded Afghanistan, Carter responded by boycotting the Olympics. And thus was a fearsome blow struck at little fourteen-year-old American girls who had spent their lives training for the Olympics.

In the great Democratic tradition of taking the nation to war without a plan to win, only the Democrats could have produced Vietnam. The Democrats' miserable prosecution of that war has tended to overshadow that it was, as Ronald Reagan said, a noble cause. It is also a textbook case of how Democratic equivocation about the use of American power leads to catastrophe. Republican confidence and determination in waging war do not preclude occasional missteps and errors, but in the end, they win the war. Democrat presidents are the opposite. Battles are won, but somehow Democrats always manage to wrest defeat from the jaws of victory.

When media darling President Kennedy first sent troops to Vietnam, liberals thought he was a genius. Having already demonstrated his derring-do at the Bay of Pigs by losing a scuffle with a banana-boat despot, Kennedy sought to prove America could win someplace in the world. After the North Vietnamese had attacked our ally, the South Vietnamese, both the *New York Times* and the *Washington Post* thought war with Vietnam was a splendid idea.[1] But soon the media would make the startling discovery that war is hell. War is especially hell when we lose, and we will always lose when the commander in chief is an irresolute Democrat. For some reason that connection has consistently eluded liberals.

No-Air-Cover Kennedy committed American troops to Vietnam, but didn't want to be too tough with the enemy. When the U.S. could have easily won, Kennedy refused to order an invasion of the North.[2] At a press conference on November 5, 1965, his brother Bobby said America should donate blood to the North Vietnamese as a gesture of goodwill toward the enemy. (Oddly, sending blood to the enemy in the middle of a war was a military strategy never mentioned in General Carl von Clausewitz's seminal 1832 war treatise, *On War*.)[3]

Soon, President Kennedy was consumed with doubts about our ally. Democrats spend a lot of time being consumed by doubts about our allies. Much as liberals had attacked Chiang Kai-shek and would one day attack the Northern Alliance in Afghanistan for not being Thomas Jefferson clones, Kennedy decided the South Vietnamese premiere, Ngo Dinh Diem, had his shortcomings. As allies go, there was nothing the matter with Diem, especially compared to Ho Chi Minh— or the "Vietnamese George Washington," as liberals called our enemy. As historian Paul Johnson put it, Kennedy was simply blaming "the agent rather than the policy."[4] In classic Democrat fashion, Kennedy couldn't stay focused on the enemy. In the middle of a war, Kennedy dispatched the CIA to help assassinate our own ally.

President Lyndon Johnson, who inherited the war when Kennedy was assassinated, principally viewed the Vietnam War as a method of proving the Democrats could be trusted with foreign policy, which they cannot. Historian David Halberstam writes that Johnson "would talk to his closest political aides about the McCarthy days, of how Truman lost China and then the Congress and the White House, and how, by God, Johnson was not going to be the President who lost Vietnam and then the Congress and the White House."[5]

The military advised Johnson that war was winnable in Vietnam but it would require overwhelming force. Here was a novel idea for a Democrat: Provide enough force to win. It was something the Democrats have been incapable of since Harry Truman. Consequently, Johnson demurred. He micromanaged the bombing from the Oval Office and insisted on only a limited bombing campaign. He chose targets out of political calculation rather than strategic necessity. Johnson's refusal to pursue victory in Vietnam is attributed to his widely heralded "moral" qualms.[6] His pain was apparently lessened by allowing American servicemen to die while not allowing them to win. American lives were sacrificed on the altar of this hand-wringing Hamlet's much-touted moral conscience.

Johnson's pain at U.S. casualties was not so great as to distract him from his real love—creating comically useless federal welfare programs. In the middle of the Vietnam War, for the first time in U.S. history, welfare spending would exceed defense spending. You can't get Democrats to concentrate on national defense even when they have taken the country to war. In a reprise of liberal Attention Deficit Disorder, on January 29, 2002, five months after terrorists leveled the World Trade Center, *New York Times* columnist Paul Krugman wrote, "I predict that in the years ahead Enron, not Sept. 11, will come to be seen as the greater turning point in U.S. society."[7]

Johnson's inability to wage a war warmed the heart of the domestic "peace" movement, which was unabashedly rooting for the Vietcong. Rolling out all the usual arguments for treason, liberals said the conflict in Vietnam was a civil war, the Communists were really agrarian reformers, the way to fight Communism is to send money to end PID— Poverty, Ignorance, and Disease. The traitor lobby was ascendant and very loud.

The media did its part, too, sowing fear and trying to undermine patriotism. Eager to demoralize the nation, the press happily published staged photos of alleged American atrocities.[8] Enemy defeats were characterized as victories, such as the Vietcong's failed Tet offensive. The *New York Times* stylebook required the word "unwinnable" be used in any sentence about the war. As with the media's propagandistic nay-saying with the war in Afghanistan, the U.S. military was absurdly described as no match for the plucky and brave Vietcong. Democrats start wars, refuse to fight, and then insist that everyone describe the wars as "unwinnable." In an amazing coincidence, the most powerful nation on earth seems to go to war against unbeatable adversaries only when a Democrat is president.

Liberals could never figure out who the enemy was—other than an enemy called the United States of America. In the early 1970s, the current publisher of the *New York Times*, Arthur "Pinch" Sulzberger, a college student and anti-war activist at the time, was asked by his father, the then-publisher of the *Times*, whom he would want to see shot if an American soldier came face-to-face with a North Vietnamese soldier. "I would want to see the American guy get shot," Pinch said. "It's the other guy's country."[9] Today he issues traitorous editorials demanding that Bush get approval from the Vichy government before taking action against the terrorists. It's their country.

Despite the left's relentless effort to dishearten the nation, vast majorities of Americans consistently supported the Vietnam War. The myth that an anti-war movement swept the nation is preposterous. Liberals always make themselves look more popular in historical accounts than they were at the time—with the exception of the McCarthy period, when they act as if they were at constant risk of extermination. Right up until our imminent withdrawal from Vietnam, no more than 20 percent of Americans ever opposed the war in Vietnam. Contrary to hagiographic descriptions of youthful onanists smoking pot and listening to the *White Album* in their Berkeley dorm rooms, even the Worst Generation wasn't so bad after all. The under-thirty-five crowd supported the Vietnam War more than those over thirty-five. Support for war was strongest among young white males.[10]

Because of his inept handling of the Vietnam War, President Johnson's reelection campaign was over before it began. After an embarrassing showing in the New Hampshire primary, he withdrew from the race.[11] Voters opposed him, by a two-to-one ratio, for not being sufficiently hawkish in Vietnam. Paul Johnson said, "Johnson lost the primary, and with it the war, because he was not tough enough."[12]

President Nixon came into office and made the best of a bad situation. Within four years he had nearly snatched victory from the Democrats' defeat in Vietnam. Nixon withdrew more than half a million troops from Vietnam, leaving a trim twenty-thousand-troop force behind. He cut spending on the war by over 80 percent. With a fraction of the military and economic aid that had been given to the war by the Johnson administration, Nixon kept the Communist North Vietnamese at bay and protected freedom in South Vietnam by relentlessly bombing the North.

Nixon had been elected in part based on his promise to end the war honorably. He would have done so, too, but for Democrats in Congress. In January 1973, the Nixon administration negotiated a truce between Hanoi and Saigon, known as the Paris Peace Accords. The war was over and our ally would be safe as long as the agreement was enforced. The U.S. retained three trump cards to play if the Communist North violated the truce and invaded South Vietnam: Keep Haiphong harbor mined, furnish military and economic aid to South Vietnam, or resume the bombing.

In the most dishonorable chapter of the nation's history, the Democratic Congress led the United States to double-cross an ally. Using hysteria over Watergate as cover, congressional Democrats openly turned their backs on the South Vietnamese, leading to a total Communist conquest of Indochina. In August 1973—the height of liberal frenzy over Watergate—Congress demanded that the president seek their approval before resuming any bombing in Vietnam. Within a matter of months, North Vietnam invaded the South. Congressional Democrats refused to appropriate any aid for South Vietnam. Still, with no U.S. support, the South Vietnamese valiantly held off the North for well over a year.

But by 1975, the situation was desperate. Even President Gerald Ford, as weak a Republican as there ever was, repeatedly pleaded with Democratic Congress not to forsake our ally, the South Vietnamese. Ford said, "American unwillingness to provide adequate assistance to allies fighting for their lives, could seriously affect our credibility throughout the world as an ally." Congress didn't have to send troops, just aid. The Democrats ignored Ford's pleas and abandoned the South Vietnamese. Before the year was out, North Vietnamese tanks rolled into Saigon. In a triumph of liberal foreign policy, Marine helicopters had to be dispatched to airlift American officials and a few fortunate Vietnamese from the roof of the American embassy in Saigon. It was, historian Paul Johnson writes, "the gravest and most humiliating defeat in American history."[13]

The Democrats did that.

They said they were for "peace." This is what they produced: "re-education" camps, political prisoners, and gruesome bloodbaths as Communists swept through Vietnam, Laos, and Cambodia. In Cambodia, millions were slaughtered by Marxist ideologues. Cambodians were forced to watch as family members were decapitated or garroted. Students were made to hang their own teachers. In Laos, an astonishing 10 percent of the population fled the Communist regime. In Vietnam, hundreds of thousands of people were imprisoned for "re-education." Hundreds of thousands more died trying to escape their Communist slave masters on boats.

In a classic statement of liberal patriotism, *New York Times* publisher Punch Sulzberger had said in 1964, "I am not sure that what we offer the Vietnamese peasant . . . is any better than what the Communists offer."[14] Since the Communists took control, two million Vietnamese have tried to flee their country. The exodus of Vietnamese boat people was so massive it created an international humanitarian crisis. As we have come to expect, the United Nations provided crucial help. The U.N.'s idea was to send fleeing Vietnamese back to Vietnam.[15]

Democrats never had the stomach to seek more than a stalemate in Vietnam. Republicans subscribe to the quaint notion that we should at least have a plan to win before we engage. A Republican president either wouldn't have started that war or would have won it pretty fast. President Eisenhower provided economic and military aid to South Vietnam. But he also said he could not "conceive of a greater tragedy for America than to get heavily involved."[16]

Barry Goldwater ran against Johnson in 1964, saying, "I would have said to North Vietnam, by dropping leaflets out of B-52s, 'You quit the war in three days or the next time these babies come over they're going to drop some big bombs on you.' And I'd make a swamp out of North Vietnam. . . . I'd rather kill a hell of a lot of North Vietnamese than one American and we've lost enough of them."[17] The Democrats explained that Goldwater was a right-wing nut who would get us all blown up. Far better to stick with Lyndon Johnson's plan of wantonly sacrificing American lives, year after year, for the sole purpose of proving he was tough on Communism. More likely, the North Vietnamese would have reacted the way the Iranian hostage-takers did when Reagan was elected, immediately releasing their American hostages the very day of his inauguration.

The party that willingly abandoned an ally in Vietnam should never have been allowed near the Oval Office again. But instead of hanging their heads in shame, Democrats cite their own inept handling of the Vietnam War to argue that America should be paralyzed in the face of dangerous despots forevermore.

We were barely three weeks into the war in Afghanistan in 2001 when liberals started comparing Afghanistan to Vietnam with a little too much zeal. Their point was: We were going to lose. If we had taken all of Afghanistan in three weeks, they would have said it was too fast. That's what liberals said after Reagan's invasion of Grenada. That wasn't a war! It took only a weekend! But three weeks in Afghanistan and they were already complaining we hadn't won yet. So now it's official: Liberals have exactly three weeks' worth of blood, sweat, and tears.

They clamored for America to be defeated, caterwauling about the ferocious Afghan fighters and proclaiming Afghanistan a Vietnam-style "quagmire." In a front-page article in the *New York Times* about a week before Kabul fell, R. W. Apple said hopefully, "Could Afghanistan become another Vietnam?" On November 4, 2001, *Los Angeles Times* columnist Jacob Heilbrunn said, "The United States is not headed into a quagmire; it's already in one. The U.S. is not losing the first round against the Taliban; it has already lost it. Soon, a new credibility gap will emerge as the Pentagon attempts to massage the news."[18]

From the traitor lobby's women's auxiliary, syndicated columnist Molly Ivins wrote on November 1, 2001, "It now looks, with 20-20 hindsight, as though we should have taken a few more deep breaths before smacking that tar-baby that is Afghanistan." Still angry at men like Bush because she wasn't invited to the prom, *New York Times* columnist Maureen Dowd wrote, "The question was suspended like a spore in the autumn air: Are we quagmiring ourselves again?" Confident we were "getting bogged down" in Afghanistan, Dowd sneered at Bush, "Polo at Yale is a bit different than the Afghan version." She said, "The Taliban have the psychological edge on three fronts: military, propaganda and bioterror."[19] Yes, the Taliban had us right where they wanted us!

About a week later, our forces had taken Kabul. By November 15, the Taliban had fled from 80 percent of Afghanistan. So much for the "quagmire." A week after Kabul fell, the cover story on the *Times*'s "Week in Review" section was titled "Surprise: War Works After All." This came as a surprise to precisely no one except *Times* readers. After America's "surprise" victory in Afghanistan, liberals began desperately trying to regroup and claim that they were too for the war, with scant evidence to support that claim. Maureen Dowd wrote, "Many who came of age during the Vietnam War, wincing at America's overweening military stance in the world, are now surprised to find themselves lustily rooting for the overwhelming display of force against the Taliban."[20]

But in the news pages, Johnny Apple was still sanguine about the prospects for defeat. As the American-led forces swept through all of Afghanistan, R. W. Apple said, "That made a lot of people think once more about Vietnam."[21] Liberals spend a lot of time thinking of Vietnam. It was becoming clearer and clearer that we could have won that war, too.

Cowering, defeatist hysteria was nothing new for liberals. We had just won the Gulf War in about ten minutes flat in 1991, when the

Washington Post ran an article with the headline "Logistical Short-comings of 'Desert Storm' Cited; GAO Report Details Operation's Problems."[22] The media feign objectivity while trying to demoralize the country with their endless nay-saying. They showed more photos of an empty Red Cross building hit by American forces in Afghanistan than they ever did of the scores of men, women, and children gassed at Waco.

In an editorial after Bush's post–9-11 State of the Union address, the *New York Times* warned nervously that America's unrivaled military force "must be used sparingly and wisely." The editorial was somberly titled "The Limits of Power." It urged the president to "guard against the temptation to use power promiscuously as the war evolves."[23] Why? What are they saying? The more immediate threat seemed to be the promiscuous use of lurid adverbs in *New York Times* editorials.

It seems that Bush's strategy of "power and intimidation" against America's enemies reminded the *Times* of Vietnam. All uses of American military might remind liberals of Vietnam. "Not since America's humiliating withdrawal from Vietnam more than a quarter-century ago," the *Times* leered, "has our foreign policy relied so heavily on non-nuclear military force, or the threat of it, to defend American interests around the world."[24]

Every military action since World War II except Reagan's nuclear buildup against the Soviet Union—opposed by liberals—has involved non-nuclear military force, including but not limited to the Grenada invasion, the Gulf War, and Clinton's misadventure in the Balkans. Not only that, but some months later, Bush would warn the world that the nuclear option was not, in fact, off the table. That should make the *Times* happy. Liberals just love saying the words "America's humiliating withdrawal from Vietnam." They will raise "America's humiliating withdrawal from Vietnam" at the slightest provocation or with no provocation at all. If you read too many editorial pages, preemptive surrender began to sound like a serious foreign policy.

In adducing proof for the likely success of war with Iraq, Reagan's invasion of Grenada was surely more relevant than Vietnam. These weren't college lecture courses on the history of anti-war protests, but commentary about an ongoing war. Grenada showed the value of Republican resolve to use military force—even when unpopular with hysterical liberal elites. The Gulf War was the most germane comparison, involving virtually the same adversaries only ten years apart.

Yet, from the 9-11 terrorist attacks to the end of 2002, the *New York Times,* the *Los Angeles Times,* and the *Washington Post* mentioned Vietnam almost as often as they mentioned the Gulf War. Meanwhile, Reagan's triumphant Grenada invasion was barely mentioned at all. The *New York Times* editorial pages cited Vietnam 120 times, the Gulf War 127 times, and Grenada only 8 times. In the *Los Angeles Times,* the Gulf War was mentioned 165 times, Vietnam 144 times, and Grenada only 9 times. In the *Washington Post,* the breakdown was Gulf War, 141 mentions; Vietnam, 116 mentions; and Grenada, 3 mentions.[25] Somehow, the farther the Vietnam War fades into history, the fresher and fresher a memory it becomes.

College professors have spent untold years trying to concoct alternative theories to Democrat ineptitude at foreign policy. They produce convoluted arguments proving that the key to success is "national dialogue" or "political grounding," but there are always more exceptions than there is theory. The various schemata purportedly demonstrating that outside forces have caused the Democrats' foreign policy debacles are long and moralistic, full of contradictory little bons mots, but lack what we used to call a point.

In the fall of 2001, weeks before American and Afghan liberators swept through almost all of Afghanistan, Berkeley professor and journalist Mark Danner wrote an upbeat piece in the *Los Angeles Times* predicting America's defeat. Hoping to erode the nation's resolve, Danner reminded Americans why they ought to be demoralized and frightened. He said American foreign policy was a story of "bluster and flight and uneasy forgetting." To prove it, he cited the following examples:

- the Bay of Pigs (Kennedy);
- Vietnam (Kennedy, Johnson, and finally congressional Democrats who refused to enforce the peace treaty);
- the Iranian hostage crisis (Carter);
- the flight from Beirut after the American embassy and Marine barracks bombings in 1983 (Reagan);
- the abandonment of Mogadishu, Somalia, after the deaths of eighteen American servicemen in 1993 (Clinton).[26]

It was a list to strike fear in the heart of any American. Fortunately, President Bush is not a Democrat.

Apart from the withdrawal of troops from Lebanon, all these foreign policy debacles occurred under Democratic presidents. Even Lebanon was a Democrat policy. Soon after American barracks were bombed, Democrats in Congress set to work drafting a joint resolution demanding that Reagan pull the Marines out of Beirut. Carter's national security advisor Zbigniew Brzezinski supported retreat, explaining that, "We must not lose sight of the fact that the Lebanese problem cannot be solved by itself, but must be tackled in the context of a wider accommodation between Syria and Israel which the United States should actively mediate."[27] In accordance with their party's preemptive surrender policy, all seven Democratic presidential candidates urged that our troops be removed from Lebanon.[28]

Senator Joe Biden (D-Del.) called for "immediate withdrawal" of the troops. He said, "There is no longer anything remotely approaching a bipartisan consensus to let the marines stay for 18 months."[29] The Democratic House Speaker Tip O'Neill said the Lebanon policy had failed: "The marines don't know why they're there and the American people don't know why they're there."[30] Representative Mike Lowry, Democrat of Washington, said, "The latest thing in Lebanon proves absolutely that it's futile and hopeless to have these people stationed in Lebanon. There's no possible way we can achieve stability."[31] Representative Ted Weiss, Democrat of New York and member of the Foreign Affairs Committee, said: "The longer we delay, the worse the time gets."[32]

Reagan responded to the Democrats' hysteria, saying Democrat House Speaker Tip O'Neill "may be ready to surrender, but I'm not." He warned that the Democrats' resolution would aid and abet our enemies in the region. He dispatched Lawrence S. Eagleburger, undersecretary of state for political affairs, to tell the fainthearted congressional Democrats that walking away from Lebanon "only postpones the day of reckoning."[33]

According to the *New York Times,* the Democrats delayed their withdrawal resolution in part because of "the criticism expressed by Republicans throughout the day."[34] But the Democrats had leapt on the bombing of the Marine barracks as a political issue and would not let go. Though Reagan claimed he wasn't going to pay any attention to the Democrats' carping, unfortunately he did.[35] Reagan gradually withdrew our troops, while simultaneously bombing Syrian-controlled areas that were firing into Beirut and on our troops. The Democrats complained about that, too. They had voted for deploying American troops to Lebanon, but claimed to have no idea that this meant American forces were authorized to shoot back. Speaker O'Neill denounced Reagan's policy of shelling Syrian artillery positions, saying the bombing was "absolutely not" within the authorization Congress granted to the president under the Lebanon War powers resolution.[36] Senator Claiborne Pell of Rhode Island, demonstrating his usual firm grasp of the world around him, said the military's use of force was a total shock: "What concerns me is that while we have withdrawal of the marines, we'll have an increase in the firing."[37]

In light of Reagan's spectacular execution of foreign policy, prevailing over an evil empire to win a half-century war with the USSR, to complain that he did not also defy the Democrats in an election year and retaliate more forcefully in Lebanon is like the complaint that the framers of the Constitution, after defeating the British Empire and creating the greatest government ever known to mankind, did not also give women the right to vote. Reagan had bigger fish to fry in the 1980s. He invaded Grenada. He bombed Libya. His administration nourished a long, internecine war with many casualties between Iran and Iraq. He gave Israel plenty of aid and a long leash to combat Islamic crazies. All this, while winning a final victory over Soviet totalitarianism. By contrast, American failure was the centerpiece of the Johnson, Kennedy, and Carter administrations. Where on the globe was President Johnson winning a war for America while losing one in Vietnam?

Danner dismissed Reagan's annihilation of the Soviet Union as merely "the triumphant cold war narrative we have shaped for ourselves." How about "the defeatist Vietnam narrative liberals have shaped for the rest of us"? Reagan's victory in the Cold War is more than a comforting bedtime story. For fifty years, Americans lived under the threat of nuclear annihilation by the Soviet Union. Now they don't. I think that goes in the "Victory" column.

It's interesting how, in their endless reminiscing about Vietnam, the Iranian hostage crisis, or Black Hawk Down, liberals tend to shy away from mentioning who was president. Indeed, Danner's entire summary of Vietnam is "the panicked retreat from Saigon in 1975." Didn't something happen before 1975? A war or something? No. Liberals treat a war started by Kennedy, lost by Johnson, and ended honorably by Nixon as a Republican war. Here's a little secret academics may not have mastered in their exhaustive study of U.S. history: Forty-nine states reelected Nixon in 1972. It wasn't because they thought he was doing a lousy job in Vietnam.

Nor, despite endless reminders of Vietnam, were Americans feeling particularly frustrated and vulnerable in the war on terrorism. Danner insisted that America was at a "grave disadvantage" because the enemy had attacked the "vulnerability in the American mind."[38] He said the terrorists "who gave their lives on Sept. 11 and those who sent them have precise objectives and a clear plan to achieve them." Meanwhile, America was beset by "the frustrations of the powerful." Danner explained that beating al-Qaeda would "require much greater power than America has shown itself to possess."

Except that—oops, wrong again. Outside of the nation's faculty lounges and editorial boards, the "vulnerability in the American mind" never materialized. Americans were so committed to the war in Afghanistan that even the Democrats could pony up only a single vote in Congress against it. Repeatedly throughout the next year, large majorities of Americans would tell pollsters they also supported attacking Iraq. Every obstructionist objection the Democrats raised to the war on terrorism would instantly vanish through lack of popular support.

In another *Surrender Now* piece in the *Los Angeles Times,* Robert Dallek and Robert Jervis, of Boston University and Columbia University respectively, argued against invading Iraq. (Jervis is the "Adlai E. Stevenson professor of international politics," which I suppose is a step up from the Alger Hiss chair at Bard College.) They argued that Saddam Hussein posed merely a "speculative and future" threat and claimed the nation's preventive actions always fail, while preemptive actions succeed.[39]

Discounting their brusque assertion that Saddam Hussein was merely a "speculative" threat, the professors' schemata almost sounded plausible until you realize the professors had simply defined all actions that failed as "preventive" and all actions that succeeded as "preemptive." Thus, for example, the professors defined the Gulf War— launched in response to Saddam Hussein's invasion of Kuwait—as a "preemptive" action. But the Vietnam War—launched in response to Ho Chi Minh's invasion of South Vietnam—they called a "preventive" action. Even Dallek and Jervis didn't have the nerve to characterize the Grenada invasion as "preemptive." Instead, Grenada was quickly dismissed as an exception to their otherwise watertight theory. Interestingly, all the successful "preventive" actions—such as American interventions in Grenada, Angola, and Nicaragua—seemed to cluster in Republican administrations. Instead of calling these exceptions to a theory that would, by then, explain nothing, a more useful method of distinguishing successful interventions from failed interventions is that the successful ones were taken by Republicans and the failures were executed by Democrats. The preventive/preemptive framework is nothing but a smoke screen for the Democrats' unblemished record of disaster in national defense since World War II.

Predictably, all three failed military interventions cited by Dallek and Jervis were undertaken by Democrats. The professors listed the Bay of Pigs (Kennedy); the invasion of the Dominican Republic (Johnson); and Vietnam (Kennedy, Johnson, and the Democratic Congress that ultimately abandoned South Vietnam under cover of "Watergate," trashing America's honor and word). In Johnson's defense, only a liberal could consider the invasion of the Dominican Republic a failure. It was over in about a week, there was minimal loss of life, and we overthrew a lousy Communist, Juan Bosch.

The professors' lone example of a "preventive" action by a Republican president that failed was the CIA's role in helping return the Shah of Iran to power in 1953. Professors Dallek and Jervis claimed that installing Shah Mohammed Reza Pahlavi was a failure because—I quote—it "helped create the conditions for the eventual triumph of Islamic militants in 1979 who remain hostile to us."

Wow. That's an interesting theory of causation. We're not talking about the Kerensky government here (Alexander Kerensky, head of Russian provisional government July 8, 1917–November 7, 1917). The loss of the Shah in 1979 was an unarguable disaster, but it's rather a stretch to blame it on Dwight Eisenhower. The Carter presidency was somewhat closer in time to the Iran an Revolution. In 1978, future Nobel Peace Prize–winner Jimmy Carter ostentatiously withdrew American support for the Shah and then stood idly by when, weeks later, the Shah was deposed by a mob of Islamic fanatics. But according to professors Dallek and Jervis, the proximate cause of the Ayatollah Khomeini's rise to power was not Jimmy Carter's abandonment of the Shah, but the fact that the Shah ever held power at all. The CIA installed the Shah in 1953, and then—wham!—twenty-six years later, Islamic fanatics deposed him.

On the professors' idea of cause and effect, forget Eisenhower. Eve was responsible. Professor Dallek also claims Harry Truman—not

Reagan—won the Cold War. And let us always honor President McKinley's indispensable role in crushing the Nazi war machine (William McKinley, twenty-fifth president 1897–1901).

Liberals didn't express much dismay about Carter dumping the Shah at the time. To the contrary, the left had always hated the Shah and was happy to see him go. Liberals prefer the sort of comical Third World despot one reads about in Evelyn Waugh novels. They think the rest of the world should be their Disneyland. The Shah was pro-Western and didn't dress like a clown. He did not threaten to hurl Scud missiles at Israel. Liberals found him a bore. Most of all, they could never forgive the Shah for replacing the left's beloved Mohammed Mossadegh—the sort of authentic Third World ruler the left admires. Mossadegh may have impoverished his country, but he was lifey: He cried, fainted, and consulted his two-year-old grand-daughter before making government decisions.[40]

For decades, liberals campaigned tirelessly against the Shah, eagerly awaiting the day that Iran would be ruled by a legitimate Third World tyrant. Richard Falk of Princeton famously praised the Ayatollah Khomeini, predicting that he "may yet provide us with a desperately needed model of humane governance for a third-world country."[41] Carter's U.N. ambassador Andrew Young pronounced that Khomeini would "eventually be hailed as a saint."[42] Ramsey Clark, avid "peace" activist in the war on terrorism and President Johnson's attorney general, returned from a meeting with Khomeini in Paris in 1979 urging the U.S. government to take no action to help the Shah. He argued that Iran should be able to "determine its own fate."[43] Clark implored members of Congress not to come to the Shah's defense.

So by helping install the Shah in 1953, forcing liberals to attack him and Carter to betray him, the Eisenhower administration set in motion an inevitable chain reaction that would cause Islamic fanatics to come to power. This from the people who snickered about the domino theory in Vietnam.

Soon after Carter allowed the pro-Western Shah to be deposed by a raving anti-American Islamic mob, the mob seized the American embassy and took fifty-two Americans hostage. It was a living testament to liberal "diplomacy": American citizens being held captive by angry barbarians in a frightening land for 444 days. Carter's strategy of patient suasion with lunatics finally worked and the hostages were released—the day President Ronald Reagan was inaugurated. Showing the results diplomacy gets, Carter had so warmed the hearts of the Islamofascists that twenty years later, Iran denied Carter's son a visa to visit the country.[44]

The release of American hostages the day Ronald Reagan became commander in chief had no impact on liberal thinking about foreign policy. No matter what the evidence, liberals insist that only their tender ministrations are capable of calming murderous dictators. Negotiation and engagement are said to "work" because, after Democrats spend years dillydallying with lunatic despots who threaten America, eventually a Republican president comes in and threatens aggressive military action. In a fascinating fifty-year pattern—completely indiscernible to liberals—murderous despots succumb to "engagement" shortly after a Republican president threatens to bomb them. This allows liberals to hail years of impotent negotiation and engagement as a foreign policy "win."

Naturally, therefore, Professors Dallek and Jervis cited Libya as a "case in point" for negotiation rather than military intervention. Muammar Qaddafi came to heel, they claimed, only as a result of a meticulous policy of engagement. Qaddafi "mended his ways in the face of a Western policy that combined military threats with U.N. economic sanctions while holding out the possibility of better relations." Also, Reagan bombed him.

After Libyan agents set off bombs in a West Berlin discotheque frequented by American servicemen in April 1986, Reagan retaliated with air strikes against Qaddafi's living quarters, missing Qaddafi, but killing his daughter. The Americans hit military targets in Tripoli and Benghazi. Our "allies," the French, denied America the use of its airspace for the attack. Tired from the long flights and showing a puckish sense of humor, the pilots bombed the French embassy by accident.

Pow! So sorry, our mistake. Our "allies" in Europe were duly mortified, uttering the usual litany of horrors—the bombing raid would
strengthen the hardliners, it would lead to yet more terrorist attacks, it
would drive Qaddafi closer to the Soviet Union. But since the bombing
raid we haven't heard much from Qaddafi. That got him out of the terrorism business in a hurry. Qaddafi was alleged to have been involved
in the bombing of Pan Am Flight 103 in 1988, but that is speculative
at best, in that Iran's former minister for terrorism has claimed credit.[45]
Qaddafi has openly cooperated with the U.S. in the war on terrorism.
It's unlikely that Qaddafi warmed to the Great Satan because of diplomacy and engagement. In January 2003, as the United States prepared
to attack Iraq, one of Qaddafi's senior officials nervously asked a
British diplomat, "Will they come after us?"[46] As Ronald Reagan said,
peace through strength is an idea that never goes out of style.

　　For fifty years, America's foreign policy failures have not been
problems of "national dialogue" or "preventive" action or the national
psyche. There is one simple problem: Democrats can't handle foreign
policy. You could almost forgive the Democrats for their spectacular
record of failure in foreign policy. But then they have the audacity to
cite their own derelict handling of the military to argue that it is always
a fool's errand to deploy troops in defense of the nation. Remember
Vietnam!

　　We should remember Vietnam. This is what we should remember:
Whenever Democrats dabble in military affairs, America suffers
relentless defeats, entire continents fall to Communism, America loses
wars, invasions fail, Americans are taken hostage, American soldiers
are dragged through the streets, and the nation is demoralized and
humiliated. It is a fact that the Democrats have been responsible for
every unmitigated foreign policy disaster since World War II.

8

HOW TRUMAN WON
THE COLD WAR DURING
THE REAGAN
ADMINISTRATION

Liberals dispute that Ronald Reagan won the Cold War on the basis of their capacity to put mocking quotation marks around the word "won." That's pretty much the full argument: Restate a factual proposition with sneering quote marks. It used to be "evil empire" that took the derisive punctuation. But after Reagan vanquished the evil empire, it's "won" that gets the quotes. Sometimes the whole phrase is put in quote marks—"won the Cold War." This is meant to prove not only that no one "won," but that there was no "war." Ironically, though there was no "Cold War," and nobody "won" it, the true hero of the Cold War was Harry Truman. It was the process of "containment" set in motion by reliable old Dean Acheson that just needed time to work. Or at least it was someone—anyone—other than Reagan who won the Cold War.

Thus, liberals insist that the true heroes of the Cold War are various great Democratic presidents such as Franklin Roosevelt, Harry Truman, John Kennedy, and Jimmy Carter. As Martin Walker, author of *The Cold War: A History*, sneered in a *Washington Post* book review, "It is useful to be reminded, amid so many florid Republican claims that they alone were the patriotic party, of the great truth that Democrats also fought the Cold War, from Truman to Kennedy to Carter."[1]

Liberal luminary Stanley Kutler mocks the boast that Reagan "won" the Cold War (his quotes), saying it "minimizes events and actions of the previous 40 years." "Kutler" (my quotes) cites, for example, that brilliant Cold War tactician Harry Truman, who "initiated the national-security state, built up American military power and resisted Soviet expansion."[2] "Kutler" also credits "Eisenhower, Kennedy, Johnson, Nixon, Ford and Carter" for having "maintained [Truman's] policies."

Gannett News Service cites "historians, diplomatic analysts and academics" who credit Truman and Kennedy—as well as Reagan—with winning the Cold War.[3] Professor Dallek informed listeners of NPR that "if you want to give one single president the most credit, I think you'd give it to Harry Truman."[4] Similarly, William Hyland, editor of the gaseous quarterly *Foreign Affairs*, claims: "If you're handing out medals, Truman should get the first one."[5]

Truman is the Democrats' choice for the true hero of the Cold War only because of their supreme confidence that no one remembers the Truman administration. Giving the Truman administration credit for standing up to Communism is like giving Clinton credit for welfare reform. Truman supported fighting Communism (and Clinton reforming welfare) at the precise instant, and not a moment sooner, that Americans put a gun to his head and forced him to take a stand.

Until the earth-shattering Republican landslide of 1946, Democrats didn't even pretend to be anti-Communist. In the seminal 1946 election, the Republicans took both houses of Congress by "link[ing] the spread of global communism to the policies of Presidents Roosevelt and Truman."[6] With the slogan "Had enough?" the nearly moribund

Republican Party swept both Houses of Congress. It was a more startling upset than the Republican Revolution of 1994 would be some
forty-eight years later.

The Young Turks of the 1946 Republican landslide were a new
breed of Republican. The pre-1946 Republican Party would confuse
young right-wingers today. At the end of the Second World War,
the Republican Party was an institution in transition. The leading
Republican of that era was Robert Taft—who voted against NATO and
opposed the Nuremberg Trials (for which John F. Kennedy would give
him a chapter in *Profiles in Courage*). Taft saw the Democrats' interest
in international affairs as part of their love of One World Government.
After the pointless slaughter of World War I, Republicans were not big
on rallying American strength for new wars in Europe. Odd as it seems
now, Democrats had been quicker to respond to Hitler than the Republicans were. Before World War II, ironically, it was the Democrats who
supported a massive military establishment. But after that war, the parties began to reverse roles, culminating in a Democratic Party that
openly seeks to render America vulnerable to nuclear attack rather
than deploy a missile shield. When Taft challenged Dwight Eisenhower for the Republican presidential nomination in 1953, Republicans from the class of '46, such as McCarthy and Nixon, backed
Eisenhower. Eisenhower's victory would shut the door on Republican
isolationism until the end of the Cold War. Meanwhile, Democrats were
consistently incapable of grasping the Soviet threat.

Noticeably, all the anti-Communist initiatives eventually taken by
the Truman administration came after the 1946 election—that is, after
Truman had been president for almost two years. It was only in
response to this extraordinary electoral event that the Democratic Party
began to dump its Popular Front element. The '47 Truman Doctrine,
the Marshall Plan, and the policy of containment (aka, a "substitute for
victory") were Democrat track covering. As even David Halberstam
admits in *The Fifties*, it had come about "under pressure from the
right." Only after the 1946 election was anti-Communism "picked up
by the incumbent Democrats."[7]

It is possible Truman would have championed "containment" in the absence of the stunning Republican landslide of 1946. And it's possible that President Bill Clinton would have signed welfare reform without the Republican landslide of 1994. But it is a fact that neither Truman's anti-Communism nor Clinton's welfare reform were in evidence until Republicans swept Congress.

Truman's natural instinct toward Stalin was goo-goo-minded liberalism. After cheerfully carving up Germany with Stalin at the Potsdam Conference in 1946, President Truman told Henry Wallace, "Stalin was a fine man who wanted to do the right thing." He later wrote in his diary that the Russians "have always been our friends and I can't see any reason why they shouldn't always be."[8] At the Nuremberg Trials, Truman connived with Stalin to cover up Soviet war crimes and flush the Hitler-Stalin Pact down the memory hole.

Most breathtakingly, in March 1946, Truman ostentatiously rebuffed Winston Churchill after his famous "Iron Curtain" speech in Fulton, Missouri. Immediately after Churchill's speech, Truman instructed his secretary of state Dean Acheson not to attend a reception for Churchill a week later in New York. Acheson himself was "deeply troubled by Churchill's call for an Anglo-American partnership that would seem to be directed against Moscow."[9] Whether the dictator is Joseph Stalin or Saddam Hussein, Democrats always warm to the idea of appeasing murderous dictators. Truman apologized to Stalin and invited him to the United States for a rebuttal speech. He graciously offered the mass murderer the services of the U.S.S. *Missouri* for the trip. Paradoxically, much of this is recounted in a book about the Cold War titled *Architects of Victory*—which hails Truman as one of those architects.

Even after the Republican landslide of '46, inspiring a "major change" in Truman's foreign policy, as historian David Halberstam puts it, the Democrats' newfound anti-Communism was based more in "internationalism" than in principled anti-Communism.[10] These sniffing pantywaists were more loyal to the well-heeled internationalist elite than they were to ordinary Americans.

When Truman created the Loyalty-Security Program—in 1947—he openly admitted to his friends he had done it only "to take the play away from" anti-Communist Republicans,[11] whom he called "the animals."[12] Similarly, Acheson referred to the growing disgust with Democrats for coddling Communists as the "revolt of the primitives." An article in *Foreign Affairs* described Acheson's dismay at having to play into the hands of the "primitives," but said he believed the Democrats' pretend-anti-Communism was "useful for domestic political purposes."[13]

The term "primitives" has popped up repeatedly throughout the years. It refers to Americans who express an unseemly enthusiasm for defeating America's enemies. In 1980, the *New York Times*'s Flora Lewis said Reagan aide Richard Pipes had a "reputation for primitive anti-Bolshevism."[14] This was as opposed to the more sophisticated view taken by liberals, which was pro-Bolshevism. In 1982, nuclear freeze supporter Noel Gayler wrote a long piece in *The New York Times Magazine* sneering about "the primitives in American politics" who would "not be satisfied with anything less than the unattainable—American nuclear 'superiority.'"[15] And then we attained it, and the Soviet Union was no more. Demonstrating the uncanny political savvy that netted him a whopping thirteen electoral votes that November, Democratic presidential candidate Walter Mondale criticized Reagan in 1984 for his "naive and primitive notion of national strength."[16] (Maybe it's not so bad to be called naive by a guy who ran for president on the promise that he would raise taxes.) It was not until the war on terrorism that liberals' use of "primitive" as an epithet for right-wingers finally fell out of fashion, presumably in deference to the feelings of an enemy that travels by camel.

Eventually, Truman responded to the public's anger with the Democrats' intransigence on Communist subversion with hysterical overreaction typical of Democrats. In 1948, Truman's Justice Department began prosecuting CPUSA leaders for sedition under the Alien Registration Act. The law was later thrown out by the Supreme Court.[17] At least he didn't put them in Japanese internment camps—another brilliant Democrat idea.

In a searingly honest 1996 article—so honest that he's probably been forced by the thought police to disavow it—liberal journalist Nicholas von Hoffman summarized the Democrats' flaccid approach to Communism.

And where was Harry Truman? His hagiographers today present him as the plucky, courageous, little guy who stood up to world communism and led America into a new age of cosmopolitan internationalism. It is a description that millions of his adult contemporaries would have found unrecognizable. In fact, the public conduct of the Truman administration became the affirmation of people who said Truman was soft on communism.[18]

Curiously, Democrats cheerfully cite Truman's doctrine of "containment" as if it were an aggressive hawkish stance. At the time, it wasn't viewed that way. To the contrary, conservatives ridiculed the idea of "containment," preferring the idea of "victory." Nixon called it the "Dean Acheson College for Cowardly Containment of Communism."[19]

The theory of "containment" sounded a bit rougher in theory than it was in practice. By 1950, Truman's sly strategy of "containment" had led to Communist takeovers of all of Eastern Europe and more than a billion people in China. Truman's defenders hail his abandonment of Chiang Kai-shek—without "hesitation"—by proudly boasting that the "decision avoided a bloody and futile war, and has made the recent improvement of Sino-American relations possible."[20] So by not opposing a Communist takeover, Truman helped pave the way to warm relations with the resulting Communist dictatorship, and the only downside was that China was then a Communist dictatorship. Even after explaining how losing China was a brilliant tactical maneuver on Truman's part, liberals denounce anyone who says Truman "lost China."

In one of the great moments of American statesmanship, in January of 1950, Truman's secretary of state, Dean Acheson, gave a speech at the National Press Club writing off South Korea. He excluded South Korea from America's defensive perimeter, saying, "It must be clear that no person can guarantee these areas against military attack."[21] The speech made quite an impression on Stalin: With his blessing, North Korea attacked South Korea just five months later.[22] But don't call them "Democrat wars." It could have happened to anyone. . . .

As the whole liberal establishment was busily formulating "containment" and "equilibrium" doctrines that preached not victory, but stalemate, General Douglas MacArthur was turning the Korean War from a devastating defeat to a glorious victory. His troops swept north, eventually crossing the Yalu River—when the Chinese Communists attacked. MacArthur responded by ordering the Chinese off the peninsula. Truman was terrified at this show of manly force: It upset the delicate diplomatic steps he had been engaged in to appease the Red Chinese. Truman believed MacArthur's crossing of the Yalu River had unnecessarily antagonized the peace-loving Chinese Communists and dragged them into the Korean War.

Like everything else Democrats ever believed about Communist motives and objectives, subsequently released documents have proved Truman wrong. The Chinese always planned to get into the Korean War. They were waiting for MacArthur to cross the Yalu River for strategic reasons only. As one of Mao's generals said: "To hook a big fish, you must first let the fish taste your bait."[23] Truman began placing political constraints on MacArthur's military strategy. Foreshadowing the Democrats' traitorous execution of the Vietnam War, military strategy was overridden from Washington based on Truman's paramount goal of not upsetting the Red Chinese. MacArthur complained publicly that he was not being allowed to win the war. So Truman fired him for insubordinately fighting the Korean War to win.

Americans erupted in fury at MacArthur's firing. Already disgusted by Truman's policy of retreat, effigies of Truman burned all over the country.[24] The International Longshoreman's Union held a work stoppage to protest MacArthur's dismissal.[25] When MacArthur arrived at the San Francisco airport, half a million people lined the streets from the airport to the city to cheer the returning hero. Seven million people turned out for a ticker tape parade in MacArthur's honor in

New York City—twice as many as had come out for Dwight Eisenhower after his return from Europe after World War II.[26] Gallup polls showed 66 percent of the nation opposed to MacArthur's firing.[27] Republicans invited MacArthur to address a joint session of Congress. Many called for Truman's impeachment.[28] Senator McCarthy took a dim view of MacArthur for his showboating, but a dimmer view of Truman's decision to fire a general for winning a war, saying Truman had hatched the idea in a "midnight bourbon and Benedictine session."[29]

Only by the media's unyielding assertion that Truman was an aggressive anti-Communist have people come to believe it. But as it was happening, Americans, who were also "present at the creation" (as Acheson pompously titled his autobiography), were not exactly bowled over by Truman's and Acheson's anti-Communism. The esteemed political philosopher Sidney Hook described the Truman administration's foreign policy solons as men of "mediocre intelligence or the most extraordinary ignorance of the nature of the international Communist movement—an ignorance, sad to say, accentuated by stubbornness in refusing to admit that any errors have been made."[30] The 1952 presidential election would finally end the Democrats' twenty-year lock on the White House when General Dwight Eisenhower was elected president. In the last patriotic act of either newspaper, the *Washington Post* and *New York Times* endorsed Eisenhower.[31]

In *The Best and the Brightest*, David Halberstam argues that, contrary to public perception at the time, Truman and Acheson were aggressive anti-Communists. The evidence he adduces for this claim is Acheson's tough talk on China at private luncheons *after Acheson was out of office.* Might have been a bit more helpful when he was in office. As Halberstam also says, when Acheson was *in* office, he did not see Ho Chi Minh as a threat, but viewed him "as a nationalist" and armed the anti-Communist forces "more as an afterthought."[32]

Halberstam sarcastically concludes this discussion of Acheson's eventual anti-Communism, saying: "Soft old Dean Acheson. Soft old Democrats."[33] It's interesting that no one ever feels compelled to point out that the Republican Party was not soft on Communism. Indeed,

Halberstam says, "Democrats would spend the next thirty years . . . proving that they were not soft on Communism, and that they would not lose a country to the Communists."[34] Years later, as President Lyndon Johnson contemplated war in Vietnam, he was murmuring about how the Roosevelt and Truman administrations had been accused of losing China.[35]

The left's whitewash of history worked so well that in the war on terrorism fifty years later, liberals were openly proposing that President Bush follow President Truman's example. In a panic that America might defend itself, Thomas Mann of the liberal Brookings Institute wrote in the *New York Times* in October 2002, "Is George W. Bush another Harry S. Truman? He and we should surely hope so."[36] Yes, if Bush were another Truman, the entire continents of Africa and Europe would be under Islamic rule by 2007. But Mann went on to describe Truman's masterful handling of foreign policy during the Cold War: "[Truman's] consultations with Congress on national security matters were early, continuous and substantive." As we have seen, these "consultations" consisted mostly of Truman's pretending to oppose Communism in order to quell "the animals."

Mann praised Truman for "resist[ing] pressure from those advocating more aggressive actions against the Soviet Union and China."[37] Resisting pressure to be tough with the Communists was how Truman was tough on Communists. As with the war on terrorism, Democrats thought preemptive surrender constituted an aggressive national defense strategy. They are genetically incapable of grasping the basic idea of self-defense. Someday, liberals will be patiently explaining to a bewildered public how Tom Daschle won the war on terrorism, just like Harry Truman won the Cold War.

Dean Acheson was especially deft at "resisting pressure" to play rough with the Reds. The very same month the Truman administration was freezing out Churchill for his "Iron Curtain" speech, the Acheson-Lilienthal Report was released. Acheson's mind-boggling plan was to put atomic energy under the control of an international authority— which would include the Soviet Union.

Tellingly, Mann also commended Truman for taking "the long view." Liberals are very big on taking "the long view" when evaluating their foreign policies. They create horrendous foreign policy disasters, but then, eventually, a Republican is elected president and cleans up the mess. They said containment would work and, lo and behold, forty years later—right at the end of the Reagan administration—the Soviet Union was stopped dead in its tracks! That's taking "the long view." Praise God President Bush is not "another Harry Truman."

To review the record, as part of Truman's yeoman work on the Cold War, he cooperated with the Soviets at the Nuremberg Trials, whitewashing their joint aggression with Hitler under the Nazi-Soviet Pact. He looked the other way when the Soviet Union murdered three million Russian prisoners of war returned home by the Allies. On his watch, the Soviet army consolidated its control over nine countries, China became a Communist dictatorship, and tens of millions of people were murdered under Communist tyrannies. Truman defended Communist spy Alger Hiss as a patriot who was framed by Republicans, and he tried to indict Whittaker Chambers for perjury.[38] He refused to remove members of his administration identified to him by J. Edgar Hoover and others as Communist agents, including Harry Dexter White, whom Truman appointed top U.S. representative of the IMF. Among the Soviet spies advising Truman on China was Frank Coe, who refused to answer the question: "Are you a Soviet agent, Mr. Coe?" Soon thereafter Coe fled to Communist China, where he became a top policy-maker to Chairman Mao, helping the Chinese murder tens of millions of their own people. Truman was considered such a dupe of the Communists that the Army refused to tell him about the Venona Project. And that's how Truman won the Cold War!

We should, of course, be duly grateful to other American presidents for their feeble and impotent public statements in opposition to Soviet expansionism—except Jimmy Carter, who was not remotely opposed. But in terms of actual results, other American presidents rarely won a scuffle in the Cold War. Simply in terms of territory lost, here's how other American presidents were waging the Cold War until Reagan. See if you detect a pattern.

Under President Woodrow Wilson (1913–1921), the October Revolution brought the Communists to power in Russia. The Soviet Union quickly seized Armenia, Azerbaijan, and Georgia and starved about five million people to death.

Under President Calvin Coolidge (1923–1929), the Soviets added Mongolia, Turkmenia, Uzbekistan, Tajikistan, and Kirgizia to their empire.

Under President Herbert Hoover (1929–1933), the Soviets captured no new countries, but did starve another five to fifteen million people within the Soviet Republic (leading Lady Astor to ask Stalin in 1931, "When are you going to stop killing people?").[39]

In his first diplomatic act of office, President Franklin Delano Roosevelt (1933–1945) officially recognized the Soviet Union. He chummed around with Joseph Stalin, one of history's greatest mass murderers, calling him "Uncle Joe." With Stalin's agent Alger Hiss at his side, Roosevelt sold out Eastern Europe at Yalta and promised Stalin three votes in the U.N. General Assembly, plus the right to name the No. 2 U.N. official. On Roosevelt's watch, the Soviets took eastern Poland, Moldavia, Lithuania, Latvia, Estonia, and Albania. "Uncle Joe" murdered an estimated twelve to twenty million people, and forced at least ten million into slave labor.

Under President Truman (1945–1953), we lost China, the most populous nation on earth. The Red Chinese occupied Tibet. Over the next four decades Chinese Communists would murder between 34 million and 64 million Chinese and an estimated 1 million Tibetans. Also as part of Truman's tireless battle against Communism, he was in office for two years before he put into place a strategy of even partial resistance to the Soviets. On his watch, the Soviets consolidated their control over Poland, Czechoslovakia, Hungary, Romania, Bulgaria, eastern Germany to the Elbe River, Yugoslavia, and North Korea to the 38th parallel. He started the Korean War when the Soviet-backed North Koreans attacked South Korea. Ho Chi Minh announced Communism in Vietnam. Stalin had nearly 100 million people under his rule.

Under President Dwight Eisenhower (1953–1961), the Korean War was concluded with a truce, winning no territory back, but holding the Communist North Koreans at the 38th parallel. Cuba fell to Communism under Fidel Castro, establishing the first Soviet-backed Communist regime in the Western Hemisphere. The Communist Vietcong instigated a violent insurrection to conquer South Vietnam. John Foster Dulles's "rollback policy," aimed—in theory—at rolling back Soviet power in Eastern Europe, was quickly abandoned as the hot air that it always was after the Red Army crushed a popular uprising in Hungary in 1956 and the U.S. refused to intervene. The Soviet Union launched *Sputnik 1,* exploded their first thermonuclear weapon, and successfully tested the first intercontinental ballistic missile (almost a year ahead of the United States). In 1956, Soviet premier Nikita Khrushchev warned visiting ambassadors from the West, "We will bury you!"

Under President John F. Kennedy (1961–1963), in just two short years, the U.S. was humiliated in the Bay of Pigs incident, lost a standoff with the Soviet Union resulting in U.S. missiles being pulled out of Turkey, and began the Vietnam War to ill effect. The Soviet Union detonated a fifty-eight-megaton thermonuclear device—the largest manmade explosion in history. The USSR also beat the United States in space, sending the first man into orbit. East Germany erected the Berlin Wall.

Under Lyndon B. Johnson (1963–1969), Communist regimes were established in South Yemen and Congo-Brazzaville. China exploded its first hydrogen bomb.

Under President Richard Nixon (1969–1974), a Marxist regime was established in Benin. Providing the first serious resistance any American president had put up to Communist advances, South Vietnam was saved from Communism for another few years—until Watergate allowed the Democrats to abandon Vietnam.

Under President Gerald Ford (1974–1977), the Imperial Congress empowered by Watergate turned its back on our allies in Southeast Asia. South Vietnam, Cambodia, and Laos fell to Communism. Communist regimes were also established in Guinea-Bissau, Ethiopia, Angola, and Mozambique. Over the next decade, hundreds of thou-

sands of Vietnamese "boat people" risked death at sea to flee Communism. In Cambodia, Khmer Rouge leader Pol Pot murdered between
one million and four million out of a population of seven million.

Under President Jimmy Carter (1977–1981), there wasn't much
territory left for the Soviets to conquer, but Carter did what he could to
help. Soviet-backed Marxists came to power in Nicaragua, the Seychelles, and Grenada. The Soviet army invaded Afghanistan. Carter
lifted the ban on travel to Cuba and North Korea. With his impeccable
sense of timing, Carter gave a speech on May 22, 1977, exhorting
Americans to abandon their "inordinate fear of Communism." Days
later Cuba dispatched a military force to Ethiopia.[40]

Under President Ronald Reagan (1981–1989), for the first time
since the Russian Revolution, Communist countries began to become
free. Not one country fell to Communism on Reagan's watch. Three
Soviet-backed regimes began to crumble, one was taken back outright,
and by the end of Reagan's presidency, the USSR was negotiating the
terms of its surrender. In 1980, months before Reagan would be elected
president, Harvard Sovietologist Adam Ulam ruefully remarked that
the Soviets' expanding empire could not be stopped unless faced with
"a power strong and determined enough to make Soviet foreign adven-
turism too risky and expensive."[41] Under Ronald Reagan, America was
that power. He came to the presidency audaciously announcing that
the Soviet Union was an evil empire "whose last pages even now are
being written."[42] By the end of Reagan's second term, the last page had
been written.

Reagan had always known he could destroy the Soviet Union if he
could only be given two terms in the White House. In 1964, Reagan-
backer Holmes Tuttle mapped out the future with mind-boggling accuracy: Reagan would run for governor of California in 1966, serve two
terms, run for president in 1976, and "by 1985, with God's grace,
Communism would be vanquished at home and abroad." As Edmund
Morris writes, Reagan "repaid Tuttle in kind and in full, only four
years late."[43] Had Reagan won the Republican primary in 1976,
America would have been accepting surrender from Konstantin Cher-

nenko in 1985 and *Time* magazine could have made him "Man of the Year."

The most that can be said for U.S. presidents before Reagan is that they generally avoided the temptation of rooting for the other side—a temptation intellectuals found irresistible. But it's a long way from saying American presidents, by and large, were not traitors to giving them equal credit with Reagan for winning the Cold War. Apart from Reagan's inner circle, no one alive between World War II and the Reagan presidency could have imagined such a magnificent conclusion to the Cold War. Reagan was the first authentic conservative in the White House in more than fifty years. That's all it took.

It was not a coincidence that Reagan succeeded where his predecessors had failed. Contrary to "Kutler's" claim that Reagan "shared the assumptions and deeds of his seven predecessors," Reagan took an approach to the Cold War dramatically different from any other U.S. president. To wit, he thought we should win. This was a fresh concept. At the time, it was widely ridiculed as a dangerous alteration of U.S. policy. Only after it worked was Reagan's dangerous foreign policy recast as merely a continuation of the policies of his predecessors.

In 1984, the *New York Times*'s national security correspondent Leslie Gelb described Reagan's transformation of Cold War tactics: "'Fight' and 'win' are new words in the lexicon of governmental nuclear strategy." Prior administrations, Gelb said, had "used words like 'preventing defeat' or 'avoiding an unfavorable outcome' to describe their belief that there could be no winners in a nuclear war." The Reagan administration proposed something different. Reagan was "actually seeking to win a nuclear war."[44] Gelb labeled this shift "lamentable." The *New York Times* stylebook expressed contempt for the idea of winning the Cold War by requiring these words to be placed in quote marks: "superiority," "win," "evil empire," "freedom-fighters," "soft" (on Communism), and "backing down."[45] This was in contradistinction to precise adjectives like "warmonger," "unwinnable conflict," "dangerous," or "simple-minded"—none of which took quotes. There is no question but that the Reagan Doctrine was completely at odds with those of his predecessors—and no question but that liberals were hopping mad about it.

Reagan had been floating the idea of victory for years. When he challenged President Ford in the 1976 Republican primary, he accused Ford of fighting the Cold War like a Democrat. The media instantly leapt to Ford's defense, with the *Economist* pompously intoning, "The accusation that Mr. Ford neglects defense is absurd."[46] The *Economist* also presciently dismissed Reagan as an irrelevant crank, saying he represented "a clear minority in the country at large and probably in the Republican Party itself."[47] Reagan almost beat a sitting president that year, and would go on to win the next two presidential elections in electoral landslides.

Reagan attacked Ford's secretary of state, Henry Kissinger, with particular vigor.[48] In 1976, Kissinger proclaimed, "We cannot prevent the growth of Soviet power." Kissinger promoted what he called the "imperative of coexistence" and cautioned Americans not to "mesmerize themselves with the illusion of simple solutions." Reagan had one of those "simple solutions." He thought we should win and the Soviets should lose. Detente, Reagan said, is "what a farmer has with his turkey—until Thanksgiving day."[49] Reagan's ridicule of Kissinger's policies was so successful that President Ford had to order his campaign to stop using the word "detente."[50]

In his book *Diplomacy*, Kissinger stated categorically that Reagan was the first American president to present "a direct moral challenge" to the Soviet Union—which he described as an "enormous difference" from prior administrations. Reagan had abandoned the "gradualism" of every other Cold War president and took the offensive "both ideologically and geopolitically." Reagan was fighting "for a final outcome."[51] As Reagan himself put it, "We want more than deterrence." We won, the Soviets lost, and Reagan's interchangeable predecessors in the Oval Office had nothing to do with it.

Reagan waged the Cold War with relish. For every missile the Soviets built, America would build two. Despite the caterwauling of liberal peace protesters, Reagan installed Pershing missiles in

Europe. He invaded Communist-controlled Grenada, clearing out a nest of Marxists in a few days. He openly supported anti-Communist forces around the world—in Angola, Afghanistan, Ethiopia, Poland, and Nicaragua. In May 1982, Reagan signed a secret order, National Security Decision Directive 32, to destabilize the Communist regime in Poland. In a covert compact with the pope—what Reagan's first national security advisor Richard Allen called "one of the great secret alliances of all time"—Reagan provided aid to Solidarity, the anti-Communist union outlawed in Poland.[52] With money from the CIA, the National Endowment for Democracy, secret Vatican bank accounts, and Western trade unions, Solidarity stirred up a lot of trouble for the Soviets in their Polish republic.[53]

The Reagan administration relentlessly opposed Moscow in every part of the world, in every way, on every front, in every form imaginable. Aiding anti-Communist efforts abroad raised the price of Soviet expansionism and weakened the USSR militarily, economically, and psychologically. The Soviet Union was already devoting a huge proportion of its anemic Gross National Product to military production. The Kremlin couldn't compete with the Reagan buildup. Contrary to cheery reports in the American media, the Soviet economy was a basket case. Reagan made it worse. He imposed a trade embargo on Russian goods. He deregulated oil and slashed the Carter-era inflation rate from 10.4 percent in 1980 to 4.2 percent in 1988.[54] When oil prices plummeted under Reagan, the Soviets were strapped for hard currency. Reagan's unrelenting pressure on the Soviet economy forced the USSR to begin withdrawing its troops and largesse from aspiring Marxist dictatorships abroad.

Still, the Soviet Union could have stumbled along for a few more decades, waiting out the Reagan administration and hoping for a Democrat president to come in and help the Soviets restore their hegemony. But Reagan wasn't going to let the USSR outlast him. The last great battle of the Cold War was fought in Reykjavik, Iceland, on October 13, 1986. That was the day Reagan refused to accede to Mikhail Gorbachev's demand that the United States abandon the Strategic

Defense Initiative. The Soviets were terrified of Star Wars—a terror that was palpable on the editorial pages of the *New York Times*. For the Soviet Union to survive, Gorbachev had to snooker Reagan into abandoning a missile defense system. This was not offensive weaponry—Reagan even offered to share the technology with the USSR. But without the credible threat of being able to launch a nuclear strike against the United States, the USSR was just another Third World country. Star Wars would make the USSR's nuclear weapons obsolete. The Soviet Union would be no more threatening than Switzerland and less appealing a place to live.

Consequently, Gorbachev offered vast, unprecedented arms reductions at Reykjavik—on the sole condition that Reagan abandon a missile defense system. Reagan refused. As he boarded Air Force One out of Reykjavik, Reagan said his aim was not agreement, but victory. The "ultimate goal of American foreign policy," he said, "is not just the prevention of war but the expansion of freedom." At Reykjavik the world saw the difference between Reagan's doctrine of victory and his predecessors' policies of deterrence, detente, and containment.

All major U.S. media went berserk at Reagan's refusal to give up the Strategic Defense Initiative. The *New York Times* angrily lashed out at SDI, calling it "utopian" and "inconceivable." The *Times* complained bitterly that Reagan had not proved his case that "this visionary bird in the bush is worth the sacrifice of the Soviet bird in the hand."[55] Gorbachev's turgid response was highlighted as the *Times*'s Quotation of the Day: "After Reykjavik, it is clear to everyone that SDI is a symbol of obstruction to the cause of peace, the epitome of militarist schemes, and the unwillingness to remove the nuclear menace to mankind. There can be no other interpretation of it and this is the most important lesson from the meeting in Reykjavik."[56] The *Times*'s foreign journalist Flora Lewis was simply bewildered by Gorbachev's hard-line stance, wondering why Gorbachev had spent his time at Reykjavik "concentrating practically all its propaganda ammunition on space defense." Gorbachev, she concluded cluelessly, "must have his own reasons."

Time magazine ran a cover story titled "Sunk by Star Wars." The magazine petulantly snipped that Reagan could have signed "the most sweeping arms control agreement in the history of the nuclear age." Alas, he had queered the deal for the sake of his "cherished Strategic Defense Initiative."[57] *Newsweek* asked, "Is Star Wars Testing Worth the Price?"[58] The *Los Angeles Times* ran an article by John Tirman—head of a "World Peace" organization and coauthor of *Empty Promises: The Growing Case Against Star Wars*—calling Reagan's defiance at Reykjavik a "colossal mistake," a "fumble," a "debacle."[59] Star Wars, he said, was a "colossal blunder" and Reagan's refusal to abandon it was a "colossal failure of leadership."[60]

Members of the scientific community did their part for America by vowing to accept no research funds to help the United States develop a missile defense shield. As the *Washington Post* reported, "thousands of scientists nationwide" pledged not to "accept or solicit research funds for so-called Star Wars projects." One scientist quoted in the article, physics professor David Roper at Virginia Polytechnic Institute and State University—whom, the *Post* pointedly noted, "occasionally votes Republican"—declared, "We don't need a huge, multimillion-dollar weapons system. . . . We need more of what they were trying to do at Reykjavik."[61] (Star Wars is not a "weapons system." It is an anti-weapons system with no offensive use.)

It wasn't clear why Reagan's idea of protecting America from incoming missiles was such a bad idea—except from the perspective of America's enemies.[62] The opinion cartel's insistence that Reagan capitulate on Star Wars leaves no doubt as to whose side they were on. When contemplating a shield that would protect America from incoming missiles, Democrats suddenly became hardheaded fiscal conservatives. For the first time in recorded history, liberals were concerned about the cost and usefulness of a government program. These people believe federally funded art therapy for the homeless will pay for itself. That you can take to the bank. But a shield to repel incoming nuclear missiles from American soil, they said, was too expensive and wouldn't work.

Reagan had spent six years bleeding the Soviet Union from every limb. By walking away from the table at Reykjavik rather than abandon SDI, Reagan consigned the USSR to the dustbin of history. His victory over the evil empire was complete. The rest was paperwork. In 1988, the American people paid Reagan one final tribute by electing his vice president, George Bush, to the presidency in a landslide vote. In 1989, the Soviets pulled their troops out of Afghanistan. On November 9, 1989, the Berlin Wall came down. On July 6, 1990, NATO announced that the Soviet Union was no longer an adversary. The rest of the year, one by one, the republics of the Soviet Union declared their independence. Finally, on December 26, 1991, the USSR was formally dissolved. To be sure, by refusing to compromise on Star Wars, Reagan had abandoned hope of ever winning a Nobel Peace Prize. It must have provided some consolation to know that he had forever destroyed the Soviet war machine on behalf of the entire free world.

Perhaps recognizing the futility of claiming that the USSR collapsed when Truman's containment policy kicked in three decades later, some liberals give all the credit to Mikhail Gorbachev for deciding to surrender. Liberals viewed Gorbachev as a "reformer" because he was the first Soviet leader whose wife weighed less than he did. By the time Gorbachev came to power in March 1985, he took the reins of a severely weakened USSR faced with a formidable adversary. Still, Gorbachev didn't surrender right away. He kept Russian troops in Afghanistan and, most important, in 1986, demanded that Reagan abandon his plan for a missile defense shield. But Gorbachev is supposed to be a hero because, in lieu of launching a banzai nuclear attack, he surrendered. Thus, Joseph Nye, director of the Kennedy School of Government's Center for International Affairs, sportingly admitted that Reagan "deserves some of the credit" for ending the Cold War. But Gorbachev, he said, "probably deserves twice as much credit for his blunders."[63]

A columnist for the *Chicago Tribune* quoted an erstwhile Soviet apparatchik for the proposition that Reagan actually played a "negative" role in ending the Cold War. The Soviet official credited Reagan only for being "ready, when Gorbachev initiated his new policy, to join in."[64] And the Soviets really did have seventy years of barren harvests because of bad weather. *Newsweek*'s Jonathan Alter praised Mikhail Gorbachev in terms that would make the Soviet toady blush: "He's only the most important political leader alive in the world today, historically speaking. . . . If you look over the course of our lifetimes, who was the most, well, you go back to Lincoln and Franklin Roosevelt. . . . If I look back over my lifetime, who is the world leader who changed things the most, and I don't actually think it is a close call."[65] It's curious that no Soviet premier had grabbed this opportunity for glory by relinquishing his empire in the previous seventy years. Geopolitical strategist Phil Donahue also disputed that Reagan won the Cold War, saying, "I do not think Gorbachev got up on a Tuesday morning"—liberal straw-man arguments frequently begin with someone getting up one morning—"and said, 'Holy cow! Reagan's got Star Wars, he's got all these submarines and intercontinental . . .' I think Gorbachev got up and said, 'Holy cow! Look at my country.' "[66]

If you were setting a half-bright trap to collect a half-bright menagerie, you couldn't do better than saying, "Reagan won the Cold War" and waiting to see who argues with you. It's the verbal equivalent of a box, a stick, and a piece of cheese. *Oh look! I caught a Jonathan Alter! And here's a Phil Donahue!* Even the *New York Times* essentially admitted Reagan won the Cold War in a 2002 news article that said, "President Reagan's aggressive posture against the former Soviet Union in the 1980's [was] a stance that succeeded so well it is now beyond debate."[67] More poignant is the assessment of Ladislav Jakl, a founder of the Czech Society for Ronald Reagan, formed ten years after the formal dissolution of the Soviet Union in honor of Reagan's nineti-eth birthday. Calling Reagan "one of the most important figures of the 20th century," Jakl said, "My life in the last 10 years in a free country, it's mainly due to the work of Mr. President Reagan."[68]

When Whittaker Chambers left the Communist Party, he said Communism would triumph because conservatives could never match the Communists' intensity of faith. The only hope, he said, was for the free world to discover "a power of faith which will provide man's mind, at the same intensity, with the same two certainties: a reason to live and reason to die." After he wrote those words, a Hollywood actor read them and would soon register as a Republican for the first time. Some three decades later, that actor would become president of the United States. In his first press conference as president, Reagan said of the Soviet Union: "The only morality they recognize is what will further their cause, meaning they reserve unto themselves the right to commit any crime, to lie, to cheat." Reporters were duly mortified by such gaucherie and asked Reagan if he wouldn't like to clarify his remarks. He did, but not the way they had in mind. He continued, saying the Soviets "don't subscribe to our sense of morality; they don't believe in an afterlife; they don't believe in a God or a religion. And the only morality they recognize, therefore, is what will advance the cause of socialism."[69]

Reagan's victory was more than a dry calculation of throw-weights and ICBMs and nuclear bombs. He did nothing less than transform America's mission. Under Reagan, Kissinger wrote, "America's goal was no longer relaxation of tensions but crusade and conversion."[70] After receiving mash notes from the *New York Times* for forty years, the Soviets were ill-prepared for Reagan's moral assault. In one of the great speeches of Western civilization, on March 8, 1983, Reagan addressed the National Association of Evangelicals and said America was at war with an "evil empire." Echoing Whittaker Chambers, Reagan said the Cold War would "never be decided by bombs or rockets, by armies or military might."[71] It was America's belief in God that would "terrify and ultimately triumph over those who would enslave their fellow man." We would prevail because our strength "is not material but spiritual."

Sovietologist Seweryn Bialer reported that by 1984, Reagan's rhetoric had "badly shaken the self-esteem and patriotic pride of the Soviet political elites." The Reagan administration's "self-righteous moralistic tone, its reduction of Soviet achievements to crimes by international outlaws from an 'evil empire'—such language stunned and humiliated the Soviet leaders." Bialer said the Kremlin was astounded to discover that Reagan seemed "determined to deny the Soviet Union nothing less than its legitimacy and status as a global power." This was something "they thought had been conceded once and for all by Reagan's predecessors."[72]

For twenty years the country had been on a downward spiral of defeat and demoralization. Race riots, civil rights battles, rampant drug use, sexual promiscuity, Vietnam—all these had crushed the moral certainty that the free world could win or even that it should. Reagan's invincible faith in God and freedom ignited the will of the American people to defeat Soviet totalitarianism. He said Communism was not merely an improbable economic system, but evil. The final lines in Reagan's 1987 speech at the Berlin Wall were these: "Across Europe, this wall will fall. For it cannot withstand faith. It cannot withstand truth. The wall cannot withstand freedom." Reagan supplied the intensity of faith that Whittaker Chambers despaired of the free world ever mustering. "The Western world does not know it," Chambers said, "but it already possesses the answer" to Communism—but only if its faith in God "is as great as Communism's faith in man." In 1984, Reagan posthumously awarded Whittaker Chambers the Presidential Medal of Freedom, the nation's highest civilian honor.[73]

Liberals still don't understand the role religious faith played in the West's victory over Communism. Reagan's moral crusade is smirkingly dismissed as if it amounted to nothing more than bright and sunny optimism—the equivalent of a peppy Madison Avenue jingle selling dog food. It wasn't just military might or a preference for the materialist bounty of capitalism that drove Reagan's victory over Communism. It was Americans choosing faith in God over faith in man. Only Reagan could give Americans "a reason to live and reason to die." He wasn't lucky; he was indispensable.

9

LIBERALS IN LOVE: MASH NOTES TO THE KREMLIN

Reagan came to power announcing that the last chapter of Communism was then being written. He said the West would "transcend" the Soviet Union, which would soon be remembered as only "a sad, bizarre chapter in human history."[1] The sophisticates said he was out of his mind and would blow up the world. Then when he won, Reagan was no longer frightening, merely nongermane. Columbia University history professor Alan Brinkley said the belief that Reagan "won the Cold War" (his quotes) was an "article of faith among many Reagan admirers." But "historians," he said, believe the end of the Cold War had "more to do with the grave internal weaknesses in the Soviet system."[2] Patton didn't "win" the Battle of the Bulge: It had more to do with Hitler running out of gas.

And that's why every college professor, editorial writer, and Hollywood activist in America was howling about Reagan's Cold War policies throughout his eight years in office. That's why they were screeching that "Ray-gun" (get it?) was leading us to the brink of nuclear holocaust. That's why they were demanding unilateral nuclear disarmament—and passing out Nobel Peace Prizes to one another for their piercing conclusions that Reagan was scaring the Soviet Union and must be stopped. All that was because the Soviet Union was a dreary old collapsing wreck of an empire anyway. *Just kidding about our hysterical jeremiads.* If the Soviet Union was disintegrating under the force of its own "grave internal weaknesses," as Professor Brinkley summarized the modern view, no one seemed to know it at the time. That theory first emerged after the Soviet Union collapsed when and how Reagan said it would.

In 1994, *Newsweek*'s Eleanor Clift explained why liberals had been completely wrong about everything they ever said about the Cold War. Apparently, there was a vast CIA cover-up during the Reagan administration that cunningly concealed facts only from liberals: "People who want to give Ronald Reagan the entire credit for the collapse of the Soviet Union ignore the fact that the Soviet economy was collapsing and the Reagan Administration covered it up. . . . The CIA concealed what was happening over there so they could keep the defense budget over here high."[3] The CIA will not cease its infernal efforts to conceal information about Communist dictatorships from Eleanor. Discussing whether Elian Gonzalez should be sent back to Cuba on April 12, 2000, she said, "Frankly, to be a poor child in Cuba may, in many instances, be better than being a poor child in Miami."[4]

If Reagan was just the night watchman for an empire in decline, it would have saved everyone a lot of trouble if liberals had told us that at the time. Quite the contrary, liberals were in a state of hysterical paranoia at the totemic symbol of Ronald Reagan. President Jimmy Carter's principal campaign theme against Reagan was to repeatedly use the words "dangerous" and "disturbing" in connection with Reagan's foreign policy. In its typical sanctimony, the *Economist* praised Carter for accusing Reagan of offering "extremely dangerous" ideas "in a quiet voice."[5] That "scored well" according to the *Economist.* Both the *Washington Post* and the *New York Times* and the rest of the elite press endorsed President Jimmy Carter and then Walter Mondale over scary warmonger Reagan—on the express grounds that Reagan's policy toward the Soviet Union put the world in imminent danger.

Strobe Talbott—*Time* magazine's Washington Bureau chief, arms control expert, U.S. deputy secretary of state under Clinton, and pompous octogenarian blowhard before he was nineteen years old—analyzed American foreign policy just one month into Reagan's presidency.[6] He began by noting that the Soviet Union was "stronger and bolder than ever before."[7] This was Reagan's first year in office, when—as we are now told—the Soviet Union was collapsing of its own "grave internal weaknesses." Stronger than ever! Thus, Talbott advised, "The U.S. must learn to live with parity. Whether America likes it or not, Leonid Brezhnev is quite correct in describing any U.S. quest for nuclear supremacy as misguided. The U.S. cannot get there from here—not against a Soviet Union that is ready and able to match America in any kind of arms race."

Again in 1982, Talbott wearily proclaimed that it was "wishful thinking to predict that international Communism some day will either self-destruct or so exhaust itself in internecine conflict that other nations will no longer be threatened." As Talbott explained it, "The Soviet Union still has plenty of resources" and Communism is "deeply entrenched in Eastern Europe." Moreover, the Soviet Union was "peculiarly constituted" and "well designed to be impervious to the consequences of the economic failure."[8]

A widely cited 1983 study conducted by thirty-five Soviet experts from Harvard, Columbia, Cornell, and other elite institutions predicted, "The Soviet Union is going to remain a stable state, with a very stable, conservative, immobile government. . . . We don't see any collapse or weakening of the Soviet system."[9] In 1983, Walter Laqueur, chairman of the International Research Council at the Center for Strategic and International Studies at Georgetown University, announced that "there is no real solution in sight for the dilemma facing East and West alike." He, too, confidently stated that "the Soviet Union is now stronger" than in the past.[10]

The Soviet Union was certainly not behaving like a power in decline when Reagan entered the Oval Office. Soviet hegemony had been steadily advancing for sixty years. More than a billion people lived under Communism. The USSR had nuclear weapons pointed at U.S. soil and outnumbered the United States in conventional arms by a ratio of about 3:1. Unaware of the revisionist history liberals would someday be trying to pawn off on an unwitting public, in the early years of the Reagan presidency the Soviet Union carpet-bombed Afghanistan, smashed Solidarity in Poland, shot down a civilian plane with Americans aboard (KAL 007), and then decorated the pilot who did it. There is powerful evidence that the Soviets, working through the Bulgarians, put out a murder contract on the pope—who was collaborating with the Reagan administration to support Solidarity.

American policy toward the Soviets had gone from "rollback" to "containment" to "detente," and was rapidly approaching acceptable defeat. In 1980, Soviet expert Adam Ulam of Harvard remarked, "For the last three or four years [the Soviets] have been led to believe they can get away with anything."[11] (That's how Carter won the Cold War.) About the same time, former president Richard Nixon published a book, *The Real War*, in which he announced that World War III had already begun and the Soviet Union was winning. The Soviets' relentless expansionism and prodigious military buildup, Nixon wrote, would force Americans to face "two cold realities for the first time in modern history" in the coming decade: "The first is that, if war were to come, we might lose. The second is that we might be defeated without war."[12]

To be sure, Communism's capacity to produce goods and services was not without flaw. Even liberals were beginning to question whether the Soviet farmer had really suffered seventy years of bad weather. But the Soviet Union was never a superpower because of its booming economy. It was a superpower because of its military might.

The experts browbeat the public into believing nuclear war was imminent. Citing a "variety of recent opinion polls," the *New York Times* reported that "a substantial plurality of Americans believe a nuclear war will occur within the next few years."[13] In 1984, Leslie Gelb, then national security correspondent for the *Times,* said the prospect of nuclear war was "becoming less remote all the time."[14] There was no nuclear war and now there is no USSR. So powerful was the liberal instinct to surrender that many liberals can't shake their Cold War cowardice even long after Reagan vanquished the Soviet Union. In 1996, a writer in *Foreign Policy* darkly intoned that winning the Cold War "would have been a great deal less glorious . . . if a few more of those nuclear weapons had actually been used."[15] The "fact that these things did not happen does not establish that they could not have happened."[16] So Reagan deserves no credit for winning the Cold War without firing a shot, because what liberals frantically said might happen didn't happen, but it could have happened. Oh, okay.

The opinion cartel was not just wrong: It was selling a bad product. To be sure, the world stage might not have permitted much hope that the Soviet Union was headed for the "ash heap of history"—as Reagan had said. But liberals weren't angry at Reagan's policies; they were angry at his objectives. Judging by their positions at the time, rather than their post hoc allegations, Democrats adored the Soviet Union. Congressional Democrats repeatedly opposed funding anti-Communist rebels, they opposed Reagan's military buildup, they opposed developing a shield to protect America from incoming missiles, they opposed putting missiles in Europe. As a rule of thumb, Democrats opposed anything opposed by their cherished Soviet Union.

The Soviet Union did not like the idea of a militarily strong America. Neither did the Democrats! In 1982 Senator Edward Kennedy said, "The arms race rushes ahead toward nuclear confrontation that could well mean the annihilation of the human race."[17] *(Run, natives of Swaziland, run!)* Former secretary of state Cyrus Vance said Reagan was not "dealing seriously with the problems" but was engaging in "needlessly provocative . . . bear-baiting."[18] Walter Mondale—whom the Democrats considered presidential material—steadfastly opposed defense spending. In the 1984 presidential debates, Mondale explained that he had opposed the F-14 fighter, the M-1 tank, the B-1 bomber—even an increase in military salaries—because he wanted "to make certain that a dollar spent buys us a dollar's worth of defense."[19] Democrats are never so penurious about taxpayer money as when it comes to the defense of the nation.

Celebrated windbag George Kennan had been haranguing Americans for over a decade to unilaterally reduce nuclear weapons by 10 percent, be nice to the Soviets, drop our demands for human rights improvements in Russia, and cut America's "external commitments to the indispensable minimum."[20] There was a surefire path to victory! Sophisticates hailed Kennan as the "designated intellectual of the postwar foreign policy establishment and the most celebrated Foreign Service officer of his time."[21] He was praised in the *Washington Post* for his "intelligence and integrity" and the "sweep" and "cogency" of his arguments.[22] In 1982, Kennan was awarded the Peace Prize of the West German book trade, with $11,000 in award money to help him carry on his important work.[23] Stanley "Kutler" of the Derisive Quote Marks school of thought cites George Kennan as another hero of the Cold War.[24]

As Kennan continued to promote his Surrender Doctrine throughout the Reagan years, toadying articles cited his despair at Reagan's "hard line against the Kremlin" and especially Reagan's "evil empire" delusion.[25] The *Washington Post* hailed Kennan as the "Cold War guru in Washington" and the "reluctant prophet"[26]— "prophet" meaning "left-wing gasbag." The prophet denounced Washington policy-makers for "failing to heed his admonition that communism was not monolithic." He argued that it was not Marxism, but the "permanent characteristics" of the Russian national character that guided the Soviet Union.[27] In a remark calculated to make the sophisticates swoon, Kennan snippily remarked, "A great many people in an official position in this country don't seem to know that Stalin is dead."[28] In his typical, unassuming style, Kennan declared in his 1983 book about Soviet-American relations, *The Nuclear Delusion,* that nuclear war with the USSR was nearly inevitable: "The clock is ticking; the remaining ticks are numbered; the end of their number is already in sight."[29] For a "prophet" with his batting average, Kennan wasn't reluctant enough.

After Reagan won the Cold War by doing precisely the opposite of everything George Kennan had been demanding in the illustrious pages of the *New York Times,* the *Washington Post, Foreign Affairs,* and other elite publications, it turned out that love of tyranny was not a native characteristic of the Russian people after all! The beautiful mosaic of Eastern European Communism, Central American Communism, and African Communism vanished without a trace. Why are people never ruined by subsequent revelations proving that they were completely wrong?

Indeed, all organs of elite opinion were in hysteria about Reagan's military buildup—the very buildup that ultimately defeated the Soviets. In 1980, the *New York Times* self-righteously sniffed that Reagan "seems genuinely to believe that the vain pursuit of arms superiority will bring the Russians begging to the bargaining table."[30] (It did.) The *Times* sneered at Reagan's "bluster, bravado and refusal to recognize that America is no longer, if it ever was, king of the world." (We weren't, but thanks to Reagan, now we are.) Reagan "is easily caricatured as a bellicose ideologue," lacking "depth," "complexity," and "subtlety." And yet, the *Times* said, Reagan was "dangerous." (What danger? The Soviet Union was on its last legs.) In a follow-up editorial the next day, the *Times* again reminded its readers for the four billionth time that Reagan was dangerous and stupid: "Mr. Reagan still pretends that a rapid buildup of nuclear weapons could frighten the Russians with the specter of American 'superiority.'"[31] (It did.) Without Reagan, we would still be listening to Helen Caldicott drone on about nuclear winter.

Throughout the Reagan administration, there was no tin-pot Communist dictator who did not instantly become the latest celebrity accoutrement in Beverly Hills and the Hamptons. Nicaraguan despot Daniel Ortega was the ne plus ultra dinner guest in Hollywood—

forcing him to cut back on denouncing "Zionists" for a while. Hollywood entertainers formed the pro-Ortega Committee of Concern, chaired by actor Mike Farrell, whose wisdom in foreign policy was, reassuringly, shaped by his years as a costar on TV's *M*A*S*H*. They held lush poolside fund-raisers at celebrity homes for this Man of the People. Mrs. George Slaff, wife of the former mayor of Beverly Hills, hosted one of the star-studded events for Ortega. She explained to a reporter that she was not bothered by the Marxist enthusiasm for eradicating the rich, because that's "their business. I don't regard them as a threat to my way of life, or to the United States."[32] Mrs. Slaff was insulated from Communist tyranny herself, but she thought it might be nice for the little brown brothers. There was no reason to imagine anyone else might want to live in a Beverly Hills estate, with the rhododendrons, and the pools, and Juanita the maid serving bottled water.

Other Hollywood Celebrities for Communist Dictators included actors Ed Asner, Michael Douglas, Susan Anspach, Diane Ladd, Robert Foxworth, Elizabeth "Bewitched" Montgomery; singer Jackson Browne; director Bert Schneider and his wife, Greta; and producers Haskell Wexler, David Hanna, Daniel Selznick, and Joan Keller Selznick.[33] Following protocol, the celebrities were duly praised for "risking their careers by taking a public stand on a politically controversial matter."[34] It was a display of raw courage not seen since George Washington's shivering troops endured the winter at Valley Forge. All the pot they were smoking in those Beverly Hills haciendas must have made them think they were huddling next to the horses for warmth. If Reagan didn't win the Cold War, did Ed Asner win it?

Famous blowhards were constantly impressing other famous blowhards with the greater calamity they could predict resulting from Reagan's support for anti-Communist guerrillas. Joan Didion hysterically berated the Reagan administration for the "wreckage" it was leaving in Nicaragua. Eventually, she said, it would be necessary to talk about Reagan's Latin American policy—and "when the levers would again be pulled and the consequences voided."[35] The "wreckage" left by the Reagan administration, referred to by Didion, is that

Nicaragua is a free country that now holds elections. But at the time, Didion was incoherently rambling that it was "time to talk about runaway agencies, arrogance in the executive branch, about constitutional crises," blah, blah, blah. Since Reagan won the Cold War, apparently it has never again been time to talk about Reagan's Nicaraguan policy. Years later, having completely forgotten about her eight-year postmenopausal rage at Reagan, Didion mocked the "dream notion that a U.S. president, Ronald Reagan, had himself caused the collapse of the Soviet Union with a specific magical incantation, the 'Evil Empire' speech."[36] The "Evil Empire" speech was important, but also central to Reagan's victory over the Soviets were all of his policies that had Joan Didion frothing at the mouth.

Showing all the fortitude of his ancestral forebears, Cornell University history professor Walter LaFeber said Reagan's Latin American policy was "the diplomatic counterpart of trying to use gasoline to extinguish a gasoline fire."[37] (The Creative Writing Department's loss was the History Department's gain!) Whatever Reagan was doing, it was not inconsequential. Reagan had his position and liberals had theirs. Reagan said he was going to fight the Soviets and America would win. They said if we fought Communism, it would be like "using gasoline to extinguish a gasoline fire."

But congressional Democrats hung on Frenchy LaFeber's every word. The Democrats repeatedly rebuffed Reagan's request to fund the anti-Communist Contras fighting Hollywood celebrity Daniel Ortega. In 1984, the Democratic leadership of the House of Representatives sent a "Dear Comandante" letter to the Soviet-backed Marxist despot in Nicaragua, commending Ortega for his efforts to bring democracy to his country and expressing regret that relations between Nicaragua and Washington were not better.[38] While Reagan called Nicaragua a "totalitarian dungeon," the Democrats saw Ortega as an indigenous reformer.[39] Democrat Senators Tom Harkin (D-Iowa) and John Kerry (D-Mass.) flew to Managua to meet with Ortega and returned claiming Ortega was "a misunderstood democrat rather than a Marxist autocrat."[40] In the end, the Democrat-controlled House voted down even humanitarian aid for the Contras in a vote of 248 to 180. Havana Radio hailed the vote as a "'catastrophic defeat' for Reagan."[41] Communists in Havana and the United States Congress had barely recovered from their victory party when, on April 29—less than a week after Democrats had voted down even humanitarian aid for the Contras—Ortega flew to Moscow to meet with Soviet leader Mikhail Gorbachev. Still, the Democrats put on a brave face. Christopher Dodd (D-Conn.) said glibly, "Where does a Marxist go? Disney World? West Palm Beach?"[42]

While Democrats were all but offering their daughters to Ortega, Reagan called the Contra rebels the "moral equals of our Founding Fathers." The *Los Angeles Times* complained that Reagan was practically "accusing Democrats of favoring a Soviet takeover of Central America."[43] The *New York Times* leapt in to defend the pro-Communist Democrats, saying, "The President's rhetoric notwithstanding, there is nothing unpatriotic about this resistance to the contra war."[44] Any statement in the *Times* that begins, "There's nothing unpatriotic about," is sure to end with rotten, treasonable behavior.

Reagan was so desperate to get aid to the anti-Communist rebels in 1985 that at the last minute he even agreed to sweeten the pot for Democrats by limiting the aid to humanitarian purposes—"food, medicine, clothing and other assistance." Then–Senate minority leader and former Klansman Robert Byrd (D-W.Va.) complained that the "other assistance" phrase was "big enough for an Amtrak train to go through" and "could very well involve trucks and earth-moving equipment." That's how much Democrats hated the Contras. No trucks.

The general theme of the Democratic opposition to aiding the Contras was to keep prattling about Vietnam. They wistfully longed for a Democratic president who could lose wars for America. Any aid granted the Contras was treated as the functional equivalent of putting American boys in "body bags." Senator John Glenn (D-Ohio) compared the paltry $14 million Reagan had requested to President Lyndon Johnson's expansion of the war in Vietnam: "It's an advanced Gulf of Tonkin resolution if I've ever heard one." The Democratic chairman of the House Intelligence Committee, Rep. Lee H. Hamilton (D-Ind.), said, "There is a better way to deal with our problems in Nicaragua than by fighting this nasty little war." Evidently sending money for food and medicine was not among the unspecified "better" ways. The Democrats always had mysterious objections and secret "better" ways, which they would never tell us. Then they would vote whichever way would best advance Communist interests.

The next year, Reagan again pleaded with Congress to fund the Contras. White House communications director Pat Buchanan said Congress could vote with the Contras or vote with the Communists. The reaction was predictable. The *Washington Post*'s Mary McGrory instantly denounced Buchanan for such "ugly" tactics. Was a refusal to aid anti-Communists a vote *against* the Communists? Democrat Congressman Tony Coelho (Cal.) proposed that Democrats vote against the Contras to punish Pat Buchanan, saying a vote for the Contras would be "a ratification of Buchanan's red-baiting tactics."[45] Liberals think they should be able to root for the reds without anyone being so uncouth as to point out they are rooting for the reds. Telling the truth about Democrats is an "ugly" tactic.

In one of the most stirring episodes in U.S. history, faced with the Democrats' refusal to fund anti-Marxists in Nicaragua, members of Reagan's staff devised a brilliant plan to support the Contras with private donations.[46] Funds were collected from patriotic Americans, various foreign countries, the Sultan of Brunei, and private organizations. In addition, Israel sold arms to Iran and a portion of the proceeds was diverted to the beleaguered Contras. Israel had its own reasons for wanting to sell arms to the Iranians, then at war with Iraq. Israel worked with moderates within the Iranian government, who offered— as a bonus—to pressure Islamic Jihad to release American hostages recently kidnapped in Beirut. But that was icing on the cake. The main operation consisted of helping two heinous regimes bleed each other a little longer while getting money to anti-Communists battling totalitar-

ian tyrants in Nicaragua. This is what could be accomplished by
bypassing the sedition lobby in Congress. As the MasterCard commercial says, Priceless.

When the Democrats got wind of the fact that men on the president's staff had been secretly promoting the national interest, they were
blind with rage. They would have been fine with a private operation to
fund needle exchanges for drug addicts. But diverting money to anti-
Communist rebels was a "constitutional crisis." Democrats raised a
hue and cry, alleging a technical violation of "the Boland Amendment,"
which no one could ever understand.[47] There were hearings and indictments and millions of dollars spent on a special prosecutor. Democrats
had not felt so alive since they used Watergate to abandon Vietnam in
the dark of night, relinquishing Southeast Asia to totalitarian monsters.
In retelling the glorious story of how the Democrats won the Cold War,
let it never be forgotten that the indictment in the Iran-Contra case
charged: "In or before the middle of 1985, the defendants Oliver L.
North, Richard V. Secord and Albert Hakim and others commenced an
enterprise (the 'Enterprise') that was intended, among other things, to
support military and paramilitary operations in Nicaragua by the Contras and to conduct covert action operations."[48] Democrats thought it
should be a criminal offense to give aid to anti-Communists. President
George Bush did not agree and, years later, would pardon the Iran-
Contra participants who stood accused of conspiring for freedom.

Sad to say, Reagan never knew about the Iran-Contra plan until his
attorney general, Edwin Meese, discovered it and informed the press.
The principals of the operation promptly resigned or were fired. Reagan
was hopping mad about Iran offering to pressure Islamic Jihad to release
American hostages: That was too close to negotiating for hostages, something Reagan said he would never do. But even if corners were cut, it
was a brilliant scheme. There is no possibility that anyone in any Democratic administration would have gone to such lengths to fund anti-
Communist forces. When Democrats scheme from the White House, it's
to cover up the president's affair with an intern. When Republicans

scheme, it is to support embattled anti-Communist freedom fighters sold
out by the Democrats.

Fascinatingly, the one event during the Reagan administration that
shook the Soviet leadership more than any other was the invasion of
Grenada—opposed by liberals. The *New York Times* matter-of-factly
reported that the Grenada invasion was "seen as a setback for the
Democrats." The media compared the liberation of Grenada to the
Soviet Union's invasion of Afghanistan. There were literally dozens of
hysterical op-eds in the *New York Times* denouncing the invasion. The
Times raged that Reagan was "Making the World 'Safe' for Hypocrisy"
for having the audacity to free Grenada from Soviet stooges. The *Times*
also reminded readers that Reagan was a "cowboy, ready to shoot at
the drop of a hat." College protesters openly rooted for the other side.
While the liberated people of Grenada greeted American troops with
open arms, liberals saw the invasion as American imperialism.

The Soviet press simply demeaned the Grenada invasion as a
meaningless nonevent. *TASS*, the official newspaper of the Soviet government, smirked that the Pentagon successfully seized "the tiny
island with the help of a whole armada of naval ships, helicopters,
planes, artillery and detachments of Marines." The *New York Times*,
the unofficial newspaper of the Soviet government, smirked that the so-
called "heros" had triumphed over "some 750 Cubans and their
Grenadian allies" on what "is, after all, only a tiny island." This was,
the *Times* said, not a "major gain."

The party that lost China was not exactly in a position to be complaining about the square footage of the territory Reagan won back,
but, in any event, Grenada was more significant than its size. Grenada
marked the point at which Reagan had unquestionably broken the
defeatism of Vietnam. When informed that the United Nations had
condemned the Grenada invasion, Reagan said, "It didn't upset my
breakfast at all." Despite daily harangues in the *New York Times*, polls
showed Americans overwhelmingly supported the Grenada invasion.
The Soviets were shocked and disheartened to discover that the edito-

rial positions of the *New York Times* did not accurately reflect the sentiments of the American people.

Even as Reagan's policies were working, liberals denied it. *New York Times* columnist Flora Lewis scoffed at Jeane Kirkpatrick's "remarkable" claim, made during the 1984 Republican National Convention, that "the Russians had nearly taken over until the Reagan administration." Where? Lewis demanded to know.[49] As Ambassador Kirkpatrick said in her speech—just a sentence or two later—in the decade preceding Reagan's inauguration, the Soviets had expanded their influence into South Vietnam, Laos, Cambodia, Afghanistan, Angola, Ethiopia, Mozambique, South Yemen, Libya, Syria, Aden, Congo, Madagascar, the Seychelles, Nicaragua, and Grenada. Other than that, no place really.

In addition to the military offensives, Reagan directed an unremitting stream of rhetorical attacks at the Kremlin. Liberals acted as if Reagan had launched a first strike every time he had a cross word for their beloved Soviet Union. Walter Laqueur condemned Reagan's "bluster" as "counterproductive" and counseled the president to "find an occasional word of praise for the great and talented Russian people." Laqueur described as "eloquently argued" the contention that the West should "cease to demonize the Soviet people and their leaders."[50] As Sting summarized the views of the intellectuals, "the Russians love their children, too."

Periodically, congressional hearings would have to be convened to allow progressives to denounce Reagan's rhetoric more fulsomely. At a 1982 congressional hearing, former Senator and segregationist J. William Fulbright (D-Ark.) said Reagan's tough language toward the Soviet Union was "a form of psychological warfare." He said Reagan was playing "a dangerous game" that threatened "the stability and soundness of our domestic economy."[51] Playing to the media, Fulbright added, "If it is a psychological game, it is a complex and delicate operation requiring experience and subtlety in its execution—qualities which are hardly the hallmark of this administration."[52] Calling Reagan stupid was a surefire hit with the self-identified smart set.

Liberals were horribly embarrassed by Reagan's bellicose anti-Communism. In the 1984 presidential campaign, Mondale said Reagan's support for anti-Communist rebels in Nicaragua had "embarrassed us." Supporting the Contras, Mondale said, had "strengthened our opposition and undermined [America's] moral authority." Apparently, it made our enemies mad. You wouldn't want that in the middle of an epic struggle with Communist totalitarians. Mondale said Reagan was "oversimplif[ying] the difficulties of what we must do in Central America."[53] Typically, Mondale had complicated long-term solutions that required doing short-term what our enemies would like us to do.

Even newspapers that endorsed Reagan claimed to be embarrassed by him. The *Chicago Tribune* endorsed Reagan over Mondale in 1984, but criticized the president for his "ignorance about the Soviet Union and his air-headed rhetoric on the issues of foreign policy and arms control." Reagan's policies, the *Tribune* said, "have become an embarrassment to the United States and a danger to world peace."[54] The left's idea for winning the Cold War was a nuclear freeze, opposing anti-Communist guerrillas all over the world, opposing the liberation of Grenada, opposing a missile defense shield, and engaging in sweet talk with the Kremlin. They never explained how their plan would work— but the French were impressed.

Needless to say, liberals reacted to Reagan's "Evil Empire" speech with apoplexy. After asking the Evangelical audience to pray for those who lived under totalitarian rule, Reagan said that as long as the Kremlin continued to "preach the supremacy of the state, declare its omnipotence over individual man, and predict its eventual domination of all peoples on the earth, they are the focus of evil in the modern world." Liberals now brush off Reagan's "Evil Empire" speech as slightly ludicrous and utterly irrelevant. They were not so complacent at the time—and as we now know, neither were the Russians. The *New York Times* alone ran more than a dozen articles on Reagan's "Evil Empire" speech, enraged at Reagan for criticizing their pet totalitarian dictatorship.[55] Invoking the "Evil Empire" speech became a standard laugh line on college campuses—matched only by the similarly hilarious invocation of Reagan's name. By contrast, Sting's insight that the "Russians love their children, too" really struck a chord with Sting's intellectual peers in academia.

Anthony Lewis berated Reagan for calling the USSR an evil empire, saying Reagan was using "sectarian religiosity to sell a political program."[56] It was a "simplistic theology—one in fact rejected by most theologians." Reagan was applying a "black-and-white standard to something that is much more complex." Whenever liberals start droning about "complex issues" for which there are no "simple solutions," hide Grandma and the kids: Rancid policy proposals are coming. Lewis's method of eschewing simplistic black-and-white characterizations was to call Reagan's speech "outrageous" and "primitive." Pushing all the hot buttons of the average *New York Times* reader, Lewis said Reagan could "easily call it a sin to teach evolution" and suggested with horror that Western European leaders may have reacted badly to Reagan's "Evil Empire" speech.

Liberals were appalled at Reagan's churlish words toward their beloved Soviet Union as well as his simplistic assumption that we could "win" the Cold War. Thus, Lewis wrote, "Can the concept of good and evil determine whether 10,000 nuclear warheads is enough?" It could and it did. We spent them into the ground. Liberals can never grasp why resistance works better than surrender. As Lewis blathered in utter incomprehension, "The terrible irony of that race is that the United States has led the way on virtually every major new development over the last 30 years, only to find itself met by the Soviet Union." What was "irony" to liberals was "strategy" for America. The Soviet Union wouldn't have collapsed anyway.

James Reston, also writing for the *Times*(!), was similarly baffled by the "objective" of "violent criticism of Russians as an evil society." The Russians love their children, too. He threw a little regional snobbery in with the anti-God bigotry, saying Reagan "went down South the other day and denounced the Soviet Union as an 'evil empire.'"[57] Reston said our European allies were shocked—shocked—by Reagan's unsophisticated rhetoric. He confided to readers of the *Times*'s op-ed page, "Secretary of State Shultz is talking quietly to the allies, and indirectly to the Russians, about how to get out of this dilemma."

Tom Wicker denounced the "Evil Empire" speech as evidencing a "dangerous doctrine" inviting a "repetition of the Vietnam experience."[58] Wicker also strenuously objected to Reagan's opposition to the spread of Communism in Central America. The "greater danger," he said, "lies in Mr. Reagan's vision of the superpower relationship as Good versus Evil." He slipped in the standard liberal disclaimer: "Most of what I know about the Soviet regime I find repellent." Good for you, Tom! In a long-standing liberal tradition, foreign despots must be pronounced "repellent" or "despicable" before urging a policy of appeasement toward them.

In case readers of the *New York Times* were not yet stockpiling cyanide pills in raw terror at Ronald Reagan's "Evil Empire" speech, still a *fourth* editorial writer weighed in on the speech. Russell Baker said Reagan offered only a "bleak, bankruptive vision of the American future."[59] Showing the prescience that has come to define the *New York Times* op-ed page, Baker said Reagan's Cold War policies raised the specter of "the next century" consumed with war against "the 'evil empire' of Communism." Baker, like his wildly diverse colleagues on the editorial page, confidently asserted that "most sensible people expect these war preparations to go on forever." There was "no happy ending in the cards. No ending of any variety. Just eternity stretching on and on with the bills coming in forever." A few years later, a Democratic Congress would be cheerfully blowing Reagan's "Peacetime Dividend" on laughably useless domestic programs.

Further obscuring the idea that the Soviet Union was a moldering old corpse of a country, when Reagan made a joke about the Soviet Union in August 1984, the entire liberal cult went ballistic. The jokester Reagan warmed up his radio mike before a presidential address by saying, "My fellow Americans, I am pleased to tell you today that I've signed legislation that will outlaw Russia forever. We begin bombing in five minutes." From the panic in the media, you would have thought it was 1914 and Reagan had accidentally shot the Austro-Hungarian crown prince.

The *New York Times* rushed to print with a thousand-word article on "Reagan's Gaffe." The article earnestly detailed the grave threat to world stability that Reagan's joke had provoked. A Mondale strategist—"speaking in private"—told the *Times* "that Mr. Reagan had undercut diplomatic efforts of recent months."[60] John B. Oakes, former senior editor of the *New York Times,* warned that Reagan's joke "reflects an instinctive feeling that the only good Russian is a dead Russian, which is a rather dangerous sentiment to be boiling along under the Presidential skin in this hair-trigger age."[61] Serving the same function as the *Times*'s man-on-the-street interviews, anonymous "Republican strategists" and "high officials" in the Reagan administration admitted to the *Times* that they had "winced over the remark." Unnamed State Department and White House officials called the incident "an embarrassment." In general, there was a lot of indignation about a country that was—as we are now told—teetering on the brink of collapse completely independently of anything Reagan said or did.

The argument that Reagan didn't know what he was doing when he won the Cold War proves nothing more than that liberals will lie about anything. There is not a shred of evidence to support it, other than the left's all-consuming hatred for Ronald Reagan. For a man who was buffeted on all sides with contradictory advice for eight years in office, Reagan certainly had a knack for always choosing to take the right advice at just the right moment.

When an advance copy of Reagan's "Berlin Wall" speech was circulated, it was vehemently opposed by "virtually the entire foreign-policy apparatus of the U.S. government," according to the draft's author, speechwriter Peter Robinson.[62] The sophisticates said it was "crude" and "unduly provocative." Robinson says, "There were telephone calls, memoranda, and meetings. State and the NSC submitted their own, alternative drafts. . . . In each, the call for Gorbachev to tear down the Wall was missing." Right up until the moment Reagan boarded Air Force One for Berlin, the State Department and National Security Council were faxing over alternative drafts.

The problem was, Robinson says, Reagan liked the speech. He

especially liked the part about the wall. When initially asked for his comments on the speech, Reagan said, "Well, there's that passage about tearing down the Wall. That Wall has to come down. That's what I'd like to say." So that's what he said. The phrase remained, Robinson says, "solely because of Ronald Reagan." Moments before giving the speech, Reagan was told that a crowd of East Berliners gathered on the opposite side of the wall to hear his speech had been scattered by the East German police. So when he came to the passage about the wall, he pounded out each syllable: "General Secretary Gorbachev, if you seek peace—if you seek prosperity for the Soviet Union and Eastern Europe—if you seek liberalization, come here, to this gate. Mr. Gorbachev, open this gate. Mr. Gorbachev, tear down this wall."

Reagan not only ignored the liberal elite throughout his administration but, when necessary, he ignored his conservative base, too. He did so rather famously in 1987, when his apocryphal senility should have been in full bloom—if that hadn't been a vicious lie. A little more than a year after Reagan walked away from the negotiating table in Reykjavik, he suddenly switched course and began playing good cop with Gorbachev. He even agreed to sign a treaty banning medium-range missiles from Europe. Conservatives went bananas. They finally thought maybe liberals were right about Reagan's encroaching dementia.

William F. Buckley, Jr.'s *National Review* called the prospective treaty a "catastrophic" venture in "utopianism." The *Wall Street Journal* criticized Reagan for making "a bad deal" and subjecting our European allies to Soviet intimidation.[63] Conservative Caucus Chairman Howard Phillips ridiculed Reagan as "a useful idiot for Kremlin propaganda," saying he was "little more than the speech-reader-in-chief."[64] This was one of the rare instances when the *New York Times* allows the likes of a genuine conservative like Phillips to grace its editorial page—to attack Reagan. Conservative fund-raiser Richard Viguerie called Reagan an "apologist" for Gorbachev.[65]

Reagan ignored his fellow conservatives. He knew he had already won at Reykjavik and that it was time to make overtures to Gorbachev.

Once again, Reagan was right and others were wrong. But this time, those who opposed Reagan were his own conservative allies. This was at the very end of Reagan's presidency, when liberals claim he was losing his grip on reality. But the doddering old figurehead disregarded his closest allies. By pursuing his own course, Ronald Reagan achieved the final triumph over Soviet Communism.

If liberals wanted to attack conservatives, this was the one brief moment at the end of the Cold War when virtually all conservative opinion was wrong. Liberals would sooner believe that it was pure dumb luck—or that trusty old Harry Truman's containment policies had finally kicked in—than they would believe that Reagan knew what he was doing. They would pass on the chance to attack Richard Viguerie and William F. Buckley simply to avoid admitting Reagan was right. If Reagan won the Cold War, liberals had been monumentally wrong on the matter of America's national security.

After Reagan brought down the Iron Curtain—by steadfastly ignoring everything liberals said—you would think erstwhile Soviet enthusiasts would stay mum on the subject of their prior positions. Instead they tell wild, bald-faced lies about how they had recognized, early on, the true nature of Soviet Communism. As Norman Mailer remembered it, he had been dubious about the Soviet Union all along. In 1996, he claimed he had always seen that the Soviet regime was "endlessly hollow."[66] Strangely enough, there is no record of Mailer ever having said that until after Reagan vanquished the evil empire.

To the contrary, in 1984, Mailer was cheerfully extolling the USSR as a free, churchgoing, middle-class haven. He said the Soviets had created an "inexpensive working economy" in which only one class was visible in Moscow, "and that is the middle class." Somewhat like Six Flags. Religious freedom reigned, Mailer said, with churches "filled to capacity." Indeed, he wrote, "I do not know if I ever attended a Catholic service that was more intense." Mailer denied the existence of a police state, recounting how he "would leave the hotel and walk around for miles" without surveillance. Mailer jeeringly criticized American propaganda that portrayed the Soviet Union as "an evil force."[67] The truth, he explained, was that the Soviet people "do not necessarily decide in advance that they are working for a doomed and evil machine." The Russians love their children, too.

But the way Mailer remembered it years later, it was conservatives who had been the naive ones because they "bought" the idea that the Soviet Union "was an expanding empire."[68] What did these conservatives have to go on, really? Sure, there were little telltale signs like the Soviets marching through Armenia, Azerbaijan, Georgia, Mongolia, Turkmenia, Uzbekistan, Tajikistan, Kirgizia, Poland, Moldavia, Lithuania, Latvia, Estonia, Albania, Czechoslovakia, Hungary, Romania, Bulgaria, East Germany, Yugoslavia, North Korea, Cuba, South Yemen, Congo-Brazzaville, North Vietnam, Guinea-Bissau, Cambodia, Laos, South Vietnam, Ethiopia, Angola, Mozambique, Nicaragua, the Seychelles, Grenada, and Afghanistan. But one could hardly call this a pattern.

Elite opinion did not part company with Reagan on his methods alone. They disagreed with the goal of winning the Cold War—or "winning," as sophisticates put it. Appallingly, after Reagan defeated the Soviet Union, America was the world's sole remaining superpower. And worse: America was going to win the war on terrorism. In 2003, Joan Didion morosely complained that "the collapse of the Soviet Union had opened the door to the inevitability of American pre-eminence, a mantle of beneficent power that all nations except rogue nations—whatever they might say on the subject—were yearning for America to assume."[69] As Didion saw it, the United States was going to harass the Taliban and Saddam Hussein for no reason whatsoever. America's imminent military victory over terrorism, Didion said, was "a dream from which there is no waking."[70]

On MSNBC, Doris Kearns Goodwin, historian and fact checker for Joe Biden, also rued Reagan's triumph over the Soviet Union. She hearkened back to the good old days when we all lived under the threat of nuclear annihilation: "At least with those two superpowers there was a balance, there was a recognition that if one acted the other would react, and there was some rationality in the minds of people. You know, but now the reaction against America being this superpower, launching itself around the world, the anti-Americanism is probably higher than it's ever been."[71] America's victory in the Cold War had taken all the sport out of global thermonuclear brinksmanship.

After having been proved spectacularly wrong in everything he ever said about the Cold War, Cornell professor Walter LaFeber felt his counsel was desperately needed in the war on terrorism. Calling American intervention abroad a "disorder" that has been "glorified, especially since the American triumph in the Cold War"—a triumph he said was impossible—LaFeber predicted "a continual war . . . to 'lead the world' to continual peace."[72] Without the highbrow sneer of sarcastic quote marks, Walter LaFeber would be unable to communicate. Liberals expect everyone to forget not only what they said during the Cold War, but the fact that there *was* a Cold War and that they were rooting for the other side.

During Reagan's magnificent prosecution of the Cold War, the Nobel Peace Prize committee unerringly awarded its prizes to Reagan's most maniacal opponents. In 1982, the prize went to Alva Myrdal and Alfonso Garcia Robles for—as the Nobel Foundation put it—"their magnificent work in the disarmament negotiations of the U.N., informing world opinion and of arousing among the general public an acceptance of its joint responsibility for disarmament."[73] Accepting her award, Ms. Myrdal said, "The crimes of violence committed on the streets are to a large extent a result of the spread of arms."[74] In 1985, the Nobel Peace Prize went to the group International Physicians for the Prevention of Nuclear War for their insistence that "both" the Soviet Union and the United States abandon nuclear weapons. The Soviet Union liked the idea since they wouldn't disarm and could execute anyone who made a fuss about it. In 1988, the Nobel Peace Prize went to the United Nations Peacekeeping Forces. Ronald Reagan never won a Nobel Peace Prize. Mikhail Gorbachev did.

Twenty years later, in the war on terrorism, the Nobel Peace Prize committee would again do itself proud. One month after the 9-11 attack on America, the peace prize was awarded jointly to the United Nations and Kofi Annan—who had once gushed that Saddam Hussein was "a man I can do business with."[75] As America prepared to attack Iraq in 2002, the Nobel Peace Prize was awarded to Jimmy Carter for his absurd objections to his own country's policies in the war on terror. Earlier peace prize–winner Mikhail Gorbachev responded to the war on terrorism by calling President George Bush and Tony Blair the true threats to world peace. Osama bin Laden apparently came in a close second. Gorbachev was particularly critical of the "unilateral" policy of the United States and Britain: "Important and serious political decisions should not be taken unilaterally."[76] That policy worked pretty well in defeating him.

Whittaker Chambers wrote, "Other ages have had their individual traitors—men who from faint-heartedness or hope of gain sold out their causes. But in the 20th century, for the first time, men banded together by the million in movements like Fascism and Communism, dedicated to the purpose of betraying the institutions they lived under. In the 20th century, treason became a vocation whose modern form was specifically the treason of ideas."[77]

All of elite opinion was in a state of high anxiety throughout the Reagan years. At every turn, Reagan's policies and statements were said to be "dangerous," promising a "bleak" future, frightening European leaders, and putting "the world's survival" at risk. Reagan was accused of engaging in "lethal leapfrog" with his "simplistic" view of the world. The *New York Times* even took shots at Reagan in the sports pages, referring to his "macho myth of American supremacy."[78] But now we're supposed to believe that these same policies were completely immaterial since the Soviet Union was collapsing with or without Reagan. For an irrelevant empire in decline, the Soviet Union sure prompted a lot of pointless hysteria.

It cannot be that Reagan's approach to the Cold War was both horribly frightening and completely irrelevant. If the Iron Curtain was crumbling, American academics, reporters, editors, and the entire *New*

York Times staff perpetrated a vast conspiratorial fraud on the American people throughout Reagan's presidency. Either that, or they were wrong and Reagan was right.

Liberals said Reagan was dangerous and his rhetoric scary. They ridiculed him as an idiot for believing the Soviet Union could be toppled. They opposed him on every front—strengthening the military, aiding and arming anti-Communist rebels around the world, invading Grenada, preparing to win a nuclear war, building a nuclear shield, and waging a spiritual crusade against Soviet totalitarianism. Reagan said the Soviet Union was an evil empire and we would prevail. He called the ball, the shot, and the pocket, and he won the game. But now we're supposed to believe he was lucky. Liberals lie about Reagan's victory because when Reagan won the Cold War, he proved them wrong on everything they had done and said throughout the Cold War. It is their last defense to fifty years of treason.

10

COLD WAR EPITAPH: THE HISS AFFAIR AT THE END OF THE COLD WAR

In the year 2003, the *New York Times* cheerfully announced the introduction of a new, "lighthearted" journal about Communism. This is an ideology responsible for nearly 100 million murders, or—as the *Times* put it—a "divisive" ideology.[1] How about a "lighthearted" journal about suicide bombing or Nazism, also "divisive" ideologies? Or must an ideology commit ten times the murders of Hitler's Nazi Germany before liberals call it lighthearted? In the inaugural issue of the "lighthearted" *American Communist History*, Robert Lichtman and Ronald D. Cohen wrote, "Is it ever justifiable in a democracy for the government to maintain a stable of paid witnesses to testify on its behalf about the political affiliations (almost always lawful and First Amendment protected) of individuals holding unpopular views?"[2] They won't quit. Paid agents of Moscow are described simply as individuals with "unpopular views."

Incomprehensibly, there is no stigma to having wittingly supported a totalitarian regime that committed monstrous crimes and had atomic weapons pointed at U.S. soil. In a stunning demonstration of the power of propaganda, accusing someone of having been a Communist makes you the nut. You may as well intone darkly that someone was a "vegetarian" as a "Communist." To this day, the label "Communist" is rather favorable, a little jaunty. After Nixon was destroyed, Hiss rehabilitated, and Barbra Streisand and Robert Redford made the movie *The Way We Were*, there was warm nostalgia for Communist traitors. They were hailed as martyrs, victims of "McCarthyism."

When Republican Senator Trent Lott uttered a single off-the-cuff remark in praise of Senator Strom Thurmond on his hundredth birthday, there were urgent calls for Lott's resignation as Senate majority leader. Fifty-four years earlier, Thurmond had run for president and, in a moment of bonhomie, Lott said the country would be better off if Thurmond had won. The problem was: Thurmond had run as a segregationist. A huge brouhaha ensued. If we had gone to war with Iraq around the time of Lott's comment, no one would have noticed. The fuss was about one former Democrat praising another former Democrat for what was once a Democratic policy. (When asked who should replace Lott, Jesse Jackson said, "How about that hymie Lieberman?")

Thurmond's Dixiecrat Party was not the only extremist spin-off from the Democratic Party in 1948. In the apex of Moscow-directed subversion of U.S. politics, Henry Wallace, FDR's vice president and agriculture secretary, left the Democratic Party that same year to form the Communist-dominated and Soviet-backed "Progressive Party." Wallace's Progressive Party was expressly pro-Soviet, excluding even the mildest criticism of Soviet aggression.[3] Wallace met personally with KGB agents.[4] And his platform, naturally, was supported by "many of America's leading cultural celebrities."[5] The Progressives received one million votes nationwide, about the same as Thurmond's Dixiecrat Party. Thurmond went on to reject segregation, become a Republican, and serve his country well as a United States senator. By contrast, running a Communist-dominated presidential campaign was Wallace's last hurrah. An off-the-cuff remark praising Thurmond's presidential campaign is the career-destroyer; fawning references to Wallace's Soviet-backed presidential campaign are utterly blameless.

Just two years before Lott's remarks, a former Democratic senator from Iowa published a hagiographic work on Wallace's life titled *American Dreamer*. How about a book about a segregationist titled *American Dreamer*? The dust jacket on *American Dreamer* featured a nauseating statement of praise by Democratic Senator Edward Kennedy, saying the book deserved "to be read by all who care about the American Dream." Wallace's version of the American "dream" was Communism every bit as much as Strom Thurmond's dream was segregation. Aren't dreams of murderous dictators, gulags, and death camps at least comparable in evil to segregated lunch counters? In 1999, the Clinton administration dedicated a room at the Agriculture Department to Wallace. At the dedication ceremony, former Democratic presidential candidate George McGovern gave a speech openly praising Wallace.[6] McGovern recalled fondly that he himself had voted for Wallace and had run for president in 1972 "on a similar platform"—with the help of a young Yale Law School graduate named Bill Clinton.

Inasmuch as Trent Lott was in kindergarten in 1948, he did not vote for Thurmond. He did not run on a "similar" platform to the Dixiecrats. He did not write a jacket-flap endorsement on a book that called a segregationist an "American Dreamer." But Lott was promptly removed as Senate majority leader. The only thing that could have saved him was some last-minute exculpatory evidence like proof that he was merely trying to obstruct justice after being caught with a chubby intern performing oral sex on him in his office. Liberals are utterly unabashed about their seventy-year pattern of rooting for America's enemies. Praise for Stalinist stooges is blameless. Even the Stalinists themselves are viewed merely as mistaken, but lovable, idealists.

On his way to Baghdad on the eve of war, Sean Penn eagerly pointed out that his father had suffered terribly under Joe McCarthy.

Yes, and a lot of racists suffered when Eisenhower sent federal troops to enforce desegregation. Liberals titter about conservatives imagining Communists under every bed, while they hysterically claim to see racists under every bed. If, in addition to murdering tens of millions of people, Stalin had maintained "Whites only" water fountains, America would now celebrate a national Joe McCarthy Day.

It is a curious fact that the most ridiculed public figures in America in the twentieth century have been those who posed the gravest threat to Communism: Joseph McCarthy, J. Edgar Hoover, Richard Nixon, Whittaker Chambers, and Ronald Reagan. The left's shameful refusal to admit collaboration with one of the great totalitarian regimes of the last century—like their defense of Clinton—quickly transformed into a vicious slander campaign against those who bore witness against them. Caught absolutely red-handed, liberals started in with their typical bellicose counterattacks.

McCarthy died censured and despised at forty-eight years old, his name a malediction. Hoover is maligned for having been a mad spymaster and is lyingly smeared as a cross-dresser—by people who admire cross-dressers. Nixon was forced to resign the presidency in disgrace. Though persecuted in his day, Whittaker Chambers is not hated today only on a technicality: The MTV generation doesn't know who he is. They'd hate him, too, but it would require research. By contrast, Ronald Reagan has prevailed over the left's campaign of lies because the American people do remember him—so far. Notwithstanding the left's fantastic lies, these men won a fifty-year war because of the abiding anti-Communism of the American people. These are the heros of the Cold War, and all have been personally reviled for their trouble.[7]

Absurdly, liberals claim to hate J. Edgar Hoover because of their passion for civil liberties. The left's exquisite concern for civil liberties apparently did not extend to the Japanese. As President Franklin D. Roosevelt rounded up Japanese for the internment camps, liberals were awed by his genius. The Japanese internment was praised by liberal luminaries such as Earl Warren, Felix Frankfurter, and Hugo

Black. The national ACLU didn't make a peep.[8] Joseph Rauh, founder of Americans for Democratic Action—and celebrated foe of "McCarthyism"—supported the internment.[9] There was one lonely voice in the Roosevelt administration opposed to the Japanese internment: that of J. Edgar Hoover. The ACLU gave J. Edgar Hoover an award for wartime vigilance during World War II. It was only when he turned his award-winning vigilance to Soviet spies that liberals thought Hoover was a beast. Liberals deemed it appropriate to throw Japanese citizens into internment camps on the basis of no evidence of subversive activity whatsoever. But it was outrageous for the FBI director to spy on high government officials taking their orders from Moscow. As we now know, Hoover didn't need to engage in much surveillance to determine who the Soviet agents were—he already knew from decrypted Soviet cables. The relentless attack on Hoover's reputation has nothing to do with civil liberties concerns. It has everything to do with his pursuit of Soviet spies.

Liberals sheltered Communists, Hoover was onto them, so they called him a fag. With precisely as much evidence as they had for McCarthy's alleged homosexuality, the left giddily gay-baited J. Edgar Hoover. While Hoover was alive, any journalist who could have proved he was gay would have won a Pulitzer Prize. But they couldn't get Hoover on a jaywalking charge. Only after he was dead did liberals go hog-wild inventing lurid stories of Hoover showing up at Washington cocktail parties in drag (perhaps not recognizing their own Pamela Harriman). In 2003, the Aspen Comedy Arts Festival put on a musical comedy about Hoover's apocryphal homosexuality, *J. Edgar! The Musical*, written by Harry Shearer and Tom Leopold.[10] While slandering a dead man with impunity, rich celebrities—in Aspen, no less—paid tribute to their own dauntless courage. For the second year in a row the festival celebrated the First Amendment, giving its "Freedom of Speech Award" to college dropout Michael Moore, in an event hosted by Joe Lockhart, former press secretary to Bill Clinton, a president whose IRS audited people who engaged in free speech against him.[11] The executive director of the festival, Stu Smiley, said the purpose of the festival was "to reacquaint ourselves with people who have sacrificed for their right to express themselves."[12]

Liberals wouldn't take their revenge on Richard Nixon for twenty years, but when they did, it was spectacular. The left's consuming hatred for Nixon is incomprehensible disassociated from his anti-Communism. Carl Bernstein, the *Washington Post* reporter who, along with Bob Woodward, saved the world by exposing Watergate, said he grew up thinking of Soviet spy Ethel Rosenberg as a "Jewish madonna."[13] After Nixon exposed Hiss and his Democrat patrons, liberals would not rest until he was ruined. This is the true story of Watergate.

Adding insult to injury, Nixon had the audacity to make a campaign issue of the Democrats' treasonous stupidity. In 1950, the very year Alger Hiss was convicted of perjury for denying he was a Soviet spy, Nixon was in a Senate race against Helen Gahagan Douglas, the Cynthia McKinney of her day. Douglas's positions on national security were so absurd, John F. Kennedy privately supported Nixon against Douglas.[14] Not long after Hiss was convicted, Douglas said, "We all know that communism is no real threat to the democratic institutions of our country."[15] She scoffed at fighting "the windmill of communism in America," saying the true battle was against "intolerance."[16] She was consistently ranked one of the most valuable members of Congress by liberal journalists.[17] Demonstrating just how low he could sink, Nixon told voters about Douglas's record. His supporters called her the Pink Lady. Liberals are still in a huff about it. A 1992 article in the *New York Times* called Nixon's campaign in that race "one of the dirtiest campaigns in American political history."[18] Nixon's sneaky ploy of alerting voters to Douglas's positions was characterized as "an opportunism focused on the unreasonable and unreasoning terror of Communist subversion."[19] It was outrageous for Nixon to make a campaign issue of a Democratic candidate's position on national security.

Anti-Communism was Nixon's original sin. Nothing he did could exonerate or excuse it. Except for his proud red-baiting days in the fifties, Nixon was the sort of politician normally cited admiringly in the *New York Times* as a "moderate Republican." Nixon imposed wage and price controls, established relations with Communist China, engaged in detente with the Soviet Union, created the Environmental Protection Agency, expanded the federal food stamp program, hired Henry Kissinger, and put Harry Blackmun on the Supreme Court. Many of the government regulations and spending programs that would be cut by Ronald Reagan a decade later were, as the *New York Times* admitted, "products of the Nixon Administration."[20] The Reagan camp tried to block Nixon's presidential nomination at the 1968 convention. In 1972, Nixon was primaried by a conservative Republican, John Ashbrook, with the motto "No Left Turn." M. Stanton Evans said there were only two things conservatives didn't like about Nixon: his domestic policy and his foreign policy. For conservatives, Watergate was a rare bright spot of the Nixon administration. Pat Buchanan claims it wasn't until the details of the Watergate scandal were unfolding in the press that a contrite Evans said to him, "Pat, I want to apologize for all the attacks upon your administration. I would never have done anything like that if I had known you were into all that good stuff we've been hearing about lately."[21]

The gravamens of Watergate were "dirty tricks" as commonplace as lobbyists in Washington. Consider the hysteria-inducing question "What did he know and when did he know it?" The "it" was wiretapping and spying, activities with a long and illustrious pedigree in Washington. Historian Paul Johnson provides a short history of presidential skulduggery in his book *Modern Times*.[22] President Roosevelt pioneered covert surveillance in the Oval Office, building a secret room off the office where stenographers would transcribe all his conversations. He engaged in mad surveillance to the far recesses of the White House, even secretly listening in on his own wife in her hotel room. FDR "created his own 'intelligence unit' responsible only to himself, with a staff of eleven and financed by State Department 'Special Emergency money.'" He tapped the phones of unfriendly members of the press as well as political opponents, such as John Lewis of the United Mine Workers.

President Kennedy and his brother Robert, the attorney general, wiretapped Martin Luther King's adulterous liaisons and arranged for the tapes to be played for reporters. They "plotted against right-wing radio and TV stations." Robert Kennedy retaliated against executives of U.S. Steel who had "defied his brother's policies" by raiding their homes at dawn.

President Johnson took surveillance of his enemies to a new level, using "secret government files, the Internal Revenue Service and other executive devices to protect himself against exposure in the Bobby Baker scandal of 1963, potentially the biggest scandal since Teapot dome." Johnson bugged Goldwater in '64. NBC TV bugged the Democratic Party headquarters in '68.

The press blithely covered up scandalous behavior of presidents they liked. These constitutionally protected guardians of the truth lied to the public about Kennedy's pill popping and pathological womanizing. JFK kept a secret apartment for his mistresses—"one of whom he shared with a gangster." This was never reported. President Johnson's prodigious bribe taking as vice president was hidden from the public. In Johnson's Bobby Baker scandal, the *Washington Post* "actually helped [Johnson] blacken his chief accuser." Historian Paul Johnson concludes this shameful record with the fabulous understatement "Nixon enjoyed no such forbearance from the media."[23]

The media detested Nixon, and his popularity made them loathe him even more. In 1972, President Nixon ran for reelection against the media's dream candidate, George McGovern. As Nixon said, "The Eastern Establishment media finally has a candidate who almost totally shares their views . . . amnesty, pot, abortion, confiscation of wealth (unless it is theirs), massive increases in welfare, unilateral disarmament, reduction of our defenses and surrender in Vietnam." Now, he said, we'd see what the American people think.[24] McGovern was smashed in a forty-nine-state landslide for Nixon.

Nixon's enemies were powerful and he was hunted. Despite giddy assertions in the society pages, Nixon had no "enemies list." It existed only in the fantasy lives of liberals. Three Nixon staffers created a so-called enemies list—never requested or seen by Nixon.[25] If liberal logic requires imputing to Nixon the unauthorized acts of his assistants, then Bill Clinton owes Kathleen Willey new tires and another cat. The very idea that Nixon needed a "list" to know who his enemies were is preposterous. And yet, even when ruthlessly destroying people, liberals must pretend to be the ones who are oppressed. All liberals of a certain age claim to have marched with Dr. Martin Luther King and to have been on Nixon's "enemies list," as if every liberal alive during the Nixon administration narrowly escaped the concentration camp. Reviewing a book by Daniel Schorr, Andrew Ferguson wrote that the biggest surprise was that "the author waits until his second page before mentioning the enemies list."[26] A *New York Times* obituary from May 27, 2001, boasts of the dearly departed: "Mr. Shearer was critical of the war in Vietnam and made President Richard M. Nixon's enemies list."[27] In twenty years, homeless peace protesters will be claiming to have been on John Ashcroft's "enemies list."

Nixon's true crimes were that he exposed Alger Hiss, he redbaited a red, he beat media darling McGovern in a forty-nine-state landslide, and he was winning the war in Vietnam. Most egregiously, Nixon spied on the anti-war felon Daniel Ellsberg. Ellsberg stole classified material from the State Department and gave it to a traitorous press in hopes of undermining the Vietnam War. Nixon had no self-interest in preventing the publication of the "Pentagon Papers": They covered his predecessors' administrations, not his. But, unlike the press, Nixon thought it would be bad if Communists swept through Southeast Asia. For stealing the "Pentagon Papers," Ellsberg was the left's most storied hero since Alger Hiss. Nixon's associates, the "plumbers," broke into Ellsberg's psychiatrist's office to get dirt on him—a more noble cause, one might add, than the Kennedy brothers' skulduggery against Martin Luther King. Nixon's spying on Ellsberg would not stand. From Hiss to Ellsberg, Nixon would not give traitors a break. Watergate was the left's final revenge.

Liberals remember nothing but their resentments. Just as Watergate was payback for Hiss, Bill Clinton was payback for Reagan. When Reagan won the Cold War, he won a fifty-year argument with liberals.

Liberals had been on the wrong side of the Cold War for most of the twentieth century. They were wrong about Hiss, wrong about Communist infiltration of the government in the forties and fifties, wrong about China, and wrong about Reagan. Liberal moaning about "indigenous peoples" and "inevitable revolutions" was finally exposed as the nonsense it always was. Even their extravagant plans for a government takeover of every American industry suffered a bit of a setback with the fall of their precious Soviet Union. The remarkable material accomplishments of a market system could no longer be denied. Liberals had completely failed ever to marshal one serious response to Communism. In Reagan's victory lay the left's defeat. Only after appreciating how defeated the Democratic Party was does their defense of Clinton finally make sense. Bill Clinton was liberalism's last gasp.

Republicans had just vanquished the gravest threat to freedom since Adolf Hitler, with liberals bleating throughout. After a triumphant twelve-year Republican reign, the Democrats managed to trick the American people into putting the smarmy son of a traveling salesman into the White House (on a plurality vote). From the moment they first laid eyes on Clinton, Republicans had screamed that he was a liar. And then it turned out they were right about that, too. If, once again, Republicans had been proved right, the Democratic Party would have become the functional equivalent of the Tories in Canada. The zeitgeist would have been overwhelming. Democrats could not allow Republicans to be vindicated again. At a strategic moment in history, Democrats had no choice but to defend Clinton with everything they had. For a party that had defended Stalin, this wasn't such a bitter pill.

The left's phony objections to Clinton's behavior at the beginning of the Lewinsky scandal were frauds from the outset. The *Washington Post* and *New York Times* had to fake indignation in order to lull the American people into believing liberals have scruples. This is the way liberals always avoid taking action against other liberals. They furrow their brows and dutifully register some vague consternation, for which they expect great admiration. With their impeccable consciences duly placed on the record, they believe no further action should be required of them. Only after uttering their sham indignation could the inexorable mantras begin: *It's just about sex, right-wing Republicans, sexual McCarthyism, it's about sex, everyone lies about affairs, Ken Starr is a dangerous man, it's just about sex.* . . . The only reason liberals did not mount an immediate defense of Clinton was that it wouldn't have worked. If they had tried to defend Clinton in the initial shock of the scandal, liberals would have lost all credibility. The *Washington Post* and *New York Times* might as well have flown the hammer and sickle outside their newsrooms. Their purported scruples were nothing but strategic calculation. Early, tepid statements of consternation about Clinton would provide cover for the subsequent counterattack.

At every critical moment for the Democratic Party for the last fifty years liberals would wage monstrous campaigns of disinformation and liberal agitprop. Clinton was the Hiss affair at the end of the Cold War. The unbearable facts would have to be buried under a mountain of calumnies. As with all liberal behavior tropes, you could tell what they were up to by what they accused conservatives of. Liberals can't help projecting their own malevolence onto others. The spontaneous and genuine outrage at Clinton was written off as the work of a "conspiracy." The media pretended to search desperately for clues. Who was the leader of this "vast right-wing conspiracy"? Was it Lucianne Goldberg? Richard Mellon Scaife? The Federalist Society? Liberals waged a conscious conspiracy directed from the White House, and then acted as if conservatives were part of a conspiracy. The tactics once used to prop up Soviet spies were later deployed to save a cheap flimflam artist. Threatened with ultimate defeat, the Democratic Party would stay in the game through massive, all-out counterattacks.

In a speech at the University of Notre Dame in the first year of his presidency, Reagan told the students that, someday, their hour would come "to explain to another generation the meaning of the past and thereby hold out to them the promise of the future."[28] Liberals wrote the history of the Hiss-Chambers battle and it took forty years to prove Chambers was telling the truth. Liberals wrote the history of McCarthyism and to this day no one knows that McCarthy was right. Liberals wrote the history of Watergate and consequently, no one has the first idea what that even was. Already liberals are trying to rewrite the history of the Cold War to remove Reagan from its core, to make him a doddering B-movie actor who happened to be standing there when the Soviet Union imploded. They have the media, the universities, the textbooks. We have ourselves. We are the witnesses.

11

NEVILLE CHAMBERLAIN HAD HIS REASONS, TOO: TREMBLING IN THE SHADOW OF BRIE

While the form of treachery varies slightly from case to case, liberals always manage to take the position that most undermines American security. Demonstrating their commitment to the war on terrorism, for example, liberals strenuously opposed America doing anything. Like their delayed-reaction defense of Clinton, liberals were tepidly supportive of war with Afghanistan immediately after 9-11, but were adamantly opposed to war with Iraq. There was no real organization to the Democrats' arguments against deposing Saddam Hussein, but a lot of hot indignation. Liberals demanded endless "inspections" and "dialogue" and yet more U.N. resolutions. They confidently asserted that Saddam was not an "imminent threat," but then said we couldn't attack because he might use weapons of mass destruction against our troops. They would try the preemptive action argument for a while and then drop that and insist with real earnestness that we work through "the allies." Then, they'd forget about the allies and say we should be attacking Saudi Arabia. They stamped their feet demanding discussion and then had nothing in particular to discuss, except to say that "of course" Saddam Hussein is detestable, but why didn't George Bush sign Kyoto? And then after one year of all their blather, liberals complained we were "rushing" to war.

For purposes of artful dodging, liberals would always insist that *of course* Saddam was despicable and must go. Just not yet! First, there were many worthless objections to be raised. Every single Democrat called Saddam Hussein "despicable." "Despicable" is evidently what Democrats call problems they have no intention of addressing. Republicans should start referring to inadequate arts funding and large class size as "despicable." The Associated Press reported, "The Democrats always preface comments on Iraq with a general statement that Saddam must go."[1] Whenever a liberal begins a peevish complaint with a throat-clearing equivocation like "Of course, we all agree," your antennae should go up. This is how liberals couch statements they assume all Americans would demand they make, but which they secretly chafe at. Liberals are masters at simulating agreement with normal people when they believe just the opposite. *I disagree with the American people but you can't catch me.*

Liberal sophistry required pretending they supported America's winning the war on terrorism—and before that, winning the Cold War. They just have a different plan of action. Fascinatingly, liberal proposals for achieving the goals—about which "of course, we all agree"—are invariably the opposite of what any normal person might think would work. Instead of punishing bad behavior and rewarding good behavior, liberals often feel it is the better part of valor to reward bad behavior and punish good behavior. Of course, we all agree that Fidel Castro is a bad man. That's why we need to lift travel restrictions and trade with Cuba! Of course, everyone would like to see Saddam Hussein removed from power. That's why we must not do anything to

remove him from power! Only in the case of smoking do liberals enthusiastically embrace the otherwise mystifying concept of punishing bad
behavior. The "of course, we all agree" hedge at least proves that liberals are under no illusions about the popularity of what they really
believe.

Both living former Democratic presidents, as well as the man liberals thought should be president—Al Gore—argued strenuously
against invading Iraq. Carter said even if the United States produced
compelling evidence that Saddam Hussein possessed weapons of mass
destruction, "this will not indicate any real or proximate threat by Iraq
to the United States or to our allies."[2] After a decade of Iraq ignoring
U.N. Security Council resolutions and lying to weapons inspectors,
Carter urged that we stick with U.N. inspectors.[3] Bill Clinton said, "I'm
all for fighting and staying in Afghanistan and getting bin Laden and
being tough about that—that's fine."[4] That's "fine"? America was in a
death match with dagger-wielding savages, and the ex-president acted
as if he was doing us a favor by not opposing all antiterrorism efforts.
Gore said that "all Americans should acknowledge that Iraq does,
indeed, pose a serious threat to the stability of the Persian Gulf
region." But before invading Iraq, Gore said we needed to establish
peace in the Middle East, create a perfect Jeffersonian democracy in
Afghanistan, and get the America-hating French and Germans on
board. Also cure baldness and put a man on Mars. Then the time
would be ripe for a preemptive attack! Unless liberals could find something in outer space that demanded our attention.

To show we really meant business, Gore said we should not get side-
tracked by a madman developing weapons of mass destruction who
threatened his neighbors and once tried to assassinate the president of
the United States. Rather, Gore said the U.S. military should spend the
next twenty years sifting through rubble in Tora Bora until they produce
Osama bin Laden's DNA. "I do not believe that we should allow ourselves to be distracted from this urgent task," he said, "simply because
it is proving to be more difficult and lengthy than predicted."[5] Al Bore

wanted to put the war on terrorism in a lockbox. This was the man Democrats claim—in their sportsmanlike way—"won" the presidential election. He was the Democrats' most esteemed political figure after Saddam
Hussein. Men don't begrudge women their chattering fearfulness, but
these are people who think they should be running the country.

Democrats made a big point of opposing every antiterrorism initiative on the grounds that Bush should be single-mindedly focused on
capturing Osama bin Laden. They seemed to imagine that President
Bush was supposed to be spending his time in Arab bazaars offering
bribes to people who might have known where Osama was. It would
have made more sense to carp about sending troops to Normandy when
we really needed to be "focusing on Adolf Hitler." Bernie Sanders,
Socialist congressman from Vermont, said, "The man who killed 3,000
innocent Americans, his name is not Saddam Hussein. His name is
Osama bin Laden."[6] Representative Dennis Kucinich, Democratic
presidential candidate and strange-looking little man, said, "Iraq was
not responsible for the attack on the World Trade Center or the Pentagon." These were perilous times for the Democrats: What excuse would
they use to oppose the war on terrorism after Osama bin Laden was
captured? With each additional capture of a major al-Qaeda leader, it
turned out that, unlike the Democrats, a Republican administration
could chew gum and walk at the same time. The Democrats' infantile
obsession with Osama bin Laden to the exclusion of all other Islamic
terrorism allowed them to sound like hawks while opposing every
aspect of the war on terrorism.

If America's entire national defense effort came down to the capture of one man, then the only justification for war was a connection to
Osama bin Laden. For this there was "no evidence." What liberals
mean by "no evidence" is always that there's plenty of evidence,
though arguably not enough to convince an O.J. jury. The *New York
Times* assured its readers that there is "no reliable evidence" that Saddam is connected to the September 11 attack or to al-Qaeda and
opposed war with Iraq until a "future link between Iraq and terrorism"
could be established.[7] The *Times* also cheerfully announced that there

was "no evidence so far that Baghdad means to share its deadly arse-nal with others." So the only guy with the deadly arsenal was a mad-man who gassed his own people, murdered his family members, and passionately yearned for the total annihilation of the United States. Well, that's a relief.

Days before the *Times*'s "No Evidence" editorial ran, Khidir Hamza, a former member of Iraq's weapons-building program, told the Senate Foreign Relations Committee that Saddam was actively devel-oping weapons of mass destruction and would have accumulated enough enriched uranium to have three nuclear bombs by 2005. The *New York Times* dealt with this information by not reporting it. Sworn statements given to a Senate committee by a former member of Sad-dam's government presumably constitute "no evidence." It was undis-puted that Saddam Hussein had used chemical and biological weapons in the past.[8] There was some "evidence" that he was working feverishly to create a nuclear bomb. Apparently it would take a mush-room cloud over Manhattan and Washington to satisfy the exacting threshold of "evidence" demanded at the *Baghdad Times.*

ABC's *World News Tonight* ran a breathless report titled "Reality Check: No Evidence Whatsoever of Iraq–Al Qaeda Connection." ABC's Martha Raddatz assured viewers: "A senior intelligence official tells ABC News there is no smoking gun. There's not even a smoking unfired weapon, linking al Qaeda and Iraq."[9] On National Public Radio, John Mearsheimer, a University of Chicago professor, said Bush had not been able to provide "credible evidence" that "Osama bin Laden and Saddam Hussein are joined at the hip."[10] Is that what lib-erals were waiting for?

On *The McLaughlin Group,* Michael Barone fleshed out the "no evidence!" talking point with Eleanor Clift:

> **MR. BARONE:** Eleanor, if you read Michael Ledeen's book,
> *The Terror Masters,* you will find that the secular and the
> religious terrorists and the terror masters work together all
> the time.

MS. CLIFT: No evidence.

MR. BARONE: You ought to take a look at the book. There is a great deal of evidence.

MS. CLIFT: No evidence![11]

Barone could have said Saddam Hussein was a "very bad man" and Eleanor Clift would have shouted, "No evidence!"

Even accepting the ludicrous idea that Saddam's weapons of mass destruction posed no threat to America unless Bush could produce cell phone records connecting Saddam to Mohammed Atta, by September 2002, there was at least some evidence of a link between Saddam and the September 11 terrorists. Czech intelligence claimed that five months before his monstrous attack, Atta met with an Iraqi agent in Prague. The CIA discounted that claim, but it's not "no evidence."

There was more. Former director of the CIA James Woolsey was sent by the U.S. government to England soon after 9-11 to investigate any connections between Iraq and al-Qaeda's terrorist attacks on the U.S. Woolsey concluded there were, saying the evidence was "about as clear as these things get."[12] Amid a raft of disclaimers, ABC's *Nightline* interviewed two Iraqis imprisoned by the Kurds, both of whom asserted that there was a working relationship between al-Qaeda and Iraq. Abu Aman Amaleeki said, "There is a relationship between the leaders of al-Qaeda and the Iraqi government. It began approximately after the invasion of Kuwait."[13] Another captured prisoner, Muhammed Mansur Shihabili, said he had killed "for the Iraqi intelligence and al-Qaeda."[14] *No evidence!*

In addition, people arguably as credible as anonymous officials quoted in the *New York Times* kept saying Iraq was working with al-Qaeda. National Security Advisor Condoleezza Rice said, "Yes, there are contacts between Iraq and al-Qaeda."[15] Defense Secretary Donald Rumsfeld said, "Iraq provided unspecified training, relating to chemical and/or biological matters, for al-Qaeda members."[16] He specifically said, "If you're asking, are there al-Qaeda in Iraq, the answer is yes, there are. It's a fact."[17] ABC News questioned the objectivity of Rumsfeld and Rice, noting their "clear" motive for connecting al-Qaeda to

Iraq: "It provides yet another rationale—terrorism—for American military action."[18] Okay, but denying a connection between al-Qaeda and Iraq provides yet another rationale for America *not* taking any military action. So where does that get us? Why are only the statements of anti-war Democrats treated as objective statements of the truth?

Liberals so loved the sound of the ringing peroration "No evidence!" that they began popping up all over to pronounce that there was "no evidence" supporting this or that argument for war. Senator Dianne Feinstein (D-Cal.) said there was "no evidence" that Saddam was "an imminent threat," "no evidence" that he was "nuclear-capable today," and "no evidence" that China is covertly assisting the Iraqis to develop any weapons, including nuclear.[19] So Saddam was merely a future threat who would soon have nuclear weapons. Representative Jim McDermott (D-Wash.) told CNBC's Brian Williams, "We do not need to invade to destroy the weapons. There's no evidence for that."[20] Representative Diana DeGette (D-Colo.) said, "We have been in briefings for the last week and we have seen no evidence of imminent danger."[21]

During the Senate debate, Senator Jim Jeffords (I-Vt.) said that, while there was "much speculation" about Saddam Hussein's weapons of mass destruction, there was "no evidence that he has developed nuclear capability and less that he could deliver it."[22] Less than no evidence. Jeffords, whose earlier history-making moment was to leave the Republican Party after Bush was elected president, also said Saddam wouldn't use weapons of mass destruction after he has "paid so dearly" to acquire them. As the saying goes, when Jeffords switched parties, it improved the average IQ of both parties.

"No evidence" became the Democrats' battle cry. It was used as often as the impeachment-era phrase "does not rise to the level of," often applied to utterly absurd scenarios. Representative Dennis Kucinich (D-Ohio) astutely pointed out, "They have no evidence or even a reasonable suspicion that Saddam Hussein was involved in any way with the anthrax attacks."[23] Was that the crucial question in the debate on Iraq? Whether Saddam had sent the anthrax? These people didn't want a smoking gun: They wanted a smoking U.S. city.

Liberals also denounced Bush for staging a "preemptive" attack against Iraq. Gore claimed Bush was "proclaiming a new, uniquely American right to preemptively attack whomsoever he may deem represents a potential future threat." He warned, "The apprehensions in the rest of the world" were "not calmed down any by this doctrine of preemption that they are now asserting."[24] Once Gore hit the tuning fork, all the Democrats started vibrating in harmony. Giving a speech in London, Clinton said, "A preemptive action today, however justified, may come back with unwelcome consequences in the future."[25] Senator Tom Daschle worried about the "message" it would send to the rest of the world, saying to act "in a preemptive manner would be a terrible tragedy and set all the wrong precedents and send the wrong messages to the world community."[26] What message would that be? That the U.S. will act decisively to prevent rogue nations from developing nuclear weapons? Isn't that the message we were trying to send? It's clear why America's enemies wouldn't care for that message, but why would any American be against it?

A writer for the *Los Angeles Times* summarized the Democrats' argument, explaining that "attacking Iraq now would give license for other nations to invade antagonists they consider potential threats. Think India and Pakistan, or China and Taiwan."[27] That's a blockbuster of an argument. It is like the brilliant riposte "Who are you to say?" *Who are we to say when America can attack another country?* I don't know, why not us? If the French found the Eiffel Tower and Arc de Triomphe in rubble, would they seek our permission before launching their cheeses of mass destruction?

The *New York Times* ("Europe's Best Newspaper") was in a panic over the shocking Bush policy of deploying American troops in order to protect American interests. The only just wars, liberals believe, are those in which the United States has no stake. Thus, the *Times* and various McTimes across the nation kept touting the idea that invading Iraq "only" to produce a regime change was unjustifiable, contrary to international law, and a grievous affront to the peace-loving Europeans. As the left's new pet, Henry "No Longer a War Criminal" Kissinger, said, "Regime change as a goal for military intervention challenges the international system established by the 1648 Treaty of Westphalia. . . . And the notion of justified preemption runs counter to modern international law, which sanctions the use of force in self-defense only against actual, not potential, threats."[28]

The idea that America would be transgressing the laws of man and God by invading Iraq—unless and until Saddam nukes Manhattan—was absurd. Did no one remember Clinton's misadventure in the Balkans? Liberals loved that war because Slobodan Milosevic posed no conceivable threat to the United States. To the contrary, as President Clinton put it, "This is America at its best. We seek no territorial gain; we seek no political advantage." Deposing Milosevic, Clinton explained, vindicated no national interest, but was urgent because it was akin to stopping a "hate crime." One searched in vain for a description of some American interest in the Balkans. For the record, there was no U.N. Security Council approval for Clinton's unprovoked attack on the Serbs.

Instead of droning on about "human dignity" and "human rights," why shouldn't American foreign policy be based on the national interest? When did self-defense become a less respectable cause for war than liberation of oppressed peoples? As it turned out, the Democrats were overhasty in their use of the word "genocide" in connection with Milosevic. Clinton's defense secretary, William Cohen, estimated that 100,000 Albanian civilians "may have been murdered." In the end, the International Criminal Tribunal for the former Yugoslavia found fewer than 3,000 bodies, most of them men of military age. That doesn't make Milosevic a hero, but he's a piker compared to Saddam, who has gassed tens of thousands of his own people and God knows how many enemy troops. So it's especially striking that liberals opposed a war with Iraq, despite Saddam's far more impressive credentials as a mass murderer.

If they were enthusiastic about deposing Milosevic, liberals should have been burning with desire to take out Saddam Hussein. But they were not: Deposing Saddam was in the self-interest of the United

States. Only a war that serves no conceivable national interest gets the *New York Times*'s endorsement. Liberals warm to the idea of American mothers weeping for their sons, but only if their deaths will not make America any safer. The point—which is always the same point—is that we must not protect ourselves. Liberals believe they are best qualified in war and peace and forced busing because they aren't going to suffer the consequences. They seemed not to understand that—unlike their other insane policies—keeping Saddam Hussein in power would affect their children, too. Nuclear annihilation cannot be safely confined to the outer boroughs.

The left's counterintuitive national security positions are always backed up with long, complicated explanations about the dire risk of encouraging "hard-liners," inciting the enemy's "paranoia," or annoying what are comically known as "the allies." The arguments not only make no sense ab initio, but openly contradict one another. Though the Democrats would later decide that for their defeatist objectives, Saddam Hussein was irrelevant to the "war on terrorism," immediately after the terrorist attack, they began complaining that former president Bush had not "finished off the job" with Saddam Hussein in the 1991 Gulf War. The Democrats hadn't supported starting that war, much less finishing it. Forty-eight Democrats in the Senate voted against the Gulf War. Only ten Senate Democrats supported it—and the only one north of the Mason-Dixon Line was Senator Joe Lieberman. Indeed, this is Senator Lieberman's one codpiece for the claim he's a "different kind of Democrat."

Clinton's secretary of state, Madeleine Albright, opposed the 1991 war with Iraq, but a decade later she, too, was carping about the first Bush administration not finishing the job she hadn't wanted to start.[29] When America was again poised to depose Saddam in 2002, Albright was against it. As she explained in a *New York Times* op-ed, Saddam Hussein had used chemical weapons, he probably had "significant quantities of biological warfare agents and some chemical munitions," and he was "striving to acquire or develop nuclear weapons." But America should do nothing. Iraq, Albright said, was not "the right focus" in the war on terrorism. The "right focus" was getting the United Nations to issue yet another useless ultimatum.[30] Saddam had ignored scores of such ultimatums throughout Albright's tenure as secretary of state to no ill effect. But she confidently asserted that Saddam "must surely be aware that if he ever again tries to attack another country he will be obliterated."[31] By whom? Not us—our liberals wouldn't let us. Democrats always assure us that deterrence will work, but when the time comes to deter, they're against it.

A *New York Times* editorial urged patient suasion with the harmless and misunderstood Saddam Hussein, demanding that "every available diplomatic option" be exhausted. In the breezy style the *Times* uses for all its crackpot ideas, it explained that America need only "ensure that Iraq is disarmed of all unconventional weapons." Meanwhile, the same editorial warned against invading Iraq on the grounds that "there may be no way to deter Iraq from using unconventional weapons against American forces."[32] Weren't we easily disarming Saddam of unconventional weapons a couple paragraphs back? They wanted to play a game of cat and mouse with Saddam Hussein and his weapons of mass destruction. Liberals said we didn't have to worry if Saddam gets nuclear weapons because he is a reasonable man. He would never use them, they assure us, because he "knows" the U.S. would destroy him. We could just disarm him—but that wouldn't be fair! That wouldn't even give him a sporting chance to build a nuclear weapon.

Liberals longed to create a nuclear standoff with a madman feverishly developing weapons of mass destruction, who gassed his own people and watched torture videos for fun. On the basis of how liberals reacted to Mutually Assured Destruction with the Soviet Union, Americans should have been terrified that they were recommending it again with Iraq. MAD was bad enough with the Soviet Union but there was a certain illiterate logic to it. Most obviously, the Soviet Union already had nuclear weapons. Saddam Hussein didn't. Why did liberals want to let him get there? It was at least vaguely credible that the U.S. would use nuclear weapons to stop the Soviets from rolling into Paris.

The French may not have been willing to fight for Paris in 1940, but we kept assuring our NATO "partners" that we would defend them with our nukes. It is not very credible that the U.S. would risk nuclear attack on our forces to defend Kuwait. Liberals weren't too keen on defending Europe; the Middle East has fewer attractions and the people are no more charming than the French. With all of the gnashing of teeth over attacking Iraq *before* Saddam had nuclear weapons, how much worse would it be if he did? Would liberals favor risking a nuclear attack on our troops "just for oil"?

The last time we faced a horrible adversary with nuclear weapons, towns throughout Vermont declared themselves "nuclear free zones."[33] Brown University students demanded cyanide pills in the event of a nuclear attack. There were glowing portraits in the *New York Times* about groups like European Nuclear Disarmament, calling for unilateral nuclear disarmament.[34] There were endless op-eds about the "suicidal" arms buildup of "these doomsday weapons."[35] In theory, peaceniks claimed they wanted "both sides" to disarm. But as George Orwell said during World War II, "Since pacifists have more freedom of action in countries where traces of democracy survive, pacifism can act more effectively against democracy than for it." In practical effect, the "pacifist" was pro-Nazi.[36]

With Iraq we had a chance to avoid a nuclear standoff with a totalitarian despot and avoid the insane stasis of Mutually Assured Destruction, but liberals counseled restraint. Put that off for another day—when the despot has a nuclear weapon and liberals can scream about nuclear winter while letting Saddam run wild throughout the Middle East. Democrats were panicked at the idea that America might defend itself by attacking Iraq, but were perfectly copacetic about living in a radioactive world. What liberals were really saying was that the U.S. should get out of the region and resign itself to whatever happens. Don't rush into war when you can console yourself with preemptive surrender! So what if Saddam eventually gets control of half the world's oil? That would be a fitting punishment for the U.S.'s rejection of the Kyoto Treaty!

Liberals didn't want to talk about what would happen if Saddam acquired nuclear weapons, but kept claiming they did want to talk about something before invading Iraq. They said they wanted more "discussion" and that they had lots and lots of questions. The insistent demand for "more discussion" about Iraq tended to leave the impression that these Democrats had something on their minds. But they never had anything to say—except that we needed "more discussion."

In September 2002, "legendary newsman," "national treasure," and pompous liberal gasbag Walter Cronkite complained on *Larry King Live* that there had not been sufficient "discussion" of the plan with Iraq. He said, "We haven't had the discussion yet. We've had unilateral approach by this administration to a unilateral solution." Uttering the classic liberal equivocation that Saddam Hussein was cause for "deep concern," Cronkite stated categorically, "We don't have adequate evidence now" to invade Iraq. This is evidently what passes for "discussion" in Manhattan salons. It was "very important," "terribly important," and "terribly important" again, that there be "wide open discussion" in Congress and by the public "as to the wisdom of the Iraqi program." The quiescence of the Democrats left Cronkite "very, very surprised." But he looked forward to their pointless nay-saying in the future. (He wouldn't have to wait long.)

Walter Cronkite was inconsolable that the press hadn't succeeded in demoralizing the country in the war on terrorism. During the Vietnam War, the "most trusted man in America" managed to persuade America that the Tet offensive had been a defeat. After watching Cronkite's coverage of the Christmas bombing of Hanoi in December 1972, Ronald Reagan told President Nixon that "under World War II circumstances, the network would have been charged with treason."[37] On *Larry King* in 2002, Cronkite was hearkening back to the halcyon days when the media could control the public's perception of a war. The president of the Ho Chi Minh Admiration Society said the media were not "adequately skeptical" of the information they were getting from the administration and "passing that skepticism along to the American people." Frustratingly, Americans were supporting America.

He was disappointed that the press had not been able to suppress President Bush's soaring approval ratings: "When [Bush] speaks, he's listened to. When he speaks, he gets time on the air. . . . So you've got to expect some of that."[38] Uncle Walter explained the widespread support for war, saying the public was "not very keen, not very aware, not very sophisticated about getting the information it needs."[39]

After liberals had nearly tired themselves out discussing the need for more discussion, on October 7, 2002, the president of the United States gave a speech on the precise topic they all claimed to be burning with desire to "discuss." Fox was the only broadcast network to cover it. ABC, NBC, and CBS—Cronkite's old network—did not cover the president's speech. According to the *New York Times*, the major networks did not run Bush's speech because "the administration did not expressly ask them to."[40] And thus ended the We-Need-More-Discussion argument.

Among the constantly scrolling series of objections to disarming Saddam Hussein, liberals argued that al-Qaeda hated Saddam because he was a secularist, but also warned that if we attacked Iraq, al-Qaeda would retaliate with new terrorist attacks against America. They said Saddam Hussein was not the enemy because he wasn't a real Muslim. But they also said the terrorists weren't real Muslims. They made the singular argument that only the rich clamored for war with Iraq because their children wouldn't fight it. If only the rich were for the war, Central Park West and Amagansett would have been ablaze with war fever as peace marches swept through humble middle-class neighborhoods. It was the effete rich who yearned for appeasement. But it was touching to have liberals claiming to be worried about "our" fighting boys, inasmuch as the left had never shown themselves to be particularly enamored of the military before. It would be enough if liberals would just pipe down a little the next time "our" fighting boys are caught pinching a few giggling drunks at Tailhook. CNN's Judy Woodruff made the remarkable argument that Iraq was simply too small to attack. In response to Bush's 2003 State of the Union address, Woodruff said, "Maybe I'm the only one here, but I'm still marveling at the notion that one-third of the president's State of the Union address was devoted to a country the size of California."[41] Who cares if Saddam was developing nukes to hand over to al-Qaeda? Iraq doesn't have the square footage to rate!

In an amazing ruse, the left simultaneously blamed Israel and used Israel as an excuse not to take out Saddam Hussein. While secretly yearning for the extermination of Israel, liberals demanded that Bush resolve the Israel-Palestinian crisis "first." Before taking out a lunatic developing nuclear weapons, liberals said, Bush would have to solve a problem that hadn't been solved in fifty years. Of course, if Iraq developed a nuclear bomb, the first victim would be an imperiled civil society of Jews. One way to get Yasser Arafat back to the bargaining table would have been to take out Saddam Hussein and eliminate a principal funding source for Palestinian terrorism. But liberals insisted the Israel-Palestinian problem had to be solved "first."

When none of their other arguments worked, liberals would trot out their demands for "multilateralism," and U.N.ism, and working with "the allies." The left's theory of a just war had evolved to (1) military force must never be deployed in America's self-interest; and (2) we must first receive approval from the Europeans, especially the Germans. Good thing we didn't have that rule in 1941.

Walter Cronkite considered it axiomatic that the United States would subject its survival to veto by the United Nations: "It is, I hope," he said, "the intention of the United States to take the matter to the United Nations and work with the United Nations." Meanwhile, back at the U.N., they were issuing resolutions demanding that Britain repeal a law that allows parents to spank their children. Cronkite appeared to fear that America would outlast him. Peculiarly, Cronkite insisted upon agreement from "the other Arab nations." In the sort of meaningless pontification that enthralls Martha's Vineyard matrons, Cronkite said that without the support of other Arab nations "we might win a war and never establish a peace again with those people."[42] In December 2001, Senator Tom Daschle, too, was demanding approval from the "Arab allies": "A strike against Iraq would be a mistake. It would complicate Middle Eastern diplomacy. . . . I think we have to keep the pressure on Iraq in a collective way, with our Arab allies. Unilateralism is a very dangerous concept. I don't think we should ever act unilaterally." How about Saddam Hussein? Should we have gotten him in the "coalition" before taking action against Iraq?

Assuredly, it would be better if the U.S. never had to go to war without lots of allies. It would be better if we could have precisely calibrated Saddam's progress in acquiring nuclear arms. It would also have been better if instead of greeting the Wehrmacht with open arms, the French had fought back. It would have been better. Be it so. We don't choose the circumstances in which we must exhibit our will as a nation. This is the price of manhood—acting when you must and not complaining that someone might get hurt.

Americans were solidly behind the president in fighting terrorism, so liberals went and sulked with their cheese-tasting friends. They literally had to go to Europe to get extraterritorial votes for appeasement. The demand for support from "the allies" was a classic political move: Expand the electorate to include your political allies. That's why Republicans wanted to enfranchise blacks, prohibitionists wanted to enfranchise women, and Democrats want to enfranchise felons. Indeed, the main opponents to the suffrage movement were liquor companies (apparently anticipating Mothers Against Drunk Driving). So it's interesting that, when it came to America's self-defense, Democrats wanted to expand the electorate to Europeans. The very idea of foreigners voting on America's national security is absurd. How about getting them to vote on the country's smoking policies? Public opinion in Europe was strongly against the United States. Of course, public opinion in Europe was also for pogroms. Liberals were pimping for the most despicable people in Europe, demanding that these moral paragons be given a vote on America's national defense.

The concept of "allies" had become rather elastic. We certainly didn't need countries like France for their military contributions. The Warsaw Ghetto held off the Nazis almost as long as did the entire nation of France. Perhaps they could supply our troops with their 265 brands of cheese. Still, Democrats were insistent that America had to give the Vichy government a veto over U.S. foreign policy. We had Australia, Spain, Italy, the Czech Republic, Qatar, Turkey, and Romania and dozens of others on our side. How many countries did we need? Apparently, France and Germany. Only then would it be a "multilateral coalition."

Back in December 1998, when Clinton bombed Iraq to delay his impeachment, Democrats weren't particularly worried about what the "allies" would think. Tom Daschle said, "This is a time to send Saddam Hussein as clear a message as we know how to send that we will not tolerate the broken promises and the tremendous acceleration of development of weapons that we've seen time and time again in Iraq."[43] Madeleine Albright opposed war with Iraq in 1991 and 2003. But she was solidly behind Clinton's impeachment bombing of Iraq, saying, "Month after month, we have given Iraq chance after chance to move from confrontation to cooperation, and we have explored and exhausted every diplomatic action. We will see now whether force can persuade Iraq's misguided leaders to reverse course and to accept at long last the need to abide by the rule of law and the will of the world."[44] Only when we had a president who wanted to attack Iraq for purposes of national security, rather than his own self-interest, did Democrats think he was being rash. Democrats are always hawks in the off-season.

Fortunately, Americans disagreed with the Democrats and overwhelmingly supported war with Iraq. In the first six months of 2002, the ABC News–*Washington Post* Poll showed 72 percent supporting a U.S. invasion of Iraq. The Fox News–Opinion Dynamics Poll also had 72 percent supporting it. The *Newsweek* poll showed 68 percent in favor. The least support for an attack came in an NBC News–*Wall Street Journal* Poll showing only 57 percent in favor of attacking Iraq. It was a measure of how strong support was for war that the *New York Times* couldn't even produce some phony poll supporting its own evident desire to keep Saddam Hussein in power. (In 1984, about three months before Reagan would win forty-nine states in the largest electoral landslide in history, a *Times* columnist reported that Mondale "led President Reagan in a recent Gallup-*Newsweek* poll.")[45]

Lugubrious over the vast public support in America for attacking Iraq, the media began doing push-polling for the House of Saud. ABC's *World News Tonight* optimistically reported that support for war was "highly conditional, dropping below 50 percent when tougher questions are asked."[46] Support seemed to decline with such follow-up questions as these:

Suppose it were your daughter being sent to war and she would be horribly raped and maimed and disfigured by Iraqi forces. Do you support going to war NOW?

If it meant calamitous casualties and total humiliation for the U.S., then would you STILL support war?

Should America go out into the shivering world all alone or would it be better to have our dearly beloved allies on board?

Even with their idiotic poll questions, the media could not suppress support for war, so they generally dispensed with polls altogether and ran ludicrous man-on-the-street interviews instead. Amazingly, all the random Americans interviewed by the *New York Times* were firmly opposed to war with Iraq. This allowed the *Times* to run breathtakingly dishonest headlines in a country burning with war fever, such as, "Backing Bush All the Way, Up to but Not into Iraq."[47] The media love these unrepresentative, dishonest man-on-the-street interviews because they can present 100 percent of the defeatist case against war without anyone ever being able to quote them. In October 2002, ABC's Peter Jennings proclaimed that the "country appears to be less confident than the President" about war with Iraq.[48] Jennings's assessment was based on interviews with about a dozen people. As with the average Americans interviewed by the *New York Times,* everyone consulted by ABC happened to oppose the war, offering such important insights as "I'm frightened."[49] ABC's Bill Redeker summed up the prevailing mood of the nation, saying, "Contrary to what the President says, when it comes to war, America does not speak with one voice." Maybe not, but sixty-seven percent is about as close as it ever gets.

In a country of almost 300 million people, liberals get seven men to issue an opinion from the Supreme Court and they want the rest of us to shut up about abortion forevermore. But before going to war to eliminate a potential nuclear threat, we need to convince every last American that war is necessary. Liberals seem to believe total unanimity is possible from watching Iraqi elections. Reporting on an election in Iraq in which Saddam Hussein won 99.96 percent of the vote, ABC's David Wright said, "It is impossible to say whether that's a true measure of the Iraqi people's feelings."[50] Really? Impossible to say? ABC knew exactly how "the country" feels about war with Iraq ("less confident than the President") but were unsure about the accuracy of an election in which Saddam Hussein won 99.96 percent of the vote.

Finally, after nine months of the media's demoralization techniques, the *Times* took its first poll in September 2002, asking Americans if they supported war with Iraq. Sixty-eight percent supported war, and only 24 percent were opposed. The headline was "Poll Finds Unease on Terror Fight and Concerns About War on Iraq."[51] One month later, the *Times* again polled Americans on support for military action against Iraq. Again, 67 percent of Americans favored a U.S. invasion to depose Saddam Hussein and only 27 percent were opposed. This time, the headline was "Public Says Bush Needs to Pay Heed to Weak Economy."[52] An editorial about the poll the next day was titled "A Nation Wary of War."[53] The *Times* characterized a poll that showed 67 percent of Americans in favor of war with Iraq as showing the country was "reluctant" to go to war and "uncertain how best to deal with Iraq."[54] That's if you didn't count the two-thirds who wanted to attack. When liberals get a poll result they like, they instantly seize on it to demand that the entire country "move on." But when they get a poll result they don't like, it means we need to have a national discussion. The editorial said Bush "still has work to do if he hopes to persuade Americans of the need to use military force to disarm Iraq." Sixty-seven percent! Do we have to have 100 percent approval before defending America's security?

Of course, it is impossible to have 100 percent support for defending America because some Americans are liberals. Journalists in particular simply could not make a psychological connection between

America's defeat and their dying. National Public Radio reporter Nina Totenberg described Saddam Hussein as a personal bugaboo of the president. Of Bush's focus on Saddam Hussein, she said, "Maybe . . . one ought not pick one's targets based, at least in part, on who tried to kill one's dad."[55] Maureen Dowd also viewed war with Iraq as merely a grudge match for the president, saying Bush had left "poor Tony Blair to make the case against *his foes* for him, and treat[ed] policy disagreements as personal slights" (emphasis added). Saddam Hussein is merely Bush's personal foe. Liberals so adored Islamic terrorists they assumed the feeling was mutual. After 9-11, college dropout Michael Moore indignantly wrote, "If someone did this to get back at Bush, then they did so by killing thousands of people who did not vote for him! Boston, New York, D.C., and the planes' destination of California—these were places that voted against Bush! Why kill them?"[56]

There were other subtle hints that the media were not keen on America. The *New York Times* was in a rapture when it discovered that nine days after September 11, Fox News chairman Roger Ailes had sent a letter to the Bush White House recommending we get rough with the terrorists.[57] This was even bigger than Enron: A highly placed member of the news establishment wanted America to win the war on terrorism. As far as the *Times* was concerned, Ailes's recommendation that harsh measures be taken against the terrorists was the smoking gun of partisanship. The paper railed that Ailes purports to be an "unbiased journalist, not a conservative spokesman." Fox News is "the self-proclaimed fair and balanced news channel." But now the *Times* had caught him red-handed, pursuing "an undisguised ideological agenda."[58] Ailes was rooting for America! It's so obvious that liberals root against their own country that it didn't even occur to anyone at the *Times* that its attack on Ailes's "partisanship" had given up the ghost on their faux patriotism. At least we finally had it from the horse's mouth.

Lawyers did their part for America, too, quickly changing their letterhead from anti-impeachment slogans to anti-war slogans. On the

"Law Professors for the Rule of Law" webpage, you could read either the professors' indignation about war with Iraq or their indignation about the Supreme Court's ruling in *Bush* v. *Gore*.[59] Also performing a vital service for America, on the first night of the war in Afghanistan, the Army's lawyer instructed the U.S. military not to shoot Talibanist Mullah Omar. Reportedly, when Secretary of Defense Donald Rumsfeld found out about this, he kicked in a glass door.[60]

Even for a naturally gaseous body, Democrats in Congress outdid themselves with their palaver about Iraq. Unlike the typical liberal cocktail party pedant, members of Congress would have to vote on Iraq—and then run for reelection. After spending the summer of 2002 yapping about how Bush had to consult Congress before invading Iraq, when Bush went to Congress for a war resolution, the Democrats got huffy at Bush for consulting them. Democrats were chafing at having to pretend they supported America. But they didn't want to have to say so until after the November elections. Democrats didn't think it was too close to an election to be switching Senate candidates in New Jersey, but it was definitely too close for a vote on Iraq.

On *Meet the Press*, Senator Hillary Clinton objected to having to vote on a war resolution before the elections, saying, "I don't know that we want to put it in a political context."[61] Yes, it would be an insult for politicians to have to inform the voters how they stand on important national security issues before an election. Minority Whip Nancy Pelosi (D-Calif.), the ranking Democrat on the House Intelligence Committee, said the Democrats would not have enough information to make an informed decision on Iraq—until January.[62] Even the press laughed at that one.

Senator Bob Byrd (D-KKK) tut-tutted the need for a resolution on Iraq, saying September 11 was "over a year old." What's the big hurry? Why is it so imminent? Why here and now? Why before the election? But back on August 30, 2002, Senator Byrd was denouncing Bush for allegedly bypassing Congress before taking action against Iraq. "Congress needs to act and vote," he said. "There needs to be a vote in Congress." Byrd said he had contacted "constitutional scholars, recognized constitutional scholars," and every one—"to the man and woman"—said the president was required "to ask the Congress for permission and to get authorization, new authorization to invade Iraq." The vain, ranting windbag of a kleptocrat said Bush should stop reading polls "and read this: the Constitution of the United States."[63] (Historical note: President Nixon was so enraged by the Senate Democrats' rejection of his Supreme Court nominees on the grounds that they were "mediocre," he toyed with the idea of nominating Byrd so he could really show them mediocre.)

In addition to the indignity of having to vote on a national security issue in an election year, Byrd said the resolution on Iraq was diverting attention from more important issues. Worse than "despicable," Byrd said Saddam Hussein was "lower than a snake's belly." And that's why it was very important that we do nothing. Imminent military action to remove a despot who longed for a mushroom cloud over the nation's capital was crowding out the big stuff like naming another building in West Virginia after Bob Byrd.

It was openly acknowledged that the Democrats opposed the war resolution, but that politics would force many of them to fake support for war with Iraq. CNN's Judy Woodruff told Ted Kennedy that some Democrats "are privately saying they are supporting the president, because they think it will hurt them politically if they go up against the president on this. They'll look unpatriotic." Kennedy agreed, saying there was "nothing terribly unusual" about politicians voting their "own political interests."[64] Peter Beinart of the *New Republic* said the Democrats in Congress were "terrified politically." He said many would vote for a war resolution "in the end" but that "in their heart of hearts, I think a lot of Democrats are opposed, but they don't have the intellectual self-confidence to actually come out and say so."[65]

Indeed, liberals were constantly admitting that it was the Democrat position to root against America. The *New York Times* reported: "Democratic congressmen who are visiting Iraq this week stirred up anger among some Republicans when they questioned the reasons President Bush has used to justify possible military action against

Iraq." Only Republicans were annoyed? Weren't any Democrats the tiniest bit irritated that members of Congress were meeting with a tyrant as the U.S. prepared to attack him? It is simply axiomatic that only Republicans would be irritated by treason. The raison d'etre of the Democratic Party demands the anti-war position.

In the final vote, Republicans overwhelmingly supported the war resolution against Iraq. Forty-eight Senate Republicans voted for the resolution and only one voted against (Lincoln Chafee). In the House, the vote was similarly lopsided, Republicans supporting the war by 215 to 6. House Democrats overwhelmingly opposed the Iraq resolution, voting 126 to 81 against.[66] In the Senate, where all members expect to run for president someday, the Democrats were split, with a slight majority voting in favor (29–21). The Democratic Party simply could not rouse itself to battle.

But don't call them unpatriotic. That makes them testy. Democrats believe they should be allowed to attack Bush relentlessly on foreign policy, but that it is outrageous for anyone to mention their stand on foreign policy. Gore said Bush's foreign policy "will damage our ability to win the war on terrorism" and "will weaken our ability to lead the world."[67] If any Republican says the same thing about Democrats, all hell breaks loose. As Chambers said, innocence does not utter outraged shrieks, guilt does.

Then–House minority leader Richard Gephardt bitterly criticized Vice President Dick Cheney for "saying that our nation's security efforts would be stronger if a Republican candidate for Congress were elected." Well, wouldn't it? When Senate Democrats refused to pass a Homeland Security bill unless it included the standard federal government proviso prohibiting incompetent workers from being fired, President Bush criticized the Democrats, saying they were "more interested in special interests in Washington and not interested in the security of the American people."[68] This was absolutely factually correct: The Democrats wanted standard civil service protections (special interests) to trump having competent workers at the Homeland Security Department (the security of the American people). Looking like an angry squirrel, then—Senate majority leader Tom Daschle marched to the Senate floor and passionately denounced George Bush for making an indisputably true statement. "You tell those who fought in Vietnam and in World War II they're not interested in the security of the American people! That is outrageous! That is outrageous!"[69] Democrats were beside themselves with indignation when they heard Karl Rove planned to raise the Republicans' demonstrable superiority on national security as a campaign issue. Inasmuch as vast majorities of Americans consistently rank Republicans as better on national defense, Rove evidently believed this was an argument that would resonate with voters.

At least when Republicans "politicize" the war, you know which side they're on. Republicans were for war with Iraq. The Democrats pretended to support the war when they were forced to vote before the November elections, but then instantly started in with their Neville Chamberlain foot-dragging. In a sea of umbrellas, they said they were for peace in our time. As President Abraham Lincoln said during the Civil War, the Democrats can "nominate a Peace Democrat on a War Platform or a War Democrat on a Peace Platform and I personally can't say that I much care which they do."[70]

Democratic presidential candidate and senator John Kerry voted for the war and then gave a major policy address months later, saying, "Mr. President, do not rush to war!" Rush to war? We had been talking about that war for over a year and it had been three months since Kerry duly recorded his vote in favor of the war. Evidently, Kerry had learned his lesson from the 1991 Gulf War. Kerry had voted against the former President Bush's war with Iraq, saying the country was "not yet ready for what it will witness and bear if we go to war." Having been taunted for that vote ever since, in 2002 Kerry made sure to vote in favor of war with Iraq—allowing the *New York Times* to call him a "moderate"—before he began attacking it.

Kerry explained his attack on a war he had voted for, saying he thought a resolution authorizing the president to use force against Iraq meant that the United Nations would have to approve. He claimed he was foursquare behind disarming Saddam Hussein, but not "until we have exhausted the remedies available, built legitimacy and earned the consent of the American people, absent, of course, an imminent threat requiring urgent action." Liberals believe all the results are in on global warming, but the situation in Iraq consistently required further study. By the time a threat from Islamic terrorists is "imminent," Chicago will be gone. This was the fundamental problem of the anti-war Democrats. They couldn't bring themselves to say it was a mistake to depose Saddam Hussein, and "don't hurry" was not much of a rallying cry.

Dianne Feinstein said she voted for the resolution assuming it meant we would invade only if "our allies" approved. Joe Biden made the terrific argument that if we didn't wait for U.N. approval, it would "make a mockery of the efficacy of the U.N." Perhaps the United Nations should have been more worried about that eventuality than we should. Senator Hillary Clinton voted in favor of the war resolution—and never had another kind word to say for the war. Months after her vote, Senator Clinton gave an interview on Irish TV in which she said she opposed precipitous action against Iraq. Hillary had not objected to precipitous action against Iraq when her husband bombed it on the day of his scheduled impeachment. That bombing raid was preceded by calm deliberation.

Aren't we entitled to ask: Did the Democrats support the war or didn't they? Why didn't they defend it? These Democrats wanted to have it both ways. If the war went well—a lot of them voted for war with Iraq, didn't they? But if the war did not go well, many of the very Democrats who voted for the war resolution had emerged as leading spokesmen for the anti-war position. That would be a real asset if the war went badly. On the eve of battle, Democrats were staking their political futures on the hope that their own country would falter.

In the Democrats' worst-case scenario, the United States would be acting precipitously to remove a ruthless dictator who tortured his own people. It's not as if anyone was worried we were making a horrible miscalculation and were about to depose the Iraqi Abraham Lincoln.

(Although Baath Party legend has it that a young Saddam once trudged twenty miles round-trip through the snow to rape and dismember a woman.) Either we were removing a dictator who had current plans to fund terrorism against Americans or—if Bush were completely wrong and Eleanor Clift were completely right—we were removing a dictator who planned to kill and terrorize a lot of people, but not Americans specifically. The Democrats did not merely question which was which, but were hysterically opposed to war.

They thought the important thing was to figure out why foreigners hate us. Gore said Bush had made the "rest of the world" angry at us. Boo hoo hoo. Stewing over the "profound and troubling change in the attitude of the German electorate toward the United States," Gore ruefully said that the German-American relationship was in "a dire crisis."[71] Alas, the Germans hated us. That same night, James Carville read from the identical talking points on CNN's *Crossfire:* "The Koreans hate us. Now the Germans—you know that's one against Germany. You know what? You know what? If we had a foreign policy that tried to get people to like us, as opposed to irritating everybody in the damn world, it would be a lot better thing." Perhaps we could get Djibouti to like us if we legalized clitorectomies for little girls.

According to *New York Times* columnist Thomas Friedman, the root cause of the world's hatred for America was Kyoto: "The unilateralist message the Bush team sent from its first day in office—get rid of the Kyoto climate treaty, forget the biological treaty, forget arms control, and if the world doesn't like it that's tough—has now come back to haunt us."[72] Instead of looking into the root causes of Islamic lunacy, how about looking into the root causes of manly patriotism? Why are liberals so loath of positive testosterone? Senator Dianne Feinstein said that while she was wearing an American-flag pin on a trip to Europe, the anti-American feeling was so strong, "I was embarrassed to wear it."[73] Democrats couldn't care less if people in Indiana hate them. But if Europeans curl their lips, liberals can't look at themselves in the mirror.

If they were worried about the Europeans, liberals were in a clinical depression over what the terrorists thought of us. Liberals instinctively responded to the attack of 9-11 by imputing their own hatred of America to camel-riding nomads. The nation had been attacked on its own shores, women widowed, children orphaned, thousands of our fellow countrymen killed. Liberals saw this as an occasion to ask: Why do they hate us? Only in the case of a terrorist attack on America are liberals consumed with the assailant's motive. How about: *Until we understand why rapists would rather violently rape a woman than take her to dinner and a movie, we cannot respond to the crime of rape.*

Bill Clinton, the man who deployed the best fighting force on the globe to build urinals in Bosnia, actually said of Muslim terrorists, "They have good reason to hate us . . . after all, we sent the Crusaders to try and conquer them." They have long memories, these fascists. As I recall, the Crusades ended in 1290. We're really sorry that seven hundred years ago a bunch of Europeans responded aggressively to the sack of Jerusalem by a mob of Muslim savages. The Muslims weren't exactly shrinking violets. They had spent the prior several hundred years grabbing a lot of territory that wasn't theirs. Perhaps the Europeans were still smarting over the Muslim onslaught at Tours four hundred years earlier. But okay, let's stipulate: "We" were wrong and "you" were right. There is no grudge worth holding for seven hundred years.

Gore said America will only create more enemies if "what we represent to the world is an empire." We must mollify angry fanatics who seek our destruction because otherwise they might get mad and seek our destruction. He also complained that we have "abandoned almost all of Afghanistan"—rather than making it part of our empire, evidently. He seemed to think it was our responsibility to "stabilize the nation of Afghanistan," "pacify the countryside," and send them valentines. Liberals think war is a Miss Congeniality contest.

One could mine every war-making text throughout history—Sun Tsu, Carl von Clausewitz, Alfred Thayer Mahan—without finding a single reference to being liked by your enemies as a tactic associated with winning a war. Gore said foreigners are not worried about "what the terrorist networks are going to do, but about what we're going to do." Good. They should be worried. They hate us? We hate them. Americans don't want to make Islamic fanatics love us. We want to make them die. There's nothing like horrendous physical pain to quell angry fanatics. So sorry they're angry—wait until they see American anger. Japanese kamikaze pilots hated us once, too. A couple of well-aimed nuclear weapons got their attention. Now they are gentle little lambs.

America is fighting for its survival and the Democrats are obsessing over why barbarians hate us. Instead of wondering why foreigners hate Americans, a more fruitful inquiry for the Democrats might be to ask why Americans are beginning to hate Democrats.

12

NORTH KOREA—
ANOTHER OPPORTUNITY
FOR SURRENDER

The Democrats' approach to national security consists of a series of incoherent gibes that add up to a totally contradictory account. Conservatives are devastatingly clear, consistent, and logical, while liberals are whirling dervishes of inconsistent positions. There are few more riveting examples of this than the left's palaver about North Korea over the past decade. When President Bush included North Korea in his "axis of evil," liberals explained he was a moron. On the basis of years of scholarship and close study, the foreign policy experts pointed out that Iran, Iraq, and North Korea were— I quote—"different countries." Tony Cordesman, an expert at the Center for Strategic and International Studies, said, "These are three very different countries here."[1] *USA Today* said, "An axis? Hardly. The countries have more differences than similarities." Koreans don't even look like Iranians. Robert Scheer wrote in the *Los Angeles Times* that Bush had grouped "the disparate regimes of Iraq, Iran and North Korea as an 'axis of evil'" but "no such axis exists."[2] The axis of appeasement had seized on an alternative definition of "axis" (colluding coconspirators) to engage in semantic nit-picking. The country was at war and we got word games from liberals.

To be sure, North Korea was not all sunshine and song. But the real danger, as liberals saw it, was Bush's evident inability to grasp that these were "different countries." Clinton's secretary of state, Madeleine Albright, said, "We know that North Korea is dangerous, but lumping those three countries together is dangerous."[3] Soon the whole chorus was singing the same tune. Former president Jimmy Carter said the "axis of evil" term was "overly simplistic and counterproductive."[4] Interestingly, however, while stressing the texture and nuance of the point that these are "different countries," the left's plan for action with both was identical: Be nice. Otherwise we might upset them.

The experts were in a panic that Bush's harsh words might compromise the pathbreaking peace deal negotiated by President Clinton in 1994. The Clinton administration was in the middle of negotiating with North Korea, when suddenly Carter popped up in Pyŏngyang, where he was meeting with the then-ruler, Kim Il Sung. Before Clinton could figure out what this idiot was doing in North Korea, Carter began issuing paeans to Kim Il Sung like a giddy girl meeting Brad Pitt. He pronounced the crazy despot "vigorous, alert, intelligent and remarkably familiar with the issues." He said Kim was "very friendly toward Christianity."[5] Carter is such a profoundly irritating person, he even got on Clinton's nerves. In case the pot-smoking draft-dodger couldn't compromise America's national security interests on his own, Carter was there to help. With assistance from the architect of the Iranian hostage crisis, Clinton got this great deal for America: North Korea would get 500,000 tons of fuel oil annually and $4 billion to construct a pair of nuclear reactors for "electricity," and, in exchange, North Korea promised not to build nuclear weapons.

In what is always a prelude to disaster, the *New York Times* was exultant. A 1994 editorial called the deal "a resounding triumph" that had brought an end to "two years of international anxiety and put to rest widespread fears." The *Times* cited the soon-to-be-broken pact as an object lesson on the virtues of appeasement, jubilantly proclaiming that Clinton had "defied impatient hawks and other skeptics who accused the Clinton Administration of gullibility and urged swifter, stronger action."[6] As the *Times* said, "From the start, the hawks' alternative to diplomacy was full of danger. Their solution—economic sanctions and bombing runs—might have disarmed North Korea, but only at the risk of war." Clinton and his trusty assistant Jimmy Carter "deserve warm praise for charting a less costly and more successful course."[7] *Times* columnist Nicholas D. Kristof wrote that the U.S. "came within an inch of going to war with North Korea, in a conflict that a Pentagon study found would have killed a million people, including up to 100,000 Americans." In retrospect, he said, "the hawks were wrong about confronting North Korea. Containment and deterrence so far have worked instead, kind of, just as they have kind-of worked to restrain Iraq over the last 11 years, and we saved thousands of lives by pressing diplomatic solutions."[8] Jimmy Carter was awarded the Nobel Peace Prize for his masterful negotiation of the 1994 deal, though, in candor, he got the prize for North Korea only because the committee couldn't formally award a prize for Bush-bashing, which was the stated reason.

As is now well-known, about six seconds after the deal was signed, the North Koreans began feverishly building nuclear bombs. In October 2002, the regime admitted it had a nuclear weapons program and, in fact, had been working on it at least since the "mid- or late-1990's," according to the *New York Times*.[9] But right up until the Bush administration caught the North Koreans red-handed, the experts were assuring us that the 1994 "peace" deal had been a smashing success.

This was the deal liberals were claiming Bush's "Axis of Evil" speech had thrown off track. After Bush called the Pyŏngyang regime evil, Clinton complained that Bush was wrecking the great strides his administration had made with North Korea: "I figure I left the next administration with a big foreign policy win."[10] If Clinton had had a few more years, he could have brought the Owen Lattimores back, the *New York Times* could be complaining that all the attacks on the State Department had squelched creative thinking at the North Korea desk, the fashion industry could introduce the North Korean equivalent of Mao jackets, and the Discovery Channel would start producing specials on this exotic faraway land.

Madeleine Albright, who had daintily proposed that terrorist nations such as North Korea should not be called "rogue nations" but rather "states of concern," was duly mortified by Bush's "Axis of Evil" speech. She said, "When we left office, we left on the table the potential of a verifiable agreement to stop the export [from North Korea] of missile technology."[11] Experts like Tony Cordesman worried that Bush had closed "options opened by the Clinton administration with North Korea."[12] *USA Today* complained that the "Axis of Evil" speech was "a simplistic policy of hubris that alienates allies and inflames problems that can be managed more benignly."[13] As *USA Today* saw it, Bush's "hot-war posturing" was ridiculous because even "critics" of the regime—as opposed to its admirers like Jimmy Carter—"concede the regime seems to have kept its promises so far regarding nuclear weapons and missile tests."[14] As the experts were hysterically attacking Bush, Kim Jong Il was hard at work developing nuclear weapons.

The principal area of disagreement among the ponderers was why Bush had called North Korea part of the axis of evil in the first place. Liberals were simply stumped. With impeccable timing, just two weeks before North Korea admitted it had been developing nuclear weapons, *New York Times* columnist Bill Keller called North Korea one of "the countries the White House insists on calling 'the axis of evil.'"[15] *New York Times* reporter Elizabeth Bumiller said that what Bush meant by calling Iran, Iraq, and North Korea evil "has been left open to guessing."[16] I think I know what he meant. I believe he meant that the three nations were evil. The experts discounted that explanation out of hand.

NBC News military analyst Bill Arkin claimed that Bush had thrown North Korea into the mix as window dressing for Muslim countries. Bush did not "want to stigmatize the Middle East . . . [or] Muslim nations."[17] David Albright of the Institute for Science and International Security made the fascinating argument that Bush had called North Korea part of the axis of evil based in part on "a hatred of the Clinton administration policy across the board."[18] Robert Scheer claimed Bush's axis of evil drivel was "the rationale for a grossly expanded military budget." He said an expanded military budget made sense only as part of Bush's "pseudo-religious quest to create a super-dominant Pax Americana." Far better to live under a Pax North Koreana.[19]

Others attributed Bush's axis of evil phrase to . . . Enron! Clinton national security staffer Antony Blinken said Bush's axis of evil phrase was a gambit to distract the public's attention from "things less comfortable, like the economy and the Enron scandal."[20] Journalist Jack Germond said, "It's hard to understand what President Bush was intending to accomplish with some of the extravagant rhetoric he used the other night," except that "compared to an 'axis of evil,' Enron seems like small potatoes."[21] Being a foreigner, Jack Straw, the British foreign secretary, did not grasp the unspeakable scandal of being from the same state as Enron. But he sensed a political ploy afoot. Interrupting his incessant denunciations of America's treatment of prisoners at Guantánamo, Straw opined that Bush's speech "was best understood by the fact that there are mid-term congressional elections coming up in November."[22]

After all the experts had spent months denigrating Bush for jeopardizing the brilliant 1994 deal, North Korea admitted it had ignored the deal from the beginning. A few months after that, U.S. intelligence forces tracked an unmarked ship carrying Scud missiles from North Korea to Yemen—this despite the fact that they were "different countries." The North Koreans were not only making missiles but trafficking in them. North Korea was beginning to look a lot like the third member of an axis of evil.

Instead of owning up to their now-ludicrous attacks on Bush and unbridled praise for Clinton's "peace" agreement, the ponderers once again concluded that Bush was a moron. Apparently, Bush had somehow driven the North Koreans to violate the agreement by being mean to them. North Korea was a beacon of peace until Bush called it "evil," forcing Kim Jong Il to build nuclear weapons—leaving unexplained why Pyŏngyang started developing nuclear weapons while Clinton was still president. Robert J. Einhorn, who helped negotiate the 1994 "peace" deal, said Bush's "tough rhetoric and tough policies" must have "unnerved the North Koreans," forcing them into "rapidly acquiring a substantial nuclear arsenal."[23] Derek Mitchell, another veteran of the Clinton administration, said Bush had provoked the North Koreans: "We did call them the 'Axis of Evil.'"

Clintonites blaming the Bush administration for the North Koreans' breach of the 1994 deal was nothing if not audacious. It would be as if ex-Nazis were attacking Eisenhower for taking his sweet time about liberating the concentration camps. You'd think they'd just shut up about North Korea. But not only were liberals unembarrassed, they were joyful. They could barely restrain their glee that one of their boys in the Third World had checkmated Bush. America was in a pickle now. Good for Kim Jong Il! In an article titled "Outfoxed by North Korea," Leon Fuerth, Al Gore's national security advisor—and, naturally, a professor—crowed: "It is certain that the Bush administration now faces an immediate loss of credibility."[24]

To review the record, the only people in the universe who had been "outfoxed" by the North Koreans were liberals. In 1994, when liberals were heaping praise on Clinton's Peace-in-Our-Time deal with North Korea, Senate Republican leader Bob Dole dryly remarked, "It is always possible to get an agreement when you give enough away."[25] Columnist Charles Krauthammer wrote of the resulting deal: "The State Department, mixing cravenness with cynicism, calls this capitulation 'very good news.' For Kim Il Sung, certainly. For us, the deal is worse than dangerous. It is shameful."[26] Just two months into his presidency, Bush canceled ongoing "peace" talks with North Korea, stating matter-of-factly that Pyŏngyang would cheat on any agreement that was not verifiable.

But according to Fuerth, the North Koreans had hoodwinked Bush. They had put him "in the awkward position of choosing to give war with Iraq priority" over North Korea.[27] Here was the nub of the matter: North Korea had given liberals another excuse to oppose invading Iraq. Months earlier, they had hooted with laughter when Bush called North Korea "evil," but as the nation prepared to invade Iraq, liberals were suddenly overwhelmed by the evil that was North Korea. This was a country that was so evil, Iraq would have to wait. Inasmuch as liberals also wanted to wait for the second Ice Age to invade Iraq, their arguments for giving North Korea top billing lacked something in the way of credibility.

While pretending to believe the North Koreans had quickly assembled a massive Manhattan Project and developed a nuclear bomb in nine months flat, liberals insisted there was no need to worry about Saddam Hussein because he was not an "imminent threat." Of course, they had also assured us that North Korea was not an imminent threat. Joel S. Wit—who helped negotiate the celebrated "peace" agreement—said, "If we attacked Iraq next year as opposed to next month, I am not sure the situation would be that different. The North Koreans, on the other hand, seem to be moving gung-ho toward making nuclear weapons."[28] Yes, that makes it a little trickier, doesn't it? Meanwhile, according to his colleagues in the Clinton administration, it was possible for despots to develop nuclear weapons within a week of hearing President Bush call them "evil."

Weeks before the Iraq invasion, Senator Teddy Kennedy was bloviating about North Korea on CNN, saying, "Our principal focus and attention today ought to be what is happening in North Korea. North Korea has produced nuclear weapons. It has a missile that can reach the United States. We ought to be talking to a North Korea that has nuclear weapons rather than going to war with Iraq that does not."[29] In the previous eight years, Senator Kennedy mentioned North Korea only two times, according to the Lexis-Nexis archives.[30] Once was at an immigration subcommittee hearing on North Korean refugees.[31] The second time was to harangue Bush's nominee for assistant secretary of defense for International Security Policy, for having criticized the 1994 peace deal. A more hawkish approach, Kennedy warned, would be "dangerously provocative to a nation that already fears aggression from the United States and South Korea."[32] In fact, as we now know, the dovish approach had produced a terrifying threat in North Korea. But in 2002, Kennedy was urging the same approach with Iraq.

Even Democrats who had voted for the resolution of force against Iraq leapt on the failure of Clinton's 1994 peace deal to repudiate their votes. Senator Charles Schumer (D-N.Y.)—who had voted for the Iraq resolution—said, "You don't have to have a Ph.D. in foreign relations to understand that North Korea poses a greater danger to the United States than Iraq."[33] Apparently we didn't need to check with "the allies" to make that call.

Liberals were utterly hysterical with their contradictory arguments. They engaged in infantile braying about how Bush was picking the easier fight, as if national security were a game. Before the North Koreans were caught violating the 1994 "peace" agreement, the *Los Angeles Times* had carped about the use of force against Iraq, warning that it might "spring open a Pandora's box of aggression" and calling the resolution authorizing force "The Wrong Resolution."[34] But as soon as Bush exposed Pyŏngyang's nuclear program, the *Times* demanded to know why we weren't attacking it. It was so obvious that North Korea was trouble precisely because it might already have nukes—making the case for invading Iraq and dismantling their nuclear program even stronger. But try to explain that to a liberal. They had no point, only their own paralyzing fear. In the female taunting of liberals, the editorial repeatedly demanded "a better explanation" of the "strikingly different treatment of two adversaries who seem equally dangerous."[35] Despite the fact that North Korea was "just as dangerous as Iraq,

Pyŏngyang has received little more than a tongue-lashing." Liberals make sport of a serious national defense policy with their absurd quibbles. They think they can outwit adults with infantile, logic-chopping games. *You won't let me smoke pot, but you drink alcohol.* Why weren't we attacking North Korea? Why not Pakistan? Why not Saudi Arabia? The administration was supposed to be supine with contradictions.

The *New York Times* said North Korea had "blown apart the Bush administration's months-long effort to portray Saddam Hussein as uniquely dangerous." Liberals think we're not in real war unless the other side has a chance to nuke us. Gleefully brandishing Clinton's failed North Korea policy as an argument for inaction on Iraq, the *Times* announced that Washington could not "afford the luxury of deferring the North Korean problem until it has finished disarming Iraq."[36]

Barbra Streisand's political advisor, Robert Scheer, ridiculed the Bush administration's interest in disarming Iraq when North Korea posed a much greater problem, sneering: "Darn, but those weapons of mass destruction keep turning up in the wrong places."[37] He's certainly not one to be fooled by North Korea. In the late sixties, David Horowitz says Scheer returned from a trip to North Korea more starstruck even than Jimmy Carter. As Horowitz describes it, Scheer "organized a radical junket to North Korea and returned to Berkeley, saying he had seen the future that worked and praising the brain-dwarfing thoughts of Kim Il Sung."[38]

North Korea was only the latest ploy in liberals' national security shell game. As America contemplated action against Iraq, liberals kept tossing out other problems they insisted would have to be addressed "first." This is supposed to prevent anyone from accusing them of being worthless appeasers. The left is all for aggressive military action—but never against any country America is about to attack. In opposing war with Iraq, liberals variously cited Saudi Arabia, Arafat, Pakistan, Syria, Osama bin Laden, and North Korea as more pressing problems than Iraq. Bush should have called their bluff and attacked all forty countries liberals claimed to be itching to attack "before" Iraq.

In May 2002, *New York Times* columnist Maureen Dowd wrote a raving column the main point of which was that Bush was a simpleton who sees the world in black and white: "In Bushworld, especially since 9-11, it's always either good or evil."[39] She went on to explain the shades of gray, by pointing out that Russia, Germany, and Pakistan were evil, too. Russia, she said, "used to be the Evil Empire. But now we need the old Evil Empire to help us with the new Axis of Evil and the Evildoers. So now Russia is the Good Empire." While in Germany, Bush made a subtle but unmistakable reference to the specter of Hitler, describing Saddam Hussein as "a dictator who gassed his own people." This, Dowd said, showed that Bush was "oblivious" to the fact that Germany was a country that "actually had a dictator who gassed his own people." And she thinks *he's* being oblivious? The psychological term for this is "projection." Furthermore, she said, "W. has embraced Pakistan," but "Pakistan does not share our democratic values; this is a place where a young woman was recently sentenced to death by stoning." Apparently, in order for Bush to show his appreciation for shades of gray and impress the editorial board of the *New York Times,* he would have to launch a first strike against Iraq, Russia, Germany, and Pakistan simultaneously.

In the same column, Dowd admiringly quoted a German reporter —with whom we would now be at war under her plan—advising the president that "Syria, too, in U.S. terminology, is a state sponsor of terrorism" and that "Saudi Arabia is anything but a democratic pluralistic society." So now she had us attacking Saudi Arabia and Syria, too. Either that or the Pulitzer Prize–winning writer spent an entire column expressing her tenuous grasp of the word "ally." Dowd was also upset that on his European trip, Bush—quote—did "not seem curious about exploring cities he has never seen."[40] She thinks Bush should declare war on the entire world, but she also wants him to be touring European art museums.

Despite liberals' dazzling point earlier in the year that Iraq, Iran, and North Korea were "very different countries," surprisingly enough, their approach to all three was the same. Whether dealing with an evil regime that might already have nuclear weapons (North Korea) or an evil regime still trying to develop nuclear weapons (Iraq), the crucial thing, as liberals saw it, was to do nothing. Or at least to do nothing that would annoy the despots. Taking no untoward action toward America's enemies is variously known as "engagement," "negotiation," "diplomacy," "detente," "maintaining a relationship," or "working through the U.N."—all euphemisms for doing nothing. If anything, we should be giving dangerous despots nuclear reactors and billions of dollars in aid to make them like us.

While claiming we couldn't attack Iraq because we had to deal with North Korea, the *Times* also said we couldn't attack North Korea: "Military action would risk a violent North Korean response."[41] So who could we attack? And why should we listen to the *New York Times*? When North Korea later admitted that they had ignored the "peace" deal from the beginning, the *New York Times* said it had "stunned the world."[42] If history always begins this morning, the world holds exciting surprises around every corner. Having only just discovered the shocking news that megalomaniacal dictators do not always keep their promises, the *Times* again insisted that Bush rush back to the negotiating table.[43] The same approach liberals had taken with North Korea before being double-crossed should be tried again. In a single editorial, the *Times* urged "multilateral diplomacy," a "firm diplomatic response," and "diplomatic solutions."[44] It would be much better to wait for North Korea to develop lots of nuclear weapons and unify with South Korea before we tried anything too bellicose.

Demonstrating the left's dynamite combination of stupidity and arrogance, the *Seattle Times* reacted to North Korea's frenzied development of nuclear weapons by hectoring Bush to "find out what this impoverished, isolated country wants."[45] The *Washington Post* cited "experts" who said North Korea's violation of the 1994 agreement reflected "a sense of deep insecurity, compounded by Bush administration rhetoric about the 'axis of evil.'"[46] Derek Mitchell said, "People talk about North Korea being crazy, but it's not. It's purely rational for a nation with no assets being threatened by the world's major power to

develop insurance against attack."[47] Maybe he should have spoken up
when Clinton was sealing that 1994 deal. Mitchell proposed that the
U.S. not isolate the North Koreans, engage in more missile talks, perhaps find out what Kim Jong Il's favorite chocolates were.[48] The North
Koreans were "insecure." Liberals' bold plan for action was to be nice
to them.

The "insecurity" argument was straight out of the traitor playbook.
New York Times columnist Anthony Lewis had used the identical words
of surrender in the eighties when he droned on about "the bankruptcy
of Ronald Reagan's policy toward the Soviet Union." A few years
before President Reagan toppled the seventy-year-old Communist
regime, Lewis cited Soviet "insecurity" to warn that "when an American President talks of a Soviet 'evil empire,' the Russians are inevitably going to be resentful, angry, defiant."[49] What was needed—and
in a hurry—was pointless chitchat. Talk, engagement, diplomacy, consensus—it's always the same thing with liberals. Lyndon Johnson
thought he could treat Ho Chi Minh like some dumb governor and give
him a dam to make him go away. It doesn't work that way with fanatics.
It certainly wasn't going to work that way with Kim Jong Il, a brutal
Stalinist dictator. But no matter what the circumstances, liberals
demand a foreign policy of craven retreat. As Joe McCarthy said of
General George Marshall, if they were merely stupid, the laws of probability would have dictated that at least some of their decisions would
have served this country's interest.[50]

Defying the uniform demands of the nation's op-ed pages, the
Bush administration opted against spoon-feeding prepared meals to
two million North Korean troops. To the contrary, Bush said he would
not negotiate until the Pyŏngyang regime dismantled its nuclear
weapons program and threatened the North Koreans with total economic collapse. Secretary of Defense Donald Rumsfeld said any
assumption that the U.S. would not use force against North Korea
would be a mistake. Such bellicosity frightens liberals. The left's reaction to nutty despots is: *He might hit me, so I'll be nice.* Rumsfeld's idea
is: *He'll hit me? Maybe I'll hit him.* The beauty of that approach cannot

be denied. Liberals look at life from the perspective of people who feel defenseless. They shrink from bullies, have a phobia about hitting, and warn children not to play with firecrackers or they'll lose an eye. Jimmy Carter claimed to have been attacked by a giant swimming rabbit. That's really all you need to know about the Democrats. The entire liberal logic on national defense could be reduced to the following three words: *Are you sure?* Gosh, I worry about that, too.

Instead of relentlessly attacking the military as immature or testosterone crazed—meaning "braver than me"—liberals might have the good grace to realize they live in a country where big burly men are willing to protect them from bullies.[51] As far as I am aware, the military does not interfere in the fashion industry. They don't have a lot of opinions about Broadway plays or write poetry like Clinton's secretary of defense, William Cohen. Why can't liberals let men defend the country?

13

{ CELEBRITY TRAITORS: "NOW THAT I'M SOBER I WATCH A LOT OF NEWS" }

No account of the war on terrorism would be complete without mentioning the underwear models. As America embarked upon the greatest battle for its survival since the end of the Cold War, the nation cried out for the opinions of the most frivolous people in the universe—celebrities. Singers, models, actors, writers, and vegan hysteric Kim Basinger all came out against the war. Liberals see themselves as part of a deployment; Hollywood celebrities are their generals. With Vietnam, it took a while for the anti-war movement to get going. Now we have an instant sedition lobby.

The attack of 9-11 was understandably disturbing to celebrities. It created an unpleasant sensation that there was something in the world more important than them and their sybaritic doings in New York nightclubs. Their lives aren't exactly full of heroics. Most celebrities wouldn't consider working for two months for less than a million dollars. They have no idea how food and other necessities materialize in their cupboards and closets. Some couldn't even tell you how much their herpes medicine costs. As they cavort across Page Six and other gossip columns, it is important for them to imagine infatuated hillbillies agape with envy. Being a part of the anti-war crowd allowed the most overpampered elites since the czar's court to feel relevant again. They could not grasp that a terrorist attack on America meant they're in it with the rabble this time.

In general, wildly overpaid narcissists are the last people who should be commenting on subjects of any importance. But the Hollywood left insisted on airing their infantile Oedipal disorders in public. Democratic politicians operated stealthily, hoping to lose listeners in the details. They created the aroma of opposition, without giving any specifics they could get nailed on. The *New York Times* assumed people would get so bored with the turgidity of their approach that no one could take it all in and realize they were rooting for the terrorists. Meanwhile, the Hollywood set was openly blurting out their hatred for America.

Actor Woody Harrelson wrote an article in the London *Guardian*, saying, "I'm an American tired of lies. And with our government, it's mostly lies."[1] He informed the foreign audience that America intended to wipe out random "non-white" nations. Harrelson even assailed the United States' food-drop/military campaign in Afghanistan as an unprovoked act of aggression. The warmongers of the Bush administration "stole the White House" and were waging "a perpetual war on any non-white country they choose to describe as terrorist." For good measure, Harrelson tossed in an attack on Christopher Columbus.[2] For some unfathomable reason, he said, stupid Americans were angry about terrorism. As the levelheaded sitcom actor dispassionately explained, "In wartime people lose their senses." He complained about the scourge of "flags and yellow ribbons and posters." Liberals react to the American flag like Linda Blair did to holy water in *The Exorcist*. Nothing demonstrates the latent fascism of Americans to liberals so clearly as the American flag. (And had anyone *not* on drugs seen any yellow ribbons in 2002?) He said, "Every media outlet is beating the war drum." The conservative media strikes again! This was all written under his own name, as if he found his babble an entirely creditable summary of world affairs.

Actress Jessica Lange denounced the impending war with Iraq as "unconstitutional, immoral and illegal."[3] She said the "Iraq plan" was "absolutely mad"—thus outsmarting Barbra Streisand by getting the name of the country right. With only slightly less subtlety than the *New York Times*'s editorial page, she added, "I hate Bush, I despise him and his entire administration." Actress Susan Sarandon said, "Nobody is answering any of the big questions. Where's the big thing? . . . You know, I know there's going to be thousands of people injured, killed. This is something that needs rigorous debate. Nobody has said. . . . It's not a Nintendo game. This is something that, you know, what's the plan once we get in? How many people do we commit to that area? How do we get there? What happened afterwards? Nobody is discussing this, and I believe that if . . . some of these details were discussed, these statistics that they're giving us about blind following would crash, because if you ask somebody, are you willing to send your son, the whole story changes."[4]

In March 2003, not long before the war began, Iraqi soldiers heard shooting and, thinking the war had started, crossed the border into Kuwait and tried to surrender to British troops.[5] The British had to send them back. As American troops moved in to liberate Iraq, they were often greeted with open arms rather than military arms. Even the *New York Times* had to admit it.[6] The peace lobby wanted to keep these people in Saddam's prison.

After Barbra Streisand ignominiously relinquished her leadership position in the anti-war movement when Matt Drudge pointed out she didn't know which country we were invading, Janeane Garofalo became the mascot of the "Activism R Us" Hollywood coalition. She explained her newfound activism, saying, "Now that I'm sober, I watch a lot of news." When a feminist as strident as Garofalo was defending the Hussein regime, you had to wonder if her newfound sobriety had hit a rough patch. Garofalo said that "dropping bombs on the Iraqis is not going to disarm Saddam." No, it will kill him. That's good enough. Trading in her Gen-X sneer for a nitwit's hysteria, Garofalo warned, "America will pay a very, very high, irrevocable price for this!" The lemon pucker puss said extremist groups will strike us "if we do this war." Things were going just great for us before—that's if you don't count the unpleasantness of September 11—and attacks on the USS *Cole,* our Air Force housing complex in Saudi Arabia, Pan Am Flight 103, our Marine barracks in Beirut, and our embassies in Kenya, Tanzania, Lebanon, and Iran.

Garofalo demanded to know why she wasn't being taken seriously in her opposition to war with Iraq, while asserting, "There is no evidence of weapons of mass destruction." The Kurds and Iranians would be surprised to hear that inasmuch as Saddam Hussein had already used his weapons of mass destruction on them. Leftist monkeys repeat things they've heard and assume they have meaning. Garofalo also said it was "disgusting that we know more about Winona Ryder's trial than we do about the Iraqi people." One interesting fact she alone appeared not to know about the Iraqi people is that Saddam Hussein wouldn't let them talk to foreigners without an Iraqi agent present, making it difficult to get much of a feel for the Iraqi people. It's a mystery why people don't take Janeane seriously.

There was a race to the bottom in the idiotic things celebrities said. Singer Sheryl Crow summarized the views of all the celebrity pundits with a specially made sequined T-shirt that said WAR IS NOT THE ANSWER. That depends on what the question is, now, doesn't it? She elaborated on her T-shirt's insight, saying, "War is never the answer to solving any problems." War ended slavery, fascism, Soviet totalitarianism, but other than that, it has a limited repertoire. Crow explained that the "best way to solve problems is to not have enemies." War solves that problem, too: We won't have any enemies because we're going to kill them. Crow warned of "huge karmic retributions that will follow." She seemed not to understand that America going to war *is* the huge karmic retribution. They killed three thousand Americans and now they're going to die.

Three days after the September 11 attacks, Madonna was onstage in Los Angeles exhorting the audience to pray for no retaliation against the perpetrators. Between songs and simulated live sex acts, the always circumspect gay-disco chanteuse explained, "Violence begets violence." When it comes to negative reviews, Madonna's publicist takes a more sanguine view of "retaliation." In February 2003, Madonna put the world on notice: Her latest music video contained a shocking anti-war message, featuring shots of Iraqi children interspersed with mushroom clouds. It was expected to be a bigger draw than her latest movie, featuring shots of Madonna in a bathing suit.

Madonna's ex-husband, Sean Penn, was not to be out-vogued. As head of "Chain-Smoking Drunks Against War," Penn took out a $56,000 ad in the *Washington Post*, addressed to President Bush, saying, "I beg you, help save America before yours is a legacy of shame and horror."[7] Evidently Bush would be able to narrowly avert shame and horror by taking no action against barbaric despots who seek America's destruction. As Penn explained the situation, "Bombing is answered by bombing, mutilation by mutilation, killing by killing." Fundamentalist Muslim terrorists kill three thousand Americans, but America isn't supposed to respond, because if we respond, they'll respond. We always hear about "karmic retributions" and the "cycle of violence" only after we've been hit. Penn had previously demonstrated his commitment to pacifism by punching defenseless cameramen. Actors are constantly engaging in conspicuous fighting to distract from the fact that they are sissy-boys who put on little-girls' plays.

In December 2002, Penn went to Iraq to "record the human face of the Iraqi people so that their blood, along with that of American soldiers, would not be invisible on my own hands."[8] In Baghdad, Penn visited hospitals and posed in front of photos of Saddam Hussein. He looked for weapons of mass destruction, but the only bomb he found was a bootleg copy of *Shanghai Surprise*. He reminded the *New York*

Times that his family had been ravaged by McCarthyism, reflecting "on the bitter experience in the 1950s of his father, the film director and television producer Leo Penn, who was blacklisted by Hollywood studios for five years after refusing to testify during the Communist scare of the McCarthy years."[9] As millions of people were sentenced to gulags and death in Stalin's Russia, Leo Penn was forced to fire the maid. It was heartwrenching.

As war with Iraq drew closer, Saddam Hussein put the people of Iraq on an Orange alert in response to an increase in "chatter" out of Hollywood. In a frenzy over the prospect of world events preempting their appearances on *Entertainment Tonight,* by early 2003, actors were in March Hare mode. George Clooney gave Charlie Rose the inside tip that Bush had cut a deal with France so they wouldn't complain when we attack Iraq.[10] Apparently even the French have more manhood than George Clooney since they never did stop complaining.

Richard Gere opposed the war, saying, "I keep asking myself where all this personal enmity between George Bush and Saddam Hussein comes from. It's like the story of Captain Ahab and the great white whale from 'Moby Dick.'" Gere refused to comment when asked whether he had read *Moby-Dick.* Fresh from receiving a lifetime achievement award for his geopolitical insights, Dustin Hoffman said that Bush "has taken the events of 9-11 and has manipulated the grief of the country, and I think that's reprehensible." He explained that "this war is about what most wars are about: hegemony, money, power and oil." Hoffman refused comment when asked to spell "hegemony." Actors seem to think they really are the cool people they play. It's not just that, as Roy Cohn pointed out, actors' only provable skill is imitating other people. A high IQ is generally an impediment to being a good actor.

Even model Kate Moss took time out from her drug habit to really wrap her head around the war issue. Terrified that an attack on Iraq could lead to an attack on Colombia and dry up her supply, she was foursquare against the war. According to the gossip columns, her pacifism apparently does not extend to hotel furniture.

In addition to increased "chatter" from the casting-couch phi-losophers, celebrity writers quickly enlisted in the anti-American bat-talion. Right after the 9-11 attack, every idiot liberal was basically coming out and cheering for al-Qaeda. Michael Moore, creator of fic-tional "documentaries" and books that he passes off as true, sympa-thized with the terrorists' goals but complained that they had killed the wrong Americans.[11] Defending the terrorists, Moore said, "We have orphaned so many children, tens of thousands around the world, with our taxpayer-funded terrorism."[12] To follow the train of tortured logic that requires introspection about how America brought the attack of 9-11 on itself is to dance on the graves of those three thousand Ameri-cans. This is liberalism gone totally haywire.

A year later, Moore was laughing at the people on the hijacked planes, saying they were cowards for not fighting back.[13] Apparently Moore believed it was only appropriate to fight dagger-wielding savages when battling them in hand-to-hand combat, but not with high-tech precision weaponry developed by Stupid White Men. He opposed war with Afghanistan and he opposed war with Iraq.[14] Indeed, he giggled at America for bothering with al-Qaeda: "To me, al-Qaeda is a men's club. To have the world's only superpower at war with a men's club is a little ridiculous."[15] America should not fight back, but the passengers on the four planes on September 11 were cowards for *not* fighting back.

Two days after the attack, novelist Norman Mailer, whose last suc-cessful novel was written fifty-four years ago, said the crumpled World Trade Center was "more beautiful than the building was."[16] He said America was "the most hated nation on earth." Like Moore, Mailer believed the victims of the terrorist attack were simply the wrong tar-gets: "You've got that many people killed who've had nothing to do with bringing on their own death other than working in a monument to corporatism."[17] The author of *Tough Guys Don't Dance* told a German newspaper that Bush should have been a ballet dancer: "Mankind would have benefited from him more as a dancer than as president."[18] Mankind would also have been better served if Mailer had been a writer instead of a buffoon. The self-reported tough guy's only recorded physical damage to another human being was when he stabbed his wife.

As Mailer saw it, the terrorist attack was retaliation for the Happy Meal: "We come in and we insist on establishing enclaves of our food there, like McDonald's."[19] He pompously criticized Americans for refusing to recognize that "large parts of the world, particularly the most backward nations, see us as cultural oppressors and aesthetic oppressors." Giving an interview from his home in Cape Cod, the multimillionaire author said people of other nations enjoy being poor. Until America faced up to the reality that "the huge profit-making way of life is not necessarily a good fit for most countries," he said, "we are going to be in trouble."[20] Liberals adore brutal despots who keep their subjects mired in poverty. Attacking wealth from their beachfront estates makes liberals sound like bon vivants on the society pages.

Angry that Bush intended to invade Iraq, rather than send troops to surround McDonald's headquarters, Mailer sniffed that Iraq was "not a danger." He said, "It doesn't matter what they're up to in Iraq. It doesn't matter if they have nuclear bombs or not or whether they're ready to do chemical warfare." (Again, the Kurds might disagree.) The only reason we were going to war with Iraq was to build an empire, and Iraq was "absolutely a position in the world we need militarily." It would start with Iraq, then move to the Near East and then Bush would make "China the Greece to our Rome."[21] The secular saints of liberalism get crazier and crazier with age.

Fellow writer Kurt Vonnegut said the plan to invade Iraq was "nonsense" hatched by a government that had been "taken over by means of the sleaziest, low-comedy, Keystone Cops–style coup d'etat imaginable. And those now in charge of the federal government are upper-crust C-students who know no history or geography, plus not-so-closeted white supremacists, aka 'Christians,' and plus, most frighteningly, psychopathic personalities, or 'PPs.'" As evidence that the Bush administration was not comprised of "normal people," Vonnegut said they "cannot care what happens next. Simply can't. Do this! Do that!

Mobilize the reserves! . . . Attack Iraq! Cut health care! Tap everybody's telephone! . . . Build a trillion-dollar missile shield! Fuck habeas corpus and the Sierra Club and *In These Times,* and kiss my ass!"[22] That's worth a few admiring glances from Hollywood starlets.

Another author, Alice Walker, wrote in the *Village Voice* that America should shower Osama bin Laden with love: "What would happen to his cool armor if he could be reminded of all the good, nonviolent things he has done?"[23] Maybe Walker could remind us of what those things are, too. Senator Patty Murray, who is not a celebrity except for the IQ, told a group of schoolchildren that America needed to understand why Osama bin Laden was so popular and concluded that Osama was beloved because—I quote—"he's been out in these countries for decades building schools, building roads, building infrastructure, building day care facilities, building health care facilities and people are extremely grateful. He's made their lives better. We have not done that."[24] Yes, bin Laden was building day care facilities for all the working women struggling with career and family under the Taliban. It was like an April Fools' Day hoax. Murray simply assumed the whole NOW agenda was on Osama's program: self-esteem, "infrastructure," battered women's shelters, aromatherapy, the whole nine yards. It presumably goes without saying that—despite Osama's hard work for reproductive choice—the U.S. lavishes vastly more money on countries throughout the Middle East, including 80 percent of all international relief to Afghanistan.

There's something about murderous dictators who hate the United States that celebrities find irresistible. They think it makes them seem wild and randy to hobnob with mass murderers. Totalitarians make good theater. Harry Belafonte—a self-described "victim of McCarthyism"—was one of the few to live long enough to transition seamlessly from praising Bolshevik heathen to defending Islamic terrorists.[25]

The psychopathology of celebrity traitors was described in a book about poet Ezra Pound called *The Roots of Treason.* Pound was indicted on nineteen counts of treason at the end of World War II for making a series of openly fascistic and anti-Semitic radio broadcasts from Rome during the war.[26] (Or, as the *Washington Post* mystifyingly put it in 1992, Pound was "anti-authoritarian."[27] Supporting Mussolini and Hitler is "anti-authoritarian" only in the sense that America is "authoritarian" and Pound was anti-American.) He escaped trial by being sentenced to a loony bin instead. A psychiatrist at the loony bin wrote about Pound's condition, in terms that should strike a chord with many celebrities: "What is unquestionably the most outstanding feature of his personality is his profound, incredible, over-weaning narcissism."[28]

As celebrities raged with anti-American fervor in the war on terrorism, a writer for *The Nation* magazine raised the specter of "McCarthyism," saying, "Back in the 1950s, an awful lot of lives were damaged" by sloppy allegations of disloyalty.[29] He doesn't mention whether or not the allegations were true; that's not the point. Celebrities feel the lash of censorship at the mere hint of criticism. It's a very elastic definition of censorship, these people have, including, "to not be fawned over by the American Legion as you attack your country" and "to not be greeted enthusiastically by authentic Americans after you mock the passengers on the 9-11 flights." Implying there was brutal suppression of dissent in America, Woody Harrelson said, "God forbid you should suggest the war is unjust." Jessica Lange said she found the atmosphere in America "poisonous, intolerable for those of us who are not right-wing."[30] Susan Sarandon complained, "I'm tired of being labelled anti-American because I ask questions."[31] Actors seem to think they have a constitutional right to say stupid things and have no one criticize them. Public reproach is the equivalent of being thrown in a gulag.

Tim Robbins touted his bravery in opposing the war with Iraq, saying, "It takes a lot of courage in this environment."[32] Janeane of Arc proclaimed, "I refuse to allow my government and the mainstream media to bully me into accepting a war that is immoral and illegal."[33] I gave earnest speeches like that when I was twelve years old.

Meanwhile, the most desperate, powerless people in Hollywood had very different ideas about what political positions to take to boost their careers. While there was plenty of anti-war palaver from genuine celebrities, the bulk of the Hollywood anti-war coalition consisted of actors who hadn't worked since they started broadcasting TV shows in color. The has-beens and wanna-bes seemed to have signed on to the anti-war lists on the off chance that their faces might appear in some B-roll on CNN so they could get their AFTRA benefits extended another six months. Actors Mike Farrell and Ed Asner were veritable titans of the broadcast arts compared to some of the speed bumps on the motley "Win Without War" list. They at least have dental coverage. Being anti-war in Hollywood was an act of bravery on the order of the keynote speaker at a PLO awards dinner making jokes about Ariel Sharon.

But sissy actors so longed for pretend-persecution, they would have attributed a rainy day to a right-wing McCarthyite blacklist. In a modern version of the Iran-Iraq war, actor Sean Penn accused Steve Bing, Hollywood producer and general degenerate, of blacklisting him from a film in retaliation for his peacenik activities. Bing not only has donated millions of dollars to the Democratic Party but also actively supports the Democrat lifestyle by fathering illegitimate children.

While objecting to having their patriotism questioned as they attacked America, celebrities made a big point of claiming to be the superior patriots for their constant kvetching. They never change, these liberals. Ezra Pound, too, claimed that his treasonable broadcasts from Rome were his "patriotic duty" and were intended to "save the consti-tution."[34] Sharmootah Sean Penn claimed to be "serv[ing] the country" by giving aid and comfort to an enemy about to be attacked by the U.S. He said it made him feel more patriotic to dissent from the war aims of his nation.[35] It is at least a counterintuitive position. Most people would not instantly grasp how it is more patriotic to always root against America. White supremacists should try claiming that burning crosses is *more* supportive of civil rights than not burning them.

During World War II, Ezra Pound arguably did less to earn a charge of treason than many of today's Hollywood stars. Admittedly, Pound continued to make his broadcasts after Pearl Harbor, when we were at war. The war with Iraq was merely pending when the liberal elite attacked their own country from Germany, London, Baghdad, and San Sebastian—though the war on terrorism was under way. The pronouncements from Penn and Harrelson came well after a congressional resolution approving war with Iraq, but before the shooting had started. On the other hand, Sean the Sham and The Pharaohs are in a position to give far greater "aid and comfort" to America's enemies. Few people ever heard Ezra Pound's treasonous broadcasts. Certainly the American public never did. Transcripts of Pound's fascist broadcasts were not published until years after his death. By contrast, in December 2002, Sean Penn's photo in front of a picture of Saddam Hussein was instantly blasted all over the globe. Within weeks of publication, Woody Harrelson's foreign policy report, "I'm an American Tired of American Lies," was posted on more than two thousand websites.

Consider the behavior of America's premier Lord Haw-Haw, former president Jimmy Carter. Just hours after the United States Congress authorized the use of force against Iraq, Norway—the country that gave us the term "quisling"—voted to give Carter the Nobel Peace Prize, warmly citing Carter's opposition to the war.[36] Chairman of the quislings, Gunnar Berge, said the award "should be interpreted as a criticism of the line that the current administration has taken. It's a kick in the leg to all that follow the same line as the United States."[37] The "line" being criticized by the award was the congressionally sanctioned policy of Carter's own country.

The moment the quislings voted to give Carter his award in honor of his vocal opposition to the war policies of his country, the press sprang to action, calling our Lord Haw-Haw America's "greatest" ex-president. The *Wall Street Journal*'s Al Hunt called Carter the "greatest ex-president in our history."[38] MSNBC's Brian Williams—who worked for Carter—asked a history professor if it was fair to call Carter "the best former president in, at minimum, modern American history, and perhaps, well, I guess, the last 200 years?" (Absolutely, historian Marshall Frady replied.)[39] On the *Today* show, Katie Couric said, "I mean, it's so wonderful . . . and so well deserved."[40]

Carter would travel to Norway to accept the award in December 2002—two months after Congress had authorized war against Iraq. Article III's definition of treason is narrow. But after Congress's action authorizing war, for any American to accept this award on the grounds offered does sound terribly like "adhering to their enemies, giving them aid and comfort." In his acceptance speech, Carter warned against "powerful countries" adopting "a principle of preventive war." He babbled about the importance of "peace," "harmony," "international consensus," and the preeminent importance of the United Nations. He said "we"—apparently meaning Americans—"should concentrate first on the obvious threat around the world from Al Qaeda."[41] That argument had already lost in the U.S. Congress and a use of force had been authorized.

Fortunately for Hollywood liberals and former Democratic presidents, the country discontinued prosecuting treason long ago. When the country decided not to prosecute Jane Fonda after the Vietnam War, the bar was raised. As the *New York Times* put it, Fonda's case was a "lighthouse on jagged rocks" for aspiring traitors like Sean Penn.[42] World War II–era traitors were prosecuted and sentenced to long prison terms for radio broadcasts heard by no one within America. "Axis Sally" was an American actress by the name of Mildred Gillars who tried to demoralize American troops from Berlin by chipperly informing them that their wives and girlfriends were cheating on them. "Tokyo Rose"—and there were actually several of them—took a more ham-handed approach, but also used feminine wiles to try to demoralize American GIs.[43] Axis Sally was sentenced to twelve years in prison. Tokyo Rose got six years in prison.[44] Hanoi Jane makes aerobics videos.

During the Vietnam War, Fonda gave wild, inflammatory anti-America speeches from Hanoi. She mugged for photographers, posing with North Vietnamese antiaircraft guns. At the time, serious thought was given to prosecuting her, but the ruling class was equivocal about treason. The refusal to prosecute Fonda was just one more indication that we weren't fighting that war to win. To this day, Fonda's case is emblematic of what liberals think is demanded of them as Americans. Penn wasn't even worried he would be unpopular, much less charged with treason. In the war on terrorism, the most Americans could hope for was that no Hollywood actress would have an affair with Saddam Hussein. America is such a wealthy country, now even treason is cheap.

14

MODERN McCARTHYISM: THIS IS WHAT IT MEANT IN THE FIFTIES, TOO

Bitterly disheartened by the outburst of patriotism across the nation after 9-11, liberals quickly channeled their frustration into claiming that President Bush had advance knowledge of the terrorist attack. Republicans were so dumbstruck by the Democrats' mendacity, they overlooked the most stunning legerdemain of the accusation. Suppose Bush had known nineteen Muslim immigrants planned to hijack four planes on a certain day. What could he have done? Throw Arabs out of the country? Put them in preventative detention? Order airport security to take an extra little peek at swarthy men boarding planes? Liberals wouldn't let us do that *after* 9-11. Instead of demanding to know what Bush knew before September 11, the more urgent question was: What did Democrats know *after* September 11?

The left's principal contribution to stopping another terrorist attack was to go into high dudgeon every time anyone in the Bush administration talked to a Muslim. They wailed about "McCarthyism" and claimed to be "very, very concerned"—not about terrorist attacks on America but about "civil liberties."[1] Liberals' idea for fighting domestic terrorism was to hold folk-song rallies with Muslims. In May 2002, Chairman of the Senate Judiciary Committee Patrick Leahy (D-Vt.) said that it was "imperative" that Bush tell the Senate "what actions were taken in response" to an FBI report warning of a lot of Arabs in flight school.[2] Leahy hauled Attorney General John Ashcroft before the Senate Judiciary Committee, saying he was "very" upset with Ashcroft, not because he was failing to do enough to prevent the next terrorist attack, but just the opposite: He was doing too much, thereby threatening the civil liberties of Arabs.[3] If the Democrats had shown half as much indignation about Saddam Hussein as they did about Ashcroft, their convictions might rate with real Americans.

In a girly-girl, eye-poking attack, House Minority Leader Dick Gephardt (D-Mo.) demanded an investigation into "what the White House knew about the events leading up to the attack, when they knew it and, most importantly, what was done about it."[4] Gephardt's genius plan for assuring air safety after September 11 was to federalize airport security. But he refused to allow airport security to scrutinize passengers who look like the last two dozen terrorists to attack civilian aircraft. That's what he did when he knew about it.

Democrats claimed to be indignant that nothing was done in response to the memo from an FBI agent in Phoenix who had noticed a lot of Arabs enrolled in American flight schools. But as the *New York Times* reported, "F.B.I. officials said there was reluctance at the time to mount such a major review because of a concern that the bureau would be criticized for ethnic profiling of foreigners." Let's see, who might have criticized the FBI for ethnic profiling?

For Ashcroft's evident interest in immigrants of Middle Eastern descent rather than white male currency traders *after* September 11, Sheila Jackson Lee (D-Tex.) railed that the detention of Arabs "smacks of racial profiling." Maxine Waters (D-Calif.) said the Bush administration was "literally dismantling justice."[5]

Senator Richard Durbin (D-Ill.) said the memo warning of Arabs in flight school was going "to be one of the most important documents in our national debate about whether we did enough to protect America from the attack of September 11th." What's this "we," paleface? After a savage terrorist slaughter by a group of immigrants of Middle Eastern descent, Durbin hysterically denounced people who support ethnic profiling of airline passengers as troglodytes "crawling on [their] bell[ies] in the mud at a right-wing militia training camp in Idaho."[6]

Senator Hillary Clinton—whose very first act in the Senate was to sponsor a bill prohibiting ethnic profiling—also demanded an investigation into what Bush knew and when he knew it. What did she know about her husband's serial philandering and when did she know it?

The *New York Times*'s Maureen Dowd said, "I guess nothing short of a copy of Mohammed Atta's Travelocity itinerary would have stirred the F.B.I. from its stupor." But back on November 25, 2001, Dowd was snarling about Ashcroft's questioning of Arab immigrants in the United States: "The first resistance to his edict to interview five thousand Middle Eastern men came from police chiefs objecting to racial profiling."[7] After Manhattan is nuked by fundamentalist Muslims, then will it be okay for the attorney general to question Middle Eastern men? Liberals are like little children on a car trip, but not as cute, incessantly demanding to know if we're there yet. Bush was deemed an incompetent for every single day he delayed in allowing liberals to attend Broadway plays without anxiety. They complained that Bush was not doing enough, while consistently opposing every domestic security measure he took.

In the midst of their constant carping, liberals refused to attack Bush for the one real black mark on the administration's antiterrorism efforts: Norman Mineta. Bursting with bipartisan bonhomie after he was elected, Bush made Democrat Mineta his secretary of transportation. At the time, Transportation was a relatively unimportant department; it would be difficult even for a Democrat to screw it up. After nineteen Arabs turned passenger airplanes into cruise missiles, the transportation department was no longer trivial. And Bush had a Clinton-holdover in the job. If the government had hired expensive Harvard-trained consultants to try to figure out a way to make the flying experience even more unpleasant after September 11, the consultants would have thrown their hands up in despair. But chalk one up to liberals: One lone bureaucrat at the Department of Transportation did it on his own!

In classic Democrat fashion, Mineta piled on lots of useless regulations that would inconvenience the maximum number of airline passengers while, at the same time, making the planes no safer. The most important thing, as Mineta saw it, was to prohibit airport screeners from paying any extra attention to anyone who looked like the last several dozen terrorists to attack an American aircraft, embassy, or military installation. Instead, he insisted that the airlines go through the manifestly absurd exercise of strip-searching little old ladies. In some goo-goo-minded attempt to prove they are not profiling, airport security made a big show of harassing precisely those passengers they should have been ignoring. This ought to have warmed the hearts of Saudi Arabians. Too bad they would never read about it, since their newspapers were too busy polishing the theory that Zionists bombed the World Trade Center.

According to the FAA, in November and December of 2001, due solely to security precautions that treated Texas cheerleaders no differently from Saudi men, 30 airport terminals were entirely evacuated, passengers on 434 flights were ordered off their planes for rescreening, 1,180 flights were delayed, 464 flights were canceled, and 15 flights were diverted to alternative destinations.[8] An elderly white congressman was ordered to strip to his underwear because of a steel hip joint. Women travelers were being asked to remove their bras. At the Los Angeles International Airport, security personnel confiscated a tiny little gun belonging to a G.I. Joe. In June 2002, airport security searched Al Gore. There's a lot not to like about Gore, but he's not a terrorist. Gore said he was glad he was searched.[9] Why? To spare a terrorist the trouble? This is a serious national issue; why must liberals lie? Searching Al Gore is a purely religious act. It is the purposeless, fetishistic performance of ritual in accordance with the civic religion of liberalism. Usually the nonsense liberals spout is kind of cute, but in wartime their instinctive idiocy is life-threatening. In response to a Muslim's attempted shoe bombing of an American Airlines jet in December 2001, Norman Mineta sprang to action by ordering the airlines to engage in random shoe checks. According to the *New York Times*, there was no discernible pattern in the airlines' choice of passengers targeted for aggressive footwear examination. At the Atlanta airport, for example, the passengers whose shoes were searched "included a flight attendant, an elderly black man, a white man wearing a cowboy hat and boots, and an Asian woman with two small children."[10]

Here, finally, was something Bush should have been pilloried and denounced for, but the Democratic Party was the dog that didn't bark. If law enforcement officers ever dared paw through the belongings of an Egyptian immigrant named Mustaffa with the fascist intensity of airport security patting down little old ladies suspected of flying to Iowa, liberals would have exploded in righteous indignation. But they didn't make a peep.

In early December 2001, *60 Minutes* host Steve Kroft interviewed Mineta about his approach to securing the airlines from terrorist attack. Kroft observed that of twenty-two men currently on the FBI's most-wanted list, "all but one of them has complexion listed as olive. They all have dark hair and brown eyes. And more than half of them have the name Mohammed."[11] Thus, he asked Mineta if airport security should give more scrutiny to someone named Mohammed—"just going down a manifest list: Bob, Paul, John, Frank, Steven, Mohammed." The secretary of transportation said, "No." In fact, Mineta was mystified by Kroft's question, asking him, "Why should Mohammed be singled out?" The Federal Aviation Administration had a computer profiling system on passengers, but it actually excluded mention of passengers' race, ethnicity, national origin, or religion. (What *does* it have?)

Mineta explained that airport security was able to consider other more important factors than race, including asking "things like, 'Did you pay cash for this ticket or charge it on a credit card? Do you have a one-way ticket or a round-trip?'" Kroft asked the relevant follow-up question: "Did the terrorists who flew into the World Trade Center have one-way tickets?" No, Mineta said, the terrorist hijackers all had round-trip tickets they bought with credit cards. So the factors airport security was allowed to consider would not have stopped the 9-11 attack, and the factors that could have prevented the 9-11 attack were required to be ignored.

Mineta obstinately refused to consider a relevant airport screening procedure on the grounds that fifty years earlier another Democrat had put him in an internment camp. "I remember on the 29th of May, 1942"—note that he remembers the day—"when we boarded the train in San Jose under armed guard, the military guard, I was in my Cub Scout uniform carrying a baseball, baseball glove and a baseball bat. And as I boarded the train, the MPs confiscated the bat on the basis it could be used as a lethal weapon."[12] A guard took Mineta's baseball bat as a child, and as a result he was subjecting all of America to the Bataan Death March. Someone should have sent him a baseball bat.

There was no principled basis for opposition to using Arab appearance as a factor in airport screening procedures. The whole country knew that goosing little old ladies boarding planes was not making us any safer. It was so patently absurd that even the *New York Times* allowed a surprisingly sensible opinion piece through the politically correct gauntlet, titled: "Let Them Profile Me."[13] The writer described security hassles she had encountered in airports all over the world on account of her Lebanese birth, name, and looks. But she then pointed out that Arab-Americans don't want to die, either. "Does anyone really want a security official to hesitate before stopping a suspicious passenger out of fear of an accusation of bias?" Yes, in fact. There were precisely two groups of people who desperately wanted airport security to be browbeaten into giving suspicious passengers a pass: terrorists and Democrats.

Even the Supreme Court was never this crazy. To the contrary, in a 1975 case called *United States* v. *Brignoni-Ponce*, the Court held that the "Mexican appearance" of a car's occupants could be considered by border police stopping cars near the Mexican border to look for illegal aliens. This was back in the halcyon days when the Court was inventing new and preposterous "rights" every other day. But even that Court didn't invent a right to have one's ethnic appearance ignored by law enforcement. Rather, the Court noted, "The government has estimated that 85 percent of the aliens illegally in the country are from Mexico." Meanwhile, 100 percent of the terrorist attacks on commercial airlines based in America for twenty years have been committed by Muslims. When there is a 100 percent chance, it ceases to be a profile. It's called a "description of the suspect." This is not a psychological judgment about an ethnic group—it is an all points bulletin: Warning! The next terrorist to board a commercial flight in the United States will be a Muslim. If ethnic appearance can be used as a factor by the police trying to stem the dire threat of one more Mexican raking leaves in Los Angeles, it is logical to conclude that ethnic appearance can also be used to counter the threat of thousands of Americans being killed in a terrorist attack.

American lives were put at risk in the name of political correctness. Safe on Air Force One, Bush did nothing to stop this menace at the Department of Transportation. And the Democrats didn't complain. The moment Mineta raised the Japanese internment (a Democrat idea), they were paralyzed. The Democrats had one clear shot at the Bush administration, but they wouldn't take it. This is what the Democrats did when they knew about it.

New York Times columnist Thomas Friedman sniffed that racial profiling was not "civilized." He blamed twenty years of relentless attacks by Muslim extremists on—I quote—"religious fundamentalists of any stripe."[14] I don't know. Amish extremists have been rather quiet lately. If all this carnage and murder had been committed by anti-abortion extremists rather than Muslim extremists, it is unlikely that Friedman would be pussyfooting around the issue by referring to the culprits as "political extremists of any stripe." He ruefully concluded that our only choices were to "become less open as a society" or simply "to live with much higher levels of risk." I have another solution. It's a little something I like to call "racial profiling." My logic is this: In twenty years of relentless attacks on America by Muslim extremists, there is a common thread. In every one of these attacks by Muslim extremists there appears to be one or more Muslim extremists involved. This ought to help the airlines engage in more accurate risk assessment.

To review the evidence:

- On September 11, 2001, more than three thousand Americans were murdered in a savage terrorist attack on U.S. soil by Muslim extremists.
- In October 2000, our warship the USS *Cole* was attacked by Muslim extremists.
- In 1998, U.S. embassies in Kenya and Tanzania were bombed by Muslim extremists.
- In 1996, a U.S. Air Force housing complex in Saudi Arabia was bombed by Muslim extremists.
- In 1995, five Americans were killed by a car bomb set by Muslim extremists.
- In 1993, the World Trade Center was bombed by Muslim extremists.
- In 1988, another passenger jet, Pan Am Flight 103, was bombed by Muslim extremists.
- In 1986, a West Berlin discotheque frequented by U.S. servicemen was bombed by Muslim extremists.
- In 1985, an Italian cruise ship, the *Achille Lauro,* was seized and a sixty-nine-year-old American was killed by Muslim extremists.
- In 1983, the U.S. Marine barracks in Beirut were blown up by Muslim extremists.
- In 1982, the U.S. embassy in Beirut was bombed by Muslim extremists.

▶ In 1979, the U.S. embassy in Iran was stormed and American
  embassy staff held hostage for 444 days by Muslim extremists.

So naturally, Democrats refuse to allow law enforcement to look for
Muslim extremists.

While braying about what Bush knew and when he knew it, liberals had nothing but contempt for Ashcroft, the man in the Bush administration doing the most to ensure another act of domestic terrorism did
not occur. Annoyed that they didn't have enough grist for the anti-war
mill, Democrats began complaining about every reasonable national
security measure at home. Liberals were angrier at John Ashcroft for
questioning Arab visitors to this country than they were about the terrorists. Bill Goodman of the Center for Constitutional Rights called
Bush and Ashcroft the Constitution's "main enemies."[15] The attorney
general was regularly compared to the Taliban—and you aren't a
patriot until some liberal compares you to the Taliban. *Newsweek*'s
Eleanor Clift ridiculed Ashcroft for his "pomposity." She complained
incomprehensibly about the terrorism alerts: "Why did Ashcroft insist
on issuing the alerts?"[16] (Perhaps to warn of terror threats?) She complained that not enough lawyers were rushing to court to undermine
the government's monitoring of terrorists' jailhouse conversations.

These alleged civil liberties concerns had only one purpose: to
give Muslims a cushion for another attack on America. Frank Rich
began a column with this: "Cheney, Rumsfeld, Ridge, Mueller. Is there
anyone who has not warned us of Armageddon over the past week? As
far as I can tell, the only slacker in this White House game of Wag the
Dog is Spot."[17] Was Rich suggesting that the war on terrorism was a
Hollywood invention airlifted to the Oval Office? Did he even think
about what he was writing?

Unable to root for al-Qaeda openly, Democrats lodged surly objections to the Bureau of Prisons for listening to the conversations of
prison inmates suspected of plotting terrorist attacks. Whenever liberals are losing on substance, they pretend to be upset about process.
Senator Leahy complained about Ashcroft's "disappointing" failure to

run all internal guideline changes past the Senate Judiciary Commit-tee. "Instead," he said, "we're presented with a fait accompli reflecting no congressional input whatsoever."[18] Ashcroft was probably worried Leahy would take as long with procedures for investigating terrorism as he was taking with Bush's judicial nominees. If Speedy Gonzalez Leahy were required to review Justice Department guidelines, America would be an Islamic regime before he got around to holding a vote.

In June 2002, the *New York Times* editorial page was in a snit with the Supreme Court for its first ruling on the Bush administration's wartime security procedures. Despite the clearly stated position of the *Times* editorial board, the Supreme Court ruled for Ashcroft. Deporta-tion hearings of suspected terrorists would not be open to the public. This, the *Times* said, was "troubling." Sadly, the Constitution does not require that national security be compromised.

When Ashcroft announced a plan to fingerprint all visitors from terrorist-producing countries, the *New York Times* said he was going in "the wrong direction." It was a "poorly conceived and inadequate sub-stitute for the serious overhaul of the immigration system."[19] Ashcroft, the éditorial continued, "should address basic problems rather than settling for quick but ultimately ineffective solutions."[20] Liberals always want some more comprehensive reform—they will never say what ex-actly. But under no circumstances may we inconvenience the enemy. That would be an "ultimately ineffective" solution. We must address issues with a long, ponderous search for solutions that would perhaps be more effective, but we'll all be dead.

A major political party that won a plurality of the popular vote in the last presidential election wanted to treat terrorists like Martha Stewart facing an insider trading charge. A few months after 9-11, forty congressmen released a letter lambasting Bush for his plan to use mil-itary tribunals for enemy combatants. Signing the letter were thirty-nine Democrats, one Vermont Independent, and one lone Republican (who was soon voted out of office). Senator Charles Schumer (D-N.Y.) demanded Senate hearings on the tribunals so that "foreign countries like Spain will look at the process better." Representative Jerrold

Nadler (D-N.Y.) said, "These procedures belong in a Soviet state or a dictatorship, not in a free society."[21]

Representative Jose Serrano, Democrat of New York, said Ashcroft's detention of two al-Qaeda terrorists as enemy combatants was "frightening."[22] Jose Padilla had been identified by captured al-Qaeda leader Abu Zubaydah as part of a conspiracy to detonate a dirty bomb in an American city.[23] Yaser Esam Hamdi was captured fighting with Taliban forces in Afghanistan. Liberals were appalled by their detentions because both of the accused terrorists were American citizens. Heated descriptions of various Muslim terrorists as "American citizens" were getting a little tiresome. The implication was that librarians in Boise, Idaho, were at risk of being thrown in jail as enemy combatants at any moment. Yes, technically, by law, Yasser Esam Hamdi and Jose Padilla were "American citizens." Talibanist John Walker Lindh was an "American citizen," and shoe bomber Richard Reid was a "British citizen." But then you'd see the AP photo and it was always a picture of some orangutan.

Human rights groups responded to the detention of every suspected terrorist with paranoid accusations of police state tactics. The *New York Times* reported, "International support for the campaign against terrorism is weakening because of human rights abuses by the United States, Human Rights Watch charged in a report published today."[24] *The Progressive* magazine said, "Welcome to the New McCarthyism."[25] ACLU president Nadine Strossen saw "parallels between what we're going through now and McCarthyism."[26] Professional McCarthy hysteric Ellen Schrecker said, "I'm terrified." There were dark rumors that terrorists were being stripped, humiliated, strapped down, and subjected to total sleep deprivation with lights and noise. Then it turned out the hapless victims of such brutal tactics weren't terrorists, but airline passengers since September 11. No one could name one thing Ashcroft had done that would alarm any normal person. Liberals seemed to imagine that the FBI had nothing better to do than to sit around investigating how much time they were spending logged onto panties.com.

Compared to any similar circumstance in U.S. history, Ashcroft was remarkably restrained. In 1924, after the homes of eight government officials were bombed, Attorney General A. Mitchell Palmer—appointed by Democrat Woodrow Wilson, though still serving under President Calvin Coolidge—rounded up 6,000 people. In 1942, after a sneak attack on Pearl Harbor—committed by a country, not resident aliens—a Democrat president put more than 100,000 Japanese residents and citizens in internment camps. By contrast, in the months following the most devastating terrorist attack in world history, in which 3,000 Americans were killed, John Ashcroft detained 766 noncitizens, many on immigration violations. Eighteen months later, more than 100 of them had been convicted or pleaded guilty to terrorism-related offenses and another 489 had been deported or left the United States willingly.[27] Even *Time* magazine had to admit that, despite the wails of civil liberties groups, "it is clear . . . at least some of the detainees are exactly the sort of people Americans would want the FBI to zero in on."[28] But *The Progressive* magazine vowed that Ashcroft's detention of a relatively small number of lawbreaking aliens "will go down in history as the Ashcroft Raids."[29] Eventually, frustrated with Ashcroft's moderation, liberals were forced to start staging events, so they could scream about their persecution. Most popular were attacks on the American flag (they really hate that flag) and vicious anti-American T-shirts all calculated to provoke a reaction—which they would then portray as fascist oppression.[30] With very little disruption and surprisingly few arrests, Ashcroft immobilized al-Qaeda's capacity to strike again.

The FBI had been on the Arab community like white on rice with wiretaps, informants, arrests, and interrogations. By the end of 2002, the Department of Justice had disrupted terrorist cells in Buffalo, Portland, and Detroit. The arrest of a former roommate of two 9-11 hijackers led to forty more arrests in a visa fraud scheme. More than two hundred airport workers in Washington, D.C., New York City, and Dallas airports had been arrested for document and immigration fraud.

At the Dallas and Newark airports, scores of workers were charged with alarming schemes to obtain access to high-security areas of the airports.

Preventing terrorism doesn't receive as much news coverage as the alternative. But from 9-11 through the end of 2002, the Bush administration had thwarted "an estimated 100 or more attacks against the United States and its interests." That stunning fact appeared in the middle of a small news item on page A-11 of the *New York Times*.[31] Few other news outlets mentioned it at all. To be sure, the nation would not be safe from terrorist attack until the malarial swamps were completely drained—something else the Democrats opposed. But a year and a half after the attack of September 11, there had been nothing approaching the horror of those attacks. That wasn't a bet many people would have taken on September 12, 2001.

It's safe to assume Ashcroft wasn't getting a lot of help. And yet he calmly persisted in the face of caterwauling idiots. This is a country virtually designed for terrorist attacks. America is a big multicultural society full of densely packed cities with large foreign-born populations—and hundreds of thousands of illegal immigrants. Try this with another country: *Hello, Indian Embassy? I would like to emigrate to your country. I have no money, no ambition, and no prospects, but I hear you have a generous welfare program and I want to start a big family and bring my extended family with me, all of whom consider your nation the Great Satan.*

Foreigners were relentlessly staging raids on our border, which was defended by a hapless bunch of incompetents at the Immigration and Naturalization Service. But the only complaints about the INS came from conservatives. Liberals view their own noncompliance with immigration laws as a sort of friendly-neighbor program. They think America is a department store, and that no one can be denied entry. Los Angeles police officers are expressly prohibited from even questioning suspects, witnesses, or crime victims—anyone—about their immigration status. When he was the avenging law and order mayor of

New York City, Rudolph Giuliani bragged about the city's refusal to cooperate with the INS in turning over illegal immigrants. His successor, Mayor Michael Bloomberg, believes the greatest threat to public safety in New York City is passive smoke. Bloomberg would only crack down on illegal immigrants if he caught them smoking.

The nation's political ethos demands that we pretend we don't suspect Egyptian immigrant Hesham Mohamed Hadayet any more than Al Gore. The rights of the accused trump the rights of the law-abiding. Special interest groups defend the right of predators to move freely in the general population. There are bands of lawyers ready to sue in response to any incident of law enforcement—just like back in Syria. The FBI was surely more polite to Middle Eastern immigrants than people in their home countries would be to us under similar circumstances. Indeed, if the government's treatment of terrorism suspects was as brutal as the left claimed, it might remind them of home.

Sensing that screaming about the rights of terrorists was not impressing voters, about a year after 9-11, Democrats switched gears and began assailing Bush for not doing *enough* about domestic security. Leading the way were a host of presidential candidates. Senator John Edwards (D-N.C.) said, "It's time for us, without regard to party, to say what every American knows—Washington is not doing enough to make America safe." Senator John Kerry (D-Mass.) said the Bush administration had failed to make "the preparations necessary to properly deal with an obvious problem of growing terror and the threat at home." Senator Joseph I. Lieberman (D-Conn.) said, "This administration has been slow and inadequate in the response to the terrorist threat here at home." Had there been another terrorist attack the nation was unaware of? There was the shooting at the El Al counter at the Los Angeles airport and the sniper attacks. But liberals wouldn't even admit that the perpetrators of those attacks were Muslims, so by their count, there hadn't been a single new act of domestic terrorism since 9-11. How exactly would liberals have done a better job? Have John Edwards sue after every attack? Put Hillary in charge of the Armed Services on the basis of her husband's acknowledged expertise in evading armed service?

If bashing Bush on domestic security was the Democrats' winning idea, one can only imagine what ideas came in second.

The fact that Democrats were rushing to have their warnings duly placed on the record was alarming. On its face, the idea that any Democrat is meaningfully concerned with security was a joke. They consider it a bore. Unfortunately, the Bush administration was obliged to give these knuckleheads parliamentary briefings on national security. Implicit in their complaints was the Democrats' hope that something would happen so they could attack Bush for not having prevented it. Democrats were leering over the prospect of another terrorist attack to use as political fodder against Bush.

Liberals belittled every bust of a terrorist cell as an overhyped publicity stunt from that cornpone Ashcroft. They were not impressed, for example, by Ashcroft's arrest of some nice Yemeni gentlemen in Lackawanna, New York. In almost every news account, the reasons for the arrest were murky and immediately buried beneath copious rationalizations from the men's defense attorneys. Interestingly, the most forthright and complete accounts of the government's case came from a noted Muslim journalist, Anwar Iqbal, writing for United Press International.

The facts were alarming, especially after 9-11. In the summer of 2001, eight men of Yemeni descent, most U.S. citizens, flew in three groups to Pakistan. The spiritual leader of the group, Kamal Derwish, left first. The next group arrived in April and the third in May. Excited by the prospect of meeting Osama bin Laden, they crossed the border into Afghanistan and traveled to what was then Taliban-controlled Kandahar. At an al-Qaeda "guesthouse" they watched promotional videos for al-Qaeda, including speeches by Osama bin Laden and other al-Qaeda leaders. After watching videos denouncing America and Israel and boasting of attacks on the U.S., such as the bombing of the USS *Cole*, the men continued to the next level, an al-Qaeda training camp.[32]

At the al-Farooq training camp, they received training in explosives, Kalashnikov assault rifles, and long-range weapons.[33] Derwish, who had been to the camp before, was enrolled in more advanced military training. Osama bin Laden appeared and gave a fiery speech to the camp. One of the accused, Sahim A. Alwan, stayed for ten days before leaving. The rest stayed for the full five to six weeks of terrorist training. Six of the men then returned to Lackawanna, and two others were believed to have returned to Yemen. Upon their return, the men trimmed their beards. Neighbors found them oddly taciturn about a trip they had begun with great fanfare.

The FBI kept the six men in Lackawanna under surveillance from the moment of their return—months before 9-11. Not so asleep at the wheel after all, these FBI agents. Alwan had a message waiting for him from the FBI when he returned in June 2001. Asked about the trip, Alwan lied to the FBI agent, claiming they had gone for religious training and never left Pakistan. After 9-11, the FBI talked to several of the men about their trip. They all maintained they had never left Pakistan. Despite the fact the men were unemployed or had menial jobs, they never wanted for money. Each had paid $1,300 in cash for plane tickets to Pakistan. After being fired from his job as a bill collector, Yasein Taher bought a new Mustang convertible and a Ninja motorcycle.[34] The unemployed Taher and Shafal A. Mosed, a telemarketer, spent $89,000 gambling at Casino Niagara.[35] A high school classmate said, "They were driving flashy cars and buying up all this stuff."[36]

There was more. As the first anniversary of the 9-11 attack approached, one of the men, Mukhtar al Bakri, sent an e-mail titled "The Big Meal" from Bahrain to another of the men. He wrote: "There are people who have been having visions . . . This is a very strong vision. A vision nobody will be able to bear." The e-mail continued: "The next meal will be very huge. It will be so big that no one will be able to withstand it, except the people with faith." (Al Bakri's lawyer would later suggest that the "big meal" referred to a hamburger.)[37]

Operating on tips from within the community and noticing an increase in "chatter" among the group, the FBI arrested the author of the "big meal" e-mail on September 10 in Bahrain, where he was marrying a Yemeni woman. At first, al Bakri stuck to the story that the men had never left Pakistan, but after being beaten by the Bahraini police, he was more forthcoming. He admitted the group had attended an al-Qaeda training camp in Afghanistan. The five men back in Lackawanna were arrested on September 13, 2002. The FBI found a cache of weapons in one suspect's home and a brief for "martyrdom operations" in the home of another. Still, the men maintained they had simply gone to Pakistan for religious training and nothing more.

Here were men who trained with Osama bin Laden—the one enemy liberals were willing to acknowledge. It was one year after thousands of Americans were slaughtered by young Muslim men with remarkably similar curricula vitae. The men lied to the FBI about their al-Qaeda training. They had lots of unexplained cash. They had recently exchanged an e-mail about a coming "big meal" that only people of faith would be able to withstand. And this was only what the government was telling us.

Naturally, therefore, the media fanned out across Lackawanna in search of any pogrom-oriented Americans committing hate crimes against Muslims. In fact, the only provable hate crime in Lackawanna was committed by the *New York Times*, which ran a staged photo of a six-year-old boy pointing a toy gun at a sign that said "Arabian Foods."[38] In reaction to an uproar from other journalists who had witnessed the photo's production, the *Times* eventually ran a correction, admitting it had been staged.

According to the FBI, members of the Muslim community had provided crucial tips about the men. But the *New York Times* ran only lachrymose accounts of Yemeni-Americans trembling in terror and indignation at the FBI, while "staunchly" defending the terrorist trainees.[39] It was just like the *Times*'s man-on-the-street interviews on Bush's tax plan. For the *Times*, an "ordinary American" is a sociology professor in Oregon whose wife teaches tantric sex at the community college. You can imagine what the "ordinary Muslim" is like. Every Muslim the *Times* talked to believed the arrested men were innocent, saying "Mistakes have been made, risks overstated, lives ruined."[40] "Many" said the men had been "misinterpreted" and the government was "trying to find the men guilty by association."[41] One of the al-Qaeda trainees was called "a pillar of the neighborhood"[42]—also "too fat to be a trained terrorist." (Apparently *he* could not withstand the "big meal.") The aspiring terrorists were "aimless but essentially harmless American Muslims, all of them United States citizens."[43]

National Public Radio also interviewed Yemeni incensed at the arrests of the Osama acolytes. One Muslim said she felt her religion was "on trial."[44] Another said she felt "forced to defend herself." She indignantly cited Timothy McVeigh as if it were manifestly absurd to imagine Muslims were more likely to commit terrorism than anyone else.[45] In a similarly widespread phenomenon, a few years ago, a man was killed with a crossbow in Brooklyn.[46] That doesn't mean New York City cops should be focusing on illegal crossbows. Another anonymous member of the Yemeni community said he thought the arrested men were "the victims of wrong assumptions." He admitted to curiosity about what they were doing in an al-Qaeda terror camp, but he evidently overcame his curiosity.[47]

Newsweek quoted people in "the community" who said it should not be a crime to travel to Afghanistan to "learn more about Islam." To this, *Newsweek* remarked, "Maybe not in Lackawanna. In Washington, however, there are plenty of people who believe it's a crime that should get them fifteen years."[48] Perhaps training with a terrorist organization that slaughtered thousands of Americans is not deserving of the beatings that will be accorded Enron executives, but a short prison sentence might be appropriate. Explaining the genesis of the trip, *Newsweek* reported, "A Muslim evangelical group invited the men to attend a religious gathering in Pakistan."[49] Evangelism? These aren't Mormons. Al-Qaeda "evangelism" consists of flying planes into skyscrapers and decapitating journalists.

But according to *Newsweek*, Ashcroft was on a crusade. The attorney general had "vowed to root [out]" al-Qaeda sleeper cells operating in the U.S., "even if that means stretching the limits of the law."[50] That's an odd phrase. Ashcroft hadn't plowed any new legal ground in arresting people who trained with a foreign army of terrorists waging war against America. Why not: *"Ashcroft vowed to enforce the law against terrorists"*? The *New York Times* suggested that the Lackawanna case put all Americans at risk: "The prosecution's case, at least in part, is that a terrorist can be the kid next door."[51] Yes—if the kid next door trained with al-Qaeda. Mohammed Atta lived next door to somebody, too. Don't all criminals live next door to somebody? What was the *Times*'s point?

In a bizarre attempt to impress the *New York Times*, Eric Boehlert wrote in Salon.com that the Lackawanna case turned "in part" on "whether downloading a document that debates suicide attacks proves terrorist ties." The document found at the home of Yasein Taher, one of the terrorist trainees, did not "debate" suicide attacks: It came out foursquare for them. But according to Boehlert, the jihad document "seems to have questionable relevance to the terrorism allegations."[52] Maybe, as Who guitarist Pete Townshend said of his child pornography, Taher had downloaded the document for "research." Boehlert insisted that the document be put "in its proper context." The context was this: Eight Middle Eastern men attended an al-Qaeda training camp in Afghanistan, had a lot of unexplained cash, and exchanged an e-mail during an Orange alert warning of a coming "big meal" that only the faithful would be able to survive.

But for Boehlert, the mere fact that the terrorist instruction manual was "widely available" on the Internet proved "the paucity" of the government's case and showed "how the government will take anything they can get their hands on and use it selectively."[53] The charming document, titled "The Islamic Ruling on the Permissibility of Martyrdom Operations," is a paean to jihad, with page after page of religious justifications for suicide missions under Islam.[54] It says, "We have found, through the course of our experience that there is no other technique which strikes as much terror into their hearts, and which shatters their spirit as much." Citing passages from Islamic texts and the words of Mohammed, the document says, "One who kills himself because of his strong faith and out of love for Allah and the Prophet, and in the interests of the religion, is praiseworthy." It complains that

Muslims "have neglected this great duty," and says every Muslim should be a "self-sacrificer" who embarks on a suicide mission "out of strength of faith and conviction, and to bring victory to Islam, by sacrificing his life for the upliftment of Allah's word!"

After 9-11, anyone slightly darker than Tony Orlando found with this document should have been arrested. In this case, it was found in the home of an Arab Muslim who recently trained with Osama bin Laden. Two months after the Lackawanna cell was broken, the CIA launched a missile strike against a car carrying Abu Ali, a key al-Qaeda leader in Yemen. With him in the car was Kamal Derwish, the ringleader of the Lackawanna cell.[55]

Liberals took the position that unless Ashcroft told them everything and destroyed the effectiveness of his investigations, they would refuse to believe him. No matter how spectacular the arrest, liberals invariably responded with, *You call that a terrorist?* When the government arrested a suspected dirty bomber, Jose Padilla, in Chicago, *Time* magazine said most people reacted with "equal parts 'Holy crap!' and 'Hey, wait a minute—how do we know these uncorroborated threats are on the level? What's the source?'"[56] Columnist Maureen Dowd said of the dirty bomber's arrest: "Is the Bush crowd hyping things?" Evidently she thought they were: "Ashcroft, Bobby Three Sticks and Paul 'Bomb Iraq' Wolfowitz breathlessly told the nation that they had thwarted a scary radiological bombing plot." Ho, ho, ho. The arrest of Padilla, Dowd said, "was designed both to make our teeth chatter and our gratitude well up. Weren't we thankful that the Bushies were finally catching somebody and protecting us?" Dowd was in stitches over the Bush administration claiming "the military has in custody a bona fide al Qaeda operative."[57] The war on terrorism was a joke.

Liberals' main point about the dirty bomber was that Padilla was too stupid to detonate a dirty bomb. In this one case, they had been given dispensation from the *New York Times* to attack the intelligence of a Latino. Padilla thus joined a shortlist of minorities whom liberals were allowed to vent their spleens on, the others being Justice Clarence Thomas and black voters in Florida. Citing anonymous "experts,"

Dowd questioned whether Padilla had "the brains" or "know-how" to construct a nuclear bomb.[58] Ashcroft, she said, had "built up the dirty bomber into an Atta-like terrorist capable of leveling downtown Washington."[59] But of course, as Dowd repeatedly intimated, Padilla was just a dumb Hispanic.

This was as opposed to that Napoleonic genius Mohammed Atta, Master War Strategist. The 9-11 terrorists didn't design the cruise missile's targeting system, they sucker punched a sleeping giant. If shoe-bomber Richard Reid hadn't been caught in the act of putting a match to a fuse on his Paris–Miami flight, liberals would have sniffed that he didn't have "the brains" to commit a terrorist act either. Until he was sixty seconds away from blowing up an airplane, the only suspicious fact about Reid was that he had once attended an al-Qaeda training camp.

The nation's various *New York Times* wanna-bes—*All the Crusading Anger with None of the Stature!*—were similarly skeptical of every terrorist the government arrested. The Allentown, Pennsylvania, *Morning Call* said the Bush administration was "reeling in small fry and making a big deal about it."[60] Members of a suspected al-Qaeda cell in Portland, Oregon, the paper said, "sound more like countercultural malcontents, not much different from any number of groups that have had grievances with our country in the past."[61]

Only when a Muslim terrorist proved his bona fides by killing people would the media believe it. That in turn would set off a Code Orange alert in the media, requiring total suppression of the information that the perp was a Muslim. Emerging as al-Qaeda's leading spokesman in America, when Muslim terrorists first attacked the World Trade Center back in 1993, the *New York Times* ran the headline "Jersey City Man Is Charged in Bombing of Trade Center."[62] On July 4, 2002, an Egyptian living in California named Hesham Mohamed Hadayet walked into an El Al terminal at the Los Angeles airport and started shooting Jews. (Not that there's anything unpeaceful about that.) In the past, Hadayet had complained about his neighbors' flying a U.S. flag, he had a "Read the Koran" sticker on his front door, and he had expressed virulent hatred for Jews. The *Times* reported straight that his motive for the shooting may have been "some dispute over a fare."[63]

The *Times* also blacked out the information that the terrorists who seized a Moscow theater in October 2002 were Muslims. In a prolix front-page article about the "hostage siege" in Russia, the *Times* referred to the Islamic terrorists who stormed the theater exclusively as the "captors," the "separatists," and the "guerrillas." One searches in vain for a clear statement that the Moscow hostage crisis was yet another enterprise of the Religion of Peace. The only hint that the "captors" were Muslims was the *Times*'s derisive reference to Russian president Vladimir V. Putin's attempt "to cast the rebels as international Islamic terrorists."[64] The *Times* knows a cheap political ploy when it sees one.

Most neurotically, the media aggressively censored the terrorists' Muslim names. When an Arab terrorist becomes an "American citizen," that legal formality is strictly observed by the press. But when a Muslim terrorist legally changes his name to Mohammed, that legal formality is ignored. Dirty bomber Jose Padilla had his name legally changed to Ibrahim in the mid-nineties.[65] When he was arrested on terrorism-related charges in mid-2002, the media changed it back— allowing Maureen Dowd to argue that he was a dumb Hispanic incapable of assembling a dirty bomb. California traitor "John Walker Lindh" changed his name to Suleyman Al-Lindh in high school.[66] When he was captured fighting with the Taliban, he was going by the name Abdul Hameed. He hadn't used the name Lindh for years. But he was identified in the press exclusively as John Walker Lindh. Thwarted shoe-bomber "Richard Reid" was identified by the French police as Tariq Raja.[67] The name he answered to at the time he tried to bomb an airplane was his Muslim name, Abdel Rahim. Naturally, therefore, the media called him Richard Reid, the name on his passport. Indeed, the *New York Times* went the extra mile, describing him as Richard Colvin Reid, a British citizen with a "Christian upbringing."[68] The *Miami Herald* ran a headline on Reid titled: "Shoe Bomb Suspect's Motives a Mystery."[69]

Stubbornly imitating an Alzheimer's joke, when terrorist snipers in Maryland and Virginia turned out to be Muslims, the media treated it like a random crime. The older of the two Muslims had converted to Islam seventeen years earlier, changed his name to John Muhammad, belonged to Louis Farrakhan's Nation of Islam, and cheered the 9-11 terrorist attack. Indeed, he was so gung-ho about the 9-11 attack that three of his acquaintances contacted the FBI, believing he could be a terrorist. Inadvertently including relevant facts in an article, the *New York Times* reported that Muhammad registered the getaway vehicle with the DMV on the first anniversary of the 9-11 attack, writing in the time of the registration as "8:52 a.m."—the precise moment the first plane had hit the World Trade Center.

But what the media saw as the crucial, salient fact about sniper John Muhammad was that he was a Gulf War veteran. CNN valiantly insisted on calling John Muhammad by his Christian name—a name he hadn't used for seventeen years. The night the snipers' names were first released, CNN's Jeanne Meserve repeatedly called him John Allen Williams.

The *New York Times* described the snipers thus: "John Allen Muhammad, 41, a Gulf War Veteran, and John Lee Malvo, 17, a Jamaican." Inasmuch as the nation was at war with Islamic terrorists, you might think it would be of passing interest that the snipers were Muslims. But you needed a *New York Times* decoder ring to figure out that *GULF WAR VETERAN* John Muhammad was a Muslim. The only clue as to the snipers' religion was the *Times*'s repeated insistence that Islam had absolutely nothing to do with the shootings. In the three months following the capture of the Muslim snipers terrorizing the capital, the *Times* would run 128 articles about the shootings. Only 9 would so much as mention the word "Muslim."[70]

The refusal to make a connection between Muslim extremists and unending violence by Muslim extremists borders on psychopathological disturbance. Islamic fanatics were staging random acts of brutality against Americans. When the Maryland snipers turned out to be Muslims who hated America and admired the 9-11 terrorists, someone in the media might have remembered that. Instead, all news outlets aggressively hid the fact that the snipers were Muslims.

To find out what the enemy was up to, you kept having to turn to obscure little boxes at the bottom of page A9 of the Newspaper of Record. In a little-noticed story almost exactly one year after Muslims staged the most horrible terrorist attack the world has ever seen, a Muslim en route from Germany to Kosovo emerged from the airplane bathroom and tried to strangle a stewardess with his shoelaces. (Not that there's anything unpeaceful about that.) That story was squirreled away in a small box at the very bottom of page A9 of the *Times*. In the entire Lexis-Nexis archives, only three newspapers reported the incident. Not one mentioned that the attacker was a Muslim. It was a rather captivating story, too. Earlier in the flight, the Muslim responded to the stewardess's offer of refreshments by saying, "I'd like to drink your blood." (Not that there's anything unpeaceful about that.)

America was at war with Islamic fanatics, but liberals treated every new onslaught like a bolt out of the blue. If the 9-11 terrorists had been fundamentalist Christians, the shoelace strangler a fundamentalist Christian, the shoe-bomber and snipers fundamentalist Christians, the Los Angeles airport killer a fundamentalist Christian, and scores of suicide bombers fundamentalist Christians, you can be sure the media would not censor the terrorists' religion. Liberals bar the most benign expressions of religion by little America. Only a religion that is highly correlated with fascistic attacks on the U.S. commands their respect and protection.

Liberals become indignant when you question their patriotism, but simultaneously laugh at dumb Americans who love their country and hate the enemy. They think real patriotism should consist of redoubled efforts to expand welfare payments. The *New York Times* ran a "Tom Tomorrow" cartoon sneering about Americans who believe with "unwavering faith in an invisible omniscient deity who favors those born in the middle of the North American landmass." This is how liberals conceive of America: an undifferentiated landmass in the middle of North America. The point was simply to convey all the proper prejudices of elitist liberals against ordinary Americans. While hooting with laughter at patriotic Americans, liberals prattle on and on about the right to dissent as the true mark of patriotism and claim their unrelenting kvetching is a needed corrective to jingoism. (It's not jingoism, and the only people who use that word are fifth columnists.)

Through their enervating dialogues and endless concerns with process, liberals made themselves incapable of feeling hate for the enemy. The president of the ACLU said America's response to terrorism was "exactly the same phenomenon" as McCarthyism.[71] And so it was. Once again, liberals would defend people contriving plots to murder Americans. Liberals simply did not have an implacable desire to kill those who cheered the wanton slaughter of thousands of Americans. But that's the way American people felt. Anyone who could "rise above" that, anyone who had "moved on" from that, wasn't angry in the first place. Liberals are appalled by patriotism with an edge of anger because it might lead America to defend itself.

CONCLUSION:
WHY THEY HATE US

While liberals ponder the psychopathology of Islamofascists, it might be useful to examine their own psychological profile. Why do they hate America? Are liberals "humiliated"? Paranoid? Agrarian reformers? And do we have to be nice to them, too?

Whether they are rooting for the atheistic regimes of Stalin and Mao, satanic suicide bombers and terrorists, or the Central Park rapists, liberals always take the side of savages against civilization. Indeed, an attack on America by Islamic fanatics finally gave the lie to the old Communist Party line about anti-Communism being a covert form of anti-Semitism. Inasmuch as half the Soviet spies were Ivy-educated WASPs, this was always a stretch. Even the willfully stupid might have noticed that their pal Stalin wasn't exactly holding parades for Jews.

But when confronted with terrorists who despised both America and the Jews, there was no doubt whose side the left would take. The breathtaking anti-Semitism of America's enemy, and of the enemy's claque in Europe, didn't even give the traitor lobby pause. Liberals, it turned out, were perfectly copacetic with the most virulent anti-Semitism imaginable—provided it served the cause of anti-Americanism. It isn't anti-Semitism or philo-Semitism or racism that drives them. It's hatred of civilization.

The left's deep sensitivity to anti-Semitism had always been a convenient lie. The Communists' opposition to Hitler turned on whichever side Stalin was on. During the Hitler-Stalin Pact, American Communists were stone pacifists. Only when Germany attacked Russia did they yearn for American boys to go fight Hitler. In 1945, with Stalin safe, *The Nation* magazine derided the atrocity films of Hitler's death camps as a hoax. The films had been made by American GIs still reeling from what they found at Nazi concentration camps— stacked bodies, mass burials, and ditches full of human remains. Writing in *The Nation,* the novelist, poet, and film critic James Agee denounced the films as propaganda.[1] The Harvard Graduate School of Education now has a James Agee chair of Social Ethics.

But liberals would throw any pot or pan in an argument. Their zealous—if delayed—support for war with Hitler provided sufficient basis for Communists to begin calling themselves "antifascists," as if they had been any more antifascist than Senator Strom Thurmond, who helped liberate Buchenwald (the site of some atrocities denied at *The Nation*). Through their infernal word games, the supporters of one totalitarian regime identified themselves as opponents of another totalitarian regime. The words "peace" and "fascist" and "antifascist" were twisted to mean the opposite of the truth. Liberals preyed on Americans' hatred of Nazism to associate conservatives with fascism. Their loudness papered over the details.

In the war on terrorism, liberals once again are cheering for the destruction of civil society. Upon viewing widespread repression, poverty, and violence across the Middle East, liberals turned with a vengeance against Israel, the one small outpost of democracy in the entire region. College protesters began demanding that universities divest from Israel. Anti-war protests bled into anti-Israel protests and sometimes into anti-Semitic hooliganism. The divestment campaign was especially popular at America's madrasahs—"the nation's most prestigious universities, including Yale, Harvard, Princeton and Cornell."[2] The Ivy League was once again doing its part for the country.

In April 2002, a favorite of the liberal intellectual set, Irish poet Tom Paulin, told the Egyptian newspaper *Al-Ahram* that "Brooklyn-born Jews" living in the West Bank "should be shot dead." This wasn't a colorful polemic: "Brooklyn-born Jews" in the West Bank really were being shot dead. He continued in the same vein, saying of the "Brooklyn-born Jews": "I think they are Nazis, racists, I feel nothing but hatred for them." The next semester, this Oxford don and BBC commentator was a visiting professor at Columbia University. (Perhaps he and Columbia professor Eric Foner would finally be able to get to the bottom of the puzzle about whether the 9-11 terrorist attack was worse than rhetoric emanating from the Bush White House.) Among Paulin's poems is one called "Killed in Crossfire," which refers to the Israeli army as "the Zionist SS." This gem was published in the *London Observer* the day before the release of *Stupid White Men*, written by American liberal Michael Moore. On Moore's book is a jacket-flap endorsement from one and the same—Tom Paulin.[3] (Someday we'll discover 20,000 copies of *Stupid White Men* in each room of David Geffen's house.)

In November, Paulin was invited by the English Department at Harvard to deliver the prestigious—because everything associated with Harvard is prestigious—Morris Gray Poetry Reading. This is a university that wouldn't buy a cup of coffee for a conservative speaker. But Harvard officially invited a terrorist sympathizer to read his poems.[4] Only after an explosion of negative publicity, mostly from outside the university, was the offer rescinded "by mutual agreement." BBC, sharing the politics of our own television networks, posted a cheerful story about the controversy, saying Paulin's "polemical, knockabout style has ruffled feathers in the U.S., where the Jewish question is notoriously sensitive." The "Jewish question"? The BBC treated an endorsement of terrorist murder as merely a niche sectarian issue.

Our European "allies," so adored by liberals, were a maelstrom of anti-Semitism after the 9-11 terrorist attack.[5] Despite assurances from our crucial "ally" French president Jacques Chirac that "there is no anti-Semitism in France,"[6] the Simon Wiesenthal Center was soon distributing a travel advisory urging Jews to exercise "extreme caution" in traveling to France.[7] In April 2002, a synagogue in Marseille, France, was burned to the ground. It was the sixth attack on Jewish religious sites in France that week. Another synagogue in Lyon, France, was set upon by fifteen masked assailants, who smashed two cars into it before setting it on fire. A kosher butcher shop in a village near Toulouse was fired on by a man with a gun. A Jewish school at Sarcelles was ransacked. In Paris, a Jewish schoolbus was attacked with stones and two other buses were set on fire. Also in Paris, a team of Jewish soccer players were beaten with iron bars.[8] In Villeurbanne, a Jewish couple was beaten so badly the woman had to spend a night in the hospital.[9] The anti-Semitism among our "allies" got so bad that even Amnesty International issued a press release condemning violence against both "Arabs and Jews." (Examples of attacks on Arabs were a little sparse.)[10] American liberals insisted that we needed the moral authority of these paragons before disarming Saddam Hussein.

European barbarism baffles Americans, since they look like us. But what defines Western Europe—as well as the American left—is its aggressive secularism. Though cathedrals abound, Christianity is a thin membrane over the cultural and political institutions of Europe. By contrast, from the time the pilgrims landed in the New World, Americans have been defined by their belief in God. In *Democracy in America*, written in 1835, Alexis de Tocqueville observed that Europeans practiced religion from a "barren traditionary faith which seems to vegetate in the soul rather than to live," but Americans "combine the notions of Christianity and liberty so intimately that it is impossible to make them conceive of one without the other."[11] America disproved the canard from the French Revolution holding that religion and freedom were incompatible. To the contrary, de Tocqueville said: "There are certain populations in Europe whose unbelief is only equaled by their ignorance and debasement; while in America, one of the freest and most enlightened nations in the world, the people fulfill with fervor all the outward duties of religion."[12]

De Tocqueville pronounced religion "the foremost of the political institutions" in America.[13] He said there exists no country in the world "where the Christian religion retains a greater influence over the souls of men than in America."[14] As a result, "while the law permits the Americans to do what they please, religion prevents them from conceiving, and forbids them to commit, what is rash or unjust."[15] And then one day, an entire political party defended a lying felon on the grounds that "everybody does it."

While undermining victory in the Cold War, liberals dedicated themselves to mainstreaming Communist ideals at home. Soviet stooge Henry Wallace wrote in his diary that FDR had assured him that he was a few years ahead of his time, but that his vision for America would "inevitably come."[16] It has come, and in a manner Americans never expected. Betraying the manifest national defense objectives of the country is only part of the left's treasonous scheme. They aim to destroy America from the inside with their relentless attacks on morality and the truth.

The immediate consequence of the Bolshevik Revolution in Russia was a wholesale abandonment of morals. Laws against divorce were loosened, promiscuity was encouraged, and marriage was demeaned as a "bourgeois institution." Providing a battle cry for the sexual anarchists, Vladimir Lenin had famously said that the act of sex should "be as simple and unimportant as drinking a glass of water."[17] American liberals have used their hegemonic control of television, movies, glossy magazines, and newspapers to create a charming world in which women apparently cannot bear to keep their shirts on. Promoting the feminist version of Howard Stern sexuality, liberals champion joyless sex. As Irving Kristol said, a liberal is a person who sees a fourteen-year-old girl performing live sex acts onstage and wonders if she's being paid the minimum wage. All media outlets keep up the drumbeat for lesbianism, abortion on demand, and pornography. It's Jerry Springer's world. We just live in it.

Feminists led the way. In 1998, *CBS This Morning* cohost Jane Robelot cheerfully reported on the wonderful world feminists had wrought: "The women's movement brought change and power to millions of American females. Virginal brides surrendered to the sexual revolution. Modern fashions exposed body parts previously reserved for the bedroom. Entering the workforce meant the old ways that women met men were ancient history [video clip of a milkman]. And a new breed of superwoman said 'I can have it all.' . . . The search for pleasure leads some women to shop [video clip of sex toys] and some to stray. . . . And experts say many husbands and wives can become stronger individuals, and on rare occasions, might even find that cheating recharges their marriage."[18] Exhibitionism, promiscuity, sex toys, and adultery. This is women's liberation.

Interestingly, de Tocqueville attributed the strength and character of America to its women. While European women were fainting in the parlor with the vapors, in the New World women joined their husbands in conquering the American frontier. The strength and independence of American women are legendary. Most important, de Tocqueville said, women were the keepers of religious faith. "No free communities ever existed without morals," he said, "and morals are the work of women."[19] Not anymore. A large segment of American women have traded faith in the Supreme Being for faith in gun control laws and day care centers. We live in an America in which soccer moms swoon over Bill Clinton, and Larry Flynt is a cultural icon. Feminists get enthusiastic about the war on terrorism only when they think we are fighting to redeem Western licentiousness. Our men are up to the job of protecting us from foreign enemies, but our women are losing the war at home.

It is not an accident that the relentless attacks on morality spring from America's women. "The aim of the party," George Orwell wrote in

1984, "was not merely to prevent men and women from forming loyalties which it might not be able to control. Its real, undeclared purpose was to remove all pleasure from the sexual act. . . . The Party was trying to kill the sex instinct, or, if it could not be killed, then to distort it and dirty it." The Party triumphed because "so far as the women were concerned, the Party's efforts were largely successful."[20]

Obligations to family, children, and God mean nothing. Aborting children is a "constitutional right." Sex is just another activity, distinct from other activities only in that "everybody" lies about it. A marriage contract is superfluous and may be broken with impunity. Disloyalty is a matter of principle. "Trophy wives" are cheerfully written up in the *New York Times,* where four marriages are de rigueur. Unmarried biological fathers are given legal rights to their offspring, and unmarried mothers are given legal rights to the biological father's paycheck.

Marriage can't be trusted, parents can't be trusted, honor can't be trusted. The only institution that can be trusted is the government. The only promise that must be kept is Social Security. Why not: "Oh, c'mon, everybody lies about Social Security"? No, sir. Social Security is sacrosanct. Only the government's word is inviolable.

The truth is another hateful "bourgeois institution." Apart from the promise of government programs, liberals always seem to be enthusiastically defending liars. Lying is their most cherished human activity. The Democratic Party formed a cordon around Bill Clinton as hysterical fascist banshees screamed that "everybody does it!" Ezra Pound described his treasonable broadcasts in wartime in the same words Bill Clinton used to describe his presidential lies and felonies in peacetime: Both claimed to be "saving the Constitution."[21]

America's enemies, from Soviet spies to terrorists, have been defined by their effortless ability to lie. Ronald Reagan said of Soviet Communism: "The only morality they recognize is what will further their cause, meaning they reserve unto themselves the right to commit any crime, to lie, to cheat." And Ehud Barak said of Muslim terrorists: "They don't suffer from the problem of telling lies that exists in Judeo-Christian culture. Truth is seen as an irrelevant category. There is only that which serves your purpose and that which doesn't. There is no such thing as 'the truth.'" You only fully appreciate what a despicable man Yasser Arafat is when you watch him retailing lie after lie and think to yourself, *This guy is as bad as Clinton!* After 9-11, President Bush went out of his way to deal fairly with Yasser Arafat. He had plenty of practice being nice to terrorists from his dealings with the Democrats. And then Bush caught the little twerp in a bald-faced lie when a ship was captured as it was delivering fifty tons of rockets, guns, and mortars from Iran to the Gaza Strip. From that moment on, Bush refused to deal with Arafat.[22] Liberals defended them all—they'll take any liar in a storm!

In *Enemies of Society*, Paul Johnson warned: "A man who deliberately inflicts violence on the language will almost certainly inflict violence on human beings if he acquires the power. Those who treasure the meaning of words will treasure truth, and those who bend words to their purposes are very likely in pursuit of anti-social ones. The correct and honorable use of words is the first and natural credential of civilized status."[23]

The fundamental difference between liberals and conservatives is: Conservatives believe man was created in God's image; liberals believe they *are* God. All their other behavioral tics proceed from this one irreducible minimum. Liberals believe they can murder the unborn because they are gods. They try to forcibly create "equality" through affirmative action and wealth redistribution because they are gods. They can lie, with no higher power to constrain them, because they are gods. They adore pornography and the mechanization of sex because man is just an animal, and they are gods. They revere the U.N. and not the U.S. because they aren't Americans—they are gods.

Americans cannot comprehend how their fellow countrymen could not love their country. But the left's anti-Americanism is intrinsic to their entire worldview. Liberals promote the rights of Islamic fanatics for the same reason they promote the rights of adulterers, pornographers, abortionists, criminals, and Communists. They instinctively root for anarchy and against civilization. The inevitable logic of the liberal position is to be for treason.

NOTES

1. FIFTY YEARS OF TREASON

1. Arthur Herman, *Joseph McCarthy: Reexamining the Life and Legacy of America's Most Hated Senator,* New York: Free Press, 2000, p. 203.
2. Lynn Smith, "Patriotism: One Size Does Not Fit All; A New Generation of Americans Must Assess What It Means to Be Loyal," *Los Angeles Times,* October 9, 2001.
3. Phil Gailey, "Bush Campaign Takes a Disturbing Turn with Attacks on Patriotism," *St. Petersburg Times,* September 11, 1988.
4. Peter Applebome, *New York Times,* October 30, 1988.
5. David Nyhan, "A Tide of Hysteria Rolls in on Dukakis," *Boston Globe,* September 30, 1988.
6. Phil Gailey, "Bush Campaign Takes a Disturbing Turn with Attacks on Patriotism," *St. Petersburg Times.*
7. Ibid.
8. Ibid.
9. Ibid.
10. Ibid.
11. Ibid.
12. Mary McGrory, "The Bush Barrage," *Washington Post,* September 11, 1988.
13. R. W. Apple, Jr., "Playing Rough; Campaign Takes a Turn onto the Low Road," *New York Times,* September 18, 1988.
14. Michael Isikoff, "President Drops Clinton Trip Issue; Bush Denies Attacking Foe's Patriotism," *Washington Post,* October 10, 1992.
15. Harry Smith, "Senator Al Gore Discusses the Presidential Campaign," *CBS This Morning,* October 14, 1992.
16. Bernard Shaw, "In Which Section of the Country Do Bush Innuendos Work?" *CNN Inside Politics,* October 8, 1992.
17. Tom Bethell, "Bush Calls a Liberal a Liberal and Looks More Like the People's Choice," *Los Angeles Times,* September 27, 1988.
18. David Denby, "Breaking Through: *8 Mile* and *Frida,*" *The New Yorker,* November 11, 2002.
19. David Nyhan, "A Tide of Hysteria Rolls in on Dukakis," *Boston Globe.*
20. Ibid.

21. Phil Donahue, *Phil Donahue*, MSNBC, December 16, 2002.
22. Ibid.
23. Geri Nikolai, "Cuomo Talks Patriotism, War," *Rockford Register Star* (Rockford, Ill.), April 3, 2002.
24. David S. Broder, "Pave a New Road to Patriotism," *San Jose Mercury News*, May 26, 2002.
25. Bill Tammeus, "Authentic Patriots," *Kansas City Star*, October 6, 2001.
26. The *Kansas City Star* was so impressed with this point, it ran Tammeus's column twice. Bill Tammeus, "Commentary: Patriotism Requires Much More Than Flags," *Kansas City Star*, October 9, 2001; Bill Tammeus, "Authentic Patriots," *Kansas City Star.*
27. Doug Erickson, "Board Reverses Pledge Ban; Hundreds Speak at Meeting; Vote Is 6–1," *Wisconsin State Journal*, October 16, 2001.
28. Janet Hook and Greg Krikorian, "Outrage Ignited on All Sides," *Los Angeles Times*, June 27, 2002.
29. Richard Gid Powers, "The Nation: Fifth Column; The Evil That Lurks in the Enemy Within," *New York Times*, June 16, 2002.
30. Ibid.
31. Ibid.
32. Matthew Rothschild, "The New McCarthyism: Cover Story," *The Progressive*, January 1, 2002.
33. See, e.g., Maynard Good Stoddard, "'God Bless America' . . . And Irving Berlin," *Saturday Evening Post*, September 1983.
34. See generally John Patrick Diggins, "Fate and Freedom in History: The Two Worlds of Eric Foner," *The National Interest*, Fall 2002.
35. William H. Honan, "Jack D. Foner, 88, Historian and Pioneer in Black Studies," *New York Times*, December 16, 1999. In the classic trajectory for Communists, years later, Foner was put in charge of his own department at Colby College in Maine.
36. Whittaker Chambers, *Witness*, New York: Random House, 1952, p. 7.
37. Ibid., p. 16. Before ascending to heaven Christ said, "And ye shall be witnesses unto me . . . unto the uttermost part of the earth," Acts 1:8.
38. Janny Scott, "Alger Hiss, Divisive Icon of the Cold War, Dies at 92," *New York Times*, November 16, 1996.
39. Whittaker Chambers, *Witness*, p. 537. ("Innocence is a mighty shield, and the man or woman covered by it, is much more likely to answer calmly: 'My life is blameless. Look into it, if you like for you will find nothing.' That is the tone of innocence.")
40. David Horowitz, *Radical Son*, New York: Free Press, 1997, p. 167.
41. Ibid., p. 104.
42. Maureen Dowd, "W.'s Conflicts of Interest," *New York Times*, September 15, 2002.
43. Jimmy Carter, "The Troubling New Face of America," *Washington Post*, September 5, 2002.

44. Chelsea Carter, "Clinton: Get bin Laden before Pursuing Saddam," Associated Press, September 5, 2002.
45. Sabrina Miller, "Clinton Prods U.S. on AIDS," *Chicago Tribune*, July 24, 2002.

2. ALGER HISS, LIBERAL DARLING

1. Whittaker Chambers, *Witness*, New York: Random House, 1952, p. 446.
2. Ibid., p. 444.
3. Ibid.
4. Ibid.
5. Ibid., p. 461.
6. Ibid., p. 462.
7. Ibid., p. 463.
8. William A. Rusher, *A Special Counsel*, New Rochelle, N.Y.: Arlington House, 1968 (cited in Arthur Herman, *Joseph McCarthy: Reexamining the Life and Legacy of America's Most Hated Senator*, New York: Free Press, 2000, p. 60). Or, as Chambers put it, Roosevelt said, "in words which it is necessary to paraphrase, 'go jump in a lake'" (*Witness*, p. 470).
9. Ralph de Toledano, *Seeds of Treason*, Boston and Los Angeles: Americanist Library, 1965, pp. 64–65.
10. Ibid., p. 63.
11. Ibid., p. 79.
12. Ibid., p. 63.
13. Whittaker Chambers, *Witness*, p. 537.
14. Ibid., p. 544.
15. Ibid., p. 536.
16. Ibid., p. 556.
17. Ibid., p. 555.
18. John Herbers, "The 37th President: In Three Decades, Nixon Tasted Crisis and Defeat, Victory, Ruin and Revival," *New York Times*, April 24, 1994.
19. Whittaker Chambers, *Witness*, pp. 564–74.
20. Ibid., p. 707.
21. Allen Weinstein, *Perjury*, New York: Knopf, 1978, p. 179.
22. Ibid.
23. Whittaker Chambers, *Witness*, p. 618.
24. Allen Weinstein, *Perjury*, p. 58.
25. Whittaker Chambers, *Witness*, p. 710.
26. Allen Weinstein, *Perjury*, pp. 180–81.
27. Ibid., p. 183.
28. Ibid., pp. 162, 184.
29. Whittaker Chambers, *Witness*, p. 733.
30. Allen Weinstein, *Perjury*, p. 181.
31. Ibid., p. 166.

32. Ibid., p. 194.

33. Ibid., pp. 165–66.

34. Ibid., p. 179.

35. Ibid., p. 182.

36. Ibid., p. 194, quoting the "accurate" remarks of Representative Robert E. Stripling.

37. Ibid., p. 184.

38. Whittaker Chambers, *Witness*, p. 783.

39. Allen Weinstein, *Perjury*, p. 168.

40. Allen Weinstein, *Perjury*, pp. 522–23 (quoting Lionel Trilling, "Whittaker Chambers and 'The Middle of the Journey,'" *The New York Review of Books*, April 17, 1975).

41. Allen Weinstein, *Perjury*, p. 532.

42. Arthur Herman, *Joseph McCarthy*, p. 313.

43. Allen Weinstein, *Perjury*, p. 532.

44. Anthony DePalma, "The Most Happy College President: Leon Botstein of Bard," *New York Times*, October 4, 1992. The Alger Hiss chair is now held by Marxist and Green Party activist Joel Kovel.

45. Janny Scott, "Alger Hiss, Divisive Icon of the Cold War, Dies at 92," *New York Times*, November 16, 1996.

46. Allen Weinstein, *Perjury*, p. 531.

47. Ibid., p. 563.

48. Michael Wines, "Hiss Case's Bogymen Are Still Not at Rest," *New York Times*, December 13, 1992.

49. Jeffrey A. Frank, "Stalin Biographer Offers Latest Twist in Hiss Case: No Evidence Diplomat 'Collaborated' with Soviets," *Washington Post*, October 31, 1992.

50. Letter to the editor, "Was Chambers Then the Victim of a Spy Sting?: Only the Truth to Gain," *New York Times*, November 13, 1992.

51. David Wise, "Was Oswald a Spy, and Other Cold War Mysteries," *New York Times*, December 6, 1992 ("The list of cold war mysteries that might—or might not—be answered . . . is lengthy. . . . Was Alger Hiss a spy, Volkogonov's assurances notwithstanding?").

52. Richard Bernstein, "Culling History from Propaganda," *New York Times*, April 24, 1994.

53. Janny Scott, "Alger Hiss, Divisive Icon of the Cold War, Dies at 92," *New York Times*.

54. Tom Zeller, "War of Secrets; Of Hiding and Seeking," *New York Times*, September 8, 2002.

55. Ibid.

56. Allen Weinstein, *Perjury*, pp. 534–35.

57. Ibid., p. 535.

58. See, e.g., Arthur Herman, *Joseph McCarthy*, p. 147.

59. Allen Weinstein, *Perjury*, p. 531.
60. Whittaker Chambers, *Witness*, pp. 740–41.
61. Allen Weinstein, *Perjury*, 505–6.
62. David Frum, "Our S.O.B.," *National Review*, December 20, 1999.
63. Sidney Hook, *Heresy Yes, Conspiracy No*, New York: John Day, 1953, p. 11.
64. Whittaker Chambers, *Witness*, p. 541. He added that it is still "better to die on the losing side than to live under Communism."
65. Ibid., p. 427.
66. Ibid., p. 702.
67. William F. Buckley, Jr., and Brent Bozell, *McCarthy and His Enemies*, Chicago: Henry Regnery Co., 1954, p. 210.
68. Arthur Herman, *Joseph McCarthy*, pp. 185–86.
69. J. Edgar Hoover, House Committee on Un-American Activities, "Investigation of Un-American Activities and Propaganda," March 26, 1947, pp. 37, 43 (cited in Arthur Herman, *Joseph McCarthy*, p. 57).
70. See, e.g., Stephane Courtois et al., *The Black Book of Communism*, Cambridge, Mass.: Harvard University Press, 1999.
71. Ronald Radosh, "The Book Club, The Spy Who Scammed Us," *Slate Magazine*, June 23, 1999.

3. NO COMMUNISTS HERE!

1. David Caute, *The Great Fear: The Anti-Communist Purge Under Truman and Eisenhower*, New York: Simon and Schuster, 1978.
2. Ellen Schrecker, "Un-American Activities: The Trials of William Remington," *The Nation*, October 10, 1994.
3. John Earl Haynes and Harvey Klehr, *Venona: Decoding Soviet Espionage in America*, New Haven, Conn.: Yale University Press, 2002, pp. 8–9.
4. Ibid., pp. 14–15.
5. Ibid., pp. 5–7.
6. Ibid., p. 21.
7. Ibid., p. 310.
8. Ibid., p. 163.
9. Ellen Schrecker, "Un-American Activities: The Trials of William Remington," *The Nation*.
10. John Earl Haynes and Harvey Klehr, *Venona*, p. 163.
11. All years search of the *New York Times* for "venona and cable and soviet":

    1. Phil Patton, "Once Secret, and Now on Display; Declassified: A Spy Museum Opens This Week in Washington," *New York Times*, July 17, 2002.
    2. Douglas Martin, "Robert J. Lamphere, 83, Spy Chaser for the F.B.I., Dies," *New York Times*, February 11, 2002.

3. David Oshinsky, "The Informer," *New York Times*, October 28, 2001.
4. Rick Perlstein, "A Look at the Architects of America's Red Scare," *New York Times*, August 20, 2001.
5. William J. Broad, "New Books Revive Old Talk of Spies," *New York Times*, May 11, 1999.
6. Maurice Isserman, "They Led Two Lives," *New York Times*, May 9, 1999.
7. Letter to the editor, "Defending His Father," *New York Times*, February 14, 1999.
8. Christopher Lehmann-Haupt, "Books of the Times; Romantics and Hustlers with Gloves, Cloaks and Daggers," *New York Times*, January 18, 1999.
9. Ethan Bronner, "Witching Hour; Rethinking McCarthyism, if Not McCarthy," *New York Times*, October 18, 1998.
10. Sam Tanenhaus, "Secret America," *New York Times*, October 4, 1998.
11. Letter to the editor, "C.I.A., Bunker Free, Is Declassifying Secrets," *New York Times*, May 3, 1996.
12. Tim Weiner, "Decoded Cables Depict Big Wartime Soviet Spy Ring in U.S.," *New York Times*, March 6, 1996.
13. Tim Weiner, "U.S. Tells How It Cracked Code of A-Bomb Spy Ring," *New York Times*, July 12, 1995.
14. Christopher Andrew, "Unshakable Faith in Treachery," *New York Times*, August 16, 1987.
15. Thomas Powers, "Ordeal by Hearsay," *New York Times*, December 11, 1983.

12. Rick Perlstein, "A Look at the Architects of America's Red Scare," *New York Times*, August 20, 2001.

13. Perlstein's *New York Times* article ran in two other newspapers at the time, the *News and Observer* (Raleigh, N.C.) and the *Toronto Star*, but searches of "Rick Perlstein and HUAC" through January 2003 turn up no other documents in which Perlstein even mentioned HUAC. A search of "HUAC w/s records" from August 2001 through January 2003 yields only the original articles announcing the release of the records. There was no new news.

14. One of the Venona cables pointing to Alger Hiss was a 1945 cable from a KGB agent in America to his bosses in Moscow: In part, it stated:

> ALES has been working with the NEIGHBORS continuously since 1935. . . . Recently ALES and his whole group were awarded Soviet decorations. After the YALTA Conference, when he had gone on to MOSCOW, a Soviet personage in a very responsible position (ALES gave to understand that it was Comrade Vyshinsky) allegedly got in touch with ALES and at the behest of the military NEIGHBORS passed on to him their gratitude.

As Sam Tanenhaus explained in *The New Republic:* "Who was Ales? Only one name fits the profile: Alger Hiss. In 1935, when he served as counsel for a Senate committee investigating World War I profiteering, Hiss had procured military documents and passed them on to Whittaker Chambers, who microfilmed them for the Soviets (so Chambers testified). Later, when Hiss was a senior official at the State Department, he traveled to the Yalta summit and was one of four American officials who journeyed on to Moscow. Add all that to the unmistakable likeness between 'Ales' and Al(ger) (H)iss, and the spy has been unmasked" (Sam Tanenhaus, "Tangled Treason," *The New Republic*, July 5, 1999).

15. John Earl Haynes and Harvey Klehr, *Venona*, p. 139.
16. Ibid., pp. 142–43.
17. Ibid., pp. 145–50.
18. Ibid., pp. 104–7.
19. Arthur Herman, *Joseph McCarthy: Reexamining the Life and Legacy of America's Most Hated Senator*, New York: Free Press, 2000, p. 75.
20. Richard Bernstein, "Ideas & Trends; Culling History from Propaganda," *New York Times*, April 24, 1994.
21. Ronald Radosh, "Progressively Worse," *The New Republic*, June 12, 2000.
22. Ibid.
23. Arnold Beichman, "Some Dared Call It Treason," *The Weekly Standard*, May 3, 1999.
24. Andrew Stern, "Head of U.S. Muslim Charity Indicted," Reuters, October 9, 2002.
25. Arthur Herman, *Joseph McCarthy*, pp. 67–68.
26. Richard J. Walton, *Henry Wallace, Harry Truman, and the Cold War*, New York: Viking, 1976, pp. 63–64 (cited in Arthur Herman, *Joseph McCarthy*, p. 77, n. 14).
27. "Joseph McCarthy Speech, U.S. Senate, June 14, 1951," *Congressional Record*, vol. 97, part 5, p. 6602 (cited in John Earl Haynes and Harvey Klehr, *Venona*, p. 16, n. 10).
28. "Obituary: Stalin Rose from Czarist Oppression to Transform Russia into Mighty Socialist State," *New York Times*, March 6, 1953.
29. See, e.g., Allen Weinstein, *Perjury*, New York: Knopf, 1978, pp. 4–5, 357–66.
30. Ibid., p. 4 (quoting David Rees, *Harry Dexter White: A Study in Paradox*, New York: Coward, McCann & Geoghegan, 1973, p. 425.
31. Sam Tanenhaus, "Secret America," *New York Times*, October 4, 1998 (reviewing Daniel Patrick Moynihan, *Secrecy: The American Experience*, New Haven, Conn.: Yale University Press, 1998).
32. John E. Haynes and Harvey Klehr, "Two Gentlemen of Venona," *The Weekly Standard*, May 13, 1996.
33. John Earl Haynes and Harvey Klehr, *Venona*, p. 47.

34. Ibid., p. 48.

35. Janny Scott, "Alger Hiss, Divisive Icon of the Cold War, Dies at 92," *New York Times*, November 16, 1996.

36. Eleven cables identified White as a spy; eight identified Duggan as a spy. See, e.g., John E. Haynes and Harvey Klehr, "Two Gentlemen of Venona," *The Weekly Standard*, May 13, 1996.

37. Sam Tanenhaus, "Tangled Treason," *The New Republic*, July 5, 1999. ("In 1943, Duggan overcame his reluctance and resumed contact with his Soviet handler.")

38. John Earl Haynes and Harvey Klehr, *Venona*, p. 202.

39. Sam Roberts, "The Rosenbergs: New Evidence, Old Passions," *New York Times*, September 23, 1983.

40. See Walter Goodman, "Reading and Writing; The Rosenberg Cause," *New York Times*, August 14, 1983 ("In this issue of The Book Review, Alan M. Dershowitz puts the cap of 'definitive' on 'The Rosenberg File,' the new book by Ronald Radosh and Joyce Milton about a case that has called forth scores of books and articles in the 30 years since the execution of Julius and Ethel Rosenberg for conspiracy to commit espionage."); "Letters to the Editor: Reactions to 'The Rosenberg File,'" *New York Times*, September 18, 1983 (letter from Walter Schneir and Miriam Schneir, Pleasantville, N.Y., on Dershowitz review, original review removed from Lexis-Nexis files).

41. Alan Brinkley, "A Story Without Heroes," *Washington Post*, September 4, 1983 (reviewing Ronald Radosh and Joyce Milton, *The Rosenberg File: A Search for the Truth*, New York: Holt, Rinehart and Winston, 1983).

42. Ibid.

43. Robert D. McFadden, "Khrushchev on Rosenbergs: Stoking Old Embers," *New York Times*, September 25, 1990. The memoirs were tapes Khrushchev had dictated from 1964 until his death in 1971, smuggled out of the USSR by his family.

44. Ibid.

45. Ibid.

46. Laurie Asseo, "Rosenbergs Acquitted in Mock Trial," Associated Press, August 10, 1993.

47. See Ronald Radosh, "The KGB Convicts the Rosenbergs," *The New Republic*, April 7, 1997.

48. See, e.g., Mark Falcoff, "Retrying the Rosenbergs Again; Observations; Julius and Ethel Rosenberg," *Commentary*, March 1, 2002.

49. Godfrey Hodgson, "Obituary: Helen Sobell: Scientist Who Campaigned to Halt the Execution of the Rosenbergs for Spying and to Free Her Husband," *The Guardian* (London), April 25, 2002.

50. John Earl Haynes and Harvey Klehr, *Venona*, p. 300.

51. Ibid.

52. "American Patriot/Soviet Spy?" *Nightline*, ABC News, June 15, 1992.

53. John Earl Haynes and Harvey Klehr, *Venona*, p. 197.
54. Letter to the editor, "Defending Their Father," *New York Times*, November 22, 1998. ("As Tanenhaus states, Gouzenko's 'confirmation' was apparently not 'stark' enough to persuade Undersecretary of State Dean Acheson to take it seriously. Let it also be remembered that the members of a grand jury, impaneled at the time to consider the evidence against White, found the testimony of Whittaker Chambers and Elizabeth Bentley so flimsy that they refused to bring an indictment. But neither these considerations nor White's own vigorous and eloquent denial of the accusations against him can sway countless uncritical thinkers.")
55. John E. Haynes and Harvey Klehr, "Two Gentlemen of Venona," *The Weekly Standard*, May 13, 1996.
56. Colin Koopman, "Pragmatism and Truth: Toward a New Politic of Knowing" (presented for the Degree of Master of Arts in Philosophy at Leeds University in September 1999). See also Dorothea E. Olkowski, "The End of Phenomenology: Bergson's Interval in Irigaray," *Hypatia: A Journal of Feminist Philosophy*, July 31, 2000:

> I am thinking here of Derrida's attempts to assume the feminine structural position. Majorie Hass reinforces the point by arguing that in modern symbolic logic "P can represent either 'the cat is on the mat' or 'the cat is not on the mat' and in either case −P will represent the negation of the statement. But on Irigaray's model, reversibility is not possible in that the two poles of difference are not interchangeable." This argument must also have profound implications for Merleau-Ponty's reversibility thesis. Following Hass's argument, reversibility would have to be part of a masculinist Imaginary (Hass 2000).

57. Bruce Ramsey, "'Spy Who Seduced America' Tells True Tale of Espionage," *Seattle Times*, September 22, 2002 (reviewing Marcia Mitchell and Thomas Mitchell, *The Spy Who Seduced America*, Montpelier, Vt.: Invisible Cities Press, 2002).

4. THE INDISPENSABLE JOE McCARTHY

1. "Corrections," *New York Times*, August 12, 1999 ("The Crossword puzzle on Tuesday had an incorrect clue for 23 Down, "Sen. McCarthy's grp." The answer being sought, HUAC, stands for House Un-American Affairs Committee, a committee of the House of Representatives. Joseph R. McCarthy was ideologically akin to members of the House Committee, but as a Senator he had no direct connection with it.")
2. Douglas Martin, "Oscar Shaftel, Fired After Refusing McCarthy, Dies at 88," *New York Times*, May 24, 2000.

3. "Corrections," *New York Times,* September 1, 2000. ("An obituary on May 24 about Oscar H. Shaftel, a faculty member at Queens College who was fired in 1953 after he refused to answer a Senate subcommittee's questions about Communist affiliation in academia, misidentified the subcommittee and its chairman. It was the Senate Internal Security Subcommittee, headed by Sen. William E. Jenner, not Senator Joseph R. McCarthy. A letter from a reader informed The Times of the error on July 18. This correction was delayed by an editing lapse.")

4. M. Stanton Evans, "Media Myths and Joe McCarthy," *Human Events,* October 13, 2000.

5. Ibid.

6. John Diggins, "*The New Republic* and Its Times: Seventy Years of Enlightened Mistakes, Principled Compromises, and Unconventional Wisdom," *The New Republic,* December 10, 1984.

7. Julius Jacobson, "The CIO's Left-Led Unions," *Industrial and Labor Relations Review,* July 1993.

8. Michael J. Ybarra, "The Real Story of the Hollywood Ten," *The New Republic,* January 5, 1998.

9. Sam Tanenhaus, "Tangled Treason," *The New Republic,* July 5, 1999.

10. Lance Morrow, "Portrait of a Dark Lady," *Time,* March 27, 2000 (noting that this was "only slight hyperbole").

11. Thomas C. Reeves, *The Life and Times of Joe McCarthy,* New York: Madison Books, 1997, p. xi.

12. Michael Paul Rogin, *The Intellectuals and McCarthy: The Radical Specter,* Cambridge, Mass.: MIT Press, 1967, p. 251.

13. David Oshinsky, *A Conspiracy So Immense,* New York: MacMillan, 1983, p. 258.

14. Arthur Herman, *Joseph McCarthy: Reexamining the Life and Legacy of America's Most Hated Senator,* New York: Free Press, 2000, p. 248.

15. Ibid.

16. Ibid.

17. David Oshinsky, *A Conspiracy So Immense,* pp. 366–67.

18. Arthur Herman, *Joseph McCarthy,* p. 248.

19. David Oshinsky, *A Conspiracy So Immense,* p. 367.

20. The pink college dropout was Harry Gold. For his prodigious work in turning over industrial and atomic secrets to the Soviets, see John Earl Haynes and Harvey Klehr, *Venona: Decoding Soviet Espionage in America,* New Haven, Conn.: Yale University Press, 2002, pp. 288–90, 304–7.

21. See, e.g., David Oshinsky, *A Conspiracy So Immense,* p. 382.

22. *Rogers v. Communist Party of the United States,* Subversive Activities Control Board (Recommended Decision of Board Member Francis A. Cherry on Second Remand Proceeding), September 19, 1958, p. 5, n. 6 ("The Party's own records, copies of which are now in evidence, and the authenticity of which it does not dispute, show an Annie Lee Moss, 72 R St, S.W. Washington, D.C. was a Party member in the mid 1940's.").

23. Thomas C. Reeves, *The Life and Times of Joe McCarthy*, p. 568.

24. See, e.g., ibid., pp. 568–69.

25. Letter from M. Stanton Evans to William V. Shannon, *New York Post*, December 10, 1958 (describing phone calls to Anna Moss, Annie Moss, and Annie L. Moss).

26. *Rogers v. Communist Party of the United States*, p. 5, n. 6.

27. Army Signal Corps–Subversion and Espionage, Hearings before the Senate Subcommittee on Investigations of the Committee on Government Operations, 83d Cong. 2d Sess. (1954), p. 447.

28. Anita Gates, "You Can See Murrow Now, Again," *New York Times*, October 21, 1998.

29. William F. Buckley, Jr., and Brent Bozell, *McCarthy and His Enemies*, Chicago: Henry Regnery Co., 1954, p. 70 (quoting *Congressional Record*, February 20, 1950, p. 1955).

30. William F. Buckley, Jr., and Brent Bozell, *McCarthy and His Enemies*, p. 54.

31. Ibid., p. 70 (quoting *Congressional Record*, February 20, 1950, pp. 1972–73).

32. Ibid., p. 54.

33. Ibid., p. 71.

34. Ibid., p. 274.

35. Quoted in David Frum, "Harry, We Hardly Knew Ye," *The Weekly Standard*, October 30, 1995.

36. William F. Buckley, Jr., and Brent Bozell, *McCarthy and His Enemies*, p. 310.

37. Ibid., p. 310.

38. Ibid.

39. John Earl Haynes and Harvey Klehr, *Venona*, p. 135.

40. Ibid., pp. 134–36.

41. Ibid., pp. 135–36.

42. Ibid., p. 135.

43. Ibid., p. 133.

44. Douglas Brinkley, "Raging Bull," *Los Angeles Times*, November 21, 1999 (reviewing Arthur Herman, *Joseph McCarthy;* and William F. Buckley, Jr., *The Redhunter: A Novel Based on the Life and Times of Senator Joe McCarthy*, Boston: Little, Brown, 1999).

45. Hearing of the Constitutional Subcommittee of the House Judiciary Committee, Panel One Subject: History and Background of Impeachment and the U.S. Constitution, November 9, 1998.

46. Ronald Radosh, "The Book Club, The Cold War: Still a Hot Topic," *Slate Magazine*, June 24, 1999.

47. See, e.g., Gus Tyler, "The Theology of Freedom: The Legacy of Jacques Maritain and Reinhold Niebuhr," *The New Leader*, April 7, 1986.

48. See, e.g., Joshua Muravchik, "Seeing Red," *The National Interest*, Fall 1996.

49. See, e.g., Julius Jacobson, "The CIO's Left-Led Unions," *Industrial and Labor Relations Review,* July 1993.

50. Rebecca West, *The New Meaning of Treason*, New York: Viking, 1954.

51. See Jefferson Cowie, "Nixon's Class Struggle: Romancing the New Right Worker, 1969–1973," *Labor History*, August 1, 2002 (citing *Haldeman Diaries: Inside the Nixon White House*, CD-ROM, Santa Monica, Calif.: Sony Electronic Publishing, 1995).

52. Arthur Herman, *Joseph McCarthy*, p. 180.

53. Ibid., p. 181.

54. Ibid.

55. Ibid.

56. David Oshinsky, *A Conspiracy So Immense*, p. 482.

5. VICTIMS OF McCARTHYISM—THE LIBERALS' *MAYFLOWER*

1. Ellen Schrecker, *The Age of McCarthyism*, Boston: Bedford Books, 1994.

2. Patricia Holt, "The Forgotten Human Cost of the '50s Witch Hunts," *San Francisco Chronicle*, March 8, 1995 (reviewing Griffin Fariello, *Red Scare: Memories of the American Inquisition*, New York: Norton, 1995).

3. Douglas Brinkley, "Raging Bull," *Los Angeles Times*, November 21, 1999 (reviewing Arthur Herman, *Joseph McCarthy: Reexamining the Life and Legacy of America's Most Hated Senator*, New York: Free Press, 2000); and William F. Buckley, Jr., *The Redhunter: A Novel Based on the Life and Times of Senator Joe McCarthy*, Boston: Little, Brown, 1999 ["But as the 50th anniversary of McCarthy's Wheeling speech approaches, an attempt is underway among the zanies to rehabilitate the man whose name has become an 'ism.'"])

4. A. O. Scott, "The Lasting Picture Show," *New York Times*, November 3, 2002.

5. Fred Bruning, "'Incapable of Bitterness' / Blacklisted and Jailed During the Red Scare, Ring Lardner Jr. Persevered Proudly and Without Recriminations," *Newsday*, November 16, 2000. ("And then came the plum—a contract to write the script for Richard Hooker's tragicomic war novel, 'M*A*S*H.' The movie went into production in 1969. Robert Altman was the director. When the credits rolled, Ring Lardner Jr.'s name was on the screen.")

6. Denise Hamilton, "Keeper of the Flame: A Blacklist Survivor," *Los Angeles Times*, October 3, 2000.

7. In 1985, when Democrats controlled the House, the House Agriculture Committee held a hearing on suffering farmers in which not a single farmer testified. Explaining the plight of farmers to the committee were several millionaire actresses who had played farmers' wives in movies: Jessica Lange (*Country*), Sissy Spacek (*The River*), Jane Fonda (*The Dollmaker*), and Sally Field (*Places in the Heart*), whose testimony was read. Among many others to appear before congressional committees: Julia Roberts testified about a disease that strikes young girls. Denise Austin testified about childhood obesity. Meryl Streep testified about Alar on apples. Kim Basinger testified about the mistreatment of circus elephants (Bob Dart, "Lights. Camera. Action. Legislation," Cox News Service, June 3, 2002).

8. Michael J. Ybarra, "The Real Story of the Hollywood Ten," *The New Republic,* January 5, 1998.

9. Whittaker Chambers, *Witness,* New York: Random House, 1952, p. 537.

10. Michael J. Ybarra, "The Real Story of the Hollywood Ten," *The New Republic.* Richard Grenier, "Revenge of the Ratfink Front," *Washington Times,* March 21, 1991.

11. See ibid.; Patrick Goldstein, "Hollywood's Blackest Hour," *Los Angeles Times,* October 19, 1997.

12. Michael J. Ybarra, "The Real Story of the Hollywood Ten," *The New Republic* ("Edward Dmytryk, who received a nomination for the 'best director' Oscar for *The Caine Mutiny,* maintains in his recent memoir, *Odd Man Out,* that the hardcore Communists in the group—he suspects at Moscow's behest— pressured the lukewarm and disaffected former members into a united front of non-cooperation and confrontation. Which would mean that in defying Washington's authority, the Ten were obeying Stalin's.")

13. Arthur Herman, *Joseph McCarthy,* p. 5.

14. Roy Medvedev, *Let History Judge: The Origins and Consequences of Stalinism,* New York: Columbia University Press, 1989, pp. 341–42.

15. Ibid., pp. 376–77.

16. Ibid., p. 381.

17. Ibid., p. 377.

18. Ibid., p. 389.

19. Charles E. Bohlen, *Witness to History, 1929–1969,* New York: Norton, 1973, pp. 51–53; *New Republic,* quoted in Sidney Hook, *Out of Step: An Unquiet Life in the 20th Century,* New York: Harper & Row, 1987, p. 231 (cited in Arthur Herman, *Joseph McCarthy,* p. 69).

20. Joseph E. Davies, *Mission to Moscow,* New York: Simon and Schuster, 1941, p. 270.

21. Ibid., p. 43 (cited in S. J. Taylor, *Stalin's Apologist,* p. 266).

22. At the beginning of her "short book of breathtaking dishonesty" (Arthur Herman, *Joseph McCarthy,* p. 4), Hellman wrote: "I have tried twice before to write what has come to be known as the McCarthy period but I didn't much like what I wrote." (Lillian Hellman, *Scoundrel Time,* Boston: Little, Brown, 1976).

23. Joshua Muravchik, "Seeing Red," *The National Interest,* Fall 1996, reviewing John E. Haynes, *Red Scare or Red Menace? American Communism and Anticommunism in the Cold War Era,* Chicago: Ivan R. Dee, 1996; Harvey Klehr and Ronald Radosh, *The Amerasia Spy Case: Prelude to McCarthyism,* Chapel Hill: University of North Carolina Press, 1996; and Richard Gid Powers, *Not Without Honor: The History of American Anti-Communism,* New York: Free Press, 1995.

24. Arthur Herman, *Joseph McCarthy,* p. 69.

25. See, e.g., ibid., p. 65.

26. Ibid., p. 64.

27. Roy A. Medvedev, *Let History Judge,* p. 391. The quotes are from the final

report of a commission organized by Trotsky to examine the Soviet show trials that was headed by American educator John Dewey.

28. Michael Wines, "Hiss Case's Bogymen Are Still Not at Rest," *New York Times,* December 13, 1992 ("Recent revelations about Stalin's purges and other Soviet deeds now seem to have confirmed much of [Whittaker Chambers's contention that Communism was "the focus of concentrated evil."])

29. See Whittaker Chambers, *Witness.*

30. Arthur Herman, *Joseph McCarthy,* p. 223.

31. Telephone conversations with Herbert Romerstein, author of *The Venona Secrets,* Washington: Regnery Publishing, 2000, and Stan Evans, McCarthy scholar and author of a forthcoming book. See also David Oshinsky, *A Conspiracy So Immense,* New York: MacMillan, 1983, p. 271 (repeating claim that McCarthy drove Kaplan to suicide while incongruously quoting McCarthy's saying, "Mr. Kaplan had no fear of this committee whatsoever" but had "expressed the desire to appear and testify").

32. David Oshinsky, *A Conspiracy So Immense,* p. 271.

33. Ibid.

34. Susan E. Tifft and Alex S. Jones, *The Trust: The Private and Powerful Family Behind the New York Times,* New York: Little, Brown, 1997, p. 259.

35. Ibid., p. 260.

36. See, e.g., Arthur Herman, *Joseph McCarthy,* p. 190.

37. Ibid., p. 191.

38. Joseph Shattan, *Architects of Victory: Six Heroes of the Cold War,* Washington, D.C.: Heritage Foundation, 1999, p. 45.

39. Among them, Republican Senator William Jenner had attacked Marshall as a "living lie" and a "front man for traitors," David Oshinsky, *A Conspiracy So Immense,* p. 197.

40. See, e.g., ibid., p. 199.

41. See Arthur Herman, *Joseph McCarthy,* p. 189, citing McCarthy-hater Richard Rovere.

42. See, e.g., David Oshinsky, *A Conspiracy So Immense,* pp. 199–200.

43. Ibid., p. 201.

44. Ibid., p. 200.

45. Ibid., p. 197, quoting journalist and McCarthy critic Richard Rovere.

46. John Earl Haynes and Harvey Klehr, *Venona: Decoding Soviet Espionage in America,* New Haven, Conn.: Yale University Press, 2002, p. 218. Budenz identified Lattimore as a Soviet agent. See, e.g., Arthur Herman, *Joseph McCarthy,* p. 123.

47. William F. Buckley, Jr., and Brent Bozell, *McCarthy and His Enemies,* Chicago: Henry Regnery Co., 1954, p. 155.

48. See, e.g., ibid., pp. 154–55.

49. Ibid., 155.

50. Ibid.

51. Letter to E. C. Carter of the Institute for Pacific Relations, July 15, 1942 (cited in William F. Buckley, Jr. and Brent Bozell, *McCarthy and His Enemies*, p. 155).
52. "F.B.I. Kept Close Watch on Douglas," *New York Times*, July 22, 1984.
53. Orville Schell, "The Strange Ordeal of Owen Lattimore," *Washington Post*, April 16, 1995.
54. William F. Buckley, Jr., and Brent Bozell, *McCarthy and His Enemies*, p. 154.
55. Ibid.
56. John J. Stephan, "The Wild, Wild East," *Washington Post*, February 20, 1994 (reviewing W. Bruce Lincoln, *The Conquest of a Continent, Siberia and the Russians*, New York: Random House, 1994).
57. William F. Buckley, Jr., and Brent Bozell, *McCarthy and His Enemies*, p. 110 (citing McCarran Report, pp. 147–48).
58. See, e.g., David Savage, "Richard Scaife: A 'Savior' of Right, A Scourge of Left," *Los Angeles Times*, April 17, 1998. In 1998, CBS Evening News correspondent Phil Jones detailed Ken Starr's "past and continuing connections with very conservative organizations." He noted darkly that Starr was appointed "independent counsel by a three judge panel headed by Judge David Sentelle, who is a close ally of ultraconservative North Carolina Senators Jesse Helms and Lauch Faircloth." *Los Angeles Times* reporter David Savage added Richard Mellon Scaife to the conspiracy theory, reporting that Scaife's "money has funded both mainstream conservative think tanks and underground attack campaigns against President Clinton. . . . Scaife's money also has poured into the rabidly anti-Clinton *American Spectator* magazine. Editor R. Emmett Tyrell [*sic*] Jr. relentlessly derided the new President in 1993, a vilification campaign that won Scaife's support."
59. Orville Schell, "The Strange Ordeal of Owen Lattimore," *Washington Post*.
60. Ibid.
61. Ibid.
62. Ibid.
63. Ibid.
64. Joshua Muravchik, "Seeing Red," *The National Interest*.

6. BUT WERE THERE COMMUNISTS IN THE STATE DEPARTMENT?

1. Quoted in John Patrick Diggins, "Fate and Freedom in History: The Two Worlds of Eric Foner," *The National Interest*, Fall 2002.
2. Thomas C. Reeves, *The Life and Times of Joe McCarthy*, New York: Madison Books, 1997, p. xi.
3. Peter LaBarbera and Allan Ryskind, "Popular Textbook Spews Venom at Reagan," *Human Events*, 1997 (quoting Joy Hakim, *A History of US*, vol. 10, New York: Oxford University Press Children's Books, 1999).

4. S. J. Taylor, *Stalin's Apologist: Walter Duranty: The New York Times's Man in Moscow*, New York: Oxford University Press, 1990, p. 267.

5. Henry Weinstein and Judy Pasternak, "I. F. Stone Dies; 'Conscience of Investigative Journalism,'" *Los Angeles Times*, June 19, 1989.

6. Ibid.

7. Patricia Aufderheide, "Wooden Portrait of Stone," *Washington Post*, January 15, 1993 (reviewing Robert G. Cottrell, *Izzy: A Biography of I. F. Stone*, Rutgers, N.J.: Rutgers University Press, 1992).

8. Ibid.

9. Henry Weinstein and Judy Pasternak, "I. F. Stone Dies; 'Conscience of Investigative Journalism,'" *Los Angeles Times*.

10. Ibid.

11. Patricia Aufderheide, "Wooden Portrait of Stone," *Washington Post*.

12. Henry Weinstein and Judy Pasternak, "I. F. Stone Dies; 'Conscience of Investigative Journalism,'" *Los Angeles Times*.

13. See, e.g., John Earl Haynes and Harvey Klehr, *Venona: Decoding Soviet Espionage in America*, New Haven, Conn.: Yale University Press, 2002, pp. 247–49; Herbert Romerstein and Eric Breindel, *The Venona Secrets*, Washington, D.C.: Regnery Publishing, 2000, pp. 432–39; Michael Krasny, "Reviewing Joseph McCarthy and the McCarthy Era," *Talk of the Nation*, December 16, 1999 (guest: Victor Navasky).

14. See, e.g., John Earl Haynes and Harvey Klehr, *Venona*, pp. 247–49; Herbert Romerstein and Eric Breindel, *The Venona Secrets*, pp. 432–39.

15. Herbert Romerstein and Eric Breindel, *The Venona Secrets*, p. 434.

16. Michael Krasny, "Reviewing Joseph McCarthy and the McCarthy Era," *Talk of the Nation*.

17. Michael R. Beschloss, "I. F. Stone: Asking the Necessary Questions," *Chicago Tribune*, January 22, 1989 (reviewing I. F. Stone, *The Hidden History of the Korean War 1950–1951*, Boston: Little, Brown, 1989).

18. Patricia Aufderheide, "Wooden Portrait of Stone," *Washington Post*.

19. Henry Weinstein and Judy Pasternak, "I. F. Stone Dies; 'Conscience of Investigative Journalism,'" *Los Angeles Times*.

20. Ibid.

21. Thomas C. Reeves, *The Life and Times of Joe McCarthy*, p. 184.

22. David Horowitz, *Radical Son*, New York: Touchstone, 1998, p. 67. (When Horowitz's parents were fired from their jobs as public school teachers for being Communists—which they were—Horowitz's father raised the ugly specter of anti-Semitism, Nazism, and the Inquisition.)

23. Ronald Radosh, "Progressively Worse," *The New Republic*, June 12, 2000.

24. Allen Weinstein, *Perjury*, New York: Knopf, 1978, pp. 535–36.

25. Ibid., pp. 522–23 (quoting Lionel Trilling, "Whittaker Chambers and 'The Middle of the Journey,'" *The New York Review of Books*, April 17, 1975).

26. Myra MacPherson, "The Secret War Against I. F. Stone; From J. Edgar Hoover's Files, the Story of a Political Vendetta," *Washington Post*, August 21, 1994.

27. Patricia Holt, "The Forgotten Human Cost of the '50s Witch Hunts," *San Francisco Chronicle*, March 8, 1995 (reviewing Griffin Fariello, *Red Scare: Memories of the American Inquisition*, New York: Norton, 1995).

28. Ibid.

29. David Horowitz, *Radical Son*, p. 69.

30. Ibid., p. 70.

31. David Denby, "Movie Review in Brief: 'Point of Order,'" *New York Magazine*, April 20, 1998.

32. Josh Getlin, "'Public Affairs' Reporting Draws McCarthy Parallels," *Los Angeles Times*, September 27, 1998.

33. Ibid.

34. Ibid.

35. David M. Oshinsky, "Cranky Integrity on the Left," *New York Times*, August 27, 1989 (reviewing Peter Coleman, *The Liberal Conspiracy*, New York: Free Press, 1989).

36. Michael Paul Rogin, *The Intellectuals and McCarthy*, Cambridge, Mass.: MIT Press, 1967, p. 232.

37. Ibid., p. 238.

38. Ibid., p. 232.

39. See Arthur Herman, *Joseph McCarthy: Reexamining the Life and Legacy of America's Most Hated Senator*, New York: Free Press, 2000, p. 10. See also http://www.friendsofkathleen.com/meetKathleen/biography.html (for Townsend's date of birth).

40. David Oshinsky, *A Conspiracy So Immense*, New York: MacMillan, 1983, p. 489.

41. In a letter sent by the Democratic secretary of state James Byrnes to a Democratic congressmen in 1946, Byrnes said that of 3,000 State Department employees who had been screened, 284 were found to be security risks, and of those, only 79 had been removed from their jobs.

42. Memo from M. Stanton Evans, February 19, 2003. ("On this point, I think I have all the documentary evidence that exists, and can say categorically that every bit of credible data on the subject shows McCarthy was telling the truth. All the imagined evidence to the contrary was discredited by the Senate investigation of the matter in 1951 and by other collateral data.")

43. Roy Cohn, *McCarthy*, New York: New American Library, 1968, p. 244.

44. Albin Krebs, *New York Times*, August 3, 1986. "Roy Cohn, Aide to McCarthy and Fiery Lawyer, Dies at 59."

45. Thomas C. Reeves, *The Life and Times of Joe McCarthy*, p. 366.

46. Ibid., p. 407.

47. See generally ibid., pp. 409–11; Arthur Herman, *Joseph McCarthy*, pp. 199–200.

48. Thomas C. Reeves, *The Life and Times of Joe McCarthy*, p. 409.

49. Ibid., p. 411.

50. Arthur Herman, *Joseph McCarthy*, pp. 198–99.

51. Thomas C. Reeves, *The Life and Times of Joe McCarthy*, p. 369.

52. Ibid., p. 407.

53. Arthur Herman, *Joseph McCarthy*, p. 53.

54. Elias Vlanton, "Deadline," *The Nation*, March 16, 1992 (reviewing James Reston, *Deadline*, New York: Random House, 1991).

55. Arthur Herman, *Joseph McCarthy*, pp. 31–32.

56. Ed Timms, "Suicide Probe Reflects Value Placed on Medals; Doubts About Combat Service Have Ruined Careers," *Dallas Morning News*, May 20, 1996.

57. Ibid. (quoting John Sibley Butler, a University of Texas at Austin sociologist).

58. Arthur Herman, *Joseph McCarthy*, p. 31 (quoting David Halberstam, *The Best and Brightest*, Greenwich, Conn.: Fawcett Publications, 1973, p. 449).

59. Jamie McIntyre, "Truth Behind LBJ's Silver Star," *CNN Live Today*, July 6, 2001 (Ret. Staff Sgt. Bob Marshall, U.S. Army: "No way. No, that story was made up and put in there by, I think in my mind, by the author of the book because we had never seen a Zero. It was never attacked. There was nothing. . . . No, never happened. That was something I would never forget if I had to do that. We never got attacked. I had no reason to swing my guns, my turret. No, them—them was built up stories.")

60. Jamie McIntyre, "Johnson's Silver Star a Historical Debate," *CNN Sunday*, July 8, 2001.

61. Gore told the *Washington Post:* "I was shot at. I spent most of my time in the field." He told the *Baltimore Sun:* "I pulled my turn on the perimeter at night and walked through the elephant grass and I was fired upon." He said he "carried an M-16."

62. The *Los Angeles Times* finally published an article in October 1999.

63. In addition to the nonstop attacks from the media, McCarthy faced real death threats. In 1954, J. Edgar Hoover warned McCarthy that Puerto Rican nationalists intended to assassinate him. This was a crowd even rougher than the Rush Limbaugh dittoheads terrorizing Tom Daschle in the fall of 2002. Puerto Rican nationalists had already opened fire from the House Gallery and badly injured five congressmen. An informant imprisoned with the Puerto Rican nationalist who tried to assassinate Truman told the FBI about the group's detailed plans to kill McCarthy, who was by now a national symbol. David Oshinsky, *A Conspiracy So Immense*, New York: MacMillan, 1983, p. 412.

64. Michael Farquhar, "Capitol Offenses: D.C.'s Long, Unhappy History of Sin," *Washington Post*, June 5, 2002.

65. Wynne Delacoma, "We Like to Watch, and It Ain't Pretty," *Chicago Sun-Times*, July 19, 2000.

66. See John Earl Haynes and Harvey Klehr, *Venona*, p. 303.

67. The others were the Tydings Committee investigation, which was in theory an investigation of McCarthy's charges, but was in fact an investigation of him; the investigation of McCarthy's role in the Maryland election in which Senator Tydings lost his seat; and the investigation of Senator Benton's libelous charges against McCarthy. The investigation of the resolution condemning McCarthy was still to come.

68. See, e.g. Roy Cohn, *McCarthy*.

69. Arthur Herman, *Joseph McCarthy*, p. 245.

70. Arthur Herman, *Joseph McCarthy*, p. 262.

71. Richard Pearson, "Frederick G. Fisher Jr., McCarthy Era Figure, Dies," *Washington Post*, May 28, 1989.

72. See, e.g., ibid.

73. Roy Cohn, *McCarthy*, pp. 197–98.

74. William Glaberson, "F.B.I. Admits Bid to Disrupt Lawyers Guild," *New York Times*, October 13, 1989.

75. Arthur Herman, *Joseph McCarthy*, p. 276 (citing Robert Griffith, *The Politics of Fear*, Amherst: University of Massachusetts Press, 1987, p. 260, n. 46, where according to Herman the "true account is tucked away in the footnotes").

76. See, e.g., John Nichols, "Leftist Lawyer Defended All—Castro, Hiss, Hoffa," *Capital Times* (Madison, Wis.), March 14, 1997.

77. "Two Alumni Look at Harvard Law School," *Legal Times*, May 25, 1992; Erwin N. Griswold, *Ould Fields, New Corne: The Personal Memoirs of a Twentieth-Century Lawyer*, West Wadsworth, 1992; Richard D. Kahlenberg, *Broken Contract: A Memoir of Harvard Law School*, Hill & Wang, 1992; Eleanor Kerlow, *Poisoned Ivy: How Egos, Ideology, and Power Politics Almost Ruined Harvard Law School*, New York: St. Martin's Press, 1994. ("First, in 1951, Harvard was sharply attacked by leaders of the Massachusetts Bar Association for harboring a chapter of the allegedly subversive student group, the National Lawyers Guild.")

78. Lawrence Van Gelder, "Harold Cammer, 86, Champion of Labor and Rights Lawyer," *New York Times*, October 25, 1995; William Glaberson, "F.B.I. Admits Bid to Disrupt Lawyers Guild," *New York Times*.

79. David Margolick, "The Law; At the Bar," *New York Times*, December 11, 1987.

80. Arthur Herman, *Joseph McCarthy*, p. 276.

81. Luisa F. Ribeiro, "Movie Review, 'Point of Order' Directed by Emile de Antonio," *Baltimore City Paper Online*, April 29–May 5, 1998.

82. Ann Hornaday, "McCarthy Footage Absorbing," *Baltimore Sun*, May 1, 1998.

83. Robert Hunt, "Red Alert," *Riverfront Times* (St. Louis, Mo.), March 17, 1999.

84. Paul Krugman, "At Long Last?" *New York Times*, April 5, 2002.

85. Michael Farquhar, "Capitol Offenses: D.C.'s Long, Unhappy History of Sin," *Washington Post*, June 5, 2002.

86. Arthur Herman, *Joseph McCarthy*, p. 280 (quoting Richard M. Fried, *Men Against McCarthy*, New York: Columbia University Press, 1977, p. 265).

87. John Earl Haynes and Harvey Klehr, *Venona*, p. 202 (Murrow praising Duggan and denouncing suggestions that he was a Soviet spy).
88. David Oshinsky, *A Conspiracy So Immense*, p. 480.
89. Ibid., p. 483.
90. Ibid., p. 481.
91. Arthur Herman, *Joseph McCarthy*, p. 23.
92. Whittaker Chambers, *Witness*, New York: Random House, 1952, p. 529.
93. Arthur Herman, *Joseph McCarthy*, p. 207 (quoting Jack Anderson and James Boyd, *Confessions of a Muckraker*, New York: Random House, 1979, p. 260).
94. Roy Cohn, *McCarthy*, p. 243.
95. Arthur Herman, *Joseph McCarthy*, p. 505 (quoting Harrison Salisbury, *Without Fear or Favor*, New York: New York Times Books, 1980, p. 470).
96. David Oshinsky, *A Conspiracy So Immense*, p. 506.
97. Roy Cohn, *McCarthy*, pp. 264–66.

7. VIETNAM: OH, HOW THEY MISS SAIGON

1. Paul Johnson, *Modern Times: The World from the Twenties to the Nineties*, New York: Perennial, 2001, p. 637.
2. Ibid., p. 633.
3. Kenneth S. Lynn, "Bobby Kennedy's Crying Game," *The American Spectator*, October 1993.
4. Paul Johnson, *Modern Times*, p. 634.
5. David Halberstam, *The Fifties*, New York: Ballantine, 1993, p. 53.
6. See, e.g., Paul Johnson, *Modern Times*, p. 635.
7. Paul Krugman, "The Great Divide," *New York Times*, January 29, 2002.
8. Paul Johnson, *Modern Times*, p. 636.
9. Susan E. Tifft and Alex S. Jones, *The Trust: The Private and Powerful Family Behind the New York Times*, Boston: Little, Brown, 1999, p. 499.
10. Paul Johnson, *Modern Times*, p. 637.
11. LBJ won the 1968 New Hampshire primary, but what finished him was that Eugene McCarthy exceeded expectations (the birth of that media horse-race standard of primary politics).
12. Paul Johnson, *Modern Times*, p. 637.
13. Ibid., p. 654.
14. Susan E. Tifft and Alex S. Jones, *The Trust*, p. 441.
15. See, e.g., "Final U.N. Flight Returns Vietnamese Boat People," *CNN World News*, May 28, 1997 at http://www.cnn.com/WORLD/9705/28/vietnam.refugees/.
16. Paul Johnson, *Modern Times*, p. 632.
17. See http://www.cnn.com/ALLPOLITICS/1998/05/29/goldwater.obit/
18. Jacob Heilbrunn, "Opinion: The Powell Doctrine; Pinpricks Still Won't Work," *Los Angeles Times*, November 4, 2001.

19. Maureen Dowd, "Liberties; Can Bush Bushkazi?" *New York Times*, October 28, 2001. See also Maureen Dowd, "Liberties; These Spooky Times," *New York Times*, October 31, 2001. ("Despite questions of another quagmire, America is at the moment a weird inside-out image of the Vietnam era. . . . Admiral Stufflebeem may be the last to know that Afghanistan is a stubborn and durable place, whose history is a long tale of war.")

20. Maureen Dowd, "Liberties; Blessings and Bombings," *New York Times*, November 21, 2001.

21. R. W. Apple, Jr., "A Nation Challenged: Letter from Washington; A Shifting Mood, a Haunting Memory," *New York Times*, November 16, 2001.

22. John Lancaster, "Logistical Shortcomings of 'Desert Storm' Cited; GAO Report Details Operation's Problems," *Washington Post*, December 31, 1991.

23. Editorial, "The Limits of Power," *New York Times*, January 31, 2002.

24. Ibid.

25. Lexis-Nexis search of *New York Times* from September 12, 2001, to the end of 2002 for (gulf war and editorial) and (Afghanistan or Iraq): 127 documents; (Vietnam and editorial) and (Afghanistan or Iraq): 120 documents; (Grenada and editorial) and (Afghanistan or Iraq): 8 documents. Lexis-Nexis search of *Los Angeles Times* from September 12, 2001, to the end of 2002 for (gulf war and editorial) and (Afghanistan or Iraq): 165 documents; (Vietnam and editorial) and (Afghanistan or Iraq): 144 documents; (Grenada and editorial) and (Afghanistan or Iraq): 9 documents. Lexis-Nexis search of *Washington Post* from September 12, 2001, to the end of 2002 for (gulf war and editorial) and (Afghanistan or Iraq): 141 documents; (Vietnam and editorial) and (Afghanistan or Iraq): 116 documents; (Grenada and editorial) and (Afghanistan or Iraq): 3 documents.

26. Mark Danner, "The Battlefield in the American Mind," *New York Times*, October 16, 2001.

27. David Bird, "U.S. Experts Favor Pullback but Express Fears," *New York Times*, February 9, 1984.

28. Steven V. Roberts, "House Democrats Draft Resolution on Beirut Pullout," *New York Times*, February 1, 1984.

29. Ibid.

30. Francis X. Clines, "White House Says Democrats Play Politics on Beirut," *New York Times*, February 2, 1984.

31. Steven V. Roberts, "House Democrats Delay Move on Marine Pullout," *New York Times*, February 7, 1984.

32. Ibid.

33. Eagleburger told a House Committee that the "view of both Israelis and moderate Arabs is that precipitate U.S. withdrawal from Lebanon would be 'a disaster' and 'devastating'—these are quotes—for the U.S. strategic position in the Middle East and for the future of the region." See "Excerpts From U.S. Aide's Statement on Reagan's View of Marine Pullout," *New York Times*, February 3, 1984.

34. Steven V. Roberts, "House Democrats Delay Move on Marine Pullout," *New York Times*.
35. Francis X. Clines, "White House Says Democrats Play Politics on Beirut," *New York Times*.
36. Martin Tolchin, "O'Neill Says U.S. Shelling Violates War Resolution," *New York Times*, February 9, 1984.
37. Ibid.
38. Mark Danner, "The Battlefield in the American Mind," *New York Times*.
39. Robert Dallek and Robert Jervis, "Opinion," *Los Angeles Times*, October 20, 2002.
40. See, e.g., "Mohammed Mossadegh: Challenge of the East," *Time*, January 7, 1952 (Man of the Year: Mohammed Mossadegh; http://www.time.com/time/special/moy/1951.html).
41. Quoted in editorial "The Darkness Called Iran," *New York Times*, February 27, 1984.
42. Associated Press, February 8, 1979.
43. See, e.g., Kathleen Teltsch, *New York Times* Information Bank abstracts, January 23, 1979.
44. "Jimmy Carter's Son Refused Visa to Iran," Associated Press, February 20, 1999.
45. The CIA originally believed Iran had backed a group of Palestinian extremists to carry out the attack on Pan Am Flight 103 as revenge for a U.S. warship having shot down an Iranian civilian flight on July 3, 1988. Focus later shifted to two Libyan intelligence officers. Qaddafi refused to release the officers for trial for over a decade. When they were eventually tried by an international court, one was convicted and the other acquitted. During their trial in 2000, a former Iranian intelligence official, Ahmad Behbahani, told *60 Minutes* that Iran had sponsored the attack. Behbahani claimed that he had been responsible for all "terrorist" operations carried out by the Iranian government at that time.
46. Lally Weymouth, "Muammar Kaddafi on the Pan Am 103 Bombing, the Fate of Saddam Hussein and Weapons of Mass Destruction," *Newsweek*, January 20, 2003.

8. HOW TRUMAN WON THE COLD WAR DURING THE REAGAN ADMINISTRATION

1. Martin Walker, "Cold War Juvenilia; History in Black, White, Red and Pinko," *Washington Post*, July 24, 1996.
2. Stanley I. Kutler, "Edmund Morris' Unconventional Biography of Ronald Reagan Is a Confusing Blend of Fact and Fantasy," *Chicago Tribune*, October 3, 1999 (reviewing Edmund Morris, *Dutch: A Memoir of Ronald Reagan*, New York: Random House, 1999).

3. John Omicinski, "Bush, Reagan Can't Claim All the Credit for Cold War's End," Gannett News Service, August 23, 1992.

4. Dallek explained, "The containment doctrine . . . is really what one can describe as winning the Cold War, not Ronald Reagan per se," though Reagan, he conceded, deserved his "share of credit" for his "stubbornness." Lynn Neary, "New Survey Which Ranks the Presidents and What Contributes to a President's Greatness or Mediocrity," *Talk of the Nation*, National Public Radio, February 19, 2001.

5. John Omicinski, "Bush, Reagan Can't Claim All the Credit for Cold War's End," Gannett News Service.

6. Sam Tanenhaus, "Un-American Activities," *The New York Review of Books* (reviewing Arthur Herman, *Joseph McCarthy: Reexamining the Life and Legacy of America's Most Hated Senator*, New York: Free Press, 2000).

7. David Halberstam, *The Fifties*, New York: Fawcett Columbine, 1993, p. 53.

8. Richard J. Walton, *Henry Wallace, Harry Truman, and the Cold War*, New York: Viking, 1976, pp. 63–64 (quoted in Arthur Herman, *Joseph McCarthy*, p. 77).

9. James Chace, *Acheson: The Secretary of State Who Created the American World*, Cambridge, Mass.: Harvard University Press, 1998, Greenwich, Conn.: Fawcett Publications, 1973, p. 147.

10. David Halberstam, *The Best and the Brightest*, p. 340. "The architects of the major change had been the Democrats and Acheson, albeit under pressure from the right."

11. David Halberstam, *The Best and the Brightest*, p. 109.

12. See, e.g., Arthur Herman, *Joseph McCarthy*, p. 146. See also Sam Tanenhaus, "Tangled Treason," *The New Republic*, July 5, 1999 (noting that Truman's Loyalty Review Board gestures meant "to undercut a Republican-controlled HUAC").

13. John Lukacs, "The Soviet State at 65," *Foreign Affairs*, Fall 1986.

14. Flora Lewis, "Diplomatic Jitters," *New York Times*, December 16, 1980.

15. Noel Gayler, "How to Break Off the Momentum of the Nuclear Arms Race," *New York Times*, April 25, 1982.

16. Hedrick Smith, "Rivals Face Debate Deeply Divided on Approach to Moscow," *New York Times*, October 21, 1984.

17. See, generally, Sam Tanenhaus, "Tangled Treason," *The New Republic*.

18. Nicholas von Hoffman, "Yes, There Were Reds Under Our Beds," *Sacramento Bee*, April 28, 1996.

19. David Halberstam, *The Best and the Brightest*, p. 324.

20. Godfrey Hodgson, "Enduring Mark of a 'Great Little Man': The Legacy of Harry Truman," *Financial Times* (London), May 8, 1984.

21. Stanlet Kober, "The Debate over No First Use," *Foreign Affairs*, Summer 1982.

22. John Lewis Gaddis, *We Now Know: Rethinking Cold War History*, New York: Oxford University Press, 1997, pp. 72–73. See, generally, Paul Johnson, *Modern Times: The World from the Twenties to the Nineties*, New York: Perennial, 2001, pp. 447–48.

23. Arthur Herman, *Joseph McCarthy*, p. 153 (citing John Lewis Gaddis, *We Now Know*, pp. 80–81).
24. David Oshinsky, *A Conspiracy So Immense*, New York: MacMillan, 1983, p. 194.
25. Arthur Herman, *Joseph McCarthy*, p. 155.
26. David Oshinsky, *A Conspiracy So Immense*, p. 194.
27. Arthur Herman, *Joseph McCarthy*, p. 155.
28. Ibid.
29. David Oshinsky, *A Conspiracy So Immense*, p. 198. This is a good example of what historians mean about McCarthy's carelessness with facts. In *A Conspiracy So Immense*, David Oshinsky earnestly says of McCarthy's remark: "Specific as always, Joe even disclosed what Truman had been drinking: bourbon and Benedictine" (p. 194). Someday historians will report Pat Buchanan's line about Bill Clinton's foreign policy experience being limited to breakfasts at the International House of Pancakes thus, *Specific as always, Buchanan even disclosed what Clinton had been eating when he formulated his foreign policy: pancakes.*
30. Sidney Hook, *Heresy Yes, Conspiracy No*, New York: John Day, 1953, p. 10. See also Sam Tanenhaus, "Tangled Treason," *The New Republic*. ("Eventually, even George Kennan, who was loyal to Hiss, faulted the White House 'for its failure to conduct a proper and exhaustive administrative investigation' of the case at a moment when 'the American people had a need . . . to know all that it was possible to learn.'")
31. It was also in 1952 that a Hollywood actor would read Whittaker Chambers's just-published *Witness* and vote Republican for the first time in his life. A little over thirty years later, President Ronald Reagan would posthumously award Chambers the Medal of Freedom and declare Chambers's farm a national landmark. Nineteen fifty-two was a year of milestones.
32. David Halberstam, *The Best and the Brightest*, pp. 340–41.
33. Ibid.
34. David Halberstam, *The Fifties*, p. 53.
35. Ibid. See also Sam Tanenhaus, "Secret America," *New York Times*, October 4, 1998 (reviewing Daniel Patrick Moynihan, *Secrecy: The American Experience*, New Haven, Conn.: Yale University Press, 1999, describing Johnson's decisions on Vietnam as propelled by "in large part, his fear of appearing 'soft' on Communism").
36. Thomas Mann, "What Bush Can Learn from Truman," *New York Times*, October 6, 2002.
37. Ibid.
38. John Earl Haynes and Harvey Klehr, *Venona: Decoding Soviet Espionage in America*, New Haven, Conn.: Yale University Press, 2002, p. 15.
39. See, e.g., "On Soviet Morality," *Time*, February 16, 1981.
40. "Carter's New World Order," *U.S. News & World Report*, June 6, 1977.

41. Peter Osnos, "The Soviets' Military Empire May Be Stretched to Its Limits," *Washington Post,* December 14, 1980.

42. "Excerpts from President's Speech to National Association of Evangelicals," Associated Press, *New York Times,* March 9, 1983.

43. Edmund Morris, *Dutch,* p. 334.

44. Leslie H. Gelb, "Is the Nuclear Threat Manageable?" *The New York Times Magazine,* March 4, 1984, p. 26.

45. Richard J. Barnet, "America Goes It Alone," *New York Times,* October 23, 1985; and Tom Wicker, "A Game of Chicken," *New York Times,* September 30, 1983.

46. "Reagan Unleashes the Hawks," *The Economist,* May 8, 1976.

47. Ibid.

48. Reagan accused Kissinger of having said that the "day of the U.S. is past and today is the day of the Soviet Union. . . . My job as Secretary of State is to negotiate the most acceptable second-best position available." Though the State Department spokesmen issued heated denials, that was precisely the point Kissinger had been making for years in books, speeches, and congressional testimony.

49. From a 1978 radio broadcast, quoted in *In His Own Hand: The Writings of Ronald Reagan That Reveal His Revolutionary Vision for America,* edited by Kiron K. Skinner, Annelise Anderson, and Martin Anderson, New York: Free Press, 2001 ("Detente: Isn't that what a farmer has with his turkey—until Thanksgiving?").

50. See, e.g., "Reagan Unleashes the Hawks," *The Economist.*

51. Henry Kissinger, *Diplomacy,* New York: Simon & Schuster, 1994.

52. Stephen F. Knott, "Reagan's Critics," *The National Interest,* Summer 1996.

53. Ibid.

54. Disproving another liberal shibboleth, Reagan simultaneously reduced the unemployment rate from 7.0 percent in 1980 to 5.4 percent in 1988. As Reagan once said: "A friend of mine was asked to a costume ball a short time ago. He slapped some egg on his face and went as a liberal economist."

55. Editorial Desk, "The War Over Star Wars," *New York Times,* October 15, 1986.

56. "Quotation of the Day," *New York Times,* October 15, 1986.

57. James O. Jackson, Johanna McGeary, and Barrett Seaman/Reykjavik, "Sunk by Star Wars: An Impasse over SDI Zaps Gorbachev's Briefcase Full of Proposals," *Time,* October 20, 1986.

58. "Is Star Wars Testing Worth the Price?" *Newsweek,* October 20, 1986.

59. Tirman was identified as the executive director of the Winston Foundation for World Peace.

60. Op-Ed Desk, "Fixated on the Technological Fix; SDI, a Colossal Blunder, Demonstrates Failure of Leadership by John Tirman," *Los Angeles Times,* October 15, 1986.

61. Barbara Carton, "Area Scientists Join Growing Protest, Pledge to Shun SDI Funds," *Washington Post,* October 15, 1986.

62. Some of the whining then and now was over the allegation that SDI and NMD would violate the precious 1972 ABM Treaty. In fact, each party reserved the right to withdraw upon only six months' notice and a statement of reasons. This was rarely reported in the watchdog media. Here is the actual text, Art. XI, paragraph 2:

> Each Party shall, in exercising its national sovereignty, have the right to withdraw from this Treaty if it decides that extraordinary events related to the subject matter of this Treaty have jeopardized its supreme interests. It shall give notice of its decision to the other Party six months prior to withdrawal from the Treaty. Such notice shall include a statement of the extraordinary events the notifying Party regards as having jeopardized its supreme interests.

63. John Omicinski, "Bush, Reagan Can't Claim All the Credit for Cold War's End," Gannett News Service.
64. R. C. Longworth, "Who Gets the Credit? GOP Grandstanding on End of the Cold War Ignores a Bipartisan Policy," *Chicago Tribune*, August 30, 1992.
65. *Imus in the Morning*, MSNBC, April 27, 2001.
66. Larry King, "Pozner and Donahue—Putting Glasnost to Work," *Larry King Live*, CNN, October 21, 1991, Transcript # 412.
67. Todd S. Purdum, "Diplomatic Memo; A Wider Atlantic: Europe Sees a Grotesque U.S.," *New York Times*, May 16, 2002.
68. Kate Swoger, "Ronald Reagan Gets Czech Fan Club," *Prague Post*, February 14, 2001.
69. "On Soviet Morality," *Time*, February 16, 1981.
70. Henry Kissinger, *Diplomacy*.
71. "Excerpts from President's Speech to National Association of Evangelicals," Associated Press, *New York Times*.
72. Stephen F. Knott, "Reagan's Critics," *The National Interest*, Summer 1996.
73. Liberals were mad about that, too. The *Washington Post*'s Philip Geyelin called Chambers a "wimp" who "ratt[ed] on his former lackey," Alger Hiss. He snarled that Chambers appeals to the "conservative political fringe that constitutes the hard core of the Reagan constituency." Furious at Reagan for giving Chambers the award, Geyelin angrily said it spoke to "the cast of mind of the man who thinks Whittaker Chambers worthy of such an honor" (Philip Geyelin, "A Journey from Treason," *Washington Post*, March 1, 1984).

9. LIBERALS IN LOVE: MASH NOTES TO THE KREMLIN

1. "Excerpts from the President's Address," *New York Times*, May 18, 1981 (excerpts from the prepared text of President Reagan's address at Notre Dame University, as issued by the White House).

2. Alan Brinkley, "Hook, Line, and Sinker," *Slate Magazine*, October 6, 1999.

3. Eleanor Clift, *The McLaughlin Group*, January 15, 1994.

4. Eleanor Clift, *The McLaughlin Group*, April 10, 2000.

5. "The Talking's Over," *The Economist*, November 1, 1980.

6. Barry Schweid, "Reagan Calls Mondale Weak on Defense; Mondale Says Reagan Not in Command," Associated Press, October 22, 1984.

7. Strobe Talbott, "To Rebuild the Image; Needed: a Consistent Foreign Policy—and Muscle," *Time*, February 23, 1981.

8. Strobe Talbott, "The Specter and the Struggle; Marx's Theory, in Soviet Practice, Is Both Dangerous and in Danger," *Time*, January 4, 1982.

9. Statement of Robert F. Byrnes, an Indiana University history professor who directed the study as quoted in the Associated Press. Charles J. Hanley, "Despite Woes, Soviet System Will Remain, Study Says," Associated Press, May 27, 1983.

10. Walter Laqueur, "America and the World: U.S.-Soviet Relations," *Foreign Affairs*, 1983. ("Walter Laqueur is Chairman of the International Research Council at the Center for Strategic and International Studies at Georgetown University. He is co-editor of the *Journal of Contemporary History* and of *The Washington Quarterly* and the author of *Russia and Germany, The Fate of the Revolution*, and many other works.")

11. Robert G. Kaiser, "Afghanistan: End of the Era of Detente; Soviet Invasion of Afghanistan: An End to Era of Detente; Soviet Miscalculation or Calculation?" *Washington Post*, January 17, 1980.

12. Richard M. Nixon, *The Real War*, New York: Warner Books, 1980.

13. Leslie H. Gelb, "Is the Nuclear Threat Manageable?" *The New York Times Magazine*, March 4, 1984, p. 26.

14. Ibid.

15. John Steinbruner, "On the Brink," *Foreign Policy*, September 1996.

16. Ibid.

17. Stephen F. Knott, "Reagan's Critics," *The National Interest*, Summer 1996.

18. "Vance Blasts Reagan's Posture on Foreign Affairs," United Press International, June 22, 1981.

19. "Transcript of the Reagan-Mondale Debate on Foreign Policy," *New York Times*, October 22, 1984.

20. George F. Kennan, *The Cloud of Danger: Current Realities of American Foreign Policy*, Boston: Atlantic/Little, Brown, 1977.

21. Walter Isaacson and Evan Thomas, "The Reluctant Prophet," *Washington Post*, August 31, 1986 (adapted from *The Wise Men*, New York: Simon & Schuster, 1986).

22. Philip Geyelin, "A Grand Design for Peace," *Washington Post*, June 26, 1977 (reviewing George F. Kennan, *The Cloud of Danger, Current Realities of American Foreign Policy*).

23. Ann L. Trebbe, "Personalities," *Washington Post*, May 19, 1982.

24. Stanley I. Kutler, "Edmund Morris' Unconventional Biography of Ronald Reagan Is a Confusing Blend of Fact and Fantasy," *Chicago Tribune*, October 3, 1999 (reviewing Edmund Morris, *Dutch: A Memoir of Ronald Reagan*, New York: Random House, 1999). Noting that the real heroes of the Cold War, Harry Truman, followed by Eisenhower, Kennedy, Johnson, Nixon, Ford, and Carter "all subscribed to George Kennan's ideas of containment."

25. Walter Isaacson and Evan Thomas, "The Reluctant Prophet," *Washington Post*.

26. Ibid.

27. Ibid.

28. Ibid.

29. Robert W. Tucker, "Nuclear Weapons and the U.S.S.R.: The Nuclear Debate," *Foreign Affairs*, Fall 1984 (quoting George Kennan, *The Nuclear Delusion*, New York: Pantheon Books, 1983, p. 231).

30. Editorial, "At the End of the Alley," *New York Times*, October 26, 1980.

31. Editorial, "The Peacemongers," *New York Times*, October 21, 1980.

32. Joanne Omang, "Nicaraguan Leader Makes U.S. Tour; Ortega Campaigns to Boost Image of Sandinista Government," *Washington Post*, October 9, 1984.

33. See, e.g., Marc Cooper, "Postcards from the Left Under the Cloud of Clintonism; Hollywood and the Democratic Party," *The Nation*, April 5, 1999; Joanne Omang, "Nicaraguan Leader Makes U.S. Tour; Ortega Campaigns to Boost Image of Sandinista Government," *Washington Post*; Marshall Ingwerson, "From Actors to Advocates, Americans Are Flocking to Nicaragua," *The Christian Science Monitor*, November 23, 1984.

34. Marshall Ingwerson, "From Actors to Advocates, Americans Are Flocking to Nicaragua," *The Christian Science Monitor*.

35. Joan Didion, *Miami*, New York: Simon & Schuster, 1987 (quoted in Christopher Lehmann-Haupt, "Books of the Times," *New York Times*, September 28, 1987).

36. Joan Didion, "Fixed Opinions, or the Hinge of History," *The New York Review of Books*, January 16, 2003 (based on a lecture given in November 2003 at the New York Public Library).

37. Barton Reppert, "Fulbright Denounces Reagan's Soviet Policy," Associated Press, March 16, 1982.

38. See, e.g., Steven V. Roberts, "Letter to Nicaragua: 'Dear Comandante,'" *New York Times*, April 20, 1984. ("The 10 authors include Jim Wright of Texas, the majority leader; Edward P. Boland of Massachusetts, chairman of the House Intelligence Committee, and other senior Democrats in the foreign policy field.")

39. George Gedda, "Hill Vote a Rebuff to Reagan Policy," Associated Press, April 24, 1985.

40. Ibid.

41. "Havana Radio Says House Nicaragua Vote 'Catastrophic Defeat' for Reagan," Associated Press, April 24, 1985.

42. Mark Whitaker with John Walcott, Gloria Borger, and Eleanor Clift in Wash-

ington and Liz Balmaseda in Managua, "Sending Managua a Message," *News-week*, June 17, 1985.

43. Doyle McManus, "Split Vote on Aid a Stinging Defeat for the President," *Los Angeles Times*, April 24, 1985.

44. Editorial, "Contadora or 'Contra'?" *New York Times*, April 23, 1985.

45. Mary McGrory, "Democrats' Uphill Contra Fight," *Washington Post*, March 11, 1986.

46. See, generally, Jim Drinkard, "Iran-Contra Arms Deal Evolved over Three Years," Associated Press, January 24, 1987; "Key Sections of Conspiracy Indictment in Iran-Contra Affair," *New York Times*, March 17, 1988. For the best description of Iran-Contra from the man who exposed it, see Edwin Meese, *With Reagan*, Washington, D.C.: Regnery, 1992.

47. Astonishingly, the Democrats so hated these brave anti-Communist rebels, they passed the Boland Amendment expressly providing that no money from the U.S. Treasury could be sent, "directly or indirectly," to the Contras. Since the money diverted to the Contras was never in the U.S. Treasury, the Boland Amendment did not apply and could not have been violated by the Iran-Contra operation. This was admitted by Attorney General Ed Meese, who exposed the Iran-Contra operation. See Edwin Meese, *With Reagan*, pp. 258–85.

48. "Key Sections of Conspiracy Indictment in Iran-Contra Affair," *New York Times*, March 17, 1988.

49. Flora Lewis, "The Split-Level G.O.P.," *New York Times*, August 24, 1984.

50. Walter Laqueur, "U.S.-Soviet Relations," *Foreign Affairs*, 1983.

51. Barton Reppert, "Fulbright Denounces Reagan's Soviet Policy," Associated Press.

52. Ibid.

53. "Transcript of the Reagan-Mondale Debate on Foreign Policy," *New York Times*.

54. The attack on Reagan's foreign policy within the *Tribune*'s endorsement assured it wide circulation. At least seven other articles cited the endorsement's criticism. See, e.g., "Tribune Backs Reagan," United Press International, October 27, 1984.

55. Bernard Gwertzman, "Reagan Sees Hope of Soviet Sharing in Missile Defense," *New York Times*, March 30, 1983; "Transcript of Group Interview with President at White House," *New York Times*, March 30, 1983; James Reston, "Washington; White House Revue," *New York Times*, March 30, 1983; Russell Baker, "Observer; No More Bluebirds," *New York Times*, March 30, 1983; Hedrick Smith, "Would a Space-Age Defense Ease Tensions or Create Them?" *New York Times*, March 27, 1983; James Reston, "Washington; Policy and Politics," *New York Times*, March 16, 1983; David K. Shipler, "1,300 Rally in Israel to Press for Soviet Emigration," *New York Times*, March 15, 1983; Tom Wicker, "In the Nation; 2 Dangerous Doctrines," *New York Times*, March 15, 1983; Francis X. Clines, "Reagan Plays the Issues in More Than a Single

Key," *New York Times*, March 13, 1983; Anthony Lewis, "Abroad at Home; Onward, Christian Soldiers," *New York Times*, March 10, 1983; Francis X. Clines, "Reagan Denounces Ideology of Soviet as 'Focus of Evil,'" *New York Times*, March 9, 1983; Associated Press, "Excerpts from President's Speech to National Association of Evangelicals," *New York Times*, March 9, 1983.

56. Anthony Lewis, "Abroad at Home; Onward, Christian Soldiers," *New York Times*.

57. James Reston, "Washington; Policy and Politics," *New York Times*.

58. Tom Wicker, "In the Nation; 2 Dangerous Doctrines," *New York Times*.

59. Russell Baker, "Observer; No More Bluebirds," *New York Times*.

60. Hedrick Smith, "Reagan's Gaffe," *New York Times*, August 16, 1984.

61. John B. Oakes, "Mr. Reagan Bombs," *New York Times*, August 18, 1984.

62. Peter Robinson, "Tearing Down That Wall," *The Weekly Standard*, June 23, 1997.

63. Both quoted in Stephen Chapman, "Zero Option Evokes Zero Honesty in Some Conservatives," *Chicago Tribune*, June 19, 1987.

64. Editorial, "Ronald Reagan, Kremlin Dupe?" *Chicago Tribune*, December 9, 1987; and Howard Phillips, "The Treaty: Another Sellout," *New York Times*, December 11, 1987.

65. Editorial, "Ronald Reagan, Kremlin Dupe?" *Chicago Tribune*.

66. Norman Mailer, "Searching for Deliverance," *Esquire*, August 1996 (interview with Patrick Buchanan).

67. PR Newswire Association, Inc., August 16, 1984 (quoting from Mailer's upcoming article in Sunday's issue of *Parade* magazine, on his recent vacation in Russia).

68. Norman Mailer, "Searching for Deliverance," *Esquire*.

69. Joan Didion, "Fixed Opinions, or the Hinge of History," *The New York Review of Books*.

70. Ibid.

71. Brian Williams, "Presidential Historian Doris Kearns Goodwin Discusses Historical Significance of Bush's News Conference on Iraq," *News with Brian Williams*, CNBC, March 6, 2003.

72. It being of crucial importance to academics to make simple ideas sound complex, LaFeber referred to American intervention abroad to make the world safe for democracy as "Wilsonianism." Walter LaFeber, "Contradiction: Alliance with the Option to Act Alone," *Washington Post*, October 6, 2002.

73. Stephen Hume, "Nobel Honour Roll: 110 Peacemakers Who Tried to Stop the Ravages of War," *Vancouver Sun*, December 27, 2001 (citing the Nobel Foundation).

74. "Nobel Peace Laureate Denounces Big Powers," *New York Times*, December 12, 1982.

75. Judith Miller, "Arms Aide Who Quit Assails U.N. on Iraq," *New York Times*, August 1, 1999.

76. Oonagh Blackman, "Gorbachev: I Fear Bush and Blair War Plan," *Daily Mirror* (UK), July 11, 2002.

77. Whittaker Chambers, *Witness*, New York: Random House, 1952, p. 524.

78. Stanley Cohen, "A Spectacle Stirs the Jumble of Nationalism," *New York Times*, August 26, 1984.

10. COLD WAR EPITAPH:
THE HISS AFFAIR AT THE END OF THE COLD WAR

1. Emily Eakin, "Party's Over, Comrade, It's History Now," *New York Times*, January 11, 2003.

2. Ibid.

3. See, e.g, John Patrick Diggins, "Good Intentions," *The National Interest*, Fall 2000.

4. Allen Weinstein and Alexander Vassiliev, *Haunted Wood*, New York: Random House, 1999, p. 119.

5. John Patrick Diggins, "Good Intentions," *The National Interest*.

6. McGovern explicitly praised Wallace's pro-Soviet positions, such as the belief that the Cold War was "overdone" and that "problems" between the nations "could not be resolved by military means." Senator George McGovern USDA Millennium Lecture and Dedication, FDCH Federal Department and Agency Documents, September 29, 1999.

7. Internationally, those who would deserve a place on the Mount Rushmore of Cold War heroes include Prime Minister Margaret Thatcher of Great Britain and President Augusto Pinochet of Chile. Pinochet proved to the world that market economics could work in a backward Third World country on the brink of becoming the next Cuba. And the world took notice. It was a tremendous blow to the left. Pinochet did that. As with Nixon, liberals are still trying to get back at Pinochet. To this day, they are trying to put him on "trial" for "war crimes" against Communist insurgents.

8. Ralph de Toledano, "What the ACLU Doesn't Want You to Know," *Insight*, July 1, 2002.

9. Wolfgang Saxon, "Joseph Rauh Jr., Groundbreaking Civil Liberties Lawyer, Dies at 81," *New York Times*, September 5, 1992. ("For almost half a century Mr. Rauh was among America's foremost civil liberties lawyers, battling McCarthyism, laying the foundation for much of the civil rights legislation of the 1960's and serving as a leader not only of the A.D.A. but also of the National Association for the Advancement of Colored People and the Leadership Conference on Civil Rights.")

10. Georg Szalai, "'J. Edgar!' Dressed for Fest; Musical Helps Kick off Aspen Gathering," *Hollywood Reporter*, February 28, 2003.

11. See, e.g., Ann Coulter, *High Crimes and Misdemeanors*, Washington, D.C.: Regnery, 1998, chapter 13.

12. Mark Harden, "Jokers Will Be Wild at Aspen Comedy Arts Festival," *Denver Post*, February 23, 2003.

13. John Nichols, "Rosenbergs' Son Carries Banner Against Death Penalty," *Capital Times* (Madison, Wis.), April 19, 1995.

14. Richard Bernstein, "Nixon, on the Ascendant, Vs. Douglas, Eclipsed," *New York Times*, January 19, 1998 (reviewing Greg Mitchell, *Tricky Dick and the Pink Lady*, New York: Random House, 1998). By contrast, Earl Warren, liberal Republican—and mastermind of Roosevelt's Japanese internment project—pointedly refused to endorse Nixon. This, the *New York Times* said, showed "a flash of the character" the nation would see again when he nearly wrecked the country while presiding over the duly infamous Warren Court.

15. Patricia Holt, "Against the Tide," *San Francisco Chronicle*, May 17, 1992 (reviewing Ingrid Winther Scobie, *Helen Gahagan Douglas: A Life*, Garden City, N.Y.: Doubleday, 1982).

16. Ibid.

17. Ibid.

18. Herbert Mitgang, "Books of the Times; Nixon's Enemy in 1950 Had the Last Laugh in '74," *New York Times*, May 25, 1992 (reviewing Ingrid Winther Scobie, *Center Stage, Helen Gahagan Douglas: A Life*, New York: Oxford University Press, 1992).

19. Richard Bernstein, "Nixon, on the Ascendant, Vs. Douglas, Eclipsed," *New York Times*.

20. John Herbers, "The 37th President; In Three Decades, Nixon Tasted Crisis and Defeat, Victory, Ruin and Revival," *New York Times*, April 24, 1994.

21. "American Conservative Union Dinner, Transcript" and "Republican Presidential Candidates Speak to the American Conservative Union Dinner," *1996 Presidential Campaign Press Materials*, October 24, 1995.

22. Paul Johnson, *Modern Times: The World from the Twenties to the Nineties*, New York: Perennial, 2001, pp. 650–51.

23. Ibid.

24. Ibid., p. 649.

25. See Fred Emery, *Watergate: The Corruption and Fall of Richard Nixon*, New York: Times Books, 1994, pp. 27, 219.

26. Andrew Ferguson, "Television Journalism as Oxymoron," *The Weekly Standard*, June 4, 2001.

27. Joyce Wadler, "Lloyd Shearer, Longtime Celebrity Columnist, Dies at 84," *New York Times*, May 27, 2001.

28. "Excerpts from the President's Address," *New York Times*, May 18, 1981.

11. NEVILLE CHAMBERLAIN HAD HIS REASONS, TOO: TREMBLING IN THE SHADOW OF BRIE

1. Will Lester, "Democratic Hopefuls Careful on Iraq," Associated Press, August 12, 2002.

2. Dan Balz, "Carter Says Bush Has 'Not Made a Case' for War," *Washington Post*, February 1, 2003.

3. Ibid.

4. Sabrina L. Miller, "Clinton Prods U.S. on Aids; Government Urged to Spend More on Worldwide Battle," *Chicago Tribune*, July 24, 2002.

5. Remarks by former vice president Al Gore at the Commonwealth Club, San Francisco, September 23, 2002.

6. Sean Hannity and Alan Colmes, "Another Resolution Before U.N. Security Council," *Hannity & Colmes*, Fox News Network, February 24, 2003.

7. Editorial, "A Time for Candor on Iraq," *New York Times*, August 3, 2002.

8. Brian Whittaker and Jon Henley, "The Desperate Flight of Refugees from Northern Iraq Raises Questions About the Scope of US-British Air Patrols," *The Guardian*, February 20, 2001 ("In 1988 Saddam Hussein used chemical weapons to attack the Kurdish town of Halabjah, killing thousands of people."); Christine Gosden and Mike Amitay, "What We Don't Know . . . ," *Washington Post*, October 3, 2002.

9. Peter Jennings, "Reality Check: No Evidence Whatsoever of Iraq–Al Qaeda Connection," *ABC World News Tonight*, September 26, 2002. Jennings referred to the administration's repeated statements that there was a connection between al-Qaeda and Iraq as "accusations" and said, "Some people will take it on face value and the President's critics will be skeptical." ABC's Martha Raddatz reported:

> A senior intelligence official tells ABC News there is no smoking gun. There's not even a smoking unfired weapon, linking al Qaeda and Iraq. . . . At one point, the Bush Administration argued that September 11th hijacker Mohammed Atta had met in Prague with an Iraqi intelligence agent. But the Administration never found hard evidence and dropped the subject. . . .
>
> [O]nly yesterday, Vice President Cheney and CIA Director George Tenet briefed a group of Senators. Senator Susan Collins was in that briefing and was surprised by the Administration's claim today.

Contradicting her introduction, Senator Susan Collins (R-Me.) did not really sound all that "surprised": "Exactly how solid that evidence is, I'm not certain. Some of the evidence we have comes from interviews with detainees."

10. Neal Conan, "US Policy of Iraqi Regime Change," *Talk of the Nation*, National Public Radio, September 25, 2002. ("Now the administration has gone to great lengths to link Iraq with 9-11, to argue that Osama bin Laden and Saddam Hussein are joined at the hip. But they have not been able to provide credible evidence that that's the case. So basically what we have here is the opening of a two-front war. We're not going against a terrorist threat. We're going against Iraq because it has weapons of mass destruction, and we don't accept the idea that rogue states like Iraq can have nuclear weapons.")

11. John McLaughlin, *The McLaughlin Group*, Federal News Service, Septem-

ber 27, 2002 (joined by Michael Barone, Tony Blankley, Eleanor Clift, and James Warren).

12. Bill Keller, "The Sunshine Warrior," *New York Times*, September 22, 2002.

13. Chris Bury, "Dangerous Liaisons?" *Nightline*, ABC News, September 26, 2002.

14. See, e.g., Chris Bury, "Dangerous Liaisons?" *Nightline*. ("Killing is something I did. I killed, true. This was for the Iraqi intelligence and al-Qaeda.")

15. Chris Bury, "Dangerous Liaisons?" *Nightline*.

16. See, e.g., Chris Bury, "Dangerous Liaisons?" *Nightline*.

17. See, e.g., Peter Jennings, "Reality Check: No Evidence Whatsoever of Iraq–Al Qaeda Connection," *ABC World News Tonight*.

18. Chris Bury, "Dangerous Liaisons?" *Nightline*.

19. Wolf Blitzer and Bruce Morton, "Interview with John McCain; McDermott, Thompson Discuss Their Trip to Iraq; Should Congress Give President Authority to Wage War?" *CNN Late Edition with Wolf Blitzer*, September 29, 2002.

> BLITZER: Senator Feinstein, have you seen any evidence that China is covertly assisting the Iraqis in developing any of these kinds of weapons, including a nuclear capability?
>
> FEINSTEIN: No, I've seen no evidence of that. But there is no question but that this man knows no scruples.

20. *The News with Brian Williams*, CNBC, September 24, 2002 (with Howard Fineman, Jim McDermott, Bernie Sanders, David Winston, Brian Williams, Campbell Brown, George Lewis, Jim Miklaszewski, Pete Williams, Ron Insana, Robert Hager).

21. Michael Smerconish, Miles O'Brien, and Candy Crowley, "Free-for-All Friday: Iraq," *CNN Talkback Live*, September 20, 2002 (guests: Jesse Jackson, Jr., J. D. Hayworth, Mike Pence, Diana DeGette, Nabil Abu Rudeineh).

22. "Excerpts from the Debate in the Senate on Using Force Against Iraq," *New York Times*, October 9, 2002 (Statement of Senator James Jeffords).

23. Copyright © 2002 eMediaMillWorks, Inc., "U.S. Representative Christopher Shays (R-Ct) Holds Hearing on Combating Terrorism," September 24, 2002.

24. Remarks by former vice president Al Gore at the Commonwealth Club.

25. "Clinton Criticizes Bush's Iraq and Domestic Policies in London Speech," *The Bulletin's Frontrunner*, October 3, 2002.

26. Judy Woodruff, "Homeland Security Opens with Plenty of Questions Unanswered; Bush Will Make Modernizing Medicare a Top Priority," *CNN Inside Politics*, January 24, 2003, Transcript # 012400CN.V15.

27. Ronald Brownstein, "The Nation; Washington Outlook; Impending Clash with Iraq Begets a Clash of Administrations," *Los Angeles Times*, October 7, 2002.

28. Henry A. Kissinger, "Iraq Is Becoming Bush's Most Difficult Challenge," *Chicago Tribune*, August 11, 2002.

29. Mick Hinton, "Albright Calls Middle East Fighting Personal War by Two Stubborn Men," *Daily Oklahoman*, April 12, 2002.

30. Madeleine K. Albright, "Where Iraq Fits in the War on Terror," *New York Times*, September 13, 2002.

31. Ibid.

32. Editorial, "A Time for Candor on Iraq," *New York Times*, August 3, 2002.

33. "Vermont Bans the Bomb," *Time*, March 15, 1982. See also Richard Halloran, "Thoughts on the Threat," *New York Times*, August 7, 1983 (book review noting that antinuclear resolutions had been adopted in nine states, twelve counties, and twenty-two cities).

34. Judith Miller, "In Europe, Ironic Reaction to Neutron Move," *New York Times*, August 23, 1981.

35. Tom Wicker, "In the Nation: A Voice of Rationality," *New York Times*, December 1, 1981.

36. George Orwell, "Through a Glass, Rosily," *Tribune*, November 23, 1945. (He later said he would not have called pacifists "objectively" pro-Nazi.)

37. Stephen Ambrose, *Americans at War*, New York: Berkley Books, 1998, p. 212.

38. "Interview with Walter Cronkite," *Larry King Live*, CNN, September 9, 2002.

39. Ibid.

40. Jim Rutenberg, "Threats and Responses: The Coverage; Speech Had Big Audience Despite Networks' Action," *New York Times*, October 9, 2002.

41. Judy Woodruff, "CNN Coverage of the State of the Union Address," CNN, January 28, 2003, Transcript # 012800CN.V54.

42. "Interview with Walter Cronkite," *Larry King Live*, CNN.

43. "Reactions from Leaders to the Strikes Against Iraq," Associated Press, December 17, 1998.

44. Ibid.

45. James Reston, "The Battle for the Dropouts," *New York Times*, July 25, 1984.

46. Peter Jennings, *World News Tonight*, ABC News, October 14, 2002.

47. Michael Janofsky, "Backing Bush All the Way, Up to but Not into Iraq," *New York Times*, August 3, 2002.

48. Peter Jennings, *World News Tonight*, ABC News, October 14, 2002.

49. Ibid.

50. David Wright, *World News Tonight*, ABC, October 15, 2002.

51. Adam Clymer and Janet Elder, "Threats and Responses: The Poll; Poll Finds Unease on Terror Fight and Concerns About War on Iraq," *New York Times*, September 8, 2002.

52. Adam Nagourney and Janet Elder, "Public Says Bush Needs to Pay Heed to Weak Economy," *New York Times*, October 7, 2002.

53. "A Nation Wary of War," *New York Times*, October 8, 2002.

54. Ibid.

55. NPR reporter Nina Totenberg on the October 19, 2002, *Inside Washington*, reacting to the revelation that North Korea has nuclear weapons.

56. "Sontagged," *The Weekly Standard*, October 15, 2001.

57. Bill Carter and Jim Rutenberg, "Fox News Head Sent a Policy Note to Bush,"

New York Times, November 19, 2002; Alessandra Stanley, "A Letter from the Boss Contradicts Fox's Creed," *New York Times*, November 19, 2002.

58. Alessandra Stanley, "A Letter from the Boss Contradicts Fox's Creed," *New York Times*.

59. http://www.the-rule-of-law.com/

60. Seymour Hersh, "King's Ransom: How Vulnerable Are the Saudi Royals?" *The New Yorker*, October 22, 2001.

61. "Senator Hillary Clinton Discusses Iraq," *Meet the Press*, NBC, September 15, 2002.

62. Jim Vandettei and Juliet Eilperin, "Democrats Unconvinced on Iraq War," *Washington Post*, September 11, 2002.

63. "Senator Byrd Demands That the Iraq Question Come Before Congress," *Inside Politics*, CNN, August 30, 2002.

64. Judy Woodruff, "Interview with Ted Kennedy," *CNN Inside Politics*, September 27, 2002.

> KENNEDY: I'm not getting—no, I think we have to try and look to the best motives of people in this area.
>
> WOODRUFF: Well, let me finally ask you about politics on the part of Democrats, some of whom are privately saying they are supporting the president, because they think it will hurt them politically if they go up against the president on this. They'll look unpatriotic.
>
> KENNEDY: Well, people are going to make their own judgment on this issue, as they make it on any other, and they're going to make it on the basis of a variety of different factors. That's never changed in . . .
>
> (CROSSTALK)
>
> WOODRUFF: Including politics.
>
> KENNEDY: Including, I suppose, their own political interests. That's nothing terribly unusual for politicians to make. We like to believe that that's—they'll be making it for other reasons, but that's—we are dealing with some realities on this case. And I would hope that they would exercise their best judgment on it, I think the overwhelming majority will. There may be some that won't, but I think we are going to have the people that vote on it will vote their conscience.

65. Wolf Blitzer, "Interview with John McCain; McDermott, Thompson Discuss Their Trip to Iraq; Should Congress Give President Authority to Wage War?" *CNN Late Edition with Wolf Blitzer*, September 29, 2002.

66. "Threats and Responses; House Vote on Iraq Resolution," *New York Times*, October 12, 2002.

67. eMediaMillWorks, September 23, 2002. Following is the text of former vice president Al Gore's speech before the Commonwealth Club of San Francisco:

> I'm speaking today in an effort to recommend a specific course of action for our country, which I sincerely believe would be better for our country than

the policy that is now being pursued by President Bush. Specifically, I am deeply concerned that the course of action that we are presently embarking upon with respect to Iraq has the potential to seriously damage our ability to win the war against terrorism and to weaken our ability to lead the world in this new century.

68. G. Robert Hillman, "Democrats Accuse Bush of Playing Politics with Iraq, Daschle Demands Apology," *Dallas Morning News*, September 26, 2002.

69. Ibid.

70. Bruce Catton, *Never Call Retreat: The Centennial History of the Civil War*, vol. 3, Garden City, N.Y.: Doubleday, 1965, p. 3.

71. Remarks by former vice president Al Gore at the Commonwealth Club.

72. Thomas L. Friedman, "We Are All Alone," *New York Times*, October 26, 2001.

73. Warren P. Strobel and James Kuhnhenn, "Bush Will Begin Making a Case for War on Iraq; Rumsfeld: Saddam Closer to Having Bomb," *San Jose Mercury News*, September 4, 2002.

12. NORTH KOREA — ANOTHER OPPORTUNITY FOR SURRENDER

1. Barbara Slavin, "Critics Question Tough Talk on Iran, North Korea," *USA Today*, January 31, 2002.

2. Robert Scheer, "An Orgy of Defense Spending; Bush's 'Axis of Evil' Rhetoric Fabricates a Need," *Los Angeles Times*, February 5, 2002.

3. "Bush Hopeful on North Korea, Iran, Iraq," The White House Bulletin, February 1, 2002.

4. Reagan Walker, "Carter Decries Calling Nations 'Evil,'" *Atlanta Journal and Constitution*, February 22, 2002.

5. Jimmy Carter, "AJC Special: The Carter Interview: Jimmy Carter's North Korean Notebook," *Atlanta Journal and Constitution*, July 3, 1994.

6. Editorial, "Nuclear Breakthrough in Korea," *New York Times*, October 19, 1994.

7. Ibid.

8. Nicholas D. Kristof, "Revolving-Door Monsters," *New York Times*, October 11, 2002.

9. David E. Sanger, "North Korea Says It Has a Program on Nuclear Arms," *New York Times*, October 17, 2002. ("Confronted by new American intelligence, North Korea has admitted that it has been conducting a major clandestine nuclear-weapons development program for the past several years, the Bush administration said tonight. Officials added that North Korea had also informed them that it has now 'nullified' its 1994 agreement with the United States to freeze all nuclear weapons development activity. . . . If the North Korean assertions are true—and administration officials assume they are—the government of Kim Jong Il began in the mid- or late-1990's a secret, parallel program to produce weapons-grade material from highly enriched uranium.")

10. Todd S. Purdum and David E. Sanger, "Forum in New York: After Hours; It Was Clinton at Waldorf Instead of Dessert," *New York Times*, February 5, 2002.
11. Toby Harnden, "Straw Mocks Bush's 'Axis of Evil,'" *Daily Telegraph* (London), February 2, 2002.
12. Barbara Slavin, "Critics Question Tough Talk on Iran, North Korea," *USA Today*.
13. "Editorial: 'Axis of Evil' Remark Sparks Damaging Backlash," *USA Today*, February 19, 2002.
14. Ibid.
15. Bill Keller, "Masters of the Universe," *New York Times*, October 5, 2002.
16. Elizabeth Bumiller, "The World; Axis of Debate: Hawkish Words," *New York Times*, February 3, 2002.
17. Chris Matthews, "A Review of the State of the Union Address," *Hardball*, MSNBC, January 29, 2002.
18. Robert Schlesinger and Susan Milligan, "Insular Nation a Gall to West Nuclear Threat North Korea's Strongest Asset," *Boston Globe*, December 30, 2002.
19. Robert Scheer, "An Orgy of Defense Spending; Bush's 'Axis of Evil' Rhetoric Fabricates a Need," *Los Angeles Times*, February 5, 2002.
20. Ron Fournier, "Bush Uses Scary Words, Images to Rally Complacent Public, Justify War's Expense," Associated Press, February 1, 2002.
21. Jack Germond, "Bush's Numbers About Terrorists in His State of the Union Address May Have Been to Draw Attention Away from Other Topics," National Public Radio, February 1, 2002.
22. Toby Harnden, "Straw Mocks Bush's 'Axis of Evil,'" *Daily Telegraph*.
23. Michael R. Gordon, "Threats and Responses: Asian Arena; U.S. Readies Plan to Raise Pressure on North Koreans," *New York Times*, December 29, 2002.
24. Leon Fuerth, "Outfoxed by North Korea," *New York Times*, January 1, 2003.
25. Elaine Sciolino, "Clinton Ups Atom Stakes," *New York Times*, October 20, 1994.
26. Charles Krauthammer, "Capitulation in Korea; Clinton's Cave-in Makes a Joke of the NPT," *Washington Post*, January 7, 1994.
27. Leon Fuerth, "Outfoxed by North Korea," *New York Times*, January 1, 2003.
28. Michael Dobbs, "For Wary White House, a Conflict, Not a Crisis," *Washington Post*, December 29, 2002.
29. Paula Zahn, "Interview with Senator Ted Kennedy," *American Morning*, CNN, March 4, 2003.
30. Lexis-Nexis search for "north korea w/s kennedy" from January 1994 to September 2002—just before North Korea admitted it was developing nuclear weapons.
31. "Capitol Hill Hearing of the Immigration Subcommittee of the Senate Judiciary Committee," Federal News Service, June 21, 2002.
32. "Capitol Hill Hearing of the Senate Armed Services Committee," Federal News Service, June 5, 2001.
33. Richard W. Stevenson, "North Korea Begins to Reopen Plant for Processing Plutonium," *New York Times*, December 24, 2002.

34. Editorial, "The Wrong Resolution," *Los Angeles Times*, October 11, 2002.
35. Editorial, "Mixed Signals over Threats," *Los Angeles Times*, December 26, 2002.
36. Editorial, "North Korea Can't Wait," *New York Times*, December 15, 2002.
37. Margaret Carlson, "Of Barbs and Barbra," *Time*, February 13, 1995; and Robert Scheer, "Foreign Policy Loses Its Logic," *Los Angeles Times*, December 31, 2002.
38. David Horowitz, *Destructive Generation*, New York: Summit Books, 1989, p. 266.
39. Maureen Dowd, "W.'s Grand Tour," *New York Times*, May 26, 2002.
40. Ibid.
41. Editorial, "North Korea Can't Wait," *New York Times*.
42. Editorial, "North Korea's Nuclear Secret," *New York Times*, October 18, 2002.
43. Ibid.
44. Ibid.
45. Editorial, "Talk to North Korea," *Seattle Times*, December 30, 2002.
46. Michael Dobbs, "For Wary White House, a Conflict, Not a Crisis," *Washington Post*, December 29, 2002.
47. Romesh Ratnesar and Laura Bradford, "How Dangerous Is North Korea? Dictator Kim Jong Il Is Pushing the World Toward a Showdown over His Nuclear-Weapons Program," *Time*, January 13, 2003 (reported by James Carney and Mark Thompson/Washington, Donald Macintyre and Kim Yooseung/Seoul, Andrew Purvis/Vienna, and Hiroko Tashiro/Tokyo).
48. Mitchell carped that Bush had provoked the North Koreans, saying, "We did isolate them, and we didn't continue the missile talks. Any time they sent out signals or feelers, we were not prepared to engage." Robert Schlesinger and Susan Milligan, "Insular Nation a Gall to West Nuclear Threat North Korea's Strongest Asset," *Boston Globe*.
49. Anthony Lewis, "Abroad at Home; A Bankrupt Policy," *New York Times*, May 24, 1984.
50. Arthur Herman, *Joseph McCarthy: Reexamining the Life and Legacy of America's Most Hated Senator*, New York: Free Press, 2000, p. 190.
51. See, e.g., Jill Smolowe, "An Officer, Not a Gentleman; Though the Battle Against Sexism Is Now Fully Engaged, the War Will Be a Long One," *Time*, July 13, 1992.

13. CELEBRITY TRAITORS:
"NOW THAT I'M SOBER I WATCH A LOT OF NEWS"

1. Woody Harrelson, "Real Lives: I'm an American Tired of American Lies," *The Guardian* (London), October 17, 2002.
2. Ibid. Among the "lies" Americans "grew up believing" is the one that "Colum-

bus actually discovered America." In fact, Harrelson said, Columbus responded to love and peace from the savage scalping nomads with threats of subjugation. Consequently, Harrelson said, "Columbus is the perfect symbol of U.S. foreign policy to this day."

3. "Jessica Lange Lambasts the Bush Administration," *Deutsche Presse-Agentur*, September 26, 2002.

4. Phil Donahue, *Phil Donahue*, MSNBC, December 16, 2002 (guests: Edward Peck, Dan Flynn, Susan Sarandon, Tim Robbins, Bob Barr, Hugh Downs).

5. Mike Hamilton, "Saddam's Soldiers Surrender," *Sunday Mirror* (U.K.), March 9, 2003.

6. Dexter Filkins, "Muted Joy as Troops Capture an Iraqi Town," *New York Times*, March 22, 2003.

7. Quoted in John F. Burns, "Actor Follows His Own Script on Iraq," *New York Times*, December 16, 2002.

8. Rory Carroll, "We'll Have Blood on Our Hands: Former Hollywood Bad Boy Sean Penn Is the Latest Celebrity to Join the Protest Against the Threat of an American Attack on Iraq," *The Guardian* (London), December 17, 2002.

9. John F. Burns, "Actor Follows His Own Script on Iraq," *New York Times*.

10. Drew MacKenzie, "Clooney Hits Out at 'Con' Bush," *The Mirror* (U.K.), January 21, 2003.

11. See, e.g., Andrew Sullivan, "Stupid White Man Goes Gunning for America," *Sunday Times* (London), December 8, 2002; and "Sontagged," *The Weekly Standard*, October 15, 2001. After OpinionJournal.com quoted Moore's petulance with the terrorists for killing non-Bush-voters, Moore removed it from his website, using one of the classic disclaimers—"doing research," "taken out of context," or "illustrating the evil of racist jokes."

12. "Stars Speak Up on the Tragedy," *New York Post*, September 18, 2001.

13. See, e.g., David Pilditch, "I Really Do Believe That Bush Is Dumber Than Sh*T. Blair Is a Smart Guy. So What's He Doing Hanging Out with a Dumb Guy?" *The Mirror* (U.K.), November 16, 2002; Stephanie Merritt, "He's All the Rage: Michael Moore's Aim Is Mostly True—But He's Sometimes More Painful Than Funny," *The Observer* (U.K.), November 17, 2002.

14. See, e.g., "Sontagged," *The Weekly Standard*, October 15, 2001. Moore praised Representative Barbara Lee for being the one member of Congress who bravely voted against "the lemmings as they headed off to war" with the Taliban in Afghanistan.

15. David Pilditch, "I Really Do Believe That Bush Is Dumber Than Sh*T. Blair Is a Smart Guy. So What's He Doing Hanging Out with a Dumb Guy?" *The Mirror*.

16. Ann Treneman, "Ruin More Beautiful Than the Building," *The Times* (London), September 13, 2001.

17. Ibid.

18. "Jailbird Pal Targets Hillary," *New York Post*, October 14, 2002.

19. Ann Treneman, "Ruin More Beautiful Than the Building," *The Times*.
20. Ibid.
21. Julie Salamon, "Old Brawler Won't Grapple with History," *New York Times*, January 22, 2003.
22. "Kurt Vonnegut vs. the !?*!@," *In These Times*, February 17, 2003.
23. "Sontagged," *The Weekly Standard*, October 15, 2001.
24. Associated Press, "Sen. Murray Asks Students to Ponder bin Laden's Popularity," *Seattle Times*, December 20, 2002.
25. "Seeking Common Ground: Civil Rights and Human Rights," John F. Kennedy Library and Foundation, Challenges at Home and Abroad Series, March 15, 2002 (with Harry Belafonte, moderated by Anthony Lewis) at http://www.cs.umb.edu/jfklibrary/forum_belafonte.html; and see, e.g., "Communist Underground," *New York Post*, October 30, 2002. Just a few years before calling Colin Powell and Condoleezza Rice "house slaves" in Bush's war on terrorism, Belafonte made a pilgrimage to Cuba, where he tearfully spoke at a rally on behalf of proved atomic spies Julius and Ethel Rosenberg. Belafonte praised the "World Peace Concert" run by the East German Communist Party, opposed the U.S. arms-control policy, and backed the Marxist Sandinista regime in Grenada.
26. E. Fuller Torrey, *The Roots of Treason: Ezra Pound and the Secret of St. Elizabeth's*, Lucas Books, 1999, p. 220.
27. Michael York and Joseph McLellan, "Chess Star Indicted for Ignoring Sanctions; U.S. May Seek Extradition of Bobby Fischer for Match in Yugoslavia," *Washington Post*, December 16, 1992. ("[Bobby] Fischer case is beginning to resemble that of another erratic and anti-authoritarian American genius: poet Ezra Pound.")
28. E. Fuller Torrey, *The Roots of Treason*, p. 249.
29. "Some Say Anti-War Protestors Are Anti-American," *Hannity & Colmes*, Fox News Network, January 22, 2003.
30. "Jessica Lange Lambasts the Bush Administration," *Deutsche Presse-Agentur*.
31. "Star Sarandon Speaks Out," Web post, January 28, 2003.
32. Phil Donahue, *Phil Donahue*, MSNBC, December 16, 2002 (guests: Edward Peck, Dan Flynn, Susan Sarandon, Tim Robbins, Bob Barr, Hugh Downs).
33. Howard Kurtz, "No Kidding: On Iraq, Janeane Garofalo Fights to Be Taken Seriously," *Washington Post*, January 27, 2003.
34. E. Fuller Torrey, *The Roots of Treason*, pp. 205 and 196.
35. Derek McGinty, "Sean Penn in Iraq Speaking Out Against US Led Attack," *ABC News*, December 16, 2002.
36. Alison Mitchell and Carl Hulse, "The Vote; Congress Authorizes Bush to Use Force Against Iraq, Creating a Broad Mandate," *New York Times*, October 11, 2002. ("The Senate voted overwhelmingly early this morning to authorize President Bush to use force against Iraq, joining with the House in giving him a broad mandate to act against Saddam Hussein.")

37. Doug Mellgren, "As Jimmy Carter Wins Nobel Peace Prize, Bush Criticized About Iraq," Associated Press, October 11, 2002.
38. *CNN's Capital Gang,* CNN, October 12, 2002.
39. "Historian and Author Marshall Frady Discusses Jimmy Carter's Life and Winning Nobel Peace Prize," *The News with Brian Williams,* CNBC, October 11, 2002.
40. Katie Couric, *Today,* NBC, October 11, 2002.
41. Frank Bruni, "Carter Accepts Nobel and Gives Message on Iraq," *New York Times,* December 11, 2002.
42. John F. Burns, "Actor Follows His Own Script on Iraq," *New York Times.*
43. Sean Price, "War on the Radio: Tokyo Rose, Axis Sally, and Hanoi Hannah Broadcast Propaganda Aimed at Turning the Hearts of Lonely U.S. Soldiers," *New York Times Upfront,* December 10, 2001. One of Tokyo Rose's broadcasts went: "Greetings, everybody! This is your No. 1 enemy, your favorite playmate, Orphan Ann on Radio Tokyo—the little sunbeam whose throat you'd like to cut! Get ready again for a vicious assault on your morale, 75 minutes of music and news for our friends—I mean, our enemies!—in the South Pacific."
44. Tokyo Rose later quietly won a pardon from Gerald Ford after spending many years arguing that she had been visiting Japan before Pearl Harbor and, after having been stranded there, was forced by the Japanese government to issue the broadcasts. Her innocence was supported by the fact that she never became a liberal cause célèbre.

14. MODERN McCARTHYISM:
THIS IS WHAT IT MEANT IN THE FIFTIES, TOO

1. Matthew Rothschild, "The New McCarthyism; Cover Story," *The Progressive,* January 1, 2002 (quoting Professor Eric Foner of Columbia University).
2. James Risen, "F.B.I. Told of Worry over Flight Lessons Before Sept. 11," *New York Times,* May 4, 2002.
3. See, e.g., *Meet the Press,* NBC, November 25, 2002.
4. Alison Mitchell, "Traces of Terrorism: Congress; Democrats Say Bush Must Give Full Disclosure," *New York Times,* May 17, 2002.
5. Jennifer Hoyt, "Lawmakers Demand Hearings on Bush's Order to Allow Trials of Terrorist Suspects Before Military Tribunals," Associated Press, November 16, 2001.
6. Letters, *State Journal-Register* (Springfield, Ill.), January 6, 2002.
7. Maureen Dowd, "Uncivil Liberties," *New York Times,* November 25, 2001.
8. Matthew L. Wald, "Effort to Cut Flight Delays Is Put Off," *New York Times,* January 7, 2002.
9. "Gore Gets Frisked on Wisconsin Travels," Associated Press, June 14, 2002.

10. David Firestone, "A Nation Challenged: Airport Security; Few Shoes Shed in Airports' Lines," *New York Times*, December 25, 2001.

11. Steve Kroft, "That Dirty Little Word 'Profiling'; Pros and Cons of Profiling Arab-American Men at Airports After the September 11th Attacks," *60 Minutes*, CBS News, December 2, 2001.

12. Ibid.

13. Fedwa Malti-Douglas, "Let Them Profile Me," *New York Times*, February 6, 2002.

14. Thomas Friedman, "Naked Air," *New York Times*, December 26, 2001.

15. William Glaberson, "A Nation Challenged: The Legal Issues; Groups Gird for Long Legal Fight on New Bush Anti-Terror Powers," *New York Times*, November 30, 2001.

16. Eleanor Clift, "Ashcroft Is Watching Us but Who's Watching Ashcroft?" *Newsweek*, November 23, 2001.

17. Frank Rich, "Thanks for the Heads-Up," *New York Times*, May 25, 2002.

18. Panel One of a Hearing of the Senate Judiciary Committee, Federal News Service, June 6, 2002.

19. Editorial, "Preserving Liberty and Security; Handling Foreign Visitors," *New York Times*, June 6, 2002.

20. Ibid.

21. Jennifer Hoyt, "Lawmakers Demand Hearings on Bush's Order to Allow Trials of Terrorist Suspects Before Military Tribunals," Associated Press.

22. Curt Anderson, "Ashcroft Defends Holding Americans as 'Enemy Combatants,'" Associated Press, March 6, 2003.

23. Eric Lichtblau with Adam Liptak, "Threats and Responses: The Suspect; Questioning to Be Legal, Humane and Aggressive, the White House Says," *New York Times*, March 4, 2003.

24. Joel Brinkley, "Threats and Responses: Accusations; Report Says U.S. Human Rights Abuses Have Eroded Support for Efforts Against Terrorism," *New York Times*, January 15, 2003.

25. Matthew Rothschild, "The New McCarthyism; Cover Story," *The Progressive*, January 1, 2002.

26. Ibid.

27. Curt Anderson, "Ashcroft Defends Holding Americans as 'Enemy Combatants,'" Associated Press.

28. Adam Cohen, "Rough Justice; The Attorney General Has Powerful New Tools to Fight Terrorism. Has He Gone Too Far?" *Time*, December 10, 2001 (reported by John Dickerson, Viveca Novak, Elaine Shannon, and Michael Weisskopf/Washington and Daren Fonda and Rebecca Winters/New York).

29. Matthew Rothschild, "The New McCarthyism; Cover Story," *The Progressive*.

30. See, e.g., Matthew Rothschild, "The New McCarthyism; Cover Story," *The Progressive*. ("Katie Sierra is a fifteen-year-old Sophomore at Sissonville High School in West Virginia. On October 22, she notified her principal, Forrest

Mann, that she wanted to form an anarchist club. . . . The next day, Sierra came to school with a T-shirt on that said, "Racism, Sexism, Homophobia, I'm So Proud of People in the Land of the So-Called Free." The principal suspended her for three days. . . . Sierra and her mother sued the school district but lost in the lower courts and in the state supreme court by a 3-to-2 vote. . . . Because she felt unsafe at Sissonville High, Sierra is now being home-schooled.")

31. Benjamin Weiser, "Threats and Responses: The Courts; U.S. Asks Judge to Deny Terror Suspect Access to Lawyer, Saying It Could Harm Interrogation," *New York Times,* January 10, 2003.

32. See, e.g, Mitra Kalita, "Detour from Dream," *Newsday,* September 20, 2002.

33. Anwar Iqbal, "Prosecutor: Terror Suspect Knew 9/11 Plan," United Press International, September 18, 2002; and see, e.g, Mitra Kalita, "Detour from Dream," *Newsday.*

34. Mark Miller and Mark Hosenball, "The Hunt for Sleeper Cells," *Newsweek,* September 30, 2002 (with Nada El Sawy and Daniel Klaidman).

35. Ibid.

36. See, e.g., Susan Sachs, "Threats and Responses: The Buffalo Case; Murky Lives, Fateful Trip in Buffalo Terrorism Case," *New York Times,* September 20, 2002 (reported by John Kifner, Marc Santora, and Susan Sachs).

37. Mark Miller and Mark Hosenball, "The Hunt for Sleeper Cells," *Newsweek.*

38. John Kifner, Marc Santora, and Susan Sachs (written by Ms. Sachs), "Threats and Responses: The Buffalo Case; Murky Lives, Fateful Trip in Buffalo Terrorism Case," *New York Times,* September 20, 2002 ("CORRECTION: A picture in early editions on Sept. 20 showed a 6-year-old boy aiming a toy pistol alongside a sign reading 'Arabian Foods' outside a store in Lackawanna, N.Y., near Buffalo. . . . After the picture was published, two editors from other news organizations telephoned the *Times* to report that their photographers said it had been posed. . . . The editors concluded, and the photographer acknowledged, that the boy's gesture had not been spontaneous. The *Times* regrets this violation of its policy on journalistic integrity.")

39. Marc Santora, "Lackawanna Journal; Waiting Uneasily on Bail Ruling in Al Qaeda Case," *New York Times,* October 8, 2002.

40. John Kifner, Marc Santora, and Susan Sachs (written by Ms. Sachs), "Threats and Responses: The Buffalo Case; Murky Lives, Fateful Trip in Buffalo Terrorism Case," Correction Appended, *New York Times,* September 20, 2002.

41. Ibid.

42. Ibid.

43. Ibid.

44. Jennifer Ludden, "Yemeni American Community in Buffalo," *Morning Edition,* National Public Radio, October 8, 2002.

45. Ibid.

46. "Man Found in Lobby Slain with Crossbow," *New York Times,* December 29, 1987.

47. Jennifer Ludden, "Yemeni American Community in Buffalo," *Morning Edition.*
48. Mark Miller and Mark Hosenball, "The Hunt for Sleeper Cells," *Newsweek.*
49. Ibid.
50. Ibid.
51. John Kifner, Marc Santora, and Susan Sachs (written by Ms. Sachs), "Threats and Responses: The Buffalo Case; Murky Lives, Fateful Trip in Buffalo Terrorism Case," Correction Appended, *New York Times.*
52. Eric Boehlert, "Does Alleged Sleeper Cell Belong Behind Bars?" Salon.com, October 2, 2002.
53. Ibid. The Islamic Ruling on the Permissibility of Martyrdom Operations can be found at http://www.geocities.com/sadiqurnet/islamic_ruling_martyrdom. html. For a document that is so "widely available," it's a mystery why Boehlert didn't read it. This must be what liberals mean when they complain about Bush's lacking "intellectual curiosity."
54. The Islamic Ruling on the Permissibility of Martyrdom Operations, http:// www.geocities.com/sadiqurnet/islamic_ruling_martyrdom.html.
55. James Risen with Marc Santora, "Threats and Responses: The Terror Network; Man Believed Slain in Yemen Tied by U.S. to Buffalo Cell," *New York Times,* November 10, 2002.
56. Mark Coatney, "Person of the Week: Abu Zubaydah," *Time,* May 24, 2002.
57. Maureen Dowd, "Summer of All Fears," *New York Times,* June 12, 2002.
58. Ibid.
59. Ibid.
60. Editorial, "War Against Terrorism; Keep Perspective with 'Terrorist' Arrests," *The Morning Call* (Allentown, Pa.), October 9, 2002.
61. Ibid.
62. Robert D. McFadden, "Jersey City Man Is Charged in Bombing of Trade Center After Rented Van Is Traced," *New York Times,* March 5, 1993.
63. Neil MacFarquhar, "Gunman's Uncle Doubts Terror Motive," *New York Times,* July 6, 2002.
64. Michael Wines, "Hostage Drama in Moscow: The Raid; At Least 67 Captives and 50 Chechens Die in Siege," *New York Times,* October 27, 2002.
65. See, e.g., Jo Thomas and Dana Canedy, "Traces of Terror: The Bomb Suspect," *New York Times,* June 15, 2002.
66. Barrett Kalellis, "Walker Is No Benedict Arnold, but Deserves Stiff Prosecution," *Detroit News,* December 19, 2001, p. 15A.
67. Peter Kononczuk, "Plane Bomb Suspect Is British Petty Criminal: Report," *Agence France Presse,* December 26, 2001. ("French police have said he has alternately identified himself to US authorities as Sri Lanka–born Tariq Raja, born in 1973, and as Abdel Rahim, a name reflecting his conversion to Islam.")
68. Alan Cowell, "A Nation Challenged: Jailed Briton; The Shadowy Trail and Shift to Islam of a Bomb Suspect," *New York Times,* December 29, 2001. ("He

is a gangling giant of a man with immigrant roots in Jamaica, a record of crime and a sense that his Christian upbringing was not enough to shield him from the violence, poverty and racial bias of south London.")

69. Jack Hagel and Martin Merzer, "Shoe Bomb Suspect's Motives a Mystery," *Miami Herald,* December 25, 2001.

70. Inasmuch as the media used various versions of the name John Muhammad for the older sniper, the search used the name of the younger sniper, Lee Malvo. Lexis-Nexis search of *New York Times* archives from October 2002 to January 19, 2003: "lee malvo and sniper": 128 documents; "lee malvo and muslims": 9 documents.

71. Matthew Rothschild, "The New McCarthyism; Cover Story," *The Progressive.*

CONCLUSION: WHY THEY HATE US

1. Paul Johnson, *History of the Jews,* New York: Harper Perennial, 1988, p. 504.

2. Michael A. Fletcher, "Campaign for Divestiture of Investments Stirs Debate on Bias, Academic Freedom," *Washington Post,* October 12, 2002.

3. Michael Moore, *Stupid White Men,* New York: Regan Books, 2001. Back cover endorsement: "Absolutely amazing satirical wit, great journalism, great research . . . wonderful Swiftian rage . . . a total masterpiece!" Tom Paulin and Bonnie Greer, BBC Newsnight.

4. Margaret Hunt Gram, "Harvard Cancels CU Visiting Professor's Talk," Columbia Spectator Online, November 19, 2002, at http://www.columbiaspectator .com/vnews/display.v/ART/2002/11/19/3ddaoa2e52d43?in_archive=1.

5. Al Webb, "Synagogues Burn as Europeans Rage," *Washington Times,* April 22, 2002.

6. Don Feder, "European Anti-semitism Has Middle East Roots," townhall.com, May 8, 2002.

7. Al Webb, "Synagogues Burn as Europeans Rage," *Washington Times.*

8. Ibid.

9. "French Jews Demand Protection," BBC News, April 1, 2002.

10. Western Europe: "Amnesty International Condemns Attacks on Jews and Arabs," press release, October 5, 2002. The press release listed these attacks on Jews: "In Belgium, synagogues in Brussels and Antwerp were firebombed in April; the facade of a synagogue in Charleroi, Southwest Belgium, was sprayed with bullets. A Jewish bookshop and delicatessen in Brussels were destroyed by fire. Criminal investigations have been opened into these incidents, as well as into a physical assault on the Chief Rabbi of Brussels in December 2001. In April, synagogues were attacked in Berlin and Herford in Germany. In the same month two Orthodox Jews were attacked and slightly injured by a group of people on a shopping street in Berlin after visiting a synagogue." It listed this on Arabs: "In an attack in Brussels on 7 May, a Moroccan immigrant couple

was shot dead and two of their children wounded by an elderly Belgian neighbour, reportedly expressing racist views."

11. Alexis de Tocqueville, *Democracy in America*, New York: Penguin, 2000, first published in 1835, pp. 354–55.
12. Ibid., pp. 355–66.
13. Ibid., p. 353.
14. Ibid., pp. 350–51.
15. Ibid., p. 353.
16. John Patrick Diggins, "Good Intentions," *The National Interest*, Fall 2000.
17. S. J. Taylor, *Stalin's Apologist: Walter Duranty: The New York Times Man in Moscow*, New York: Oxford University Press, 1990, p. 116.
18. *CBS This Morning*, April 23, 1998 (cohost Jane Robelot reporting).
19. Alexis de Tocqueville, *Democracy in America*, pp. 733–35.
20. George Orwell, *1984*, New York: Signet Classics, 1950, p. 57.
21. E. Fuller Torrey, *The Roots of Treason: Ezra Pound and the Secret of St. Elizabeths*, Lucas Books, 1999, p. 196.
22. See, e.g., Lawrence F. Kaplan, "Torpedo Boat; How Bush Turned on Arafat," *The New Republic*, February 18, 2002.
23. Paul Johnson, *Enemies of Society*, New York: Atheneum, 1977, p. 259.

INDEX

Raw and uncensored, totally controversial, here is the essential Ann Coulter—her most comprehensive analysis of the American political scene to date.

How to Talk to a Liberal (If You Must):
The World According to Ann Coulter
1-4000-5418-4
$26.95 hardcover (Canada: $37.95)
Crown Forum

And *The New York Times* bestseller, now in paperback:
Slander:
Liberal Lies About the American Right
1-4000-4952-0
$14.95 paper (Canada: $22.95)
Three Rivers Press